STUDIES IN IMPERIALISM

General editor: Andrew S. Thompson

Founding editor: John M. MacKenzie

When the 'Studies in Imperialism' series was founded by Professor John M. MacKenzie more than thirty years ago, emphasis was laid upon the conviction that 'imperialism as a cultural phenomenon had as significant an effect on the dominant as on the subordinate societies'. With well over a hundred titles now published, this remains the prime concern of the series. Cross-disciplinary work has indeed appeared covering the full spectrum of cultural phenomena, as well as examining aspects of gender and sex, frontiers and law, science and the environment, language and literature, migration and patriotic societies, and much else. Moreover, the series has always wished to present comparative work on European and American imperialism, and particularly welcomes the submission of books in these areas. The fascination with imperialism, in all its aspects, shows no sign of abating, and this series will continue to lead the way in encouraging the widest possible range of studies in the field. 'Studies in Imperialism' is fully organic in its development, always seeking to be at the cutting edge, responding to the latest interests of scholars and the needs of this ever-expanding area of scholarship.

Royal tourists, colonial subjects and the making of a British world, 1860–1911

Manchester University Press

SELECTED TITLES AVAILABLE IN THE SERIES

WRITING IMPERIAL HISTORIES
ed. Andrew S. Thompson

EMPIRE OF SCHOLARS
Tamson Pietsch

HISTORY, HERITAGE AND COLONIALISM
Kynan Gentry

COUNTRY HOUSES AND THE BRITISH EMPIRE
Stephanie Barczewski

THE RELIC STATE
Pamila Gupta

WE ARE NO LONGER IN FRANCE
Allison Drew

THE SUPPRESSION OF THE ATLANTIC SLAVE TRADE
ed. Robert Burroughs and Richard Huzzey

HEROIC IMPERIALISTS IN AFRICA
Berny Sèbe

Royal tourists, colonial subjects and the making of a British world, 1860–1911

Charles V. Reed

MANCHESTER UNIVERSITY PRESS

Published by Manchester University Press
Altrincham Street, Manchester M1 7JA, UK
www.manchesteruniversitypress.co.uk

British Library Cataloguing-in-Publication Data is available

ISBN 978 0 7190 9701 0 *hardback*
ISBN 978 1 5261 2289 6 *paperback*

First published by Manchester University Press in hardback 2016

This edition first published 2018

Printed by TJ International Ltd, Padstow

To Jude and Oliver

CONTENTS

FOUNDING EDITOR'S INTRODUCTION

Royal Tourists are still very much with us. The September/October 2016 tour of Canada by Prince William and Kate, together with their understandably somewhat bewildered young children, Prince George and Princess Charlotte, received very prominent coverage. Even as I write, Prince Charles and Camilla, Duke and Duchess of Cornwall, are preparing for a tour of Singapore, Malaysia and India later in 2017. At the time of Queen Elizabeth II's golden jubilee in 2012, members of the royal family were despatched throughout the Commonwealth to symbolise the Queen's position as Head of that organisation. There were even celebrations in South Africa, a republic, and in Hong Kong, returned to China in 1997. All this activity reflects the continuing mystique, diplomatic leverage, and, in modern parlance, marketing power of the British royal family. These visits also indicate the ways in which things have changed dramatically since the nineteenth and early twentieth century tours examined in this book. The original tours were men-only events. Wives began to be involved in the twentieth century, and now whole families travel. The biggest change of all, of course, is that the British Empire is no longer with us. The modern tours celebrate the existence of a multi-racial Commonwealth, an international organisation, certainly no longer nominally 'British', which provides mutual aid, multilateral relationships, and elements of diplomatic connections to its membership countries. Tours also still have the capacity to make political statements. Charles and Camilla were, it was thought, going to visit Myanmar (Burma) until the Rohingya crisis clearly made such a visit internationally inappropriate.

Royal tours can perhaps be seen to have started with the Royal Navy and the British army. Both an earlier Prince of Wales, the future William IV and his younger brother the Duke of Kent, were stationed in Halifax, Nova Scotia, the former in the navy between 1786 and 1789, the latter in the army 1794-1800. Their service was inevitably punctuated with ceremonial events which rendered them in some respects the precursors of royal tourists. The service by these royal princes is still celebrated in the Citadel, the significant 'heritage' building of that city. But, as Charles Reed rightly indicates, it was notably in 1860 that the more modern concept of the royal tour was created, with the visit of the teenage Prince of Wales, later Edward VII, to Canada and his younger brother Alfred to South Africa. From that date onwards, initially hesitantly, a rapidly evolving up-to-date form of royal tourism began to develop with its ceremonies and receptions, triumphal arches, laying of foundation stones, opening of buildings, and even investitures. These tours were accompanied by multiple publications to enhance popular knowledge of and interest in their events, not to mention extensive press reporting and, often, special supplements. Such journalistic comment was invariably accompanied by engravings, later photographs, and in the twentieth century paralleled by moving newsreel shown in theatres and early cinemas. Thus such events were always highly visible, both in Britain and in the colonies themselves. This represented the extent to which they were designed as expressions of imperial identity, of the modernity of technological and economic change, paradoxically of often quasi-feudal relations with indigenous rulers and their peoples, and above all of British political and military authority. Such innovative power was represented by the vessels in which the princes arrived and, ashore, the trains in which they travelled. All this was further emphasised by their extensive entourages of often uniformed supporters as well as the troops marshalled to celebrate their materialisation on a global stage.

But the handling of the intentions and effects of such tours can take place at a variety of different levels. Those who planned them in London (initially not always with the unalloyed enthusiasm of Queen Victoria herself) invariably failed to foresee the ways in which they could be further manipulated by officials and politicians 'on the spot' nor the manner in which they might be interpreted by colonial peoples, settlers, expatriates and, above all, indigenous people and their representative rulers. For example, both in the case of the vernacular press in India and in some of the settler journals in the colonies of settlement, newspaper comment might well move on beyond celebration to more significant criticism or reinterpretations of the significance and purpose of the visit. In these ways the presence of the royal tourists was manipulated into multiple meanings and messages by the different organisers and 'recipients' of the touring members of Victoria's family and their descendants. Tours that were often designed to be principally ornamental became instrumental in the hands of imperial governors, and then again differently and conveniently symbolic – and sometimes a source of contestation – in the eyes of indigenous rulers and politicians.

This book is indeed the first one to analyse these manifold facets of the royal tours in the light of a modern historiography. Charles Reed has used a remarkable range of sources to examine the reactions of the royal tourists themselves as well as the responses of the many actors at different social and ethnic levels. His sophisticated construction of the many ways in which the tours can be interpreted takes the reader from those early 1860 princely journeys through the central significance of the Prince of Wales's tour of India in 1875-76 with its extraordinarily powerful political and social resonances, not least in respect of the relationship with the Indian princes and the later proclamation of Queen Victoria as Empress. The major climax of these tours comes with the extensive empire tour of the Duke and Duchess of York (the future George V and Queen Mary) on HMS *Ophir* in 1901, when they visited Gibraltar, Malta, Ceylon, the Straits Settlements, New Zealand, Australia (with the central event of the declaration of the new Commonwealth of Australia in Melbourne), and South Africa. They subsequently toured India in 1905-6 and, as Emperor and Empress, returned to India for the coronation durbar in 1911. The latter event received a crescendo of press and visual coverage and took place at a turning point for the development of Indian nationalism. It was, however, also to herald an extraordinary sequence of royal tours in the twentieth century, although no monarch would visit India as an imperial territory again. Perhaps their declining efficacy was beautifully illustrated by the fact that the royal family's 1947 tour of South Africa (George VI, Queen Elizabeth, later the Queen Mother, and the princesses Elizabeth and Margaret) signally failed in one of its objects – to hold back Afrikaner nationalism and perhaps save the political fortunes of the Anglophile Jan Smuts. After that, the relentless and impeccable touring of Elizabeth II was much more 'ornamental', designed initially to cement the creation of the Commonwealth and then to hold it together. Maybe we need a companion work which will examine these twentieth-century manifestations of royal tourism. But Charles Reed's volume will inevitably stand as a model study which others should follow and develop.

John M. MacKenzie

ACKNOWLEDGEMENTS

Writing a book is both a profoundly collective project and an intensely individual (and lonely) one. As goes the usual caveat, the strengths of this work can be attributed to the former and its weaknesses only to the latter. It has been produced with the assistance and support of countless people. These acknowledgements cannot fully express my gratitude to them, but I will do my best.

Richard Price was a patient and able adviser, who has shared his enormous knowledge, insight, and experience while allowing me to intellectually venture out on my own and to develop my own world-view as a historian (occasionally intervening, pulling me out of the conceptual quicksand). He personifies the kind of academic humanism that inspired me to become a historian in the first place. Paul Landau encouraged me to pursue my interest in African history. He has treated me, as a student and as a teaching assistant, with generosity and graciousness. I can only hope that this work can engage with Africanist scholars in a thoughtful and productive way that honours his intellectual influence.

I must also thank the many archivists and librarians who have helped make this dissertation possible: Pamela Clark at the Royal Archives at Windsor; the staff of the British Library, the National Archives at Kew, the Special Collections at the University of Nottingham, the University of Cape Town Archives, and Bodleian Library at Oxford University, the Queensland Women's Historical Association; Ruth Gibson at the University of Birmingham; Ian Sharpe at the Auckland Public Library; and the staff of McKeldin Library at the University of Maryland and the staff of the G.R. Little Library at Elizabeth City State University. I also thank Her Majesty Queen Elizabeth II for permission to use materials from the Royal Archives; the Department of History and the Graduate School at the University of Maryland, the US Department of Education, Elizabeth City State University, and the National Maritime Museum for funding my research and conference travel; my parents and Mary Jane Jackson for supplementing these grants; the Andrew W. Mellon Foundation, Susan Pedersen, and my fellow seminarians for their support during the 2010 Modern British History seminar at Columbia University; and the team at Manchester University Press. The work has also been informed by the advice and insights of Dane Kennedy, Anne Rush, Peter Hoffenberg, Vince O'Malley, Andrew Kellett, Julie Mancine, Chris Saunders, Hilary Green, Beccie Seaman and Jill Bender.

Finally, and most importantly, I must express my love and devotion to my family, who have supported their first college graduate in an enterprise that sacrificed financial benefits for personal fulfilment. This book is for my grandfather, who was raised on a farm during the Great Depression, served as a medic in the Pacific theatre during the Second World War, and toiled in the coalfields and steel mills of southwestern Pennsylvania. He had an insatiable interest in the world, reading the local newspaper every day from cover to cover, and it was he who first inspired and continually nurtured my interest in the past. This work is also for my parents and grandmother, who encouraged me to pursue my dreams, no matter how unreasonable they seemed to be; for my wife and friend, Tracy, who has offered more love and support than I ever could have asked for; and, for Jude, my best boy ever, and Oliver, my best kid ever. It could not have been written without them.

ABBREVIATIONS

ANZ	Archives New Zealand
BL	British Library, London
CO	Colonial Office Records, National Archives
JC	Correspondence, Diaries and Papers of Joseph Chamberlain, University of Birmingham
JICH	*Journal of Imperial and Commonwealth History*
MSS Eur	European manuscripts, British Library
NA	National Archives (formerly Public Records Office), Kew
OHBE	*Oxford History of the British Empire*, 5 vols (1998–99)
Oxford DNB	*Oxford Dictionary of National Biography*, 22 vols (Oxford, 2004)
RA	Royal Archives, Windsor

PROLOGUE: CHIEF SANDILE ENCOUNTERS THE BRITISH EMPIRE

In the winter of 1860, Queen Victoria's second son Prince Alfred embarked on a grand tour of British South Africa. When Sir George Grey, the Governor of the Cape Colony, invited Alfred to the Cape earlier in the year, his parents Victoria and Albert saw an opportunity to combine 'his professional studies as an Officer in H.M. Fleet' with the 'acquirement of such knowledge of Foreign Countries as he may have opportunities of obtaining'.[1] George Grey had his own objectives in mind for the tour, which he used to push through funding of a Table Bay breakwater against the opposition of Eastern Cape legislators and to campaign for the extension of British sovereignty in southern Africa. One of the most celebrated encounters of the visit, between Alfred and the Xhosa chief Sandile, was planned by Grey to display the wondrous effects of British civilisation on a humbled foe and to demonstrate British paramount in South Africa.

The figure of Sandile was used to symbolise the success of colonial native policy and African docility even before Alfred encountered him. In Graham's Town, Alfred was presented with a transparency of Sandile, 'in his kaross, holding forth a branch, emblematic of peace, and trampling an assegai under his foot' at the residence of the missionary W. R. Thompson.[2] Sandile and some of his people, accompanied by the Resident Commissioner Charles Brownlee, joined Alfred's entourage on its way to Queen's Town. Sandile greeted Alfred, who spent some time interviewing him, although no account of their conversation exists.

When asked by Alfred to go to Cape Town by sea, Sandile's followers apparently begged him not to go. While this was dismissed by settlers and the press as the childish fears of uneducated people, their concerns were well justified, given the history between the British and the Xhosa chiefs, including Sandile himself.[3] *King William's Town Gazette*, a settler newspaper, saw the invitation as an opportunity 'to extend [Sandile's] knowledge by visiting various parts of the colony … [and to] witness the [ceremonial] demonstrations made at Cape Town' 'where he will behold many thousands assembled to welcome [the prince]'.[4] Grey proposed the idea to the Colonial Office by arguing that 'the good feeling and confidence thus created between the two Races [by Alfred's visit] should be fully matured' by having 'some of the leading Kaffirs' travel to Cape Town so that they might have 'an opportunity of becoming tolerably well acquainted with our power, and modes of thought and action'.[5] Both Grey and the *Gazette* understood that exposing Sandile to royal ritual and the modern splendour of Cape

Town and London was a means of securing his loyalty and obedience. For them, Sandile was a symbol, representative of British progress and expansion in South Africa.

At the opening of the South African Library and Museum in Cape Town, with the Xhosa chief present, Grey gave a long speech not about the violence and destruction that had characterised Britain's relationship with men like Sandile but about the glorious possibilities of civilisation and Christianity that awaited southern Africa. According to Grey, Alfred came from an island that represented, when Egyptian civilisation prospered, 'almost the confines of the habitable earth, and was only peopled by hordes of painted and lawless savages' 'slumber[ing] in savage barbarism'.[6] Great Britain had risen over the centuries to become 'the centre of Christianity and civilisation – from that great heart, the ceaseless pulsations of which scatter truth, swarms of industrious emigrants [*sic*], crowds of traders, and streams of commerce throughout the world'.[7] The Britain of the past represented the Africa of the present in the hierarchy of civilisations. In this vein, Grey focused, in particular, on the issue of Western education, of civilising Africans and making them useful to Europeans.

This was the rhetoric of liberal imperialism, of an empire of liberty and free trade rather than one of violence and conquest. The vision of empire also reflects Grey's 'native policy' of cultural assimilation, which he pursued during his tenures as governor in both New Zealand and the Cape Colony. In his own words, the policy of cultural assimilation was designed to 'induce [indigenous people] to adopt our customs and laws in place of their own, which the system I propose to introduce will gradually undermine and destroy'.[8] The processes of converting indigenous people to Christianity and civilisation, through institutions such as Grey's 'Kaffir College' called Zonnebloem, did not so simply represent a civilising mission, whereby well-intentioned British men and women could raise African civilisation as they had their own. It was part and parcel of the broader processes of destruction and neutralisation brought on by decades of frontier wars and millennial movements, such as the Xhosa cattle killing of 1856–57, which helped make such cultural imperialism possible.

In his speech at the museum opening, Grey went on to describe the methods of this enlightenment, through the spatial expansion of European people and culture:

> Those who have preceded us here as colonists [presumably the Boers] have done much to lay the foundation for such an attempt; they have already spread over a great extent of territory, large numbers of the coloured races have accepted the doctrines of Christianity and have adopted

> some of the arts of civilised life, and many others are daily following their example in some respects. But still we are a small and scattered people, with many dangers and enemies around us and in our front.[9]

The rugged frontier settlers, 'patient of fatigues and want, self-reliant, and many of them good and pious men' stood at the vanguard of this mission.[10] Grey had his eye on the 'high plateau [that] exists in the interior of the continent, healthy and habitable for Europeans'.[11] The progress represented by the opening of the museum, the spread of civilisation and the presence of Sandile was embodied in the person of Alfred.[12] The language of the civilising mission was not always so directly tied to the more violent and expansionist tendencies of colonialism, but in Grey's case, it clearly was. He equated progress with cultural destruction and physical expansion.

Yet Sandile was not a passive symbol or prop of British propaganda, but someone with a long history of experiences with British rule in southern Africa. The idea that Sandile would experience the spectacle of imperial order and thus become a more docile subject ignored the long history of violence and British duplicity on the Eastern Cape. Yet in a letter Grey claimed was written by Sandile to the captain of Alfred's ship *Euryalus*, John Tarleton, the Xhosa chief celebrated and honoured British rule in South Africa while describing his encounter with Prince Alfred:

> The invitation [to travel to Cape Town] was accepted with fear. With dread we came on board, and in trouble have we witnesses the dangers of the great waters; but through your skill have we passed through this tribulation .... We have seen what our ancestors heard not of. How have we grown old and learn't wisdom. The might of England has been fully illustrated to us; and now we behold our madness in taking up arms to resist the authority of our mighty and gracious Sovereign. Up to this time have we not ceased to be amazed at the wonderful things we have witnessed, and which are beyond our comprehension. But one thing we understand, the reason of England's greatness, when the Son of her great Queen becomes subject to a subject, that he may learn wisdom, when the sons of England's chiefs and nobles leave the homes and wealth of their fathers and with the young Prince endure hardships and sufferings in order that they may be wise, and become a defence to their country, when we behold these things we see why the English are a great and mighty nation.... And now great chief we end by expressing our gratitude that we have had this opportunity of seeing so much. From our hearts we thank you for your kindness and attention to us. We have been cared for in every way and all our wants supplied. The chiefs under you have shown us every kindness, and the people under them have acted to us as countrymen and brothers; this we more highly esteem as it was

> unlooked for and unexpected. We feared we had come among a strange people who would look upon us as their enemies, but it has been otherwise.... What we have here seen, and all the kindness received shall never be forgotten.[13]

A forgery or not, these sentiments conveniently reflect Grey's vision of the royal tour rather than Sandile's lived experiences under British rule.[14]

Sandile was well versed in British deception. The War of the Axe concluded in 1847 when the chief was invited by the British to negotiate a settlement, only to be locked up and threatened with deadly consequences if he tried to escape.[15] He was the half-brother of Maqoma, a chief who had been publicly threatened and embarrassed by Sir Harry Smith, the Governor of the Cape Colony, in the aftermath of the war.[16] Smith had annexed their father Ngqika's territory as Queen Adelaide Province in 1835. When Smith called Sandile to a meeting in 1850, the chief wisely refused to go and was subsequently deposed. Over the next decade, warfare with the British and a millennial movement that climaxed in the Xhosa cattle killing of 1856–57 ripped the fabric of the Xhosa societies apart. The South African historian Jeff Peires describes the Sandile Alfred met as a broken man who 'existed as a mere cipher, drinking heavily and clinging ever harder to traditional customs', not a likely candidate for the conversion imagined by George Grey.[17] To add insult to injury, Sandile was required to tour 'what were once his own dominions' with Grey and Alfred.[18] Royal rituals and imperial splendour could not so easily excise the past.

In addition to attending the dedication of the new library and museum, Sandile was present at the most elaborate and celebrated ritual of the visit: the ceremonial tipping of the first truck of stone into the bay, beginning the construction of the Table Bay breakwater. He was an object of attention for the crowd, with whom he briefly interacted before the festivities began. It is unclear what exactly Sandile was supposed to get out of this ceremony. In his visit to the home of the Rev. William Thompson of the London Missionary Society, Sandile told the missionary, 'Now I see how foolish I have been, in trying to resist such a mighty power, but I will do so no longer.'[19] While perhaps no more reliable than the letter from Grey, since it passed through Brownlee's translation and was recorded by the missionary's daughter, this remark better reflects Sandile's experiences with British rule. He had been battered and bruised by it, and no level of pomp and circumstance would convert him to the progress of British rule.

Sandile had no reason to trust the British, even with the royal son present. In his performance of loyalty to the Queen, Sandile knew that he had to speak and act carefully. He interpreted the royal tour through his own life experiences and acted in a way that demonstrates the instabilities of metropolitan-produced narratives of benevolent monarchy and loyal subjects. It is also worth noting that, when Alfred and Sandile visited Zonnebloem College, George Grey's 'Kaffir College' aimed at inoculating chiefs' sons with a dose of British civilisation, the students were more excited to meet Sandile, as a symbol of resistance to colonial domination, than to meet the son of the Great White Queen.[20] This abused and broken chief could produce spectacles of his own making.

In the end, Sandile would indelibly corrupt his place in colonial propaganda. Nearly twenty years later, in 1877, the Ngqika Xhosa chief rose up against the British in support of the Gcaleka Xhosa king Sarhili in a conflict known as the War of Ngcayecibi (1877–78, also called the Ninth Frontier War). Besieged in the Isidenge forests, Sandile was killed in battle by loyalist Mfengu volunteers. As David Bunn has demonstrated, Sandile participated in another kind of imperial ritual in death.[21] His body was left to decompose in the bush for two days before British authorities collected it. As Sandile's grave was about to be filled in, Commandant Schermbrucker gave a eulogy, a warning against disloyalty to the Queen:

> [Sandile] has been denied the honours which are usually accorded even by the enemy. Had he fallen on the side of his Queen ... he would have been buried in a manner befitting his rank. This is the last chief of the Gaikas; let his life and death be a warning to you.... Instead of being lords and masters in the country they once owned, [Sandile's followers] will now be servants.[22]

His was buried between the bodies of two British troopers in order to 'keep the blackguard quiet'.[23] In life, his symbol was used to exhibit the effectiveness of liberal imperial rule in southern Africa, a powerful chief humbled by the power of the British and the generosity of the Great Queen. His encounter with Prince Alfred was interpreted in vastly different ways by his followers, Sir George Grey, and the settler press of South Africa. In revolt and death, he represented the consequences of challenging this imperial order. Sandile's rebellion may have failed, but he repossessed the meaning of his life, revealing the dissonance between the symbols and practices of rule in southern Africa.

Notes

1 John Russell to W. D. Christie, 30 April 1860, Royal Archives, Windsor (henceforth RA), VIC ADD A20/49.

2 Saul Solomon, *The Progress of His Royal Highness Prince Alfred Ernest Albert through the Cape Colony, British Kaffraria, the Orange Free State, and Port Natal, in the year 1860* (Cape Town, 1861), 40.

PROLOGUE

3 *King William's Town Gazette*, 24 August 1860.

4 *King William's Town Gazette*, 24 August 1860; Major John Cowell to Albert, 14 August 1860, RA VIC ADD/20/69.

5 George Grey to Colonial Office, 20 September 1860, National Archives, Kew (henceforth NA), CO 48/404/48–52. Grey articulated his motivations for establishing Zonnebloem, the 'Kaffir College', in very similar language: 'that England might exercise, through means of an institution which conferred great benefits upon them, her due influence over the native chiefs around us'. Janet Hodgson, 'History of Zonnebloem College, 1858–1870: A Study of Church and Society', MA thesis (University of Cape Town, 1975), 178.

6 Enclosure to George Grey to Colonial Office, 20 September 1860, NA CO 48/404/57–60.

7 Enclosure to George Grey to Colonial Office, 20 September 1860, NA.

8 Letters Dispatched by High Commissioner, Cape Archives, Cape Town, South Africa, Grey to Maclean, 17 September 1855, CH 30/4, cited in James Gump, 'Sir George Grey's Encounter with the Maori and the Xhosa, 1845–1868', *Journal of World History* 9 (March 1998), 90.

9 Enclosure to George Grey to Colonial Office, 20 September 1860, NA CO 48/404/57–60.

10 Enclosure to George Grey to Colonial Office, 20 September 1860, NA.

11 Enclosure to George Grey to Colonial Office, 20 September 1860, NA.

12 Enclosure to George Grey to Colonial Office, 20 September 1860, NA.

13 Enclosure to George Grey to Duke of Newcastle, 20 September 1860, Sandile to Chief [Captain] Tarleton, NA CO 48/404/50–6.

14 Richard Price, *Making Empire: Colonial Encounters and the Creation of Imperial Rule in Nineteenth-Century Africa* (Cambridge, 2008), 473.

15 Jeff Peires, *The Dead Will Arise: Nongqawuse and the Great Xhosa Cattle-Killing Movement of 1856–7* (Bloomington, IN, 1989), 4. A British settler named George Southey had murdered the Gcaleka Xhosa chief, Hintsa, in 1835 after Smith had lured him to his camp with the promise of negotiations. Colonists or soldiers had kept Hintsa's ears, and possibly his genitals, as souvenirs. See Alan Lester, *Imperial Networks: Creating Identities in Nineteenth-Century South Africa and Britain* (New York, 2001), 124–5.

16 Peires, *The Dead Will Arise*, 6. Also see Richard Price, 'Violence, Humiliation and Paternalism in Imperial Culture: Sir Harry Smith and the Xhosa Chiefs 1835–1850', North American Conference on British Studies, Denver, CO, 7–9 October 2005.

17 Jeff Peires, 'Sandile', *Oxford Dictionary of National Biography*, 22 vols (Oxford, 2004) (henceforth *Oxford DNB*).

18 Major John Cowell to Albert, 15 August 1860, RA VIC ADD/20/69.

19 'An Evening Visit from Sandili, the Kaffir Chief, to the Rev. W. Thompson, of Cape Town', *Juvenile Missionary Magazine* 18 (January 1861), 19.

20 Janet Hodgson, 'Xhosa Chiefs in Cape Town in the Mid-19th century', *Studies in the History of Cape Town* 2 (1980), 59. Cited in Vivian Bickford-Smith, 'Revisiting Anglicisation in the Nineteenth Century Cape Colony', in *The British World: Diaspora, Culture and Identity*, ed. Carl Bridge and Kent Fedorowich (Portland, OR, 2003), 91.

21 David Bunn, 'The Sleep of the Brave: Graves as Sites and Sins in the Colonial Eastern Cape', in *Images and Empires: Visuality in Colonial and Postcolonial Africa*, ed. Paul Landau and Deborah Kaspin (Berkeley, 2002), 78–89.

22 Quoted in Bunn, 'Sleep of the Brave', 78. Bunn reports that the London newspapers instead focused on the 'decency of funeral rites'.

23 Bunn, 'Sleep of the Brave', 79. In 1862, the last Mughal emperor, Bahadur Shah Zafar II, who was symbolically restored as the sovereign of India during the 1857 war, was buried in an anonymous grave filled with lime, to ensure rapid decomposition, in Rangoon. William Dalrymple, *The Last Mughal: The Fall of a Dynasty, Delhi, 1857* (New York, 2006), 1.

INTRODUCTION

During the summer of 2011, the Duke and Duchess of Cambridge travelled to the Commonwealth Realm of Canada to represent William's grandmother Queen Elizabeth II on their first official trip overseas as a married couple. The newlyweds met with the Governor General and the Prime Minister of Canada, memorialised the Commonwealth war dead at the National War Memorial, inspected recent veterans of the War in Afghanistan, and were entertained by an aboriginal dance put on by First Canadians. They encountered cheering crowds and were heckled by Quebecois separatists. The young royals, particularly the label and style of the duchess's clothing, enraptured the press in Canada and Britain. Royal onlookers across the globe, continuing their observations from the April wedding at Westminster Abbey, celebrated a British monarchy revitalised by the duke and duchess.

A century earlier in 1901, William's great-great-grandparents the Duke and Duchess of Cornwall and York, the future King George V and Queen Mary, were on a worldwide tour of the British Empire. The most ambitious royal tour of the empire to date, their travels had been planned by Joseph Chamberlain and the duke himself to inaugurate the new Australian parliament and to convey Britain's appreciation for imperial service to the ongoing South African War. George and Mary participated in a remarkably similar itinerary of events, from reviews of imperial troops to entertainment by indigenous peoples. Extolling the birth of a new imperial century, newspapers, and subsequently colonial subjects, across the British world carefully and anxiously followed the movements of the duke and duchess.

As young Princess Elizabeth sat on the coronation throne in 1953, she inherited a set of ritual practices that had roots in an earlier period but were developed and perfected over the course of the nineteenth century.[1] Empire Day (now Commonwealth Day), jubilees, and royal tours of empire were the 'inventions' of a nineteenth-century British state that sought to inspire obedience and loyalty in the Queen's subjects across the globe. While the tours of the twentieth century – most notably the 1911 coronation durbar and the travels of the Prince of Wales during the 1920s – are the most well-known and impressive examples, the apotheosis of an imperial-ritual state, these moments were products of the Victorians' ideological work. The royal tour of empire – the subject of this book – remains an essential function of the British monarchy, embraced by the modern Elizabethan monarchy even long after the end of empire. Queen Elizabeth II is far and away the most travelled monarch in history, having visited every country in the Commonwealth save Cameroon, a total of nearly 200 visits.[2]

Despite the remarkable similarities between the 1901 and 2011 tours, down to the intricate details of their itineraries, they were carried out in vastly different contexts. The future George V and Queen Mary encountered an empire that was still on the march and would not achieve its greatest territorial extent until after the Great War. William and Catherine, on the other hand, interacted with citizens of an independent nation-state who by and large understood their British colonial heritage as secondary to their national story as Canadians. In some sense, the royal tour of today is a relic of a previous age, an antique in a world that has moved beyond both monarchy and empire as legitimate political forms. At the same time, the 1901 and 2011 royal tours both reflect the political settlement that emerged out of the Victorian monarchy, of an imperial monarchy that embraced its ritual function and all but relinquished its political role

The royal tour

Royal Tourists, Colonial Subjects and the Making of a British World examines royal tours of empire, from the first royal visits in 1860 to George V's 1911 coronation durbar.[3] While Queen Victoria herself never travelled farther than Ireland and the Continent, her children and grandchildren travelled the world as soldiers, sailors, and ambassadors. They interacted with her colonial subjects during welcoming ceremonies, parades, balls, dinners, and durbars. Victoria's sons, the Prince of Wales, Albert Edward, and Prince Alfred, were the first royals to visit the British Empire during 1860 tours to Canada and the Cape of Good Hope, planned by Prince Albert and the Colonial Secretary, the Duke of Newcastle. While the royal tours of 1860s had some origins in the royal progress or the grand tour – intended to encourage public visibility of and interaction with the British royal family and to educate young royals in the lessons of empire – they were a decidedly novel political and cultural invention. They were made possible by new modes of transport and communication, the steamship and the telegraph. Royal movements were disseminated by an expanding culture of print in Britain and the empire and through the new medium of photography. By the mid-nineteenth century, royals could travel in comfort and safety by land and sea because of British naval dominance, the expansion of settler communities, and the 'neutralisation' of indigenous peoples. During an age of imperial consolidation, the royal tour 'create[d] a new function, purpose, and justification for monarchy' at home and abroad.[4]

Royal rituals, of course, have for some time been an important topic in the historiography of European nationalism and imperialism. Historians seeking to understand the significance and survival of archaic institution in a modern and democratic nation-empire have viewed the monarchy through various optics – from welfare monarchy to 'democratic royalism'.[5] The intersection of empire and ritual politics has emerged as one of the most fruitful and interesting lines of inquiry in recent years.[6] Eric Hobsbawm and Terence Ranger's *Invention of Tradition* theorised that historical traditions – in the case of David Cannadine's essay, the royal rituals of the British monarchy – were invented by European ruling elites to legitimise and perpetuate their political, social, and political power.[7] Their work reflected a broader movement in the historiography of modern European nationalism that understood the nation and its ideological superstructure as historical constructions of the recent past rather than as proof of timeless and organic national communities. Much more recently, Cannadine's *Ornamentalism* used the grand ritual ceremonies of empire, particularly in the Raj, to explore the reinvention of the monarchy during the nineteenth and early twentieth centuries.[8] In a rather different vein, scholars of historical anthropology and 'area studies' have understood colonial rituals as part of a larger effort to acquire and use colonial knowledge for the purposes of rule.[9]

Royal tourists, colonial subjects and the making of a British world draws from this literature and expands it into a broader imperial context. It suggest that the ritual space of the royal tour was an important site where a British imperial culture was made and remade by a diverse array of historical actors in Britain and the empire. The book is a tale of royals who were ambivalent and bored partners in the project of empire; colonial administrators who used royal ceremonies to pursue a multiplicity of projects and interests or to imagine themselves as African chiefs or heirs to the Mughal emperors; local princes and chiefs who were bullied and bruised by the politics of the royal tour, even as some of them used the tour to symbolically appropriate or resist British cultural power; and settlers of European descent and people of colour in the empire who made claims on the rights and responsibilities of imperial citizenship and as co-owners of Britain's global empire. The work suggests that the diverse responses to the royal tours of the nineteenth century demonstrate how a multi-centred imperial culture was forged in the empire and was constantly made and remade, appropriated and contested. In this context, subjects of empire provincialised the British Isles, centring the colonies in their political and cultural constructions of empire, Britishness, citizenship, and loyalty.

The Victorian and Edwardian British Empire was a space of political imagination and cultural creativity where imperial politics and cultures were forged not only by colonial administrators and British/English settlers but by ordinary colonial subjects of colour, native princes and chiefs, as well as South Asian, Dutch, Chinese, and Irish subjects of the British monarch who imagined themselves as members of a British imperial community. *Royal tourists, colonial subjects and the making of a British world* is not a comprehensive examination of the nineteenth-century royal tour as a thing in itself; scant attention is given to the extensive travels Victoria's son Prince Arthur or to the experiences of Australia, Ireland, or Canada. Instead, it follows moments when the imperial fantasy of the royal tour was challenged or destabilised – by an uncooperative monarch or a pro-empire African intellectual – in order to understand how one particular and under-appreciated site of imperial culture was imagined and used by different historical actors in Britain, southern Africa, New Zealand, and the Indian Empire. It argues that within the ritual space of the royal tour, colonial subjects not only remade and appropriated the symbols and traditions of a British imperial culture in ways that subverted or challenged the political and cultural intentions of colonial administrators in London or Cape Town but also actively sought inclusion as citizen-subjects of the British Empire.

The making of imperial culture

Through a combination of technological advances, effective propaganda and the Queen's longevity, the symbolism and mythology of Queen Victoria was widely and deeply disseminated among subjects of the British Empire. This mythology was very consciously nurtured and disseminated to Queen Victoria's colonial subjects by administrators at home and abroad and 'made real' to her subjects through encounters with Victoria's children and grandchildren during royal tours of empire. In this context, they often appealed not only to the Queen as a protector and fount of justice but also to the *idea* of Queen Victoria, as a personification of the body politic.[10] Yet despite the efforts of colonial officialdom to control and utilise the Queen's image, her subjects around the world appropriated, remade, and reimagined this representation through sometimes overlapping, sometimes competing lenses of social class and status; political rights and citizenship; personal experiences; and local histories, traditions, and mythologies.

The powerful and lasting image of Queen Victoria demonstrates both the employment of cultural symbolism by British colonial states as a strategy of imperial rule and its appropriation by the Queen's subjects, from colonial governors to 'traditional' political elites, from settlers of European descent to Western-educated *respectables* of colour. While many historians have focused quite reasonably on the limits and failures of these efforts – on the unimpressed, apathetic, or openly hostile colonial subject – the embrace, appropriation, and bastardisation of Victoria as a symbol offer an equally interesting and important analytic lens through which to study British imperial culture.[11] Moreover, Victoria's malleability and adaptability as a symbol reflects the fragilities and instabilities of a British imperial culture that was made in the movement of people, ideas, and commodities through the networks of the British world and through encounters with local people in the empire.

While *Royal tourists, colonial subjects and the making of a British world* is about the royal tours, it also makes an argument about imperial culture. In this context, the book suggests that metropolitan society had no monopoly on the cultural construction of Britishness or imperial identities. It provincialises the British Isles, to centre 'the periphery' in the political and cultural constructions of ideas about empire, Britishness, citizenship, and loyalty. It thus problematises the role of the British Isles in the history of empire, to show that metropolitan culture could not dictate the contours of imperial culture. The work builds on growing historical literatures about diaspora, citizenship, and the cultures of empire. In particular, it aims to understand the British world as a complex field of cultural encounters, exchanges, and borrowings rather than a collection of unitary and unidirectional paths between Great Britain and its colonies.[12]

The development and reception of the royal tours was not shaped along a single circuit between the metropole and individual colony but connected across imperial networks.[13] Imperial rituals were developed by colonial officials through imperial networks of culture, administration, and colonial intelligence, with India often but not always serving as the model. These practices were not produced in isolation but as part of an effort by colonial officials at home and abroad to develop an imperial culture that would secure the bonds of empire in a period of rather great uncertainty.[14] The South Asian durbar, a ritual practice 'borrowed' by the British from the Mughals, was adapted for use in other colonial contexts, including New Zealand and the Cape Colony during the 1901 royal tour.

Notions of imperial identity, citizenship, and Britishness were also informed by knowledge of, communication and competition with a multi-centred British world. As I argue in Chapter 4, Western-educated 'respectable' people of colour in the Raj and the Cape Colony imagined themselves to be simultaneously British and 'natives' and advocated for their rights as citizen-subjects of the British Empire. British and 'other' (e.g. Dutch, Irish, and Chinese) settlers across the empire competed with the British metropole and each other to forge 'better Britains' on the edges of the earth. Both *respectables* of colour and non-British (or non-English) migrants used their membership of the British Empire to make claims on a non-racial, non-ethnic definition of Britishness and citizenship.

Global Britishness and imperial citizenship

Moreover, royal tours, both then and now, were interpreted by Queen Victoria's colonial subjects and Queen Elizabeth II's Commonwealth subjects respectively on their own terms and often in ways unimagined or unintended by tour architects. During the spring of 2002, the Queen and Prince Philip embarked on a royal tour of the Commonwealth countries of Jamaica, New Zealand, and Australia, to celebrate Elizabeth's fiftieth anniversary as Queen. In 1999, a few years earlier, Elizabeth's Commonwealth throne had barely survived an Australian referendum on the monarchy, the pro-monarchy vote beating out the republican cause by only a few percentage points.[15] During one carefully planned encounter on this visit, the Queen and Prince Philip met a group of natives wearing loin cloths and body paint at the Tjapukai Aboriginal Culture Park, where a fire-lighting ceremony was performed for their benefit. Prince Philip allegedly asked them if they 'still [threw] spears at each other'.[16] From the perspective of the monarchy and the Australian planners, this encounter was meant to convey British and Australian reconciliation with the Aborigine population and evidence of Australia's modernity and multi-culturalism.[17]

Yet within the ritualistic order of the tour the fire-lighting Aborigines articulated their own counter-narrative: 'This opportunity to showcase our culture to the world will perhaps influence at least some people to rethink their attitude to indigenous culture ... We are not a curiosity but a relevant and integral part of 21st-century Australia', said 'troop leader' Warren Clements. 'We here, represent a new spirit of freedom – freedom from dependence on government handouts, freedom from a century of oppression, freedom from the cycle of poverty.'[18] Clements reimagined the royal tour with his own vision – of a renewed future for his people within an Australian nation that, by the twenty-first century, had started to make amends with its native population.

Likewise, Queen Victoria's subjects at home and abroad made sense of the royal presence in complicated and profoundly different ways. Colonial administrators and local elites imagined the royal tours as instruments of imperial rule and social control, as methods of inspiring obedience and loyalty to empire; transcending the divisions of wealth, status, and class at home and in settler societies; naturalising British rule in African, Asian, and Pacific societies; and creating an illusion of consent with the 'ruled'. However, the meanings that colonial subjects attached to the tours and imperial culture itself, made in the empire, could not be dictated to or controlled by Whitehall, Windsor, or Government Houses in Cape Town or Bombay. Like Victor Frankenstein's monster, they had a life of their own and produced unintended consequences. This work is about these complex processes of reception and appropriation.

Royal tourists, colonial subjects and the making of a British world posits that colonial actors, from African and South Asian intellectuals to the neo-Britons of settlement colonies, were legitimate contributors to British culture. Against the telelogy of emerging nationhood in which the stories of both the colonies of settlement (e.g. New Zealand and Australia) and the 'dependent' empire (e.g. India and Africa) have been traditionally framed, it argues that imperial culture and identities figured importantly in the everyday lives of British subjects the world over. I argue that colonial subjects in the empire were as important to the creation of nineteenth-century British politics and culture as anyone at 'home'. Colonial subjects abroad had a formative influence on discourses on Britishness, citizenship, and empire that was as important as, or more important than, that of metropolitan society.

In particular, the book identifies the ways in which colonial subjects of colour, from princes and chiefs to the Western-educated middle class, imagined their places in a British imperial world. Recent work by scholars of the British diaspora has reconceptualised Britishness as made in the networks and movements of British and 'other' (e.g. non-British) settlers across the global space of empire, but little attention has been paid to people of colour. My work argues that imperial culture was an important, even the primary means through which some British subjects of African, Asian, and Maori descent ascribed their political, cultural, and social identities and status. By examining the role of empire – particularly in the construction of citizenship and social status – for colonial subjects in the Cape Colony, South Asia, and New Zealand, the book contributes significantly to a developing historiography on imperial networks and a global Britishness.[19]

Britishness, and ideas about British liberty and constitutionalism, informed how many colonial subjects imagined their political, cultural, and social universes. This work proposes that a notion of imperial citizenship, a brand of loyalism that made claims on the rights and responsibilities of Britishness and a co-ownership of a global British Empire, profoundly shaped the politics and identities of many colonial subjects. 'Respectable' people of colour in the empire, such as colonial subjects of African and Asian descent, appealed to their status as loyal subjects and imperial citizens to challenge the injustices of imperial rule and to appeal to the unredeemed promises of imperial citizenship (Chapter 4). For white and 'other' settlers, such as people of South Asian or Chinese descent living in South Africa or New Zealand, manifestations of Britishness and imperial citizenship were used to make and claim community identities and mythologies and to challenge perceived injustices, whether its source was the imperial government, land-hungry settlers, or a competing colony or settlement (Chapter 3).

As usual, a few caveats are in order. Because royals, colonial administrators, and colonial subjects recognised the comparability of different groups and colonies *across* the empire and because the royal tours were developed within this larger context, the book's analysis is framed in such a way as to compare the experiences of different 'kinds' of colonies and their populations and to explore their interconnectedness through the imperial networks of the British world. An eagerness to engage with a comparative approach should not be confused with a belief in the interchangeability of these sites. For instance, British India was an empire in itself, a rather different beast, comparatively speaking, from sparsely populated islands at the end of the world. But to restrict our imaginations and see these sites as incomparable does not harmonise with how the historical actors presented here imagined the royal tours. From the perspective of colonial subjects, for example, Prince Alfred's 'small' visit to the frontiers of southern Africa was as important as the grand ceremonies of the Raj. Categories of inclusion and exclusion – of whiteness or indigeneity, Britishness and respectability – transcended these colonial boundaries.

Chapter overview

Chapter 1 examines the conceptual space between the projection of Queen Victoria as a symbol of empire and nineteenth-century royals' often ambivalent attitude toward the empire and, particularly, the royal tours. Nineteenth-century colonial administrators and imperial activists sought to use the vision of a justice-giving Great Queen during the royal tours in order to promote imperial solidarity and to encourage loyalty and obedience on the part of colonial subjects. Queen Victoria herself was a reluctant participant in the tours and had little to do with the political and cultural fashioning of the Great (White) Queen as a symbol. Using the extensive correspondence of Queen Victoria, I argue that the royal tours went forward *in spite* of her rather than *because* of her. It also describes the experiences of royal tourists of empire between the first royal tours of 1860 and the coronation durbar of 1911. Using correspondence to, from, and about travelling royals – including two future kings – the chapter examines Victorian and Edwardian royals' encounters with the empire from their daily routines to their participation in Mughal-inspired durbars with Indian princes. Through the writings and experiences of royal travellers such as Prince Alfred or the future George V, I argue that Queen Victoria's children and grandchildren were generally bored as royal tourists and rarely considered the tours' political and cultural implications for empire. They complained of the tedious and demanding ritual practices and often remained, mentally, 'at home' in Britain. Nevertheless, I also show that it was also over the course of these visits that young royals were educated in the idea of imperial monarchy and came to accept their purely symbolic role in the political and social worlds of Britain and the empire, a development that Queen Victoria had long resisted.

Chapter 2 examines how 'native' princes and chiefs in Africa, South Asia, and New Zealand encountered the empire and British royals during the tours of empire. In particular, the chapter focuses on the ways that princes and chiefs, through the royal tour, symbolically resisted British appropriation of local political traditions or used connections with the British to invent or accentuate their own status and authority. At the same time, it also explores how colonial administrators, such as Lord Lytton in India or Theophilus Shepstone in Natal, sought to naturalise British rule by reimagining themselves as Mughal governors or African chiefs within an imperial hierarchy. When these 'imagined traditions' confronted complicated and messy realities of colonial rule, as they did during the royal tours, the results reflected the degree to which British colonial administrators were captives of their own fantasies about 'native' political cultures and how local elites could capitalise on, or suffer at the expense of, this captivity of mind. Moreover, they demonstrate the conceptual dissonance between the imagined traditions of rule, as products of colonial knowledge, and the slippery and elusive nature of local political cultures, which could never be fully grasped or controlled.

Chapter 3 examines how colonial settlers imagined their relationships with a British 'homeland' and a larger British world. By examining the robust English-language print cultures in South Africa and New Zealand, the chapter explores how colonial settlers used the forum of the royal tour to self-fashion communal mythologies and identities in the languages of Britishness and imperial citizenship not only in individual colonies – in New Zealand or the Cape Colony – but also in provincial and urban cores – in the Eastern Cape or Dunedin, for instance. While the royal tours were used by colonial officials and local elites as instruments of propaganda and social control, colonial subjects in the empire often used the languages of Britishness and imperial citizenship to protest at injustices, whether local or imperial, or to challenge racial or ethnic determinism. Irish, South Asian, and Chinese 'other' (i.e. non-British, settlers not from the British Isles) settlers used visits as an opportunity to contest their political and social exclusion and to claim the rights of imperial citizens. Over time, political and technological change ended the localism and provincialism that undermined the role of the 'imperial factor' in southern Africa and New Zealand, and discourses of nationalism and whiteness came to dominate local politics and traditions at the expense of imperial identities. Nevertheless, British and imperial identities remained – and remain – culturally relevant long past the end of empire.

Chapter 4 explores how a modern politics and mass culture were mobilised by Western-educated *respectables* of colour in southern Africa and the British Raj to make claim on Britishness and imperial citizenship. In particular, it explores how historical actors such as Francis Z. S. Peregrino, Viswanath Narayan Mandalik, John Tengo Jabavu, and Mohandas Gandhi participated in the networks of a British imperial world and in the making of a British imperial culture. Through the circuits of empire, *respectables* of colour came to identify themselves as members of a global community of 'natives' and Britishers and invested their notions of respectability in the promises of an imperial citizenship. Using the rich resources of independent African and South Asian newspapers, which covered and editorialised the royal tours with enthusiasm and at length, the chapter examines how South African and South Asian *respectables* claimed a more genuine understanding of British constitutionalism than the governments in Cape Town or Calcutta and through this understanding advocated a non-racial respectable status and an imperial citizenship. It claims a political and intellectual space for colonial subjects of colour in a British imperial world.

Chapter 5 brings the book's conceptual framework full circle by examining a different kind of 'royal tour', the pilgrimage of colonial subjects 'home' to Great Britain in order to petition the Queen/King for justice. Culturally imbued with the notion of the Great (White) King/Queen, colonial subjects brought their cases against British or settler governments in the colonies to the metropole in hopes of inspiring imperial intervention against colonial injustices and abuses. Through an examination of two visits by British subjects – the 1884 visit of the Maori King to London and the 1909 delegation in opposition to the Union of South Africa – and their failures to inspire change in imperial policy (in the case of the Union of South Africa) or even an audience (in the case of the Maori king), the chapter demonstrates how 'imperial networks' short-circuited when the empire came home. Moreover, the chapter explores the ways imperial culture failed – contrary to the traditional narrative – as a result of the lack of interest and ambivalence of metropolitan politics and culture.

Note on terminology

I have chosen to consistently use 'British' and 'Britishness', rather than 'English' and 'Englishness', throughout the work to reflect the general historiographic consensus. Conceptually, Britishness has been understood as more open-ended and less prone to ethnic or racial determinism. Englishness is seen as more ethnically and racially exclusive, representative of a 'Little Englanderism' that ignores or rejects the role of the Celtic fringe, of Scotland, Wales, and Ireland, in the making of modern Britain and the British Empire as well as the ways that Britishness was appropriated and claimed non-white and non-British people around the world.

I use the term 'people of colour' to cover a wide array of origins and ancestries, to explain what might be construed as a negative category of people who understood themselves or were seen as by settlers as non-white and non-European, including indigenous people (who themselves were often the product of 'mixing'), Indians, and people who saw themselves as a product of multiple ancestries (e.g. Cape 'Coloured'). Even so vaguely defined, these groupings are still unstable and uncontained, so I will attempt, whenever possible, to use more specific terms and to use identifiers, such as status or profession, that are not racial or ethnic in origin.

It is also important to recognise that group identifications were self-fashioned and imposed by different historical actors. They also changed over time. In the Cape Colony, the chattel slaves of the early nineteenth-century colonial culture were the 'Cape Malays' of the second half of the nineteenth century and the 'Cape Coloureds' of the twentieth century. I sometimes use contemporary language, both to reflect historical usage and to challenge the ethnic and racial determinism of twentieth-century ethnography. For instance, I describe Moshoeshoe, the paramount chief of modern-day Lesotho, as the 'Basuto' king to destabilise Sotho as a natural category and to reflect on the role of Moshoeshoe in the invention of a 'Basuto'. When I use

Xhosa or Zulu, I am referring to a language group and not a timeless tribe of Xhosa or Zulu peoples. I also use 'South Asian' and 'Indian' interchangeably, not to impose a colonial construct on 'the colonised' but to identify someone as a subject of British India, which included the modern nations of India, Pakistan, and Bangladesh.

Notes

1 David Cannadine, 'The Context, Performance and Meaning of Ritual: The British Monarchy and the Invention of Tradition, c. 1820–1977', in *The Invention of Tradition*, ed. Eric Hobsbawm and Terence Ranger (Cambridge, 1993), 101–64.

2 'The role of the Monarchy in the Commonwealth', *The Official Website of the British Monarchy*. www.royal.gov.uk, accessed 12 May 2010.

3 The scholarship on the royal tours is thoughtful and important. This book, however, considers the development of the royal tour over time and space and its role in the making of an imperial culture. See Phillip Buckner, 'Casting Daylight upon Magic: Deconstructing the Royal Tour of 1901 to Canada', *JICH* 31 (May 2003): 158–89; Phillip Buckner, 'The Royal Tour of 1901 and the Construction of an Imperial Identity in South Africa', *South African Historical Journal* 41 (1999): 326–48; Ian Radforth, 'Performance, Politics, and Representation: Aboriginal People and the 1860 Royal Tour of Canada', *Canadian Historical Review* 84 (March 2003): 1–32; Ian Radforth, *Royal Spectacle: The 1860 Visit of the Prince of Wales to Canada and the United States* (Toronto, 2004); Henry Wade, 'Imagining the Great White Mother and the Great King: Aboriginal Tradition and Royal Representation in the "Great Pow-Wow" of 1901', *Journal of the Canadian Historical Association* 11 (2000): 87–108. Also see Cindy McCreery, 'Telling the Story: HMS *Galatea*'s 1867 Visit to the Cape', *South African Historical Journal* 61 (December 2009): 817–37; Cindy McCreery, 'The Voyage of the Duke of Edinburgh in HMS *Galatea* to Australia, 1867–8', in *Exploring the British World: Identity, Cultural Production, Institutions*, ed. Kate Darian-Smith, Patricia Grimshaw, Kiera Lindsey, and Stuart Mcintyre (Melbourne, 2004), 959–78; Hilary Sapire, 'African Loyalism and its Discontents: The Royal Tour of South Africa 1947', *Historical Journal* 54, no. 1 (2011): 215–40; Hilary Sapire, 'Ambiguities of Loyalism: The Prince of Wales in India and Africa 1921 and 1925', *History Workshop Journal* 73 (Spring 2012): 37–65. Two popular histories have also been useful to me in conceptualizing this project: Theo Aronson, *Royal Ambassadors: British Royalties in Southern Africa, 1860–1947* (Cape Town, 1975); John Fabb, *Royal Tours of the British Empire, 1860–1927* (London, 1989). Neil Parsons has skilfully explored the reversal of the royal tour, when African 'royals' came to Britain. See Neil Parsons, '"No Longer Rare Birds in London": Zulu, Ndebele, Gaza, and Swazi Envoys to England, 1882–1894', in *Black Victorians/Black Victoriana*, ed. Gretchen Holbrook Gerzina (New Brunswick, 2003), 110–41; Neil Parsons, *King Khama, Emperor Joe, and the Great White Queen* (Chicago, 1998).

4 David Cannadine, *Ornamentalism: How the British Saw Their Empire* (London, 2001), 101.

5 See, for instance, Frank Hardie, *The Political Influence of the British Monarchy*, 2nd edn (London, 1963); William Kuhn, *Democratic Royalism: The Transformation of the British Monarchy, 1861–1914* (New York, 1996); Frank Prochaska, *Royal Bounty: The Making of a Welfare Monarchy* (New Haven, 1995); Frank Prochaska, *The Republic of Britain: 1760–2000* (New York, 2000); David M. Craig, 'The Crowned Republic? Monarchy and Anti-Monarchy in Britain, 1760–1901', *Historical Journal* 46 (March 2003): 167–85; Tom Nairn, *The Enchanted Glass: Britain and Its Monarchy* (New York, repr. 2011); Vernon Bogdanor, *The Monarchy and the Constitution* (New York, 1995); John Cannon, *The Modern British Monarchy: A Study in Adaptation* (Reading, 1987); Margaret Homans, *Remaking Queen Victoria* (Cambridge, 1997); Marilyn Morris,

The British Monarchy and the French Revolution (Princeton, 1997); John Plunkett, *Queen Victoria: First Media Monarch* (Oxford, 2003); Anthony Taylor, *'Down with the Crown': British Anti-Monarchism and Debates about Royalty since 1790* (London, 1999); Dorothy Thompson, *Queen Victoria: The Woman, the Monarchy, and the People* (New York, 1990); Alex Tyrrell and Yvonne Ward. '"God Bless Her Little Majesty." The Popularising of Monarchy in the 1840s', *National Identities* 2 (July 2000): 109–25; Richard Williams, *The Contentious Crown: Public Discussion of the British Monarchy in the Reign of Queen Victoria* (Brookfield, VT, 1997); Andrzej Olechnowicz, ed., *The Monarchy and the British Nation, 1780 to the Present* (Cambridge, 2007).

6 Walter Bagehot's distinction between the 'efficient' (political) and 'dignified' (symbolic) represents an early assessment of ritual's importance to the modern monarchy's relevance. Walter Bagehot, *The English Constitution*, ed. Paul Smith (New York, repr. 2000). Also see Cannadine, 'The Context, Performance and Meaning of Ritual'; Cannadine, *Ornamentalism*; Duncan Bell, 'The Idea of a Patriot Queen? The Monarchy, the Constitution, and the Iconographic Order of Greater Britain, 1860–1901', *JICH* 34, no. 1 (March 2006): 3–21; Freda Harcourt, 'The Queen, the Sultan, and the Viceroy: A Victorian State Occasion', *London Journal* 5 (Winter 1979): 35–56; Anne Rush, *Bonds of Empire: West Indians and Britishness from Victoria to Decolonisation* (Oxford, 2011); Philip Murphy, *Monarchy and the End of Empire: The House of Windsor, the British Government, and the Postwar Commonwealth* (Oxford, 2013); Jim English, 'Empire Day in Britain, 1904–1958', *Historical Journal* 49, no. 1 (March 2006): 247–76; and the numerous works on royal visits (cited above).

7 Cannadine, 'The Context, Performance and Meaning of Ritual', 120–1.

8 Cannadine, *Ornamentalism*, 4.

9 Bernard Cohn, *Colonialism and Its Forms of Knowledge* (Princeton, 1996); Nicholas Dirks, *Castes of Mind: Colonialism and the Making of Modern India* (Princeton, 2001); C. A. Bayly, *Rulers, Townsmen, and Bazaars: North Indian Society in the Age of British Expansion, 1770–1870* (Cambridge, 1983).

10 This understanding of Victoria's place in the empire is obviously inspired by Ernst H. Kantorowicz, *The King's Two Bodies: A Study in Mediaeval Political Theology* (Princeton, repr. 1998).

11 For instance, the Tswana people of southern Africa called her *Mmamosadinyana*, or 'Mrs/the little woman'. Parsons, *King Khama*; see also Justin Willis' excellent work on the response of the king of Bunyoro in Uganda to the British gift of a signed portrait of King George V. 'A Portrait for Mukama: Monarchy and Empire in Colonial Munyoro, Uganda', *JICH* 34 (March 2006): 105–22.

12 These contributions include the work of the New Imperial historians (most notably Catherine Hall), the British world 'movement', and the more traditionally minded works of imperial history by John Darwin, James Belich, Chris Bayly, Thomas Metcalf, and Richard Price.

13 Alan Lester, *Imperial Networks: Creating Identities in Nineteenth-Century South Africa and Britain* (New York, 2001); Elizabeth Elbourne, 'Indigenous People and Imperial Networks in the Early Nineteenth Century: The Politics of Knowledge', in *Rediscovering the British World*, ed. Phillip Buckner and R. Douglas Francis (Calgary, 2005), 59–86.

14 Thomas Metcalf, *Imperial Connections: India in the Indian Ocean Arena, 1860–1920* (Berkeley, 2008).

15 54.4 per cent of Australians voted against the republican referendum.

16 'Prince Philip's spear "gaffe"', BBC News: Asia-Pacific. http://news.bbc.co.uk/2/low/asia-pacific/1848813.stm, accessed 30 October 2007.

17 Of course, this narrative ignores the difficult legacies of colonial rule and settlement still experienced by First Australians.

18 'Prince Philip's spear "gaffe"', BBC News.

19 See, among other examples, Sukanya Banerjee, *Becoming Imperial Citizens: Indians in the Late-Victorian Empire* (Durham, NC, 2010); Duncan Bell, *The Idea of Greater*

Britain: Empire and the Future of World Order, 1860–1900 (Princeton, 2007); Saul Dubow, 'How British Was the British World? The Case of South Africa', *JICH* 37, no. 1 (2009): 1–27; John Lambert, 'An Identity Threatened: White English-Speaking South Africans, Britishness, and Dominion South Africanism, 1934–1939', *African Historical Review* 37 (2005): 50–70; Bill Nasson, 'Why They Fought: Black Cape Colonists and Imperial Wars, 1899–1918', *International Journal of African Historical Studies* 37 (Winter 2004): 55–70; Rush, *Bonds of Empire*.

CHAPTER ONE

British royals at home with the empire

> We were so frightened to hear that our husbands were going to war.... We had no slight idea what the war was about, the thing is, we only heard that Queen [Victoria] has asked for help, so they are going to fight for the Queen. We then know that this involves us, if they [the Germans] are fighting the Queen, as we were her people. We were under her, and she helped us against our enemies and with other things, so we had to help her. We didn't know how long they were going to take there. Even if we were afraid we just encouraged them to go in the name of God, we will also pray for them whilst gone, so that they can help the Queen as she helped us.
>
> Miriam Pilane of Bechuanaland, post-war interview[1]

As Miriam Pilane saw it, the Tswana-speaking peoples of southern Africa were motivated to serve the British war effort during the Second World War because of their loyalty to a long-dead British Queen. While her invoking of the Great White Queen was, at some level, simply an instance of confusion, it also demonstrates the longevity of Queen Victoria as a symbol of British justice and benevolence, the image carefully nurtured by colonial officials and imperial stakeholders of the Queen as the mother of empire. Despite anti-colonial movements of the interwar period and imperial betrayals from the Union of South Africa to the Amritsar Massacre, this image managed to survive, a testament to the effectiveness of imperial propaganda.

Through the ideological work of colonial officials, Queen Victoria's subjects across the empire imagined her to be a justice-giving imperial mother. There are perhaps more statues of Victoria on earth than of any other non-religious figure in history. She sits or stands among whizzing automobiles in Auckland, in front of neo-Gothic façades in Mumbai, and near the waterfront that bears her name in Cape Town – in bustling metropolises and provincial towns, near churches, mosques, and temples. In 1876, using the successes of the Prince of

Wales' tour of India in 1875–76, she persuaded Disraeli to style her Empress of India, an event celebrated by a royal durbar in Delhi. Her children and grandchildren travelled extensively through the empire. Her son Edward was the first Prince of Wales to visit the empire. Her grandson as King George V would become the first reigning monarch to visit the empire. As David Cannadine has argued, the empire lent itself to a monarchy in need of cultural refashioning, and the monarchy in turn gave itself to the empire.[2] Place names, monuments, and royal visitors all commemorated this developing solidarity, through which the 'imperial monarchy intruded itself into the individual lives and collective consciousness' of its subjects.[3] During her lifetime, Victoria was a ubiquitous symbol of Britain and its empire, made real to people across the world through images, statues, and visits. Her image as a maternal and justice-giving Queen was disseminated, used, and appropriated by her subjects in Britain and abroad – politicians, administrators, settlers, and local people – to various ends.

Yet the reality of the Great Queen was rather different. The ornamentalism described by Cannadine, and the willing role played by the monarchy in it, was an imperial fantasy. Indeed, Victoria's attitudes to royal visits to the empire reflect a certain ambivalence and reluctance about empire that contrast sharply with the mythology. While Victoria relished Benjamin Disraeli's efforts to title her as the imagined heir to the Mughal emperors, for instance, in most other respects she played a limited and sometimes resistant role in the cultivation of her imperial image.[4] On multiple occasions, she rejected proposals from her colonial subjects for a royal visit, insisting that family and the monarchy's duties at home came first. Even when she allowed the royal tours to go ahead, her journals and correspondence about and during the tours focus on matters closer to home – that her children and grandchildren were developing into dutiful and useful young men and, above all, that they returned home safely. For her, the empire was an accepted part of life, but it was – outside of moments of national-imperial crisis – of limited or superficial interest. As an examination of the royal tours will demonstrate, Queen Victoria's participation in crafting and disseminating a vision of imperial culture that centred on her person was surprisingly limited and often unwilling.

In the end, however, her resistance to royal visits was almost always overcome, circumvented, or ignored. As this chapter demonstrates, royal tours went on with or without her blessing, and it appears that she sometimes agreed in the end simply to save face. She could not be the Great White Queen, for she lacked the political power – the efficient capacities of Walter Bagehot's *English Constitution* – to do much more than advise, even in matters that involved her children and grandchildren. On the public stage, she played the role masterfully, but she struggled, unsuccessfully, to manage the production behind the scenes. While her resistance to part with her children and grandchildren was likely personal, particularly after the death of Albert, rather than an act of rebellion against her own political impotence, she either truly believed herself to be the master of the monarchy or simply could not accept the purely symbolic role that later monarchs would embrace.

As for the royal children, they were generally bored by royal rituals and offer us limited reflections on their colonial encounters. Even as they sat in hunting camps in the Punjab or greeted cheering subjects in Cape Town or Auckland, they rarely wrote of the empire in their correspondence home. When they did, they often complained of the tedium of their ritual duties and encountered empire with a tourist's sense of distance. For royal tourists, the royal tour was a quotidian practice, a job. In time, however – through experiences in the empire – a younger generation of royals came to accept their ceremonial place in imperial culture without the struggle for political power put up by Victoria and Albert. Through these processes, the invented tradition of the 1860s and 1870s became the standardised ritual practices of the twentieth century.

This chapter aims to understand how Victorian royals thought and talked about the empire through the lens of the royal tour. As a whole, the Victorian royal family was deeply and profoundly ambivalent about the British Empire. Victoria's consort Prince Albert and her grandson George, the future George V, were the most important exception to this observation. After Albert's demise in 1861 and a decade of mourning, Queen Victoria consistently resisted the royal tours. She unsuccessfully struggled to assert her royal prerogative and to control her image, which had been, by that point, almost fully appropriated by officials at home and the empire as well as by her colonial subjects around the world. Her children, on the other hand, were at home with empire. It was the background, the *mise-en-scène* for other adventures away from controlling parents and escapes from the tedium of royal duties. That the empire was quotidian for them reflects an acceptance of its normality as part of British and royal life. For future generations of royals – represented in this chapter by Albert Edward's second son George – the royal tour as developed and perfected by the Victorian generation was embraced as a standard practice and duty. Educated principally in and about the empire, rather than the Continent, tutored by Joseph Chamberlain, and coming of age in an era of perceived imperial crisis, the future George V accepted and embraced the dignified functions of the empire without his grandmother's struggle for political power, on one hand, or bereaved ambivalence, on the other. In the end, perhaps despite themselves, Victorian royals invented the truly imperial monarchy of the twentieth century.

Inventing the Great Queen

Long before the 'imperial turn' in British history and his work in *Ornamentalism*, Cannadine radically reconceptualised the meaning of royal ritual in Eric Hobsbawm and Terence Ranger's *The Invention of Tradition*.[5] Writing in the early 1980s, when the modern Elizabethan monarchy was experiencing a period of unpopularity stemming from a series of family controversies, Cannadine sought to understand how the monarchy emerged from a transformative age of political reform as a popular symbol of nation and empire. For Cannadine, the answer was to be found in the ritual functions of the British monarchy, what Walter Bagehot had called the dignified powers of the Crown. He identified 'theatrical show' to be 'central in explaining the emergence of popular monarchy' during the nineteenth century, which 'shap[ed] a national identity based on tradition, hierarchy, and peculiarity'.[6] Under Victoria, then, the monarchy embraced a newfound *raison d'être*, to ceremonially perform as a symbol of the British nation-empire.

Queen Victoria, Cannadine argues, was fundamental to this reinvention of the British monarchy. Victoria's eventual willingness to come out of mourning and embrace her public duties in the 1870s helped transform the monarchy into a 'symbol of consensus and continuity to which all might defer'.[7] Within Cannadine's chronological frame, the golden age of royal ceremony began after 1876, when Victoria became Empress of India. The Golden (1887) and Diamond (1897) Jubilees represented high-water marks in this symbolic reinvention, during which the monarchy was celebrated in grand style in Britain and across the empire. Thus, the last decades of the nineteenth century were, he argues, 'a time when old ceremonials were staged with an expertise and appeal which had been lacking before, and when new rituals were self-consciously invented to accentuate this development'.[8]

Twenty years after his *Invention of Tradition* essay, as a younger generation of royals has embraced their ceremonial roles, Cannadine's argument about the British monarchy is more persuasive than ever. While it is true that royal ritual was not entirely new to the British monarchy – one need only revisit Elizabeth I's royal progresses to realise this fact – they were underused and largely out of practice by the time the young Victoria came to the throne in 1837.[9] If Victorian ceremonials had roots in the past, they were used in a new context and for new reasons. The royal tours, for instance, were made possible by the steamship and the railway, on which young royals could travel in safety and comfort, and their images and narratives were transmitted over telegraph wires to engage the readers of a burgeoning popular press in Britain and the colonies.

The British monarchy then and now has sought to project itself not only as ancient and timeless, and therefore indispensable to national identity, but also as modern and useful. For Victoria and Albert as well, making the monarchy a modern and useful national-imperial institution informed how they raised their children and grandchildren. For them, as this chapter shows, the royal tours were often as much or more about instilling the importance of national service in their children as they were about consciously embracing the imperial role of the monarchy.

The Queen/Mother

To suggest the limits of Queen Victoria's imperial consciousness is not to say that she did not care about her empire. As her extant letters demonstrate, she was a prolific writer on imperial affairs, particularly during the decades before Prince Albert's death (1861) when he served as her *de facto* personal secretary and exerted political influence over his wife and colonial affairs. Over the course of her long reign, Victoria wrote to prime ministers, colonial secretaries, and colonial governors frequently. She loudly voiced her (often unsolicited) approval or disapproval of colonial policies to the government, writing an average of 2,500 words on every day of her adult life.[10] She tried to learn 'Hindoostani', corresponded with several South Asian princes, and employed a trusted Indian servant named Abdul Karim.[11] She even adopted a Maori child as her godson after his parents, the Ngapuhi chief Hare Pomare and his wife Hariata, lamented the death of Albert.[12] And, after becoming Empress of India, she insisted on signing her name as 'Victoria RI', that is *Regina Imperatrix* or Imperial Queen.[13]

At the same time, her relationship with the empire was more ambivalent and complicated than these examples suggest. Her imperial interests focused on India, and the vast majority of her letters on foreign affairs are on the subject of Europe. When she wrote to her globetrotting children and grandchildren, she very rarely discussed imperial politics, focusing her attention on family, marriages, and children. Her private journals lament the absence of her children and rarely reflect on the larger implications of the tours for the monarchy or the empire.

And after the death of her beloved husband Albert, her interest in governance and policy wavered significantly, to be rekindled during the 1870s by political and public pressure. Even then, she, like the British public, rediscovered the empire during periods of crisis. Despite her outward interest in empire, she was always reluctant to allow her children and grandchildren to take long journeys abroad.[14] For her, family and the domestic duties of the monarchy came first.

Her ubiquity across the British world as a symbol of Britain and 'her' imperial dominions largely reflected an effort by government and colonial officials to use her image to their own ends, rather than any ideological work on her part. Victoria could certainly be described as an *imperialist*, if of the banal variety. She was fascinated by India, but mostly out of nostalgia for Albert, who himself demonstrated a keen interest in the subcontinent. While she did write prolifically on imperial affairs, particularly during crises, she was far more interested in European politics.

Colonial propaganda presented her as the maternal and justice-giving Great Queen, an idea many dispossessed peoples clung to well into the twentieth century. She was frequently visited by colonial subjects and did, at times, exhibit a strong interest in their welfare. Walter Arnstein argues that she demonstrated a brand of Victorian multiculturalism, seeing 'herself far less as the head of a homogenous nation-state than as the head of a multi-ethnic and multi-religious Empire' and 'insist[ing] time and again that other traditions and religions and even rulers in the Empire deserved respect'.[15] At the same time, she believed that the expansion of British rule (rather than German, French, or Russian) would serve to push civilisation forward. As a constitutional monarch, she had little power to live up to her mythology as the Great Queen, defender of subject peoples, and did not choose to spend what little political capital she had on defending her subjects.

With the exception of Ireland in 1849 and 1900, Queen Victoria never visited her empire.[16] She did travel around the British Isles and to the Continent extensively. Because of these limits, one useful way to truly understand how Victoria felt about her colonial subjects is to examine what happened when the empire came to visit her (see Chapter 5). During these encounters, Victoria was regularly used to convey and legitimise decisions made by the government regarding imperial affairs. When the Bechuana chiefs Khama, Sebele, and Bathoen came to Britain in 1895 to appeal for imperial justice against the land-hungry Cecil Rhodes, Queen Victoria met with them at Windsor Castle. She addressed the chiefs, her words presumably approved in advance by Joseph Chamberlain, telling them that she was 'glad to see [them], and to know that they love[d her] rule' and confirming their settlement with Chamberlain, which reaffirmed imperial protection in their dispute with Rhodes.[17]

For Victoria, these colonial encounters in the imperial metropole and those of her children and grandchildren in the empire infrequently registered in her letters and diaries. Above all, Victoria was a nation-imperial symbol, one that was used and remade by her subjects at home and in the empire. Despite her interest in colonial subjects, her concerns, and those of Albert, centred principally on salvaging what remained of the monarchy's domestic prerogatives and raising their children and grandchildren to be useful to the British nation. Future monarchs, including her grandson George, would embrace imperial rituals and the royal tour, developed however reluctantly during the reign of Victoria, as principal functions of the British monarchy.

Victoria's struggle to maintain control of royal travels and the projection of her image was part and parcel of a larger effort by both Victoria and Albert to recover the political prerogatives of the British monarchy. Victoria's uncle, William IV, was the last British monarch to dismiss a prime minister (Viscount Melbourne in 1834). In *The English Constitution* (1867), Walter Bagehot unofficially demarcated the limits and rights of the constitutional monarchy inherited by Victoria – to be consulted, to advise, and to warn; he went as far as to suggest that the political transformations of the nineteenth century had allowed a 'Republic [to] insinuate ... itself beneath the folds of the monarchy'.[18] But, like so much of the British constitution, these were unwritten agreements, forged over centuries of political and cultural negotiation. To Victoria, they were suggestions at best. In one letter to her eldest daughter Victoria, she lamented what a 'miserable thing [it was] to be a constitutional Queen'.[19]

The true litmus test of this nineteenth-century constitutional settlement was whether or not politicians could willingly ignore or circumvent Victoria's imagined prerogative. William Gladstone, about whom the Queen expressed the bitterest sentiments, rarely shared what he considered Victoria's political meddling with his colleagues. Similarly, as we shall see, when Joseph Chamberlain wanted the Duke of York to go on a royal tour during the South African War, he circumvented the Queen's objections by collaborating (or conspiring?) with the duke to persuade her. The fact that the Queen's protests and attempted interventions rarely altered plans or policies is telling.

Both Gladstone, the grand old man of nineteenth-century liberalism, and Chamberlain, the former Birmingham radical turned imperialist, embraced and co-opted the monarchy as a national-imperial symbol compatible with their political worldviews, perhaps the clearest evidence of the monarchy's extremely limited political prerogative by the *fin de siècle*. What the 1860s and early 1870s proved was that Queen Victoria *could* refuse her public services, but only at grave risk to the monarchy's existence as an institution. The Great Queen became a symbol to be managed and manipulated, a process that Victoria unsuccessfully sought to limit and control. As the royal tours demonstrate, Victoria was a reluctant and often unwilling participant in the projection of her image – but she had little choice in the matter. Despite the failures of Victoria and Albert in this regard, both participated – willingly at times, unwillingly at others – in the reinvention of the British monarchy as a symbol of the nation-empire, a role that was accepted and embraced by her descendants.

The Prince Consort

The German-born Prince Albert (1819–61) proved himself to the British political establishment as a thoughtful and efficient political operator. Albert was, as Cannadine puts it, 'fascinated by statecraft' and 'determined to play a full part in the political life of his adopted country'.[20] He paid visits to politicians, was always present when Victoria met with her ministers, and drafted most of her letters. He quickly established himself as a patron of culture and the sciences and worked endlessly on his various projects. He was hardworking, tireless, and ruthlessly efficient. In the historical record, it is often extremely difficult to tell where Victoria ends and Albert begins. His influence as Victoria's closest adviser and personal secretary over this period (1840–61) is undeniable. It was also comparatively short.

Albert was the cultural engineer of the Victorian monarchy and, in the context of this work, of an imperial culture centred on the monarchy.[21] Long before Disraeli's Crystal Palace speech (1872) or the Royal Titles Act of 1876, Albert conceived of a new place for the monarchy in British society, namely a British imperial culture that was culturally anchored in the monarchy and monarchism. Albert's personal involvement in the design of the Star of India, which itself became an essential part of royal visits to India, offers some insight to the role he played in imagining a new role for the monarchy:

> The 'Eastern star' will perhaps on [the] whole be the best denomination. The Centre of the badge of the Order might then be the Queen's image surmounted by a star & surrounded by an appropriate motto & the star of the Order might be the star surrounded by flames on a glory.... The Badge to be worn suspended from a Collar which might be composed of stars, Lions and Unicorns or the sunflower, or Lotus & ordinarily from a Ribbon. The presiding Idea would be contained in the Angel's salutation 'Glory to God, peace on earth & goodwill towards men'.[22]

While Victoria grew reluctant to participate in this new role after his premature death, his efforts unleashed irreversible changes to the way the monarchy did business. Most significantly, he had willingly and enthusiastically promoted the first royal tours of empire by his sons in 1860.

It was Albert who encouraged the Duke of Newcastle to accept the invitation from Canada and his wife to embrace George Grey's proposal for a South African visit. It was Albert who worked through the arrangements and negotiations for the visits and imagined the ideological work that they would achieve.[23] He wrote to his close friend Baron Stockmar: 'What a cheering picture is here of the progress and expansion of the British race, and of the useful co-operation of the Royal Family in the civilisation which England has developed and advanced!'[24] In a toast given at Trinity House in June 1860, Albert remarked:

> It will be a curious coincidence, that at the same time – a few weeks hence – though almost at the opposite poles, the Prince of Wales will inaugurate, in the Queen's name, that stupendous work, the great bridge over the St. Lawrence in Canada, while Prince Alfred will lay the foundation stone of the breakwater for the harbour of Cape Town. What vast considerations, as regards our country, are brought to our minds in this simple fact! What present greatness! What past history! What future hopes! And hope important and beneficent is the part given to the Royal Family of England to act in the development of those distant and rising countries, who recognise in the British Crown, and their allegiance to it, their supreme bond of union with the mother country and each other![25]

Albert's careful planning of both of his sons' tours indicates the importance of the visits to him. His public excitement and the laborious private negotiations over the royal tours reflect a concerted effort to reshape the monarchy and to create a new kind of imperial culture. While Albert may have been the 'uncrowned King' of the United Kingdom, Victoria was the reigning monarch and the official author of most correspondence on the subject of the royal visits. The obvious change in the Queen's tone regarding the travels of her children and grandchildren after his death reflects both the loss of his voice and the profound personal and psychological trauma that she experienced over his death.

Through public patronage, national service, and royal ritual, Albert sought to connect the monarchy to notions of progress and improvement. He spent his years as a British royal nurturing an image of the monarchy as a patron of the arts and sciences, most famously in organising the Great Exhibition of 1851. To Albert, the monarchy needed to excise the demons of excess and decadence associated with the previous two reigns and make a new image for itself of a respectable and moral royal family, one that echoed the reign of George III. In this vein, he demanded that his children be useful – to commit to a difficult regimen of learning and improvement and to serve their nation in Her Majesty's military forces.

Victoria and Albert raised their children to be useful, both to their family and to the nation. There was nothing particularly imperial about their or their children's upbringing. Victoria and Albert considered the royal tradition of military service most important.[26] In an age before proconsular apprenticeship, service in Her Majesty's armed services was the primary route through which royal sons could earn their spurs and see the world.[27] Their children Alfred (navy) and Arthur (army) served, as did their grandchildren Albert Victor and George (both in the navy).

For this reason, royal visits could not, he decided, invoke images of the royal progress of past times (with some exception for India). Royal children were to visit the empire as respectable and upstanding subjects, who dressed in the respectable and simple clothing of modern royals, rather than the effete regalia of monarchy's past. India was different, because colonial administrators identified the need to appeal to an 'Oriental mind' that yearned for medieval spectacle. But most of this was left for imperial durbars, where the viceroy rather than royal children represented the Queen in an official capacity.

Victoria and Albert had very specific ideas about how their children should behave and represent the monarchy while abroad. As we shall see, governments and colonial administrators were also deeply concerned with the dynamics of royal rituals in relation to the legitimacy of imperial hierarchy. Who would represent the sovereign and how she was represented were crucial questions for both the monarchy and for governing elites who ran the empire.

Thus, royal children were to appear in the empire as first subjects of the Queen rather than as her representatives. In 1875, for instance, the Queen and the Viceroy of India, Lord Northbrook, agreed that there could be no durbar when the Prince of Wales visited India.[28] When her sons and grandsons travelled as royal sailors, they were expected to perform their duties, much to the surprise of the Queen's colonial subjects. Propriety demanded that only the governor of a colony, the Queen's official proxy, could represent her, and this fact had to be reflected in imperial ceremonies. On certain occasions, tour planners made certain that the governor and the royal visitor were not seen together, so as to avoid any confusion in the minds of colonial peoples.[29] Seeking to avoid the perception of excess that characterised Continental monarchies and past British monarchs, Victoria and Albert sought to project the image of a respectable and modern royal family both as a means of raising dutiful and respectful children and protecting the monarchy from the fate of its Continental brethren.

While Victoria dictated that royal children could not represent her in an official capacity, this conceptual distinction was not easily maintained on the ground. When royal children arrived, they immediately became the centre of attention. Sometimes exceptions were granted for Princes of Wales to pass out medals or honours, but never without a debate about the precedents and consequences of doing so. In 1875, the Queen opposed the idea of the Prince of Wales rather than Lord Northbrook distributing the Star of India.[30] During the investiture ceremony, as things turned out, Edward and Northbrook sat together, and Edward awarded the Star of India to the guests of honour under 'special warrant from the Queen'.[31]

This standard also made sense in the context of the royal tours as an educational experience. As didactic tools, the royal tours were imagined as grand tours of empire, not leisurely tourist expeditions. Victoria – and particularly Albert – wanted the monarchy to be *useful.* Before Alfred's travels in 1860, Queen Victoria sent off countless letters to naval and colonial officials, explaining that her son was to receive no special treatment (once sailor reached land, this never happened, of course). For instance, Lord John Russell wrote to the Foreign Office regarding:

> Her Majesty's desire and intention that HRH should apply himself more particularly to his professional studies as an officer in HM Fleet, combining with those studies the acquirement of such knowledge of Foreign Countries as he may have opportunities of obtaining.... You will explain the nature and objects of HRH's visits to the Ports of the Country, and, unless otherwise informed, you will state in the most respectful manner ... that His Royal Highness should decline formal civilities.[32]

While the protocols established by Victoria and Albert were focused on shaping their children's attitudes, colonial subjects took note. It was said that the Xhosa chief Sandile – who was brought to Cape Town by Governor George Grey to be awed into obedience – was impressed most not by Cape Town or its works of progress but by the sight of Prince Alfred swabbing the deck. When the Prince of Wales returned from Canada in 1860, under the 'delusion that the tumultuous welcome [he experienced] was for [him]', Albert forcefully reminded him that 'it was nothing of the kind. It was simply an expression of loyalty to the Queen.'[33] For royal sons serving in the military, the tours were as much about discipline and service as seeing the world. For the heirs to the throne, they were meant to give them public responsibilities and to see the empire over which they would one day rule.

Victoria and Albert took a particular interest in carefully selecting fellow travellers for their children and grandchildren. The Prince of Wales went to Canada, as Ian Radforth describes, with a group of middle-aged men and was prohibited from interacting with the younger midshipmen abroad the HMS *Hero*.[34] Albert made sure that General Robert Bruce, the Prince of Wales' governor, was always 'under the same roof' with Edward while in North America so as to avoid any moral wandering on the prince's part.[35] There was a long conversation between the monarchy and Indian administrators over Alfred's travelling companion for his 1870 visit to India. The Queen thought that the young prince was 'rather easily led away' and thus in need of a 'steady, firm' travelling companion who would 'exercise a good influence'.[36] For the Queen, this was one of the few prerogatives that she could dictate during later tours.

Royal children

On 12 March 1868, Prince Alfred – royal spare to Albert Edward the Prince of Wales and second son of Queen Victoria – was shot in the back with a pistol at Clontarf, north of Sydney in New South Wales, by an Irishman named Henry James O'Farrell in a Fenian-inspired assassination attempt.[37] Months earlier, three Fenians, who became known as the Manchester Martyrs, had been executed for killing a policeman. The assassination plot aroused trepidation across the British world that an empire-wide Fenian conspiracy was underway, a fear best illustrated by the draconian Treason Felony Act passed by the parliament of New South Wales six days after the attack and modelled on the British Treason Felony Act of 1848 (11 & 12 Vict. c. 12).[38] Without question, ethnic and sectarian tensions informed the political, social, and cultural discourses of the nineteenth-century colonies of settlement, as the outburst of anti-Irish rhetoric and violence in the aftermath of O'Farrell's attempt demonstrates. During Alfred's visit, Irish Catholics in Melbourne had rallied outside the Protestant Hall, evoking the Battle of the Boyne in illumination form.[39] On the other hand, the Sydney Catholic newspaper *Freedman's Journal*, fearing that an Irishman would soon be revealed as the shooter, affirmed that, if such were the case, 'Irishmen must bow their heads in sorrow, and confess that the greatest reproach which has ever been cast on them, the deepest shame that has ever been coupled with the name of our people, has been attached to us here in the country where we have been so free and prosperous'.[40] The act was condemned by Irish communities across Australia and the empire.

Curiously enough, even O'Farrell's commitment to republicanism appears questionable, and in interviews he advocated a future for the Irish within the British Empire. Excerpts from his diary and the transcript of an interview he had with the Colonial Secretary of New South Wales, Henry Parkes, were published in 1868 as *Fenian Revelations: The Confessions of O'Farrell who Attempted to Assassinate the Duke of Edinburgh.*[41] During his confession, O'Farrell claimed that he was part of a Fenian cell in Sydney ordered from England to assassinate the prince.[42] While he condemned the execution of the Manchester Martyrs and damned England, he also expressed little sorrow for having failed, indicating that he 'rather liked' the duke and voted against the plan to kill him in the first place.[43] When Parkes interrogated him on his political beliefs, O'Farrell advocated not an independent republic of Ireland but a united republic of the British Empire.[44] He expressed concern that the prince would be in grave danger should he steam on to New Zealand, only for the purposes of 'a few more addresses'.[45] While perhaps an extreme example, O'Farrell's apparent loyalty to the empire, despite his hatred of the English and the monarchy, complicates more traditional narratives of ethnic and sectarian conflict in the British world.

On the other hand, Alfred received an outpouring of outrage and concern from Australians and colonial subjects from across the empire. The Royal Archives and National Archives at Kew contain an impressive array of these letters, odes, and declarations to Alfred, which demonstrate the sincere concern felt by colonial subjects for the young prince. Recovering in Australia, Alfred wrote to his mother about the aftermath of the attempt on his life, expressing how deeply touched he was by the outpouring of loyalty and concern, not from her colonial subjects but from his crewmates:

> I shall never forget ... the manner in which I was spontaneously cheered by the whole squadron especially by my own ship's company & the manner they received me on board. I was very much overcome by it & had to go to my cabin & remain there.... I think it was the proudest moment of my life, to find that the nearly 600 men I command really loved me.[46]

Of course, Alfred did convey his thanks to his mother's subjects, but his deeply emotional response had little to do with what happened on land. He was not ungrateful to his mother's colonial subjects, but the relationships that he had developed on board his ship made naval life more meaningful to him.

While the Great Queen and Empress of India had never travelled outside of the British Isles or the Continent, her children and grandchildren travelled the world as servicemen and royal ambassadors. Their encounters with the Britain's subjects across the globe importantly shaped how the monarchy was received and understood in the empire. As British ambassadors within and beyond the borders of British *imperium*, Princes Alfred, Albert Edward, and George actively participated and became part of local mythologies of imperial community in the empire. Alfred, for instance, became memorialised as South Africa's prince, a hybrid tradition that appealed to both local and imperial narratives of belonging. Foreshadowing later proconsular appointments held by royal children, there were calls for Victoria to install her sons as governors or kings of the white colonies of settlement. More profoundly, colonial subjects often used the forum of the royal tour to profess a membership in the political and cultural community of empire, inspiring – even if quite accidently – the development of decidedly modern notions of political identity and belonging in the British Empire.

A generational difference arose through these experiences, through their participation in royal tours and their extended contact with the empire: a younger generation of royals – exemplified by Edward VII's son George – came to willingly embrace and accept their ceremonial place in imperial culture without the political fight put up by Victoria and Albert. While Victoria's sons Alfred and Albert Edward travelled extensively throughout the empire, they expressed in their letters a limited appreciation for their mother's dominions. Prince George, the future George V, developed the model embraced by the twentieth-century monarchy, of a royal with a keen interest in imperial matters and who embraced his ritual role without contention. Based on the experiences of the royal tours, it is of little surprise that George V would be the first reigning monarch to visit the British Empire. Victoria and Albert set in motion a tradition – albeit one that was embraced reluctantly and ambivalently at times – that would have the consequence of shaping their grandchildren into true imperial rulers who embodied concerns that were only mythical for Victoria herself.

Alfred

Victoria's second son Alfred is perhaps best known in European history for almost becoming the Greek King. He was selected in a Greek plebiscite to fill the throne left vacant by the deposition of King Otho. The prospect of accepting this 'election' was interpreted by the British government to be a violation of the 1830 London Protocol, designed to limit the influence of any individual 'protecting power' on an independent Greek state.[47] He married the daughter of Tsar Alexander II and later became the hereditary duke of Saxe-Coburg Gotha. He lived a somewhat uninspiring life as a German duke and died an early death.

Yet Alfred's teens and twenties, when he toured the world as a royal sailor, are the far more interesting and, arguably, historically significant episodes in his life. He was the one of the greatest royal travellers in history. In terms of distance travelled and places seen, he ranks with the greatest of Victorian adventurers. In August 1870, Lieutenant-Colonel Arthur Balfour Haig, Alfred's equerry, estimated that, since leaving Wellington sixteen months prior, the prince's ship had travelled more than 31,000 nautical miles, or one and a half times the circumference of the world.[48] This astounding figure represents a mere segment of Alfred's life at sea. He travelled to Australia, New Zealand, South America, South Africa, China, India, Japan, and many other places in his twenty-year-long naval career. Alfred was probably seen in the flesh by more people in the colonial empire than any royal before the advent of the jet age.

By 1860 when he set sail for South Africa, Alfred had become the great hope of Victoria and Albert. He was not the most intellectually gifted boy, Victoria frequently observed, but he demonstrated a curiosity and common sense that his older brother rarely did. Having passed his naval exams by age 14, Alfred was sent off to sea by his father and spent the next decade of his life travelling the world. Queen Victoria, less guarded in her letters to daughter Vicky, abandoned her usual reverence for Albert in expressing her anger over Alfred's departure:

> I have been shamefully deceived about Affie.... It was promised to me that the last year before he went away to sea, he should be with us, instead of which he was taken away.... Papa is most cruel upon the subject. I assure you, it is much better to have no children than to have them only to give up![49]

By the time Sir George Grey, the Governor of the Cape Colony, invited Alfred to South Africa in 1860, his mother had accepted his fate, and both parents recognised an opportunity. They imagined his naval apprenticeship and his royal visit would combine 'his professional studies as an Officer in H.M. Fleet' with the 'acquirement of such knowledge of Foreign Countries as he may have opportunities of obtaining'.[50] His first voyage out, in 1860, took him to South Africa, with stops at South American ports on the trip out and on the West African coast on the journey back. On Alfred's sixteenth birthday, which he spent in southern Africa, Victoria lamented his first birthday apart and prayed 'May God bless & protect him, & may he become like his beloved father!'[51]

His governor Major Cowell was given full discretionary powers over him, and Alfred was expected to be treated as a normal sailor in the Royal Navy, except in instances approved in advance.[52] The message was relayed in letter after letter penned by Victoria to local officials and to the officers of his ship, HMS *Euryalus*. Some exception was intended for the Cape Colony, where it was planned Alfred would inaugurate the construction of a new Table Bay breakwater.[53] While these rules were rarely, if ever, followed on land, they were followed at sea: Alfred was seen on duty at the gangway when the ship arrived in Table Bay. While this performance of the work ethic was meant to shape both Alfred and his audience, to nurture a particular image of the monarchy, it also represented the childrearing philosophy of Victoria and Albert, who sought to nurture the merit of service in their children and grandchildren.

Victoria and Albert intended for the *Euryalus* to be a royal classroom, where their son could learn discipline and see the world, while avoiding the various digressions of his older brother. For his parents, the trip had clear didactic purposes, with welcomed political side-effects for the empire. Toward the end of the 1860 tour, Major Cowell reported to Albert that the desired results were 'purchased ... very cheaply' and that Alfred had reflected on and understood the state of affairs in southern Africa.[54] Victoria reflected in 1860:

> Affie was greeted [in southern Africa] by endless savage Tribes, with a loyalty & enthusiasm highly gratifying. He travelled 1000 miles, chiefly on horseback & returned all the better for it ...they say that the benefits produced by this journey will be immense & interesting, that the 2 Brothers should just at the same time be making their triumphal and peaceful progress, in such very opposite parts of the Globe![55]

As for Alfred himself, the personality of the young man who had visited southern Africa in 1860, demonstrating a keen interest in whatever Governor George Grey had to show him, was quickly transformed by life in the navy. He became far more interested in the hyper-masculine culture of the sea and far less interested in the cultures of the empire. He shared his father's love of hunting and often completed his duties as a royal visitor with the expectation that he might be rewarded with a hunt. He even tried to divert the itinerary of his 1869 tour in order to stop in Natal for a hunting expedition.[56] Of course, these interests were important components of a British imperial culture, but they represented a subconscious, banal imperialism rather than an explicit, ideological one.[57]

Between 1860 and the early 1870s, Alfred transformed from an active and intellectually curious young prince into an adult far more settled in his ways, the boor that his mother frequently described. Despite his early curiosity, Alfred's worldview on empire and the royal tour can be detected from his earliest tour and retained a significant degree of consistency over time. Alfred wrote frequently to his mother, and these letters offer valuable insights into his understandings of his travels. Details about colonial cultures or his experiences were rarely reported back to Victoria by Alfred, but were usually conveyed by his co-travellers and through newspapers sent back by colonial officials. Victoria and Alfred most frequently discussed family and European politics. Home life, impending marriages, and Continental affairs rather than the empire dominated these conversations. As his letters illustrate, Alfred's expressions of interest in his mother's colonial subjects were rarely articulated explicitly (which is not to say that he had none). Indeed he found meaning in the royal tours not in his role as an imperial prince but in the masculine culture of the navy and in his favourite pastime, hunting.

Growing up in the navy, Alfred's life was shaped by its culture. The homosocial space of a Royal Navy ship cultivated a brand of masculine camaraderie and friendship that Alfred cherished, to such a degree that he later had trouble socialising back on land in Europe. Despite the highly regimented nature of the navy, life aboard ship for Alfred was one of playful, and sometimes violent, horseplay and a fair dose of taunting and vexation. Once, when he arrived at Malta, his fellow midshipmen aboard the *Euryalus* 'bumped him on the deck' with each shot of the royal salute.[58] This playfulness was somewhat of a departure from his strict upbringing by his parents.

Feelings of camaraderie eased the strict regime and social separation of a navy life. Lieutenant-Colonel Haig reported to Queen Victoria the profound isolation of life at sea and the importance of human connections. One night per week, part of the main deck was transformed into a stage, lit by a row of lanterns.[59] With an 'orchestra' of a piano and a fiddle, the sailors performed songs, readings, and recitations to entertain their audience, who, 'determined to be amused … sit there, and laugh, and cheer to their hearts' content'.[60] The ship even had its own band of minstrels, who would perform 'Negro melodies'.[61] On other nights, Alfred might be found playing the violin while other men sat or lay about reading or doing crochet.[62] Alfred grew very comfortable and content with this life and these relationships.

When off the ship, hunting was never far from Alfred's mind. In this, he was like his father, who had adored the royal estate at Balmoral, in part because he could spend hours stalking deer in the Scottish

Highlands.[63] Alfred frequently and excitedly reported to his mother his hunting adventures while on tour. In South Africa, he and George Grey awaited a rumbling herd of wild animals, rounded up and driven toward them by a group of local natives, and began firing upon them *en masse* during a rather grotesque 'hunting' trip in 1860.[64] He went hunting with the Maharajah of Benares in 1870 and 'rolled over an enormous tiger' that 'got away very badly wounded'.[65] He hunted antelope, elephants, ostriches, partridges, pheasants, deer, and many other exotic animals. While encountering his mother's subjects, it seems, his mind often wandered to the hunt.

Like other royal children, when he did write to his mother about his visits, it was often to complain. He openly complained to his mother during his visit to India in 1869–70. From Calcutta in 1869, he griped that 'ever since my arrival it has been one unceasing state ceremony, Levées, large dinners, state receptions, visits, balls, & drawing rooms in rapid succession'.[66] He reported that the previous day the festivities began at 8.30 in the morning and continued until 1.30 that morning.[67] Early in January 1870, he again wrote to his mother complaining of his duties:

> I received the Native Princes on board this is a very tedious ceremony. They each come separate with the Viceroy's agent who is attached to him and a few native attendants, he is brought in by the foreing [sic] secretary & sits down on my right with the foreign secretary & his attendants on his right & my staff on my left. The conversation consists of asking after one another's health, the beauty of the weather .... The only difference in the seven [?] visits was the number of guns in his salute & the number of steps.[68]

Royal children routinely complained about such visits and their tedium. His letters home reflect boredom with his imperial duties, preferring his shipmates to local dignitaries and hunting trips to dinners at Government House.

Alfred was not wholly uninterested in the empire, but it often represented an irritating interruption of the life he most enjoyed. He probably travelled more than any royal before or after him, yet he hardly thought about or commented on his role as one of the British Empire's greatest travellers. While colonial subjects who met him often commented on his warmth and graciousness, on his skill as a royal ambassador, these encounters virtually never registered in his letters home. For his parents, travelling the world as a sailor in the Royal Navy was a method of teaching Alfred a profession and giving him an opportunity to see the world. For everyone else who was touched by the visits, he was a symbol of diverse manifestations of imperial identity and citizenship. For Alfred, the meaning of his royal tourism was found in the joys of navy life and the pursuit of his favourite pastime.

Albert Edward, the Prince of Wales

Victoria and Albert had high expectations for young Albert Edward (the future Edward VII), the heir to the throne, and his parents' rigorous educational programme for him reflected these desires. They sought to avoid the decadent excesses of his uncles and to train Edward as an informed and thoughtful King in the model of Albert. The young prince, however, was not an intellectually curious child and was rather quickly considered somewhat of a lost cause by his parents. He was not Albert, and more closely resembled his polar opposite. Victoria and Albert favoured his older sister Victoria, and later Alfred and Arthur.[69] Edward wrote very little and left historians very little textual evidence, other than what was written on his behalf by his private secretary Francis Knollys and in the official histories of the monarchy.

In British history, Edward has come to represent cultural and moral excess, a reaction against the strictness and austerity of Victorianism. Yet his reaction was initially to his father, not his mother, with whom he had much in common. He found his father's rules and morals stifling and his expectations unachievable. In this regard, the image of the Savile Row Prince of Wales, wearing midnight blue dinner-jackets, smoking, attending the theatre, philandering, and generally living up to his reputation as a rakish playboy is accurate. He was, as Bagehot suggested, 'an unemployed youth', with no obvious role in life other than waiting to be King.[70] He performed adequately at Oxford and Cambridge, matriculating at Trinity College in 1861. He unsuccessfully tried out life in the army during the summer of 1861, only for gossip about his romantic encounter with the actress Nellie Clifden to be spread around London. And, when his father died, his mother would blame him and all of his trouble-making for his death.

As a royal tourist, however, Edward proved rather successful in carrying out his ceremonial duties in the empire, which required more in terms of charm and far less in terms of intellect. His performance in the 1860 royal tour of Canada was a rare occasion when his parents openly expressed satisfaction in his performance.[71] He was the first heir to the throne to visit the empire and was very well travelled, taking frequent trips to the Continent; travelling to North America in 1860; cast off to Jerusalem, Cairo, and Constantinople in 1862 after his father's death; and making a trip to India in 1875–76. Even if he was far out-travelled by his younger brother Alfred, he was the most 'globalised' Prince of Wales in history (though this honour would immediately pass to his son, George). Jane Ridley, writing about his tour of India in 1875–76, argues that the royal tour 'was royalty as theatre, and he excelled in the role. His passion for uniforms and dressing up coupled with his addiction to the London stage meant that he knew his lines perfectly and understood instinctively how the role of the prince-emperor should be played.'[72] Despite his success as a royal ambassador, his mother did not trust him to act as her representative in performing the monarchy's public duties, despite her own refusal to perform them.[73]

In 1860, Queen Victoria was invited by the Canadian colonies to inaugurate the Victoria Bridge over the St. Lawrence River. Victoria did not want to go but agreed to send her oldest son, Albert Edward, the Prince of Wales. His father, the Prince Consort, and the Colonial Secretary, the Duke of Newcastle, conceived of the tour as a historic moment in the history of the British Empire. Newcastle travelled with the prince and acted as his handler. Albert Edward spent several months in Canada and the United States. He watched Charles Blondin cross the Niagara Gorge on a tightrope and stayed with the President James Buchanan at the White House.

Like Alfred's tour, the idea for his older brother Albert Edward's royal tour of Canada in 1860 came from the empire, at the invitation of the Canadian legislature.[74] Victoria had been invited to Canada several times in the 1850s, a prospect that she considered to be impossible.[75] She proposed that once the Prince of Wales was old enough, he would visit Canada.[76] As was the case during the Duke of Cornwall's royal tour forty years later, it was intended to thank colonials for their contributions to an imperial war effort, in this case the Crimean War.[77] Moreover, the idea of the heir to the throne inaugurating the new Victoria Bridge across the St. Lawrence River, one of the Victorian era's greatest engineering marvels, as his younger brother across the Atlantic tipped the first truck of stone into Table Bay built on much of the ideological work Albert had done as the Prince Consort – to connect the monarchy to notions of progress.

There is little sense that Edward realised the importance his parents and the Canadian government placed on the visit. He wrote to his mother in the mode of a tourist, rather than as a future imperial monarch. He performed well and impressed his handlers. Yet he was a teenager who was simply performing the duties being asked of him. He wrote to his mother after performing his first public duties as a royal ambassador in Newfoundland: 'I had to receive fourteen addresses, rather a large number for the first time.'[78] He commented on an encounter with First Peoples in the language of a sightseer, which would be repeated during his 1875 tour of India; he noted that they treated him civilly and wore 'more modified costumes than those that are generally represented in pictures'.[79]

While in North America, he often reported on the beauty of the New World and matter-of-factly on his experiences with colonial people. Even his official biographer, Sidney Lee, admitted a complete lack of imperial consciousness by Edward: 'If the Prince's descriptions of his experiences ... proved bare and informal, they were relieved by some naïve comments on the persons whom he met, by comparisons of scenes which were new to him with familiar places at home, and by occasional notes on surviving memories of his grandfather.'[80] Even while in the empire, his mind remained very much at home.

In 1875, when the Council of India raised the idea of a royal visit by the Prince of Wales to India, however, the Queen was reluctant to grant her permission.[81] While his younger brother Alfred had recently visited India, Edward had survived a bout of typhoid fever in 1871, the disease that likely killed his father, and the Queen was unwilling to part with him. The Queen had not always opposed the idea of Edward travelling to India; before his father died, Albert had imagined India to be on the itinerary of his planned travels in the Near East.[82] But now, perhaps understandably, the Queen did not want to give up her son.

Victoria was surprised and angered, then, when Lord Salisbury, the Secretary of State for India, announced to her his plan for the prince's tour of India. The Prince of Wales himself was determined to go to India, although his motive, other than escaping his mother's grip, is unclear. Upon finding out, Victoria wrote to Lord Salisbury to articulate her unhappiness about the plans: 'The Queen has received Lord Salisbury's letter of the 17th relative to the Prince of Wales' going to India and she wishes him to know that while she gave her consent, she did so very reluctantly as she thinks the risk and responsibility very great for the Prince of Wales is no longer in his former health and invariably over does his powers of endurance & fatigue and the distance from home is enormous!'[83]

Two months later, she explained in a letter to Lord Northbrook, the Viceroy of India, that she had given 'a very unwilling consent' and that 'she had expected it ... would have been very carefully considered and weighed in the Cabinet before being announced to the Viceroy'.[84] She indicated that she wanted to convey her 'real feelings and views on this subject' to him and sought his 'impartial opinion' on the visit. Noting these reservations, Salisbury and Northbrook continued to forge their plans for the visit.

The Queen grew irritated by her exclusion from the planning process. She complained to Salisbury that she had personally 'received no information' from the Secretary of State about the tour arrangements, even though 'the newspapers are full of them'.[85] Victoria demanded that she be 'accurately informed on every point' and that 'her sanction may be obtained before anything is decided'.[86] She focused her efforts on preserving Edward's health over the duration of the visit by trying to limit his engagements. She also sought to approve of the prince's party, mainly so she could excise any of his troublesome friends from the list. According to Derby, one letter from Victoria to Disraeli was written 'with so much violence and so little dignity that to hear it read with gravity was impossible'.[87] Furthermore, the Queen insisted, in agreement with Salisbury, that the Prince of Wales was to travel to India as first subject rather than as a representative of the Queen. Northbrook was her true representative, as she understood imperial hierarchy. Her son could not, then, hold a durbar or take any ceremonial precedence over the viceroy.

The Prince of Wales and the government forged ahead despite her reservations, and although the Queen came to imagine herself as the proper master of the planning process, this notion was very much an illusion. As the responses to her protests reflect, planning Albert Edward's tour of India continued with or without her blessing. As the case of the Prince of Wales' second son George will demonstrate, Victoria could refuse and obstruct plans, but proponents would collude – as we shall see, Prince George, the Colonial Secretary, and the Queen's personal secretary – to convince her to put aside her reservations.

While he never developed a well-defined knowledge or consciousness of the empire, Edward did express an interest in local peoples, particularly the Indian princes, during his visits and sought to recast himself more visibly as an imperial monarch once King. In a sense, he became a better-travelled version of his mother, captured by the *idea* of being an imperial monarch but without an obvious understanding of what exactly being one meant.

The extant letters of Edward offer some limited insight into his understanding of the royal tour of India. In terms of his imperial consciousness, he had much in common with his mother. While he articulated an interest in local people, he also demonstrated a certain naivety about the empire, seeing it as an uncomplicated place. He recounted, for instance, his encounter with the Gaekwad of Baroda (see Chapter 2) in simple terms to his mother: that he gave the young gaekwad, 'a very intelligent boy, quite overloaded with jewels', some gifts, which pleased the boy, and received in return 'some very pretty things'.[88] In conveying an image of Bombay to his mother, he described his travels through the streets of the city in the language of a tourist: 'You see mixed together natives of all classes, creeds & origin. Their Houses are very picturesque & they are all painted different colours. The lowest classes & children hardly wear any garments at all.'[89] This assessment reflects a limited knowledge of his surroundings and enough cultural distance to avoid the moral implications of his sightseeing.

Like his mother, Edward expressed a much more profound interest in the hereditary princes of India than anything else in the Raj. He complained to his mother about the abuse of the princes by colonial administrators:

> What struck me, most forcibly, was the rude and rough manner with which the English 'Political Officers' (as they are called, who are in attendance upon them) treat them. It is indeed much to be deplored, and the system is, I am sure, quite wrong. Natives of all classes in this country will, I am sure, be more attached to us and to our rule, if they are treated with kindness with firmness at the same time, but not with brutality & contempt.[90]

While the dynamics of ornamentalism and imperial rule will be discussed in Chapter 2, Cannadine's notion that the British 'saw' their empire in terms of an imperial social hierarchy, rather than race or colour, is useful in this context.[91] In the looking-glass of empire, did Edward see, in the behaviour of British officials toward native princes, a mirror image of the Victorian monarchy, deprived of its power and pushed around by government officials? It would not be a conceptual leap to suggest that royals recognised some semblance of *similarity*. This does not mean that his sympathy did not also invoke *difference* (racial or otherwise) or that what he imagined reflected anything but an invented 'idea' of India. Yet Edward's simple imperialism represented a limited kind of imperial consciousness; deprived of any real power in the imperial hierarchy, he may well have recognised that he was not all that different from the princes with whom he sympathised.[92]

Much like Victoria, Edward delighted in the idea of being an imperial monarch in name. The effect of travelling twice to the empire, to Canada in 1860 and to India in 1875, indelibly informed his notions of what it meant to be the British monarch. Upon the death of Victoria, Edward proposed a revision to the royal title that included 'Greater Britain'. The request was certainly influenced by his reading of Dilke but was more directly inspired by the suggestion of Sir Alfred Milner, the Governor of the Cape Colony and High Commissioner for Southern Africa. Ironically perhaps, he would never set foot in the empire again.

George

Prince George had much in common with his uncle, Alfred. Between 1879 and 1882, George travelled the world as a royal cadet aboard HMS

Bacchante with his older brother Albert Victor.[93] As a reaction against his own austere and 'over-pressured intellectual education', Albert Edward encouraged a less rigorous and more limited educational programme for George and his brother.[94] George had a limited knowledge of French and German and had little exposure to the Continent. During his 1879–82 tour of the world, George visited many places, both British and not: among them, Gibraltar, the Mediterranean, the West Indies, the Falklands, the Cape, Australia, Fiji, Japan, China, the Straits Settlements, Ceylon, Egypt, and Palestine. His understanding of his royal duties was profoundly informed by his years in the Royal Navy, where he legitimately earned his spurs as an officer, and he felt a deep respect for and connection with naval culture and with the people with whom he developed relationships during this period of his life. Unlike his parents and grandparents, he expressed a certain discomfort with Europe, despite his marriage to the English-born Mary of Teck. As the second son of the Prince of Wales, he had little prospect of becoming King, that is until his older brother Albert Victor died suddenly of influenza in 1891. Despite the similarities, George developed a different and more complex understanding of empire than his uncle, in part through his relationship with Joseph Chamberlain.

His consciousness of the empire as grandson and son of a monarch and later as King George V represents a generational difference with his grandmother and father and reflects broader changes in British society. His coronation at Westminster Abbey in June 1911 was celebrated by a Festival of Empire in London, and he was the first reigning monarch to visit the overseas empire, holding a coronation durbar in Delhi in 1911. Growing up in the high age of European imperialism, his understanding of the empire represents a turning point between a nineteenth-century monarchy that struggled and failed to retain its political relevance and a twentieth-century monarchy that came to accept its ceremonial role in British and imperial culture, best illustrated by Elizabeth II's frequent travels in Britain and abroad. Ironically, George V reigned over the beginnings of the transformation of the British Empire from an empire on which the sun never set into a collection of associated states (later institutionalised as the Commonwealth) and the decline of Britain as a global power.

The Queen soundly rejected Prince George's first invitation to the empire as an adult royal. Apparently enthused by the outpouring of colonial loyalty to the Queen during the Diamond Jubilee celebrations of 1897, the government of New Zealand invited the Duke and Duchess of York to visit New Zealand and Australia.[95] Queen Victoria very quickly refused, citing her reluctance to allow a prince so close to the throne to travel so far away from home.[96] She scolded the Cabinet for even considering the proposal and asserted that she would 'never give [her] consent to this idea'.[97] George, in a letter to the Colonial Secretary Joseph Chamberlain, wrote that he was sorry about his grandmother's decision, considering that 'it is so very important to do all we can to please the Colonies at this moment, and to so bind them more closely to the Mother Country'.[98] The government's unquestioning acceptance of the Queen's refusal was extremely rare, if not unheard of, during this period. The fact that neither Chamberlain nor the Duke of York took a particular interest in the visit and or the Queen on the issue, as was usually the case, perhaps explains this capitulation.

In 1900, Chamberlain again proposed a royal tour, this time in response to an Australian invitation to inaugurate the new federal parliament in Melbourne. While his initial proposal focused on Australia, but quickly incorporated a Canadian invitation, he imagined a much larger global tour of empire. Chamberlain conceived of the tour as an opportunity to thank the colonies for their service in the South African War and to forward his own ideas about imperial unity. Prince George was very enthusiastic about the prospect of this trip and corresponded frequently with the Colonial Secretary about the state of the negotiations with his grandmother. As on previous occasions, Queen Victoria was extremely reluctant to allow the Duke of York to go to Australia.[99] Chamberlain and George, assisted by the Prince of Wales and the prime minister, Lord Salisbury, spent several months negotiating with the Queen and, in effect, conspiring with one another to convince the Queen to permit the tour.

In 1900, the Australian colonies invited the Queen to send her grandson George to the inauguration of an Australian federation, an offer that she declined. Over the course of several months, Victoria had to be coaxed and convinced by the government and by her family to allow George's visit. George took the lead in advocating in favour of the visit to his grandmother. He wrote to Chamberlain in early July 1900 to indicate that he had made some progress with his grandmother on the subject of the royal tour, since she 'seemed less unfavourable to the suggestion than on a former occasion', and that his father the Prince of Wales would speak to her on the importance of the visit, 'a most important event connected with the birth of the Empire'.[100] By mid-August, George found her to be 'not adverse' to the idea of a brief visit to Australia, though she refused any consideration of a stop in Canada.[101] He wrote in the manner of an intelligence-gatherer, suggesting to Chamberlain that 'it would be better if you did not mention that you had heard from me'.[102] For George, his prospects of his royal tour looked promising. Far more than his grandmother, he understood the importance of the royal tours and actively participated in convincing the Queen.

The Queen, however, would waver and then refuse, again. Two days later, the Queen's personal secretary Sir Arthur Bigge wrote urgently to Chamberlain, explaining that 'Her Majesty did not seem to be so much in favour of the proposal as the Duke assumed her to be after their conversation two days ago.'[103] She was unhappy that the prime minister or the Cabinet apparently had no knowledge and thus no opinion of the proposal and concluded, according to Bigge, that 'if [she] was asked now [she] should feel inclined to refuse'.[104] The Queen's age and the need to have royal children on hand to attend ceremonies in her place further discouraged her willingness to consent.[105] Despite collaboration between George, the government, and the Queen's personal secretary, she was more reluctant to grant permission for royal visits than ever before.

Bigge, a personal servant of the Queen, informed Chamberlain that he sensed that, when the proposal was put clearly and formally to the Queen, she would realise the importance of the visit to Australia, 'the practical birthday of a new Empire'.[106] Lord Salisbury feigned ignorance, Bigge informed Chamberlain, because the Prince of Wales wished to first speak to her on the matter. If the government was respectful of her concerns and appealed to her through official channels rather than through her grandson, he encouraged, she would be far more receptive. Even the Queen's personal secretary, it seems, conspired with George and Chamberlain in the scheme to bring a royal son to the empire.

After receiving a formal proposal from Salisbury, the Queen finally agreed to the visit, with very specific stipulations. She agreed to the visit if the South African War had concluded by the time of the tour; if she remained in good health; if his visit was no longer than five months; and if George agreed to visit Canada and India another time.[107] Bigge confided to Chamberlain that she 'does not like the idea' but was convinced of its importance by Salisbury.[108] While worried that he might be considered a disloyal servant of the Queen, he even suggested that the limitations set by the Queen might be overcome with time. Chamberlain would assure him of his loyalty and indicated that other proposals for visits, from Canada, for instance, could still be considered until later stages in the planning process.[109] George similarly proposed to Chamberlain that Canada might be reconsidered at a later time.[110] They had got what they wanted and could seek more concessions from the reluctant imperial monarch later.

Despite the Queen's reluctance and obstructionism, the semi-official account of the tour, written by fellow traveller Joseph Watson, was curiously titled *The Queen's Wish*.[111] The idea of the Queen as a willing and enthusiastic participant reflects a key ideological component of the royal tour, principally that Queen Victoria sought to share her children and grandchildren with her colonial subjects as a gesture of maternal goodwill. Yet, even though she was the iconic symbol of the empire, the Queen was always a reluctant partner in royal visits. She wished to keep her children and grandchildren close to home. Only through the work of others, including young royals, was she ever persuaded to allow such travels.

George's letters to Joseph Chamberlain before and during his 1901 tour demonstrate a deep knowledge of and interest in imperial politics. He had enthusiastically promoted the tour to his grandmother, in part because he foresaw 'the greatest possible benefits to the Empire'.[112] Before the tour began, he articulated a desire to distribute medals to colonial troops, this while expressing concern over the sack of Kumasi on the Gold Coast.[113] He might be compared to his grandmother in his interest in empire, except that George had been to the empire and understood many of the political and cultural intricacies that would have been lost on Victoria.

Other than describing the loyalty of Australians, which he attributed to the rule of his grandmother, the South African War, and the work of Chamberlain, he articulated a sophisticated understanding of colonial policy.[114] His letters reflect a profound knowledge of Australian politics, particularly after such a short time in the country: the rivalries between the different states, trade policy, policies regarding 'Black' and Chinese labour, drought and agricultural production, and many other topics. His correspondence reads like colonial intelligence, a seismic shift from previous royal tours. To describe George's more developed awareness of empire is not to romanticise his knowledge or concern for empire.

The royal tour – the most extensive to date – only developed George's sense of being better connected to the empire than his predecessors and the rest of British society. Returning to Britain late in 1901, he gave a speech at Guildhall on 5 December that he claimed reflected the colonial mood, asserting 'that the Old Country must wake up if she intends to maintain her old position of pre-eminence in her Colonial trade against foreign competitors'. This sentiment reflects the political work of his imperial tutor, Joseph Chamberlain.[115] In this regard, George represented a departure from his father and grandmother, in having a clear sense of his role as an imperial monarch. He advocated imperial unity and defence and travelled to the empire once he became King. Yet it was in George that the British monarchy took on its familiar twentieth-century form, as an institution that had come to accept its purely symbolic role in both British domestic society and at the centre of a global empire and Commonwealth.

Prince George would be a monarch in a much different mould from his grandmother. As the first reigning monarch to visit the empire, he embraced its importance to the monarchy and his own role in its ritualistic order. As a teenager, he had written on Bagehot's *English Constitution* and had internalised the notions of the monarchy's 'dignified' and 'business' (rather than 'efficient') capacities.[116] He returned from the 1901 tour as a vocal advocate of imperial unity. As Prince of Wales, he visited India in 1905–06, and echoing his father's complaints of 1875–76, argued that 'the Ruling Chiefs ought to be treated with greater tact and sympathy, more as equals than as inferiors'.[117] He also wrote to the Commander-in-Chief of the Indian army, encouraging improved pay and conditions for Indian soldiers, and in his Guildhall speech called for 'wider sympathy' on the part of colonial administrators in relation to their colonial subjects.[118] As George V, he travelled to India in 1911 to be crowned King-Emperor at the Delhi durbar and Imperial Assemblage (see the Postscript). What Victoria resisted and refused would be embraced by a new generation of royal children.

Conclusion

Victoria died a few months after George and Chamberlain secured her reluctant commitment, in January 1901. The South African War would not end for another year. Edward VII was slow to allow the heir to the throne to go ahead with the tour but ultimately approved it, at the insistence of Arthur Balfour, the Conservative Party leader.[119] George would visit not only Australia but also New Zealand, Mauritius, South Africa, and Canada, with stops in Aden, Ceylon, and Singapore. This world tour was hardly the 'Queen's wish'. While those who planned and participated in the tour regarded a federated Australia as representing the symbolic beginnings of a new imperial century, it more clearly represented the newly developed role of the monarchy in a British world, forged and refined over the previous four decades. George and his successor would embrace Bagehot's 'dignified' powers and the importance of empire in a way that Victoria never did.

The image of Queen Victoria was transmitted to and appropriated by Britain's colonial subjects around the world. It was used by colonial administrators to support and legitimise imperial rule and by colonial subjects to demand imperial citizenship as loyal subjects to the Queen. It spread to the farthest reaches of the British colonial empire, often far beyond the zone of effective military or political control. And, long after her death, subject peoples continued to appeal to her memory in demanding rights and fairness. Queen Victoria was the most potent cultural symbol in the history of the British Empire.

The British monarchy was reinvented as an imperial monarchy through the efforts of colonial officials and Victoria's subjects across the globe. The Great Queen was a reluctant participant in the royal tours and demonstrated a limited interest in her empire after the death of Albert. While her children frequently embraced a similar attitude toward the empire, of distance and reluctance despite their own encounters with it, her successors would ultimately accept the monarchy's ritual and cultural role in the empire as vitally important. By the crowning of George V as King-Emperor, and certainly by the coronation of his granddaughter Elizabeth, the myth of the imperial monarch became real.

Notes

1 Miriam Pilane interview, undated, Botswana National Archives, Gaborone, Tape 36. Translated from Setswana. Cited in Ashley Jackson, 'Motivation and Mobilisation for War: Recruitment for the British Army in the Bechuanaland', *African Affairs* 96, no. 384 (July 1997), 401.

2 David Cannadine, *Ornamentalism: How the British Saw Their Empire* (London, 2001).

3 Cannadine, *Ornamentalism*, 103.

4 According to Miles Taylor, before 1876 Victoria 'thought she was Empress of India already'. Miles Taylor, 'Queen Victoria and India, 1837–61', *Victorian Studies* 46, no. 2 (Winter 2014), 264.

5 David Cannadine, 'The Context, Performance and Meaning of Ritual: The British Monarchy and the Invention of Tradition, c. 1820–1977', in *The Invention of Tradition*, ed. Eric Hobsbawm and Terence Ranger (Cambridge, 1983), 101–64.

6 David M. Craig, 'The Crowned Republic? Monarchy and Anti-Monarchy in Britain, 1760–1901', *Historical Journal* 46 (March 2003), 170.

7 Cannadine, *Ornamentalism*, 133.

8 Cannadine, 'The Context, Performance and Meaning of Ritual', 108.

9 See Natalie Mears, *Queen and Political Discourse in the Elizabethan Realms* (Cambridge, 2005); Anna Keay, *The Magnificent Monarchy: Charles II and the Ceremonies of Power* (New York, 2008); Robert Bucholz, *The Augustan Court: Queen Anne and the Decline of Court Culture* (Stanford, 1993).

10 Christopher Hibbert, 'Introduction' in *Queen Victoria in her Letters and Journals* (London, 1984), 1.

11 Michael Alexander and Sushila Anand, *Queen Victoria's Maharajah: Duleep Singh, 1838–93*, 2nd edn (London, 2001); Neil Parsons, *King Khama, Emperor Joe, and the Great White Queen: Victorian Britain through African Eyes* (Chicago, 1998), 227.

12 Alison Drummond, 'Queen Victoria Had a Maori Godson', *Te Ao Hou: The New World*, no. 24 (October 1958): 60–1; Miles Taylor, *Queen Victoria and India* (New Haven, forthcoming). Taylor argues that Victoria was intensely engaged with her Indian empire, a fact that I do not dispute here. I do contend that her interest was limited and ambivalent and was most often focused on moments of crisis or celebration.

13 John MacKenzie, 'Introduction', in *The Victorian Vision: Inventing New Britain*, ed. John MacKenzie (London, 2001), 19.
14 Royal visits to the empire, with the exception of the Prince of Wales' visits to Canada and India in 1860 and 1875–76 respectively, are virtually ignored in the historical biographies and the published letters of Queen Victoria and Prince Albert, as well as those of their children and grandchildren.
15 Walter Arnstein, *Queen Victoria* (New York, 2003), 202.
16 James Murphy has written a very skilful study of the British monarchy and Irish society, particularly Victoria's royal tour of 1900, the insights of which will be revisited in the later chapter on imperial rule. See James Murphy, *Abject Loyalty: Nationalism and the Monarchy in Ireland during the Reign of Queen Victoria* (Washington, DC, 2001). For more on Victoria's travels see David Duff, ed., *Victoria Travels: Journeys of Queen Victoria between 1830 and 1900, with Extracts from her Journal* (New York, 1971). A very curious, if interesting, volume about Victoria's imaginary visit to Jamaica was published in the 1980s by Doubleday, republished by Random House in 2002: Jonathan Routh, *The Secret Life of Queen Victoria: Her Majesty's Missing Dairies* (Garden City, NY, 1980).
17 Parsons, *King Khama*, 227–8.
18 Walter Bagehot, *The English Constitution* (Project Gutenberg e-text). http://www.gutenberg.org/dirs/etext03/thngl10.txt, accessed 10 February 2009.
19 Quoted in Hibbert, *Queen Victoria in her Letters and Journals*, 4.
20 David Cannadine, *History in Our Time* (New York, 2000), 42.
21 In her excellent analysis of Albert's significance, Karina Urbach dubs him the 'Creative Consort'. Karina Urbach, 'Prince Albert: The Creative Consort', in *The Man behind the Queen: Male Consorts in History*, ed. Charles Beam and Miles Taylor (London, 2014), 145–5.
22 Collar of the Order of the Star of India, RCIN 441295, Royal Collection, London.
23 Albert's extraordinary attention to detail can be witnessed in his lengthy letter to the Duke of Newcastle detailing arrangements for the Prince of Wales' tour of Canada. Albert to the Duke of Newcastle, 8 July 1860, Ne C 12771/1, Papers of the Duke of Newcastle, University of Nottingham.
24 Theodore Martin, *The Life of His Royal Highness the Prince Consort*, vol. 5 (London, 1880), 83.
25 'A Toast Given at the Dinner of the Trinity House, June 23, 1860', *The Principal Speeches and Addresses of His Royal Highness the Prince Consort* (London, 1862), 243–4.
26 On this topic, see Miriam Scheider, 'Royal Naval Education, Sailor Princes, and the Re-Invention of the Monarchy' (MPhil thesis, University of Cambridge, 2011).
27 In 1863, John O'Shanassy, the Premier of Victoria, suggested the Prince Alfred might become king of Australia. Cindy McCreery, 'A British Prince and a Transnational Life: Alfred, Duke of Edinburgh's Visit to Australia, 1867–8', in *Transnational Ties: Australian Lives in the World*, ed. Desley Deacon, Penny Russell and Angela Woollacott (Canberra, 2008), 59. Also see *A Proposal for the Confederation of the Australian Colonies, with Prince Alfred, Duke of Edinburgh, as King of Australia. By a Colonist* (Sydney, 1867). During the negotiations over the Royal Titles Act in 1876, Disraeli suggested that Victoria's two sons might be titled the Duke of Canada and the Duke of Australia. Extract from the Queen's Journal, 26 February 1876, in *The Letters of Queen Victoria*, ed. G. E. Buckle, Second Series, *1862–85*, 3 vols (London, 1926–28), vol. 2, 448. Arthur, Duke of Connaught would later serve as Governor-General of Canada under his nephew, George V. Also see Cannadine, *History in Our Time*, 39–40.
28 Lord Northbrook to Lord Salisbury, 29 April 1875, RA VIC/MAIN/Z/468/10.
29 Queen Victoria to Lord Salisbury, 27 May 1875, RA VIC/MAIN/Z /468/11. This problem was deemed of particular importance in India, particular because a Raj ruled by the Crown rather than a trading company was a rather new idea in the 1870s. This issue was also discussed in the preparations for Alfred's visit of 1875. Lord Northcote

to Baron Lawrence, 1 August 1868, Papers of Sir John Lawrence, British Library, London, European Manuscripts (henceforth BL MSS Eur), F90/29 no. 40.

30 Lord Salisbury to Queen Victoria, RA VIC/MAIN/Z/468/ CFP/24. Salisbury appealed to the precedent of the 1860 Canadian tour, which he saw as allowing a temporary suspension of this policy on grounds that 'there is some real danger that if the Queen's own son is put in a position of obvious inferiority, the true relation of the Viceroy to the Queen will be misunderstood or ignored'.

31 J. Fayer, *Notes on the Visits to India of Their Royal Highnesses the Prince of Wales and Duke of Edinburgh, 1870–1875–76* (London, 1879), 75.

32 Major Cowell to W. Christee (Foreign Office), 30 April 1860, RA VIC/Add A 20/49.

33 Quoted in Richard Hough, *Victoria and Albert* (New York, 1996), 157.

34 Ian Radforth, *Royal Spectacle: The 1860 Visit of the Prince of Wales to Canada and the United States* (Toronto, 2004), 44.

35 Albert to the Duke of Newcastle, 8 July 1860, Ne C 12771/1, Papers of the Duke of Newcastle, University of Nottingham.

36 Lord Northcote to Baron Lawrence, 1 August 1868, Papers of Sir John Lawrence, BL MSS Eur F90/29 no. 40.

37 Whether O'Farrell was actually a Fenian remains unclear. The Colonial Secretary of New South Wales at the time, Henry Parkes, who doubled as a police detective during the investigation, remained convinced, thirty years later, that O'Farrell was of sound mind. Henry Parkes, *Fifty Years in the Making of Australian History* (London, 1892), 190–211.

38 John Manning Ward, *The State and the People: Australian Federation and Nation-Making,1870–1901*, ed. D. M. Schreuder, B. H. Fletcher, and R. Hutchison (Leichhardt, 2001), 16.

39 Malcolm Campbell, 'A "Successful Experiment" No More: The Intensification of Religious Bigotry in Eastern Australia, 1865–1885', *Humanities Research* 12, no. 1 (2005), 70.

40 Cited in Campbell, 'A "Successful Experiment" ', 70.

41 *Fenian Revelations: The Confessions of O'Farrell who Attempted to Assassinate the Duke of Edinburgh* (London, 1868).

42 *Fenian Revelations*, 5.

43 *Fenian Revelations*, 3, 13. He told Parkes that the Fenians did not target the Prince of Wales because he was 'useful to the cause – the Republican cause, because he disgraces loyalty.... He is turning England against royalty.'

44 *Fenian Revelations*, 12–15.

45 *Fenian Revelations*, 9–10, 24. 'Perhaps he wants to make up a million exactly, or a legion, 10,000; he has received a stream now from all parts of the colony.... Will he take them all home with him? Will the *Galatea* hold them all? I think he ought to set fire to the lot and take the ashes of them all home.'

46 Alfred to Queen Victoria, 27 March 1868, RA VIC/ADDA20/1281.

47 Alfred has received surprisingly little attention from scholars. The only book-length biography of Alfred is John Van der Kiste and B. Jordaan, *Dearest Affie: Alfred, Duke of Edinburgh, Queen Victoria's Second Son, 1844–1900* (Gloucester, 1984). Van der Kiste updated his biography in short-form for *Oxford DNB*, 'Alfred, Prince, duke of Edinburgh (1844–1900)'; Cindy McCreery, who was of assistance in the competition of this work, has published several more recent works on Alfred. See McCreery, 'A British Prince and a Transnational Life'; Cindy McCreery, '"Long May He Float on the Ocean of Life": The First Royal Visit to Tasmania, 1868', *Tasmanian Historical Studies* no. 12 (2007): 19–42.

48 Arthur Balfour Haig to Queen Victoria, 27 August 1870, RA VIC/MAIN/S/27/54.

49 Quoted in Hough, *Victoria and Albert*, 162.

50 John Russell to W. D. Christie, 30 April 1860, RA VIC/ADDA20/49.

51 Queen Victoria's Journals, Princess Beatrice's copies, vol. 49, 204–5, 6 August 1860.

52 Status in this sense would be revisited again and again during the royal tours, as we shall see.

53 Gardner D. Engleheart to the Governors of the Cape, St. Helena, Sierra Leone, 5 May 1860, RA VIC/ADDA20/62.
54 Major John Cowell to Albert, 29 August 1860 and 5 September 1860, RA VIC/ADDA20/69.
55 RA VIC/MAIN/QVJ (W), 28 October 1860 (Princess Beatrice's copies).
56 Alfred to Queen Victoria, 28 December 1869, RA VIC/ADDA20/1303.
57 Several scholars of empire have argued that hunting was a function of colonialism. It reflects an imperial consciousness much different from the one being examined here, however. Most importantly, see John MacKenzie, *The Empire of Nature: Hunting, Conservation and British Imperialism* (Manchester, 1997).
58 Hough, *Victoria and Albert*, 163.
59 Arthur Balfour Haig to Queen Victoria, 27 August 1870, RA VIC/MAIN/S/27/54.
60 Arthur Balfour Haig to Queen Victoria, 27 August 1870, RA.
61 Arthur Balfour Haig to Queen Victoria, 27 August 1870, RA.
62 Arthur Balfour Haig to Queen Victoria, 27 August 1870, RA.
63 Richard W. Butler, 'The History and Development of Royal Tourism in Scotland: Balmoral, the Ultimate Holiday Home?', in *Royal Tourism: Excursions around Monarchy*, ed. Philip Long and Nicola J. Palmer (Bristol, 2007), 55–7.
64 Saul Solomon, *The Progress of His Royal Highness Prince Alfred Ernest Albert through the Cape Colony, British Kaffraria, the Orange Free State, and Port Natal in the Year 1860* (Cape Town, 1861), 86–92.
65 Alfred to Queen Victoria, 24 January 1870, RA VIC/ADD/A/20/1306.
66 Alfred to Queen Victoria, 28 December 1869, RA VIC/ADDA20/1302.
67 Alfred to Queen Victoria, 28 December 1869, RA.
68 Alfred to Queen Victoria, 9 January 1870, RA VIC/ADDA20/1304.
69 H. C. G. Matthew, 'Edward VII', *Oxford DNB*.
70 Bagehot, *The English Constitution*.
71 Queen Victoria to the Duke of Newcastle, 4 August 1860, Duke of Newcastle Papers, University of Nottingham, Ne C 12744/1.
72 Jane Ridley, *The Heir Apparent: A Life of Edward VII, the Playboy Prince* (New York, 2014), 209, 215.
73 Matthew, 'Edward VII': 'The queen, however, was strongly hostile to the prince's taking on public duties in Britain. She tried to maintain the code of behaviour which Albert had prescribed, which was one in which Albert was the chief male prince. The queen, as Sidney Lee put it, kept her son "in permanent in *statu pupillari*. She claimed to regulate his actions in almost all relations of life". Maintaining a sort of fiction that Albert was alive and active, she forbade the prince's presence on royal commissions and public bodies, and, despite her own almost total seclusion, he was not allowed to represent her at public occasions.'
74 As Prince of Wales, Albert Edward was the ranking son of Queen Victoria. In some sense, the decision to discuss Albert Edward after Alfred is decidedly subversive. After all, Alfred was a far greater traveller than Albert Edward and deserves first attention in a study such as this one. I have relied heavily on Ian Radforth's excellent history of the 1860 tour of Canada rather than retracing what he has already done. Radforth, *Royal Spectacle*, 17.
75 Radforth, *Royal Spectacle*, 17.
76 Radforth, *Royal Spectacle*, 18. Also see Sidney Lee, *King Edward VII: A Biography*, vol. 1 (London, 1925), 85.
77 Radforth, *Royal Spectacle*, 18.
78 Lee, *Edward VII*, 89.
79 Lee, *Edward VII*, 90.
80 Lee, *Edward VII*, 88.
81 Lee, *Edward VII*, 373.
82 Lee, *Edward VII*, 370.
83 Queen Victoria to Lord Salisbury, 18 March 1875, RA VIC/MAIN/Z/468/3. Emphasis in the original text.
84 Queen Victoria to Lord Northbrook, 17 May 1875, RA VIC/MAIN/Z/468/7.

85 Queen Victoria to Lord Salisbury, 27 May 1875, RA VIC/MAIN/Z/468/11.
86 Queen Victoria to Lord Salisbury, 27 May 1875, RA.
87 Vincent, *Derby Diaries 1869–78*, 221 (5 June 1875), cited in Ridley, *Heir Apparent*, 209.
88 Prince of Wales to Queen Victoria, 14 November 1875, RA VIC/MAIN/Z/468/98.
89 Prince of Wales to Queen Victoria, 14 November 1875, RA. Colonial administrators generally guarded him from the worst examples of suffering and poverty.
90 Prince of Wales to Queen Victoria, 14 November 1875, RA. A similar sentiment would later be echoed by his son George upon returning to Britain from India in 1905–06.
91 Cannadine, *Ornamentalism.*
92 Joseph Chamberlain to Edward VII, 15 April 1901, Papers of Joseph Chamberlain, University of Birmingham, JC 11/12/37/60 (henceforth JC).
93 John N. Dalton, *The Cruise of Her Majesty's Ship 'Bacchante', 1879–1882: Compiled from the Private Journals, Letters, and Note-books of Prince Albert Victor and Prince George of Wales*, 2 vols (London, 1886).
94 H. C. G. Matthew, 'George V (1865–1936)', *Oxford DNB*.
95 Earl of Ranfurly to Joseph Chamberlain, 25 November 1897, JC 29/6/6/6; extract from Address by the Governor of New Zealand to the House of Representatives, 23 September 1897, JC 29/6/6/5.
96 Joseph Chamberlain to Queen Victoria, 7 February 1898, JC 29/6/6/10; Joseph Chamberlain to the Earl of Ranfurly, February 1898, JC 29/6/6/2.
97 JC 11/38/10. This document is unsigned, undated, and was written on a plain sheet of notepaper. Context clues, however, make obvious that it conveys the Queen's opinion of the New Zealand invitation. Whether it was written by the Queen or her personal secretary Arthur Bigge is unclear. I must acknowledge Helen Fisher at the Special Collections Library, University of Birmingham, for her assistance on this matter.
98 Duke of York to Joseph Chamberlain, 15 February 1898, JC 29/6/6/11.
99 She was also unhappy about the Australians' choice of 'Australian Commonwealth' as the new federation's name because she thought that it reflected republican sentiments. Chamberlain assured her that they simply wanted to use a different name from the Canadians. Extract from the Queen's Journal, 27 June 1900, *The Letters of Queen Victoria*, ed. G. E. Buckle, Third Series, *1886–1901*, 3 vols (London, 1930–32), vol. 3, 566–7.
100 Duke of York to Joseph Chamberlain, 1 July 1900, JC 11/37/7.
101 Duke of York to Joseph Chamberlain, 15 August 1900, JC 11/38/11.
102 Duke of York to Joseph Chamberlain, 15 August 1900, JC.
103 Sir Arthur Bigge to Joseph Chamberlain, 17 August 1900, JC 11/38/12.
104 Sir Arthur Bigge to Joseph Chamberlain, 17 August 1900, JC.
105 Sir Arthur Bigge to Joseph Chamberlain, 17 August 1900, JC. Her son Alfred had died in late July 1900, and her grandson Albert Victor died in 1892. These deaths left her son the Prince of Wales and his immediate successor the Duke of York, in addition to Prince Arthur, the Duke of Connaught. She determined Arthur to be even more indispensable than George. Queen Victoria to Joseph Chamberlain, 26 August 1900, JC 11/38/17.
106 Sir Arthur Bigge to Joseph Chamberlain, 17 August 1900, JC.
107 Queen Victoria to Lord Salisbury, 26 August 1900, JC 11/38/14.
108 Sir Arthur Bigge to Joseph Chamberlain, 26 August 1900, JC 11/38/15.
109 Joseph Chamberlain to Sir Arthur Bigge, 29 August 1900, JC 11/38/18.
110 Duke of York to Joseph Chamberlain, 9 September 1900, JC 11/38/22.
111 Joseph Watson, *The Queen's Wish: How It Was Fulfilled by the Imperial Tour of T.R.H. the Duke and Duchess of Cornwall and York* (London, 1902).
112 Duke of York to Joseph Chamberlain, 15 August 1900, JC.
113 Duke of York to Sir Arthur Bigge, 15 November 1900, *Letters of Queen Victoria*, Third Series, vol. 3, 620.
114 Duke of York to Joseph Chamberlain, 2 June 1901, JC 11/12/77.

115 *The Times*, 6 December 1901. Chamberlain also gave a speech at the Guildhall celebratory luncheon, where he contrasted the current relationship between Britain and its colonies to the period of the 1860 royal tour of Canada, when the imperial connection was being questioned both at home and in Canada.
116 Harold Nicolson, *King George V: His Life and Reign* (New York, 1952), 62.
117 Nicolson, *King George V*, 88.
118 Nicolson, *King George V*, 88.
119 Matthew, 'George V'.

CHAPTER TWO

Naturalising British rule

Shortly after the Prince of Wales' 1875–76 visit to India, Lord Lytton, Viceroy of India, wrote to Queen Victoria complaining that, hitherto, British rule had relied too heavily on 'costly canals and irrigation works which have greatly embarrassed our finances, and are as yet so little appreciated by the Hindoo rustic that they do not pay the expense of making them'.[1] Instead of wasting British time through improvement projects and economic development, Lytton proposed, the British ought to hold a grand durbar to celebrate Victoria's new title, Empress of India. This chapter explores how colonial officials embraced this impulse toward ornamentalism between 1860 and 1911 by developing a shared repertoire of ritual practices across the British Empire and how these efforts were made sense of by 'native' princes and chiefs in South Africa, India, and New Zealand.[2]

During the second half of the nineteenth century, imperial ritual emerged from an era of warfare and conquest to be a principal technology of British rule.[3] The development of the royal tour, in particular, reflected both continuity with the ritual encounters that had characterised the imperial experience since the first boats arrived on the beaches and a new era of consolidation supported and legitimised by the mythology of the Great White Queen.[4] The emergence of imperial ritual also reflected a profound anxiety over the failures of imperial governance and reform during the first half of the nineteenth century. The royal tours were central to an emerging order of rule that displayed British power, nurtured the mythology of the Great Queen, and appropriated local traditions into an imperial culture. Colonial officials developed the royal tour as a site of encounter where they expected to control and display an iconic order of empire, free of the everyday politics of rule.

The royal tours also reflected efforts by imperial administrators and activists to naturalise British rule in Africa, South Asia, and the Pacific by appropriating local modes of legitimacy and systems of order into an imperial culture.[5] Colonial administrators, such as Lord Lytton in India or Theophilus Shepstone in Natal, sought to naturalise British rule by reimagining themselves as Mughal governors or African chiefs in an imperial hierarchy, atop of which sat the Great Queen.[6] The adoption of Mughal ceremonies in the Raj is the best-known example of this phenomenon.[7] Yet there were many others. 'Secret' Malay performances, usually performed in the dead of night, and Zulu 'war dances' were performed for Prince Alfred during his tour to South Africa in 1860.[8] Broken chiefs and handpicked rajas were trotted out as symbols of imperial progress and supremacy. The unknown and dangerous of an earlier era were transformed and appropriated into the known and the safe of imperial ritual. They became incorporated into an imperial culture.

Colonial officials developed customs and practices such as royal visits in a long-term cultural dance with Native Americans, South Asians, Africans, Maori, and Australian Aborigines, one dominated by Europeans but informed by the (imagined or real) demands and expectations of their colonial partners.[9] British imperial rituals were themselves a product of colonial knowledge, made and remade, translated and mistranslated through encounters with local people. At the same time, the practices and ideologies of imperial rule were produced in and disseminated through a larger imperial culture, with India often serving as the model.[10] The result was a set of cultural practices used with princes and chiefs across the empire, perhaps most spectacularly in the Raj, during the Imperial Assemblage of 1877, the 'Curzonation' of 1903, and the 1911 coronation durbar, and during durbar-inspired rituals in New Zealand, South Africa, and even Nigeria.[11]

When these imagined traditions confronted the more complicated and messy realities of colonial rule, as they did during the royal tours, the results reflected the degree to which British colonial administrators were captives of their own fantasies about 'native' political cultures and how local elites could capitalise on, or suffer at the expense of, this captivity of mind.[12] The royal tours demonstrate the conceptual dissonance between the imagined traditions of rule, as products of colonial knowledge, and the slippery and elusive nature of local political cultures, which could never be fully grasped or controlled. While the royal tour as a technology of rule functioned in the immediate term to display British power, it failed to naturalise in the long term British rule by successfully nurturing loyalty to an imperial hierarchy or a belief in an imperial culture.

This interpretation challenges David Cannadine's understanding of British 'ornamentalism' and imperial rule. According to Cannadine, the British saw the social order of the empire as analogous to their own society, that is, 'as an unequal [one] characterised by a seamless web of layered graduations'.[13] His understanding represents a fundamentally Schumpeterian vision of empire as an atavism of British society, made and ruled by conservative, rural, and hereditary elites who identified Indian princes or African chiefs as their social (but not racial) equals and partners (if unequal ones) in governance.[14] Yet, as the case studies in this chapter demonstrate, the recognition of social rank by colonial officials was a fundamentally practical consideration, aimed at producing technologies of rule. For British officials, ornamental ritual represented a less expensive and more practical method of rule more than it did any sense of shared status or values. Moreover, imperial rituals of the British imperial fantasy were performed in contested political spaces, which local political rulers often used to negotiate the terms of or contest British rule or to accentuate their own authority and legitimacy. The planning and performance of imperial rituals were also characterised by a political and cultural insensitively on the part of the British toward princes and chiefs in Africa, South Asia, and the Pacific that widened rather than narrowed the gap between the rulers and the ruled.

The colonial encounters of this chapter reveal a diverse array of experiences, all of which demonstrate the limits of imperial ritual as a technology of rule. Continuing from the experience of Sandile, it begins in southern Africa in 1860, with Prince Alfred's meetings with Moshoeshoe, the King of Basutoland, and a Zulu government chief named Ngoza. Moshoeshoe used the royal tour to demonstrate his own chiefly authority and to circumvent the authority of Governor George Grey by appealing directly to the Great White Queen. Ngoza, whose power was made by British rule, was cast (wrongly) as the paramount king of the Zulu, in service to British rule and his own political ambitions. Moving in time and space to 1868 New Zealand, I will explore the implications of Alfred's unfulfilled encounter with the Maori king, whose legitimacy and authority the British governor George Bowen sought unsuccessfully to undermine. The chapter then continues on to the Prince of Wales' tour of India in 1875–76, where the tales of the Nizam of Hyderabad and the Gaekwad of Baroda explicate the limits of the royal tour as a technology of rule. Finally, the chapter concludes with a brief discussion of the 1901 royal tour as a way of understanding the consolidation and limits of British ornamentalist politics, which had reached their developmental zenith as methods of imperial rule at precisely the moment they were being effectively transcended in imperial political culture by modern forms of citizenship and dissent.[15]

Moshoeshoe (1860)

By 1860, when the fifteen-year-old Alfred, Queen Victoria's second son, visited South Africa, King Moshoeshoe, or Moshesh, of Basutoland was an old man of over seventy. A state-builder on the southern highveld of southern Africa, Moshoeshoe incorporated a diverse array of subjects – including those fleeing the expansion of the Zulu kingdom and the growth of European settlement – under his rule by offering patronage and security. He was not a hereditary chief leading a timeless tribe, but someone who used the instability brought on by shifting local politics and colonial intervention to create political sovereignty. In this sense, the nature of his rule was not a novelty to the political culture of southern Africa but the very essence of it. In effect, his kingship was an African invented tradition.

A savvy political leader, Moshoeshoe won the fealty of his subjects through generosity, protection, and accommodation; he spoke both Sesotho and Zulu, enabling him to easily converse with most of his subjects, and rewarded loyal Basuto through a cattle-loaning system called *mafisa*.[16] In 1840, one of Moshoeshoe's Zulu-speaking subjects told the French missionary Thomas Arbousset's translator that those who had fled to Basutoland 'are no longer foreigners in your [Arbousset's] country ... [the reigning Zulu king] Dingane, I served him for a while; I have also served his father.... Believe me, friend, Dingane is nothing to me any more, nor to my family. We are Basotho.'[17] While the mythology of Moshoeshoe as the founder of a modern Basuto nation is a product of later Basuto chiefs' ideological work to fend off incorporation into the Union of South Africa, he did effectively build an identifiably modern, non-ethnic state that appealed to and appropriated both African political traditions and facets of European culture.[18]

Over the course of his reign Moshoeshoe paid tribute to the feared king of the Zulu, Shaka, with cattle and ostrich feathers and avoided conflict with later Zulu kings in the same manner; he also fended off attacks by the Nguni-speaking Amangwane and by the Amandebele, to whom he offered cattle as gifts in exchange for their retreat.[19] By the 1830s, Moshoeshoe had forged alliances with other chiefs in the region to emerge as the most powerful ruler in the region, the *Morena e Moholo* or Paramount Chief.

Conflict with white settler farmers in the fertile Caledon Valley, however, threatened his sovereignty and the territorial integrity of his kingdom. Moshoeshoe allowed European settlers, mostly Boers, to graze their herds in his territory, informing them in a 'Circular' that his permission did not constitute permanent settlement and that they were required to respect his paramountcy.[20] While the farmers had petitioned Moshoeshoe for this right, proof that they recognised his authority in the territory, they soon claimed ownership of the land as property, which had never been Moshoeshoe's intention. In 1843, the Governor of the Cape, George Napier, made a treaty with Moshoeshoe that officially recognised his sovereignty between the Orange and Caledon Rivers, and 25 or 30 miles north of the Caledon.[21] The motivations behind the protection of Basutoland as a 'colonial enclave' was not entirely or even primarily altruistic, however; it was principally aimed at checking Boer expansion in the interior of southern Africa.[22]

British intervention in Basutoland left Moshoeshoe with a quasi-sovereignty that recognised him as the Paramount Chief for the purposes of colonial rule but largely relinquished the territorial control of his kingdom to British administrators. In 1845, Governor Maitland ceded 'alienable' territories to the Boers; three years later, Governor Harry Smith annexed the territory between the Orange and the Vaal, giving more land to the Boers and separating Moshoeshoe from his African neighbours.[23]

In 1854, the British abandoned this arrangement and left Moshoeshoe to deal with his land-hungry settler neighbours on his own.[24] The British government renounced its sovereignty north of the Orange River and recognised the Orange Free State, an independent Boer republic in Moshoeshoe's backyard.[25] In 1858, Moshoeshoe's well-positioned military force was able to fend off an army mustered by the Free State. In the aftermath of this war, Governor George Grey negotiated a new boundary, but Moshoeshoe knew that the white settlers encroaching on his kingdom would not be appeased.

His requests for imperial protection ignored by George Grey, Moshoeshoe used the 1860 tour to bypass the colonial bureaucracy and appeal directly to Prince Alfred, handing him a letter to the Great White Queen herself.[26] Despite the capricious nature of British protection in the past, the Basuto king continued to assert his loyalty to the Queen and his alliance with the British as the only hope for the long-term stability and autonomy of his besieged kingdom even in the context of British abandonment. After all, Victoria was not the first powerful chief to whom Moshoeshoe had paid tribute, and the skilled diplomat understood the British to be a lesser evil than the Free State Boers.

The meeting between Moshoeshoe and Prince Alfred at Aliwal North on the Orange River was, like other royal encounters, pre-scripted by colonial officials. The meeting place was a symbolic one; it was at Aliwal North that Moshoeshoe had signed a deal brokered by George Grey in 1858 to settle Basutoland's boundary with the Orange Free State and where he would later, in 1869, be forced to cede rich territory to the Orange Free State in a second treaty. J. Austen, the Superintendent of the Wittebergen Native Reserve, brought 600 armed locals, performing war-songs and appearing appropriately 'native', to meet Alfred.[27] By inviting Moshoeshoe to meet Prince Alfred in an act of imperial theatre, complete with native warriors pacified by British rule, colonial administrators in southern Africa sought to incorporate the great chief into their understanding of imperial culture. Moshoeshoe was cast in a small role as the loyal African chief, who came on-stage to express loyalty to and submit to the Great Queen.

The British viewed Moshoeshoe in deeply ambiguous terms. Part of this ambiguity was a reflection of Moshoeshoe's uncertain relationship with the British state in South Africa, as not wholly inside or outside of its dominion. He was the unconquered sovereign of a semi-independent African kingdom. On one hand, Moshoeshoe was represented as a brave general and a skilled politician.[28] He was described as sympathetic to European missionaries and loyal to the Great Queen. His conflict with local settlers from the Orange Free State was depicted as a struggle against Boer tyranny. On the other hand, while dressed as a respectable Victorian gentleman, complete with a top hat, Moshoeshoe was described by colonial observers as a comedic product of cultural mimicry, like a child in his father's suit. It troubled the progressives in Cape Town, who otherwise petitioned on his behalf, that Moshoeshoe was 'still professedly ... a heathen', despite his openness to Christian missionaries.[29] In particular, he was judged harshly for his acquisition of many wives and for the distribution of women to loyal subjects.[30] Moshoeshoe was seen as astute but potentially menacing, cunning but absurd.

In meeting Prince Alfred, Moshoeshoe played his role but infuriated George Grey by deliberately going off script, upstaging the teenaged Alfred and openly defying Grey's authority as governor. He arrived on horseback, with 300 followers amid muskets firing, to 'the hurrahs and shouts both of Europeans and natives'.[31] When the fire and smoke cleared, the chief 'took off his hat, bowed gracefully, and stretched out his hand' in the direction of Alfred.[32] He caused much excitement, even more than Alfred did, and the assembled group of onlookers crowded around him, hoping to shake his hand.[33] When one observer, a local writer, suggested that Moshoeshoe might retire after his long ride, he said to 'let them come. I like to see them, and will tire them all out yet.'[34] While imagined as a minor player in an act of imperial theatre by colonial officials, Moshoeshoe played a major role in what he saw to be his own show.

Nevertheless, the local natives brought to Aliwal North dutifully played their roles as tamed savages. Moshoeshoe's entourage was equipped with flags and banners, with messages in Sotho about Alfred and his mother: 'God save the Queen', 'You are welcome, chief, son of the Queen', '[The] Basuto place their trust in the Queen.'[35] Local people from the native reserve were lined up on each side of the road, those dressed in European-style clothing on one side, 'the more savage-looking ones in the native war-dress' on the other.[36] The *Cape Argus* described their responses in detail:

> [Those wearing European clothing], as the Prince and his party passed, all bowed to the ground, shouting 'Khosi! Khosi! Khosi!' while the line of savages gave a simultaneous shudder and shrunk behind their shields, against which they rattled their assegais. The gesture was a very horrid one, but was meant for a very respectful and dutiful greeting, and the Prince bowed from one side to the other, as if they had been so many ladies and gentlemen in Hyde Park.[37]

Such a 'horrid' performance demonstrated the placidity and progress of previously threatening natives and the effectiveness of imperial rule. As the local natives performed 'war dances' and 'burst forth into the tune of "God Save the Queen" in their own language', Moshoeshoe, Alfred, and Grey paraded beneath the banners and arches to a house for Dutch religious services, after which the gifts were exchanged.[38]

The exchange of gifts was always an important ritual of royal encounters with indigenous people, and the meeting between Moshoeshoe and Alfred was no exception. It was a practice most clearly associated with expensive royal visits and durbars of the Raj but had been a part of British imperial culture in some form since the earliest days of British exploration.[39] Moshoeshoe gave Alfred three tiger-skin karosses, one from his brother Letsie, who was too ill to come.[40] Moshoeshoe, according to colonial accounts, asked the prince for 'some token in the prince's handwriting ... that he might take back with him and show his people'.[41] Alfred obliged, giving the Basuto king a signed photograph of himself, the gift of a royal image that was so typical of such exchanges.[42]

On the surface, this encounter appears to conform exactly to the message that Grey sought to convey through the royal tour: a rather savage, unsophisticated present from the African chief and a product of British progress and technology, if basically a trinket, from Alfred. The kaross from Moshoeshoe might be seen as a symbolic investment in British rule as Moshoeshoe ultimately appealed to Queen Victoria as a loyal ally who sought her protection and patronage. Moshoeshoe's interest in the photograph shows it offered a powerful, even magical, representation of the monarchy's efficacy. As Thomas Spear has argued, political legitimacy is always 'subject to local discourses of power', and Moshoeshoe was reascribing and inventing his own sovereignty and authority, in part by appealing to his relationship to Britain and its Great Queen.[43] While what Alfred and Moshoeshoe discussed is unknown, their interviews were translated by George Grey, giving him the power to embellish, omit, and invent the language of the encounter.[44] After the gift-giving, Alfred retired for much-needed rest as locals bustled around the illuminated village and a massive bonfire in the market square.

The next day Alfred and Moshoeshoe met again. The ceremonies commenced with more 'war-dancing and the chanting of songs in an aboriginal fashion'.[45] The settlers of Aliwal and the French missionaries from Basutoland addressed the prince, expressing their loyalty to the Queen. After delivering a letter addressed to Queen Victoria to the prince, Moshoeshoe and his counsellors sat for a photograph, which remains the best-known image of the Basuto king.[46] Photography, as scholars have argued, was a form of colonial knowledge that acquired and appropriated the 'other' into the realm of the known.[47] The photograph of Moshoeshoe represented a cultural appropriation of his image into imperial culture, proof of a civilisation-giving and liberal British imperialism.

At the same time, Moshoeshoe used his role in imperial rituals, his relationship with the Great Queen, and even his own photograph to remake his own symbolic role in the 'nation' of Basutoland. Moshoeshoe came to see the teenaged prince not because he longed to pay his respects to the Great Queen but because he understood that imperial intervention might be the only thing that stood between his kingdom and the settler 'scourge'.[48] While the British reports convey a Moshoeshoe amazed by the presence of a flesh-and-blood prince – proof that the Great White Queen did really exist – the Basuto king was no stranger to the potential risks of inviting British 'protection'. He also recognised, from experience, that the British were fickle allies and that imperial protection was limited and subject to the political winds in Cape Town and London. Thus, regardless of British policy toward his kingdom, he would continue running guns and stockpiling arms to defend his kingdom against British and Boer alike.

Yet, as a political strategist, Moshoeshoe also recognised the value of loyalty to the Queen and allegiance to the empire in fending off the settler threat. He knew that being attached to the British Empire was the only way to protect his kingdom from local settlers and sought to use it to reinvent his own political authority. As colonial administrators such as Grey sought to channel local protest into the fundamentally apolitical formulation of imperial ritual, Moshoeshoe used the opportunity to express to Alfred 'a hope that the relations which existed between him and the British government in the time of Sir

Harry Smith and other Governors might be restored', that is, some degree of British protection against the incursions of Boer settlers.[49] Grey immediately moved to end this unscripted conversation, telling the Basuto chief that 'his best course would be to embody his request in a letter to the Queen instead of addressing himself to the Prince' and that 'Prince Alfred will not hear anything further on the subject'.[50] The effect of his performance and his letter to the Great White Queen was probably nil, but the attempt reflects on the ways that the symbolic space of imperial rituals could be used and subverted by their participants.

Moshoeshoe's political genius lay not only in the creation of a 'nation' of Basutos but in his brand of *realpolitik* informed by the experiences of his long reign. His foreign policy, with both Africans and Europeans, relied on peace-making, alliances, and incorporation when possible, gunrunning and warfare when these *détentes* expired.[51] As his performance in 1860 suggests, Moshoeshoe's use of *realpolitik* prevented the complete annihilation of his sovereignty.

Despite his political achievements, he let 'the snake in the house'.[52] His successors, increasingly sewn in by European settlement, were less successful in maintaining local sovereignty. In 1871, Basutoland came under British protection, administered by the Cape Colony, and subjected to what amounted to a British residency.[53] While it remained a quasi-independent African state under British protection through the twentieth century, the most fertile lands of Moshoeshoe's kingdom, the crest west of the Caledon, were ceded to land-hungry Boers. During the late 1870s, when several chiefs including Moorosi rebelled against Cape-appointed magistrates, its administration was taken over by London. Major-General Charles Gordon's proposition to replace the magistrates with British residents modelled on India, while rejected, reflects the slow devolution of Basuto as a political state from sovereignty to quasi-sovereignty.[54] As the 1901 tour will demonstrate, Moshoeshoe's successors had few opportunities to challenge the symbolic space of the royal visit. While Moshoeshoe's political compromise with the British helped preserve some Basuto land for future generations, it created a morass for his successors, who lacked Moshoeshoe's political genius and were increasingly sewn in by more and more land-hungry European settlers.

Ngoza (1860)

Alfred met another chief while visiting Natal in 1860, who was described by colonial officials as the supreme chief of the Zulu. Ngoza had served in the Zulu army under King Dingane and entered the colony of Natal in 1843, where he worked in a settler's kitchen until he caught the attention of the Secretary of Native Affairs in Natal, Theophilus Shepstone, in 1847.[55] Working as an agent for Shepstone against a 'recalcitrant' local chief, Ngoza was installed as a native strongman (*induna*) in the Mngeni valley of Natal.[56] Shepstone placed more and more African settlers under Ngoza's authority, and he became 'a government chief, one of the *iziphakanyiswa* – those 'raised up'.'[57] The Anglican bishop of Natal, John Colenso, was most impressed with Ngoza during his tour of Natal in 1854, describing him as:

> dressed neatly enough as an European, with his attendant Kafir waiting beside him.... [He] is Mr. Shepstone's head man, and, though not an hereditary chief, has acquired considerable power, and is practically a chief of as much authority as any in the district, which he owes partly to Mr. Shepstone's patronage, partly to his own modest and amiable character. There are probably, (by reason of refugees having flocked to him, who had left their own chiefs behind,) more pure Zulus under Ngoza than under any other chief in Natal.[58]

Both Shepstone and Ngoza were participating in an African tradition of reimagining chiefship.

The appropriation of Zulu titles and political traditions, as the British imagined them, were central to the imperial culture that the royal tours were designed to nurture. When Alfred came to southern Africa in 1860, the Zulu kingdom was represented not by King Mpande and the independent Zulu kingdom north of Natal but by Shepstone's government chief Ngoza in 'war dances' choreographed by Shepstone himself. Instead of wearing the attire of a respectable African chief, he wore a dramatic costume of monkey tails, tiger skins, and ostrich feathers that borrowed from some combination of local traditions and European ideas about what a Zulu chief ought to look like.[59] Alfred encountered the Zulu assembled in a semicircle, each man carrying an oval ox-skin shield.[60] As the supreme chief, Ngoza led the dances 'under the effective management and direction of T. Shepstone':

> Goza's bands began the ball, coming up towards the spectator like a surging line of inky surf, making, at the same time, a whole hurricane of noise. They advance, they retreat, they leap aloft into the air, they kneel and crouch to the ground, placing their shields before them. They become frantic, brandishing their spear-sticks, and kicking with knee and foot against their shields. They see the enemy, and yell at him like a pack of demoniac hounds. How they would tear and rend him if they could but get him! Now they retreat, holding their shields behind them, and hissing like a host of wriggling serpents between their teeth. Awful fellows![61]

The performance represented British dominance over the feared Zulu and, therefore, the success of colonial rule over native peoples. Shepstone offered an address 'that had been agreed upon for the sake of brevity by the native chiefs'.[62] The settler newspaper *Natal Mercury* understood it as proof that 'these barbarous things' had been 'tamed' under the 'easy yoke of the British Government', which offered protection and safety from the cruelty of local chiefs.[63] The fierce dance by one young Zulu prompted the *Mercury* to explain that, while such a man would have aroused horror and fear in London, 'Natalians know [that the] poor creature is perfectly harmless, and would repeat the performance on any day of the week for a pinch of snuff.'[64] These carefully choreographed performances were designed to tout the successes of British rule and to incorporate local traditions into an imperial culture, into the realm of the safe and the knowable.

The government chief Ngoza performed as the representative of the Zulu chiefs and master of ceremonies, an act that ignored both the reality of Zulu politics and the dominant role of Shepstone and his officers in crafting the performance. The subjugated Zulu king was a former kitchen worker without regal ancestry; the legitimate kingdom of Shaka to the north was ruled by Mpande and remained outside of the British pale. Ngoza dressed for his performance in the attire of a savage rather than that of a subordinate colonial administrator. The Zulu war dances were adapted, even invented, by Shepstone, who choreographed them to maximise the intended effect.

Ngoza's chiefship, then, was a product of colonial rule, made by Shepstone to appropriate local forms of political authority. But what Shepstone and other colonial officials failed to appreciate was that political traditions in southern Africa (and elsewhere in the empire) were always in the making. Successive forms of political authority, as the transformation of minor chiefs Moshoeshoe and Shaka into great kings demonstrates, did not reflect the natural persistence of ancient traditions or tribal bloodlines but were products of innovating and reimagining local political culture. In the context of African politics, the creation of Ngoza and other chiefs reflected the profound disruption of the Shakan period on African polities in the region, a disorder that the British used to the benefit of colonial rule by organising new chiefships as a bulwark against the Zulu kingdom.[65] For Shepstone, as we shall see, making his own Zulu 'tribe' in the borderlands of the British Empire was one part of a more ambitious programme. Ngoza, a former soldier and labourer, used his invented chiefship to make a place for himself in the world, one where he was theoretically an important ruler, if in practice a low-level colonial administrator. In a sense, both Shepstone and Ngoza were participating in a local tradition of political adaptation.

Recent work on Shepstone, or Somtsewu kaSonzica (something like 'father of whiteness'), as Africans knew him, has offered a complex portrait of a colonial administrator driven by a profound opportunism, an insidious desire to control and manipulate African politics for the purposes of colonial rule, and sympathy for what he considered to be 'African interests'.[66] Jeff Guy and Thomas McClendon point out Shepstone's upbringing, speaking 'Kaffer from childhood', in Xhosa-speaking areas of the Eastern Cape by Wesleyan missionary parents equipped him to be a skilled observer of local politics and culture.[67] Guy posits that Shepstone personally occupied and monopolised a cultural space between African oral traditions and written colonial knowledge, which he used to accentuate his own status and power in both conceptual universes.[68] While the 'Shepstone system' of indirect rule angered the frontier settlers of Natal, who understood his native reserves as both inhibiting European use of the land and limiting their access to native labour, its principal objective was to 'secure white power in a colony which had never been conquered' and where European settlers represented a tiny minority.[69]

The crowning of Ngoza as a Zulu king represented Shepstone's grand designs in their infancy. His system of indirect rule and role as a king-maker would reach their maturity in 1872 when he participated in the ceremony that installed Cetshwayo as the king of Zululand.[70] During the ceremony, Shepstone performed as the great founder of the Zulu kingdom, Shaka.[71] In his official reports of the event, Shepstone overstated the importance of his presence and its implications for British power in Zululand, a reflection of his systematic attempt to mythologise himself as the great white chief in the eyes of both Europeans and Africans.[72] In this context, he played up his role as a law-giver to the Zulu, whose failure to adequately appreciate his gift later justified the invasion of Zululand.[73] As Carolyn Hamilton's skilful analysis of the event demonstrates, however, the ceremony began before Shepstone arrived, a subtle act of subversion that demonstrates that Cetshwayo and his counsellors comprehended Shepstone's intentions and sought to undermine them. Moreover, the Anglo-Zulu War (1879) reveals the limits – or the insidiousness – of the Shepstone system and British impatience with any semblance of independence on the part of local rulers.

The performances of Ngoza and his 'tribe' during the royal tour of 1860 demonstrate the colonial appropriation of local traditions for the purposes of rule and for the personal opportunism of Shepstone, as an occasion to embellish his status as the great white chief. It also shows the artificiality of indirect rule, which tried to appropriate African political traditions but failed to fully control local symbolic spaces.

Ngoza and other enterprising African men, those intermediaries and interpreters who occupied the places in between two or more cultural universes, could ascend from the white man's kitchen to become the heir to the great Shaka.

Kingitanga (1869–70)

In 1869–70, Prince Alfred, now captain of his own ship, visited New Zealand as part of a much longer voyage across his mother's empire. George Bowen, the Governor of New Zealand, worked tirelessly to schedule a meeting between Prince Alfred and Tawhiao, the Maori king, as part of a scheme designed to undermine the political and cultural legitimacy of the Maori King movement.[74] Kingitanga was a political and cultural movement that sought to create a zone of sovereignty to counter British rule.[75] It was consciously modelled after Queen Victoria, the story goes, inspired by the 1852 encounter of Tamihana Te Rauparaha, the son of chief Te Rauparaha, with Queen Victoria during a visit to Britain.[76] Founded as a pan-Maori movement, it was aimed at uniting the diverse populations of Maori people across the islands of New Zealand in a context of intensified land acquisition by the Crown legalised and institutionalised by the Treaty of Waitangi.[77] In 1858, Potatau Te Wherowhero was elected and crowned the Maori king, his kingdom centred in Waikato on the North Island and supported by a collection of local communities (*iwi*). Well into the 1860s, the King movement survived the military and political onslaught of the colonial government, much to the irritation of Bowen and the colonial government.

In time, Kingitanga developed its own cultural symbols of authority (*mana*), such as a national flag, and articulated its counter-sovereignty by establishing King institutions and an imagined community of print using government documents, in works of history, and through a series of King newspapers, including *Te Hokioi o Niu Tireni e Rere atu na* (January–May 1863).[78] For a period in the 1860s and 1870s, Pai Marire, a syncretised religious movement comparable to the cattle killing and other millennial movements in South Africa, rapidly spread among adherents of the King movement; although influenced by Christianity, it rejected European influences and interactions, and its most radical believers used it to justify violence against European settlers.[79] King territory was marked off by an almost cosmic territorial pale, or *aukati*, over which no unauthorised European could cross, and which provided a source of settler resentment and a 'constant reminder of the Crown's failure to crush Maori independence'.[80] The Maori state claimed legitimacy and sovereignty through an imagined pan-Maori community, which the British saw as a clear threat to colonial rule in New Zealand and the myth of empire.[81] Kingitanga claimed loyalty to Queen Victoria, their treaty partner, but rejected government and settler encroachments as a violation of the Treaty of Waitangi.

Potatau's son Tawhiao (r. 1860–94) would inherit the ire of the British Empire. During the 1860s, the British government sought to alienate non-aligned chiefs from the movement through diplomacy and warfare. Governor Gore Browne and his replacement Sir George Grey sought to isolate Kingitanga and 'dig around the [movement] until it fell'.[82] Browne was sacked for his failure to crush local Maori assisted by Kingite troops during the 1860–61 Taranaki War.[83] Grey would bring a native policy developed during his first tenure as Governor of New Zealand (1845–54) and his time as Governor of the Cape Colony (1854–61) and a missionary zeal to the government campaign against Kingitanga.

Using questionable intelligence-gathering tactics and relying on untrustworthy native informants, Grey built the case and 'pumped reports into London alleging a widespread Maori conspiracy to attack Auckland'.[84] An 1863 ultimatum from Grey demanded submission to Queen Victoria, but colonial troops crossed over the *aukati* before the Maori could even respond, beginning the Waikato War (1863–46).[85] Tawhiao finally retreated to Tokangamutu (Te Kuiti) in Ngati Maniapoto territory. As a consequence, the colonial government confiscated 1.2 million acres of Maori land, including most of the Waikato district in a process the Maori called *Raupatu*. In response, Kingitanga isolated itself even further from the British and from loyalist *kupapa*, or Queenite, Maori. Tawhiao sought to prevent the land court from operating within areas controlled by the Maori king by banning the surveying and selling of land. It was in this context – of an unsuppressed King movement and continued violence between Maori and the British, most often blamed on the Kingitanga – that Prince Alfred arrived to New Zealand during 1869 as part of an extensive world tour.

Governor George Bowen sought to use Alfred's royal visit to negotiate the surrender of Tawhiao, by enticing him to violate his own sacred *aukati* and to culturally undermine his claims to sovereignty by submitting to the son of Queen Victoria. Two years earlier, in 1867, George Grey had encouraged a meeting between Alfred and Tawhiao, telling the Maori king that if he was 'willing to give up [his] weapons of war to a great chief [Alfred], none greater than this chief will ever come near you'.[86] Grey sought unconditional surrender, and Kingitanga's leaders sought restoration of confiscated land and recognition of Tawhiao in King country. Both Grey and Kingitanga rejected the other party's preconditions, and the meeting did not happen.

In response to Bowen's new proposal, the King movement organised a conference at Upper Waikato at the end of April 1869.[87] The Resident Magistrate (RM) in Waikato, William Searancke, was invited to the meeting and described its composition: 1,700 armed men, 'besides some friendly natives', Maori leaders, and many civilians – a mass meeting that totalled around 3,500 attendees.[88] The RM noted that, while the Maori king's followers were considered rebels by the British government, they overwhelmingly rejected the recent violence on part of Te Kooti, a Maori guerrilla fighter on the North Island who had recently escaped from imprisonment on the Chatham Islands, some 800 kilometres off the coast of New Zealand.[89] Searancke judged Tawhiao's speech to be 'couched in ambiguous language' but 'pacific in tone'.[90] When Searancke pressed Tawhiao to meet with Prince Alfred, the Maori king agreed to consider the proposition.[91] Despite the conciliatory tone on the part of Tawhiao, Bowen noted that 'nothing can be absolutely certain in dealing with a race liable, as are the Maoris, to be actuated by sudden and fanatical impulses'.[92] Bowen's failure to make sense of Kingitanga is reflected in his troubled ethnography of Maori motives.

As diplomatic messages passed between the government, the Maori king, and other Maori chiefs, the settler press was accusing Tawhiao of planning an uprising and of supporting Te Kooti's raids on the North Island.[93] But the threat that the King movement posed to the British government was not violence, as Tawhiao had rejected violence unless directly threatened, but counter-sovereignty beyond the pale of British control. In this context, Bowen sought to used Alfred and the mythology of Queen Victoria's greatness and power to undermine this counter-sovereignty by forcing Tawhiao to submit to British rule. Bowen complained to the Colonial Office that the 'adherents of the so-called Maori king' had 'since 1860, either been in arms against the Crown, or have dwelt apart in their mountains and forests in sullen and hostile isolation, like the Jacobite clans in the Scotch Highland'.[94]

In his letter to the Colonial Office in London, Bowen focused his attention on demonstrations of loyalty by 'friendly' Maori while Kingitanga and the ongoing raids by Te Kooti were framed as fringe movements, minor disturbances far outweighed by overall Maori gratitude for British rule. The governor assessed the prince's visit as an occasion to confirm and reward 'the loyalty of the clans now in arms for the Crown'.[95] Despite his efforts to minimise Maori resistance, his dispatches to the home government also asserted the necessity of limiting Alfred's travels to the cities and avoiding the interior of the North Island, where conflict continued to rage.[96]

The chiefs of the North Island met Alfred at Auckland, those of the lower North Island and South Island at Wellington. Bowen was most interested in symbolic acts of submission by chiefs to the British Queen. During the ceremonies, 'several of the Maori Chiefs have laid at the feet of the "Queen's Son" as tokens of homage, the hereditary ornaments which had been treasured by their ancestors for many generations', which he compared to the Scottish Brooch of Lorn.[97] For instance, Tamihana Te Rauparaha, the son of the Ngati Toa chief Te Rauparaha, presented Alfred with a greenstone ornament representing Kaitangata, a character of Maori mythology, which had 'been an heirloom in his tribe for five-hundred years'.[98] The message of this exchange was abundantly clear to Bowen: that the Maori chief was giving over a traditional symbol of Maori authority to the British monarchy.

During the 1830s and 1840s, Tamihana 's father Te Rauparaha, like Kingitanga, had resisted European efforts to purchase more land and refused entry to surveyors, inciting settlers to send a vigilante expedition that tried (unsuccessfully) to arrest him.[99] Settler rumour and paranoia encouraged fear of Te Rauparaha, whose control of much of central New Zealand inspired much resentment, and in 1846 Governor George Grey had him arrested and held on the naval ship *Calliope* for ten months without charge.[100] He was released to his people in Otaki in 1849, left to live out the last year of his life as a broken man.

His son Tamihana Te Rauparaha was baptised by the CMS missionary Octavius Hadfield in 1841 and travelled the islands as an evangelical missionary.[101] He lived on a European-style estate, his lucrative sheep farm, wore European clothes, and kept servants.[102] It was in 1852, when he travelled to Britain with other Wesleyan Missionary Society missionaries aboard the *John Wesley*, that he was introduced to Queen Victoria as an example of a 'civilised native'.[103] Despite being a founding member of Kingitanga, he broke with the movement in 1860 over what he saw to be the king's antagonistic positioning.[104] By the mid-1860s, he was serving as the senior land assessor for the colonial government.[105] Tamihana was not a collaborator, but someone who sought to engage constructively with the Crown and maintained hope that it would adhere to the promises made in the Treaty of Waitangi. He also sought, however, to use new cultural and political forms inspired by Christianity and the British monarchy to invent new traditions aimed at protecting local people by uniting them.

In this context, the handing over of a sacred symbol of his father's *mana* offers a message far more ambiguous than the one imagined by Bowen. Te Rauparaha was a man broken and beaten by the British despite his earlier partnership with European settlers and his later reluctance to fight them, in spite of settler pressure to sell his land against what he saw to be the agreed terms of the Treaty of Waitangi.

His son's presentation of the Kaitangata greenstone could hardly represent a tribal submission of 'traditional' Maori rule to the great and powerful British monarchy. Tamihana imagined himself to be a modern, Christian Maori, a product of the colonial encounter. His gift to Prince Alfred might better be considered an investment. For the Maori, gifts created reciprocal bonds and obligations.

In investing his family's legacy in the British monarchy, and in effect co-opting it for Maori culture, Tamihana sought the patronage and protection of the Great Queen. He declared loyalty to the Queen, not to the colonial government. Of course, colonial officials saw the handover as the absorption of local hierarchy and tradition into imperial culture. According to Bowen, 'this last survivor in a long line of Chieftains and warriors' told him that, 'as there were none of his name and lineage to succeed him', as 'his house was gone, like the Moa [Maori birds hunted to extinction by the Maori]', he had, as it were, bequeathed this dearly prized talisman of his fathers, as a token of love and honour, to 'the Son of the Queen of England and New Zealand'.[106] His family's *mana*, like his father, had gone the way of the moa. Colonial officials such as Bowen may have imagined the royal tour as a way to incorporate Maori chiefs into the great imperial hierarchy, but the encounter on the ground reflected a far more complicated and ambiguous relationship.

* * *

Shortly before Prince Alfred's scheduled departure in May 1869, he was invited by two loyalist chiefs from Waikato, Wi Patene and Te Wheoro, to a proposed 'meeting [with Tawhiao's] Maoris, at Ngaruawahia, the old Maori capital'.[107] Its purpose, they said, was 'to tell you [Prince Alfred] and the Governor their thoughts, so that peace and goodwill may arise in this Island of troubles'.[108] The Maori king, they claimed, wanted to see *him*, the prince of the Queen, for, 'although the Governor represents the power and authority of your Mother … you are Her own Child; You are the Queen Herself; therefore it is that the Maori tribes long to see your face'.[109] The chiefs assumed that the prince's presence would be helpful to negotiations between the government and the King movement.

It is unclear if the colonial government had any role in prompting the meeting although it had worked for months to arrange a meeting between Alfred and the Maori king.[110] One letter to the editor of the *Taranaki Herald* argued later, when Alfred returned to New Zealand in 1870, that 'a chief who claims independent sovereignty' meeting Prince Alfred was 'almost equivalent to a recognition of his claim'.[111]

Perhaps the loyalist Maori recognised an opportunity for Tawhiao to make peace in the presence of British royalty. The Maori knew, as the Xhosa did, that leaders who went to negotiate with the British often did not come back. And they knew, after the Treaty of Waitangi, that the protections offered in signed treaties did not count for much. They perhaps assumed that the presence of the Queen's son might offer some insurance – that the Great Queen, knowing that the agreement was made with her son's involvement, might intervene to defend its stipulations.

Bowen was 'convinced that it is of vital importance to endeavour to arrive at a peaceful understanding, not inconsistent with the sovereignty of the Queen, with the so-called "Maori King", by which title his adherents appear to mean little more than a great Chieftain and Magistrate analogous to the semi-independent Rajahs of British India'.[112] While refusing the legitimacy of Tawhiao as a monarch, and thus comparable in some way to Queen Victoria, Bowen also lamented that the Maori king had not been militarily crushed when the government had the resources available.[113] To supplement the sword, he sought to culturally destroy the Tawhiao's legitimacy by persuading him to submit to Victoria's greatness and power. Rewi, one of Tawhiao's principal generals, urged the Maori king to attend on the grounds that he had 'long fought the Pakeha [white settlers], but that war had caused the Maoris to lose many men and much land, and that he was now as strong for peace as he had been for war'.[114]

Tawhiao never crossed his *aukati* and never met Prince Alfred, who left on 1 June.[115] *The Taranaki Herald* offered, at the royal tour's conclusion, a far more nuanced and complicated picture of this non-event than that offered by colonial propaganda:

> [Prince Alfred's] stay in Auckland was the longest, where he enjoyed himself, a greater part of the time, with pheasant shooting.... He was to have left on the 28th May, but owing to a wish expressed by some of the inhabitants of Auckland, that he should stop and visit the Maori King, who they were trying to persuade to come half-way to meet the Prince, His Royal Highness postponed his departure till the 1st June. We cannot see what good was likely to have resulted from the interview, but it might have done a great deal of harm. Old political questions would have been raised, and Tawhiao would have quoted scripture largely to bear out his arguments, which we fear, his Royal Highness would have found it difficult to refute. Altogether we think that Tawhiao (the Maori King), has shown greater wisdom in refusing.... [The prince] will ... only take away a very different impression of the Colony to what it really is; for he has *only* visited the cities of New Zealand. Had he called at some of the smaller towns, or gone where the rebellion was rife, and seen a 'real war

> dance', he would have had a better knowledge of the place, the peoples, and of the difficulties.[116]

For the next several decades, Tawhiao refused various concessions from the colonial government in exchange for an oath of allegiance. In 1884, he went to Britain to appeal directly to Queen Victoria: to ask her for an independent Maori parliament and inquiry into land confiscations. Instead, he met with the Colonial Secretary, Lord Derby, who told him that the imperial government would not intervene in local affairs. The reality of the Great White Queen fell far short of the mythology.

Inspired by the Great Queen, Kingitanga appealed to the idea of indigenous political and cultural unity as a means of challenging imperial rule. It was an invented tradition in its most real sense, a new movement that transcended older rivalries and political traditions. It did not reject the authority of Queen Victoria, but demanded a political and cultural sovereignty – one that its adherents made real in print, institutions, and symbolism, and which they saw as the rightful legacy of Waitangi. The royal tour, as imagined by colonial administrators, sought to inspire obedience and loyalty in 'traditional', 'tribal' leaders, who would submit to the authority of the Great Queen and the legitimacy of the great imperial hierarchy of rule. In New Zealand, Prince Alfred encountered a much more confusing empire, but not the Maori king, who refused to submit.

The Gaekwad of Baroda (1875)

In 1875, the Prince of Wales travelled to the western Indian princely state of Baroda to meet with its gaekwad, a ten-year-old boy named Sayaji Rao III, whom Albert Edward described as 'a very intelligent boy, quite overloaded with jewels'.[117] In Bombay, the Prince of Wales spent time talking to the lad, who was only a few years older than his eldest son Albert Victor, about 'illuminations and horsemanship' (he encouraged him to pursue his interest in the latter).[118] During the return visit to Baroda, the young gaekwad grasped the Prince of Wales' right hand and led him toward an elephant that would carry him to the durbar for local dignitaries at the British Residency.[119] Later, the British prince was treated by the young gaekwad to rhinoceros and elephant fights and a hunting exhibition for cheetahs.[120] Despite the good feelings expressed by the Prince of Wales and the Gaekwad of Baroda toward each other during the visits, a far more unsavoury reality lay behind the delicate façade of ornamental spectacle.

The practices developed during the royal tours demonstrate that the science of observing and acquiring knowledge of Indian traditions, practices, and mentalities for the purposes of rule profoundly informed the relationship between the British and their South Asian subjects. It also reveals that colonial knowledge by its very nature was a partial and incomplete reflection of reality, based on limited and flawed knowledge. Thus, when the fantasy of imperial rule became practice during the royal tours, the political and cultural distance between the rulers and the ruled often widened instead of narrowed.

Over the course of the nineteenth century, British officials constantly sought to refine and improve the elaborate and time-consuming system of imperial rituals. Without a sense of irony, British administrators sought to modernize the 'feudal' institutions of the Mughal royal tour and durbar for use by the viceroy, governors, and visiting royals during imperial visits of state. Raj officials carefully studied the historical relationships between different South Asian states and princes – as a reflection of a timeless social order rather than of the push and pull of local politics – in order to determine a proper ritual order. Philip Wodehouse, the Governor of Bombay, conveyed his 'fear that some of the Native Princes, so tenacious of their privileges, might resent any disregard of their rights in matters of ceremony & etiquette, especially with regard to the exchange of visits'.[121] British officials in India obsessed over gun salutes, ceremonial rankings, and placement to such a degree that it is rather difficult to determine where Indian practices ended and British fantasies began.

British administrators also sought to simplify imperial rituals. For instance, the Duke of Edinburgh and the Prince of Wales could not logistically pay return visits to the many rulers whom they encountered during their visits to India. To solve this problem, formal return visits were limited to the most prominent Indian princes; less important chiefs were housed in government buildings or hastily constructed tent villages, where the British prince could, in a matter of hours, pay return visits to dozens of South Asian princes at their 'home residences'.[122] In 1875, Wodehouse established that Indian rulers who received less than a seventeen-gun salute would not be granted the traditional return visit from the Prince of Wales.[123] This arrangement left Albert Edward with 'only six visits to be paid at their own houses and nine concentrated visits'.[124]

At these temporary princely hotels, royals such as Alfred and Albert Edward met with Indian rulers in rapid succession.[125] Princely elites were hurried into and out of their visits with the British prince, for which they had often travelled long distances and at great expense.[126] Moreover, their attendance was not considered optional by British officials. In Ajmere in Rajasthan, tour planners expected the Prince of Wales to meet with twelve chiefs in less than two hours, with ten minutes allotted for each prince.[127] Alfred's complaint to his mother (Chapter 1) about the tedium of imperial ceremonies was stirred by such an event.[128] Even for twenty-one-gun princes who were granted more respect and attention and who received return visits at their residences rather than in a tent or a government apartment, the royal tour represented an expression of imperial domination more than a British respect for India's 'natural rulers'.

Similarly, when the Prince of Wales complained to his mother of the 'rude and rough manner' of British political agents toward Indian princes (Chapter 1), he echoed the complaints of many Indian observers, including the independent South Asian press, about the ritual practices of the royal tour.[129] From this perspective, South Asian princes were often abused and disrespected during imperial rituals. While some princes profoundly enjoyed entertaining a fellow prince – taking the Duke of Edinburgh or the Prince of Wales hunting for game or treating him to animal fights and local cuisine – these princes often retained some semblance of sovereignty, far away from the administrative dominance of Simla, Calcutta, and Bombay.[130] South Asian elites were far more likely to visit the prince in a tent hotel temporarily designated an official residence and to experience the 'rough and rude manner' of their British handlers than to embark on a private hunting exhibition with the Queen's son. If Cannadine's *Ornamentalism* describes the British fantasy of imperial rule, the experience of the Gaekwad of Baroda reflects the reality of it.

The Prince of Wales encountered the young Gaekwad of Baroda near the end of a long political drama: the poisoning of the British Resident of Baroda and the subsequent ousting of the Malhár Rao, the previous gaekwad, by the British government of India.[131] While the British officials in India imagined the royal tour of 1875–76 as an opportunity to solidify the traditional hierarchy that they had been nurturing since 1858, the ouster of Malhár Rao coloured the meaning of the royal visit for many South Asian princes, intellectuals, and activists, for whom the British removal of an 'independent' prince revealed the rotten and corrupt core of British rule in India.

A 'quasi-independent' state ruled by an Indian gaekwad, Baroda's structure was typical of the system of princely rule invented by the East India Company, arguably in the tradition of the Mughals, and reinforced by the settlement of 1858.[132] The gaekwad was allowed to govern the internal affairs of Baroda, with the advice of a British Resident. While Indian princes were more independent in practice than African chiefs, who often acted as little more than the bottom rung of the colonial hierarchy, the gaekwad's rule was always subject to British 'advice' and intervention, though the most blatant and obvious interferences were mostly avoided. On the eve of the Prince of Wales' visit, however, the British Resident of Baroda, Colonel Robert Phayre, found arsenic in his sherbet, leading to a series of events that demonstrated the British theory of paramountcy and limits of indirect rule.

Historians have described the removal of the gaekwad as a defining moment in the relationship between the Raj and local princes. Lauren Benton has argued that British officials were deliberately evasive in defining legal and political sovereignty in 'colonial enclaves' such as Baroda, simultaneously asserting respect for local traditions ('divisible sovereignty') and claiming British paramountcy in the tradition of the Mughal and Maratha: as Benton puts it, the British sought 'to decide where law ended and politics began'.[133] Charles Lewis Tupper, a British official in the Punjab during the 1890s, argued that South Asian princes 'whether by compulsion or otherwise' had historically rendered themselves subordinate with 'the hegemony of some paramount power'.[134] To the English legal scholar John Westlake, the distinction between the princely states and 'the dominions of the Queen' became, over the course of the nineteenth century, 'niceties of speech', a strategy of rule rather than a legal or political reality.[135] The Baroda case crystallised and forwarded British claims of unlimited paramountcy. As an expression of British unlimited sovereignty, it signalled 'more than a gap between theory and practice'.[136] More importantly, the case demonstrates that colonial officials defined the relationship between the Raj and South Asian princes with a purposeful ambiguity that allowed imperial rule to expand and contract without the requirement of legal precedent.

Baroda's relationship with the British government in India was rather strained by the 1870s.[137] In 1872, Malhár Rao was accused of poisoning his predecessor's diwan (chief minister), but he refused an inquiry by the British and disposed of the body without an examination.[138] Philip Wodehouse, the Governor of Bombay, appointed Colonel Robert Phayre as the British Resident in 1873 with the intention of reining in the gaekwad; Phayre apparently had little patience for princely rule or ornamental politics and sought even greater control over the gaekwad than the British government would allow. Phayre's dogged resolution to challenge corruption and misrule in Baroda, often against the wishes of officials in Bombay and Calcutta, demonstrates the importance of local 'men on the ground' in shaping global imperial politics.

Phayre wasted no time in developing an antagonistic relationship with the gaekwad and local notables. Soon after his appointment, Phayre reported to the British government a public flogging during which one victim died and requested a commission to investigate general misrule in Baroda, including the gaekwad's treatment of the hard-pressed countryside.[139] During a meeting with the sardars of Baroda, he informed them that he was forming a revenue commission to investigate the state's finances and that if they misrepresented their wealth, he would 'find them out'.[140] Phayre 'sent increasingly alarming accounts of conditions to the Bombay Government', reporting even the most minor problems to the government.[141] Only 'latent insanity', Phayre claimed, could explain the gaekwad's 'inordinate thirst for wealth and self-gratification' but he also blamed 'evil advisers', particularly his allegedly illiterate and inexperienced diwan, Sivaji Rao, and his finance ministers for 'the positive reign of terror' in Baroda.[142] Phayre, it seems, subjected the gaekwad to an ideal of British principles of rule, constantly antagonising and prodding him: hardly the relationship between an independent ruler and a British 'adviser'.

Prompted by Phayre's alarms, the Bombay government decided to act decisively against the gaekwad, but Lord Northbrook in Calcutta disagreed, and argued that an investigation was needed to determine whether or not Phayre's claims were overstated. The struggle between the central British administration in Calcutta and the local British government in Bombay to control official policy in Baroda is a clear example of the kind of push and pull that occurred between a multiplicity of cores within the British Empire.[143] Northbrook sought to control what he saw as an overzealous policy of interference by Phayre and the government of Bombay (though the Governor of Bombay, Philip Wodehouse, was generally a restraining force in his council's desire to control Baroda's governance). Nevertheless, Northbrook established a commission to investigate Phayre's allegations, appointing Colonel Robert Meade, Chief Commissioner of Mysore, as chair, as well as Faiz Ali Kan, former Diwan of Jaipur.

Malhár Rao soon called upon the lawyer Dadabhai Naoroji, who in 1872 had unsuccessfully argued on the gaekwad's behalf on another matter and who had made a case for him in London during the current crisis, for assistance.[144] Naoroji, a Hindu intellectual educated at Elphinstone College, was a forerunner of the loyalist *respectables* examined in Chapter 4. Living much of his adult life in Britain, he dedicated his intellectual career to educating the British public about the inequity of British rule in India – most famously in *Poverty and Un-British Rule in India*, which underlined the extraction of wealth from India by the British – and became, in 1892, the first British MP of South Asian descent.[145] By recruiting Naoroji to his cause, the gaekwad, quite ingeniously, sought to utilise the emerging political strategies and tools that would soon so effectively serve Indian nationalist politics.

As Naoroji returned from Britain in 1873 to take up his position as the gaekwad's adviser, Northbrook's Baroda Commission began its meetings. The commission completed a far more limited investigation than Phayre sought. It dismissed many of the complaints put forward by Phayre but ultimately decided against the gaekwad, voting for the replacement of his ministers and more direct control of Baroda's affairs by the British Resident.[146] Northbrook held back, giving the gaekwad the opportunity to respond to the report. Northbrook warned that 'the Gaikwar himself [would be responsible] for the good government of his State under a warning that, if before 31st December 1875, he [did] not reform his administration he [would] be deposed from power'.[147] It appears that the gaekwad did aspire to reform his court, if only for the purposes of self-preservation, but was prevented by Phayre's obstructionist tactics.

On the night of 9 November 1875, Phayre noticed a strange-looking substance in his sherbet. Upon examination, the residency surgeon confirmed the presence of arsenic in the drink.[148] Phayre immediately blamed the gaekwad but ignored the advice of Northbrook to resign his post. Against Wodehouse's counsel, Northbrook removed Phayre, replacing him with the more experienced Lewis Pelly as Agent to the Governor-General, who reported directly to him.[149] Pelly, the gaekwad, and Naoroji commenced an ambitious programme of financial reform. The gaekwad and Naoroji rapidly grew apart, however, ultimately resulting in Naoroji's departure and a rather abrupt halt to the British-sponsored reform.[150]

During the following investigation, a servant soon confessed that the gaekwad had provided the poison and instructed him to use it against Phayre.[151] After the evidence was vetted by the Advocate-General of Bombay, Pelly urged the immediate removal of the gaekwad. The commission appointed by the viceroy, three British officials, and three prominent Indians from other princely states could not agree on the gaekwad's guilt; regardless, he was ultimately deposed on grounds of 'misrule'.[152] Since the British claimed no criminal jurisdiction over Baroda, the removal of the gaekwad was 'an act of State, carried out by a Paramount Power'.[153]

The arrest of the gaekwad was ritualised both by the British administrators at Baroda and by the gaekwad himself. While the reported stir of anticipation in the air on the morning of the gaekwad's arrest was partially spontaneous, it also reflected a fetish with spectacle on the part of British officials as well as a desire to make an example of the troublesome gaekwad:

> Early this morning, the cantonments were in a flutter of excitement. The newly-arrived troops, which had taken up their quarters in the maidan

> [public space] opposite the Residency, were all astir; the 9th Native Regiment marched, to the stirring music of their band, to the vicinity of the new encampment; by the red, yellow, and blue ropes, which did duty as reins and ornaments to the saddler, stood in the Residency compound; near the main gate a saluting party of the 9th infantry were drawn up, and as it was their duty to present arms, when officers or civilians passed in or out from the presence of Sir Lewis Pelly, they had plenty to do in consequence of the unusual pedestrian traffic which followed between the encampments and the Residency..... It required no soothsayer to affirm that something unusual was happening.[154]

The gaekwad surrendered in a ritual performance, which doubled as a final act of defiance. To British officials in India, the ritual arrest of the gaekwad represented the administration of British justice, the liberation of Baroda from a corrupt, Oriental despot. The removal of an 'autonomous' prince by means of ambiguous and questionable legal justifications, however, profoundly informed the meanings of another imperial ritual: the royal visit.

As the melodrama of Phayre and the gaekwad demonstrates, warm feelings on the part of British administrators toward traditional, hereditary rulers were hardly universal, and the methods of indirect rule were often unrefined, their motives conflicted and directed by multiple authorities. Moreover, while the Prince of Wales, his mother, and Lord Northbrook all scowled upon the removal of a hereditary ruler such as Rao, their reluctance was not enough to prevent the gaekwad's removal, which was justified by the British government of India despite the less-than-airtight case against him.[155]

The affair informed the meaning of the Prince of Wales' visit for urban elites and hereditary rulers of British India. For many of them, the removal of the gaekwad was not an anomaly or exception but exemplified the very nature of British rule in India. The urban elites of the Raj represented the royal visit as a logical extension of this brand of British despotism.[156] The *Rájshahye Samáchár* (East Bengal) saw the prince's visit as intended 'to create an impression of the power of the British, and to wound the feelings of Native Princes ... for the object of making a parade before others of its popularity with the natives'.[157] The *Sádháraní* (West Bengal) wondered how 'the Native public ... [could] rejoice at the visit of the Prince of Wales, at a time when their hearts are sad with the deposition and misfortunes of Malhárrao'.[158] In the minds of many of the Queen's Indian subjects, the despotism of British rule demonstrated by the Baroda Affair and the charade of the royal tour represented opposite sides of the same coin.

Both British and Indian newspapers reflected on the political significance of the meeting in the context of the removal of Malhár Rao. They drew vastly different conclusions. Many of the independent South Asian newspapers expressed a willingness to punish the gaekwad if proven guilty but argued that the evidence against him was limited.[159] No matter how charismatic or gentle the Prince of Wales was in his interactions with the child prince who replaced the troublesome gaekwad, Albert Edward could never escape the perception of the Indian press that British rule was fundamentally illiberal. To many South Asian intellectuals, the rule of law – endlessly used by the British to legitimise imperial rule over local misrule and despotism – represented a tool of imperial rule, employed when convenient and abandoned when not.

To British observers, in contrast, the encounter between Prince Alfred and the young prince demonstrated the political revolution that was afoot in Baroda, where the guiding hand of British progress was transforming a corrupt Oriental despotism. The child prince would rule over his kingdom in a manner suitable to a loyal subject of the Queen. British administrators continued to direct a policy of purposeful ambiguity when legally and constitutionally defining their relationship with the gaekwad; Pelly advocated making no new treaty with the princely state on the grounds that 'a treaty more or less implies equality, and this has ceased to exist'.[160] Meade reported to Northbrook his satisfaction that Albert Edward's visit to Baroda had been an 'entire success in every respect':

> We of course took all proper measures to ensure our being duly acquainted with any suspicious or doubtful proceedings on the part of those who are known to be dissatisfied with the new arrangements.... To the community generally the Prince's visit has given the upmost satisfaction, and I feel convinced that it will be regarded as a seal to the new settlement, and will have a very important effect in checking intrigues from any and every quarter.... We may also hope that it will leave a deep and lasting impression on the young Gaekwar, and attach him firmly to the Crown.[161]

Yet the encounter reveals the far more complex relationship between the rulers and the ruled. The removal of an Indian prince and the personal selection of his successor by the British administration demonstrate the instabilities of ornamental rule. The happy meeting between the Prince of Wales and a child prince could not undo the past or the perception by many South Asians that British rule was unjust and despotic and that imperial rituals served to legitimise it.

Nizam of Hyderabad (1875)

Tour planners marvelled at the political effects of the royal presence on South Asian princes. In their minds, it demonstrated that ornamentalism represented an ideology and a set of ritual practices absolutely fundamental to imperial rule. Sir Henry Daly, the Political Agent for Central India, described to Northbrook the 'miraculous' effects of the Prince of Wales on the native princes of British India: 'There is a sentiment in their feudalism which has been touched and reached.'[162] On the other hand, the Indian newspaper *Rájshahye Samáchár* argued that the British wrongly 'seem to think that, as Asiatics, we are very fond of glitter and sport; and it was only by such displays and demonstrations that the Mahomedan Emperors, though foreigners in both creed and language, succeeded in gaining the affections of the natives. This is not correct.'[163] Independent Indian newspapers chastised colonial officials for their abuse of the local princes and their failure to govern justly and equitably.

The worst excesses of the practices and policies crafted by tour planners in the name of Asiatic spectacle were exemplified in their treatment of the Nizam of Hyderabad. British policy toward the sickly nine-year-old nizam, prince of an expansive Muslim state in south-eastern India, reflects the continuity between the Baroda controversy and the ritual practices of the royal tour. The unwillingness of Nizam Mahbub Ali Khan's handlers to allow him to make the voyage to Bombay in 1875, in order to pay his respects to the visiting Prince of Wales, was a contentious issue in the political discourses of British India, a pitched political battle fought in the pages of the Anglo-Indian and South Asian newspapers.[164]

The nizam was an odd choice for harassment by the Anglo-Indian press, which spearheaded the public relations campaign against the young prince; after all, he had been nurtured from birth to serve as a docile agent of British rule. He was given an 'English schoolboy's education', supplemented by lessons in Persian, Urdu, calligraphy, and the Qur'an, by a British tutor. After his father died in 1869, he was led to a ceremonial rug, representing the throne of Hyderabad, and invested – hand in hand with his diwan and regent, Sir Sálár Jung, and the British Resident of Hyderabad.[165]

Yet colonial officials considered attendance at imperial rituals to be compulsory. Lord Northbrook wrote to Philip Wodehouse that, short of compelling circumstances, Indian princes were expected to attend the ceremonies.[166] When the nizam's court indicated that he was too sick to attend, Northbrook found the prince's excuse to be 'insufficient'.[167] The *Sulabh Samáchár* (Calcutta) complained that a British invitation was more akin to a summons.[168] Sir Sálár Jung attested to the nizam's inability to make the arduous journey to Bombay and even considered making overtures for compromise, offering the nizam's presence within a day's journey of Hyderabad 'in either the territory of the British Government or his own'.[169] The British Resident in Baroda, C. B. Saunders, had little sympathy or patience for the nizam's predicament and immediately doubted the claim, treating Jung, in the words of *Sulabh Samáchár*, 'like a common clerk'.[170]

Against the claims of the Anglo-Indian press, South Asian independent newspapers assumed the sincerity of the nizam's illness and argued on his behalf. Further, the editors of the South Asian press used the opportunity to express their concern that the process of attending British ceremonies was often so humiliating to Indian princes that they would often rather stay home. In other words, the press claimed, South Asia's hereditary elite would rather be accused of disloyalty by the British than experience the undignified process of being ordered around and having their status disrespected by colonial officials. Weeks later, when the Anglo-Indian *Bombay Gazette* criticised 'the refusal of the Nizam to meet the Prince of Wales' as 'holding back the hand of friendship to the Heir to the Throne of England ... [and] a sullen declaration of hostility to the British Government in India', *Native Opinion* lambasted the comments of the *Gazette* as an effort 'calculated to generate ... feelings of distrust and antipathy to British power in India'.[171]

Responding to the public controversy, Captain John Clerk, the nizam's British tutor, wrote to Lord Northbrook 'on the subject that is now before Your Excellency as to His Highness the nizam meeting His Royal Highness the Prince of Wales'.[172] Clerk was a sympathetic observer of the child prince, although his account also reflects a more general European stereotype about Asiatic rulers and their weak disposition of health and nerve:

> notwithstanding all the pressure that the Resident has brought to bear on the Regency, and notwithstanding the malignantly worded telegram (from England), and subsequent newspaper articles in the *Bombay Gazette*, &c., which the Resident seems to regard as of so great importance.... When I came out (in January last) I found His Highness extremely weak and delicate; not a week passed that he was not in the hands of the doctors, either with fever or bowel complaint, or glandular swellings of the neck, resulting from his scrofulous inheritance. By dint of constantly – daily, I may say – urging the necessity of proper diet, open air exercise, and that they would allow him to take our medicines, tonics, &c., &c., gradually an improvement set in.... But when your Excellency considers all the circumstances attendant on a journey, and for the intended purpose which must inevitably lead to great excitement and nervousness to a boy who is eminently excitable and nervous – that His Highness has never been five miles away from his capital – that he has never been absent a day from his mother....Were His Highness older, and of a sound constitution, not only do I think the Regents, but also all

> of the important Nobles of the state, would look upon the fact that His Highness is going to meet and welcome His Royal Highness in India … as conferring a very great honour on them all.[173]

British officialdom's long-standing distrust of native information required the more trustworthy information of a British observer. Even this report, however, did not dissuade most British officials involved from believing that the nizam's illness was a 'mere excuse'.[174]

Clerk's reports to the British government in Calcutta on the press and public opinion in Baroda also demonstrate the limits and instabilities of colonial knowledge. He blamed the independent Indian press for disseminating untruths about him and for encouraging the resentment of the nizam's subjects toward the British government of India: 'They set on every kind of report – that I had come to make *their* Nizam Christian – that this was the first step in upsetting all their old institutions and customs – that all would be made English in a few years in ideas – and then that the Government of India would step in and take the country.'[175] Clerk understood these fears as almost pathological, a product of the paranoid and fear-mongering enemies of the British. The nizam's court, however, was attended by Saunders and a cadre of residency staff as well as Clerk, his tutor, who complained in the very same letter that the young ruler knew very little English because he spent too much of his study time reading the Qur'an! On one hand, Clerk's account of the nizam reflects the blissful ignorance of the ambitious official on the ground, looking to enact reforms on his own model of British education and scientific rule. On the other hand, it reveals a more profound weakness in the relationship between the rulers and the ruled – that the British officials on the ground failed to comprehend the effects of their practices and policies on local politics.

The nizam was ultimately 'excused' from attending royal rituals in Bombay by Northbrook after fulfilling, in the words of *Native Opinion*, the 'humiliating' requirement of sending a 'medical certificate' as proof of illness.[176] Saunders was removed, not because of his adamancy that the nizam attend the rituals in Bombay but because he was 'injudicious and [dis]courteous' in his treatment of the nizam.[177] This controversy of treating the child prince and his diwan with such enmity infuriated the editors of the independent Indian press and initiated a battle of words between the 'native' press and the Anglo-Indian newspapers. The *Bhárat Sangskárak* (Calcutta) even went as far as to conceptually link the treatment of the nizam with the Baroda Affair, as proof to the true relationship between British residents and Indian princes.[178]

In the end, the Prince of Wales did meet the nizam's regent and prime minister, Sir Sálár Jung. Jung was, according to Albert Edward's secretary Francis Knollys, 'the most astute and far seeing politician in India'.[179] British administrators who attended to the Prince of Wales concluded that Jung was quite happy to rid himself of Saunders and would use the opportunity to pursue, 'with oriental cunning', the restoration of Berar Province.[180] The assumption that Jung's intentions were devious and insincere demonstrates why British ornamental politics could never succeed as long-term methods of imperial rule. Their culturally acquisitive processes reflected not merely the missteps they made in 'dancing with strangers' but also a more insidious desire to control political discourses that proved to be a counter-productive consequence of the interventionist nature of indirect rule.

The royal tour of 1901

The encounters between British royals and local hereditary elites at the turn of the century, during the world tour of the Duke and Duchess of York and Cornwall, illustrate the changes that British imperial culture had undergone in the previous forty years. Colonial officials increasingly closed off the limited public space created by public ritual through a developing system of colonial rule and reshaped local political cultures to serve British administrative desires, by eroding and appropriating the autonomy and legitimacy of hereditary elites. As local elites became dependants and functionaries of colonial rule, they were transcended in the realm of imperial and national politics by the 'modern' politics of Western-educated *respectables*, who often had little patience for their 'traditional' practices. Those rulers who could not be controlled or neutralised were isolated, imprisoned, or destroyed by the British.

The New Zealand welcome for the Duke and Duchess of Cornwall and York, who travelled the world in 1901 in order to celebrate Australian federation and to thank imperial troops for their service to empire in the South African War, incorporated and appropriated the symbols of local culture. In this context, Maori children singing the national anthem in their native language and battle sites of the New Zealand Wars were co-opted as symbols of a national-imperial culture. Upon the duke's arrival at Auckland, the Premier of New Zealand, Richard Seddon, presented him with an ornate box, made with native woods and decorated with a Maori 'war canoe' and kiwi.[181] On Victoria Street in Auckland, an arch welcomed the duke and duchess in English and professed 'Aroha, Tonu, Ake, Ake, Ake' (translated as 'Love for Ever and Ever').[182] Of course, triumphal arches representing different ethnicities were standard decorations for royal visits, but the 1901 empire tour was perhaps most remarkable for the ways in which local customs and traditions were remade and appropriated both for the purposes of imperial rule and as part of the development of nascent national mythologies.

The duke and duchess participated in a durbar-like ceremony in Rotorua, near the Bay of Plenty on the North Island. Colonial officials invited each Maori group to send a hundred representatives to pay tribute to the Duke of York.[183] Local Arawa Maori, in the tradition of imperial rituals, performed a 'war dance', waving ceremonial battle-axes and singing a song of welcome.[184] The main event at Rotorua, however, was the Haka, where representatives from many of New Zealand's Maori groups assembled. In the grand ceremony, the Maori chiefs 'in full battle array, faced the Duke and Duchess when they entered the Royal pavilion'.[185] Performing the role of the paramount chief, the duke wore 'across the shoulders, a kiwi mat, and carried a greenstone mere, the genuine native insignia of chieftainship'.[186]

In a colonial exhibition of the Maori nations, men and women performed, professed their loyalty, mourned the loss of Queen Victoria, and brought gifts.[187] The *Poverty Bay Herald*, commenting on the sheer number of gifts received by the duke, proposed that a 'Maori Museum' ought to be built in Rotorua so that New Zealand could preserve the 'Native relics' still left in the colony.[188] By bringing together the diverse groups and cultural practices of the Maori, which had threatened the stability of European expansion in the Pacific in previous decades, the Haka transformed them into safe and controlled symbols of imperial culture – proof of 'how completely the Maori hatchet has been buried'.[189]

Still outside of the pale, the Maori king was nowhere to be found at Rotorua. While the settler press portrayed the Maori king's absence as evidence of the colonial policy of isolation, the historical record suggests that colonial administrators retained the hope that the duke's visit might present the opportunity to penetrate the symbolic space of Mahuta, the Maori king.[190] After initially agreeing to come to the Haka with several hundred followers, Mahuta stated that he was 'not inclined' to go but invited the duke and duchess to the capital of King country.[191] The government refused to alter the duke's plan so that he might stop at Mahuta's capital.[192] Thus the Maori King movement, by resisting both military and cultural colonisation, continued to challenge the processes of acquisition so central to British rule.

Similarly, when the Duke of York visited war-torn South Africa, colonial officials adopted the ritual practices that had been perfected in the Raj, bringing together 'Chiefs of all of the principal Tribes in the

Cape Colony, of Basutoland and Bechuanaland'.[193] As Indian officials during the tours of the 1860s and 1870s had found, this method was far more effective than having the King's son trek around southern Africa, as Alfred had, and ensured the protection of an heir to the throne visiting a warzone. During earlier tours, individual attention from visiting royalty was meant to demonstrate British respect for the most important local elites, with less important notables left to meet with the prince in groups or during brief interviews. Not surprisingly, there was a significant correlation between elites deserving of personal attention and those who had not fully come under the control of British rule. By 1901, these individual visits were extremely rare outside of India.

The most prominent guests at this durbar-like ceremony in Cape Town were Lerothodi of Basutoland (Lesotho), the grandson of Moshoeshoe, and King Khama of Bechuanaland (Botswana), who had visited Britain in 1895 to ask Queen Victoria for protection from the land-hungry mining magnate and politician Cecil Rhodes.[194] Both Basutoland and Bechuanaland had effectively come under British rule over previous decades.[195]

With a dozen tiger, leopard, and silver jackal rugs, their gifts to the duke, lying on the ground, the chiefs gathered in a semi-circle, facing the duke and duchess, who were sitting under a tree.[196] Each approached the heir to the British throne and, introduced by the Resident Commissioners and interpreted with the help of John Smith Moffat, the son of Scottish missionary Robert Moffat, or African interpreters, expressed his loyalty to the King and mourned the loss of the Great Queen.[197] The gifts presented by the chiefs – cheetah or jaguar karosses, leopard and jackal skins, as well as Zulu shields and assegais – demonstrate one ethnographic accomplishment of the previous half-century, that the distinctions between different political and social groups could be collapsed into a single category of 'traditional rulers'.[198] This ceremony reflected the consolidation of colonial rule in South Africa over the previous forty years and the ways that royal ritual had been developed through encounters across the empire.

Reminiscent of the performances staged by Shepstone in 1860, S. O. Samuelson, the Under-Secretary of the Native Affairs Office, choreographed and directed Zulu war dances for the Duke of York's visit. During the spectacle, the Zulu 'chiefs and their followers advanced with leaps and wild gesticulations [toward the prince] brandishing their spears, shields, and clubs, till they reached a white chalk line which marked the place where they were to halt'.[199] The appropriation of Zulu culture had long been important to the ideological work of colonial rule in what is now KwaZulu-Natal from the days of Shepstone. This work had taken a dramatic and violent turn in 1879, when British troops defeated the Zulu under Cetshwayo at the Battle of Ulundi. Cetshwayo was deposed, and the divided Zulu kingdom erupted into civil war.[200] The colonial policies aimed at neutralisation and annexation of the Zulu kingdom in the aftermath of the war proved more important than the war itself, however, and represented continuity rather than change, part and parcel of the British desire to control and appropriate the symbols and political legitimacy of the Zulu dynasty and the legacy of Shaka.

As in other ornamental rituals, the chiefs of Zululand expressed their loyalty and mourned the loss of the Great Queen in a single address 'translated' by Samuelson and delivered through Henry McCallum, the Governor of Natal.[201] The duke's response acknowledged the Zulu as worthy opponents of the past and loyal subjects of the present, while he appealed to the mythology of the Great White Queen, most notably her adoration of her 'native children'.[202] By 1901, the ritual precedents had been firmly established, pioneered by administrators such as Grey and Shepstone. South Africa's hereditary elites resembled, in terms of their political ability to act and control their fates, Sandile far more than they looked like Moshoeshoe, and the political discourses of the colonised had been effectively usurped by the educated *respectables* of South Africa's burgeoning urban communities.

The significant exception to this decline and growing dependency of hereditary elites in the context of British imperial culture, were those political traditions that were able to resist colonial appropriation by nurturing their own proto-national identities.[203] For the Basuto, the state-building of Moshoeshoe and the development of a Basuto identity and culture centred on the mythology of Moshoeshoe helped promote imperial protection of the kingdom as different from the rest of southern Africa. The Maori King movement succeeded, with similarly limited yields, in resisting colonial appropriation and retaining some semblance of autonomy into the twentieth century. The mythology of Shaka and a Zulu national identity lingered in the historical memory of southern Africa, re-emerging most prominently in moments of crisis, such as the Bambatha 'uprising' (1906), and much later in the tribal-nationalist politics of the Inkatha Freedom Party.[204]

* * *

The royal tours and other imperial rituals were practices that reflected British fantasies more than colonial realities. After decades of colonial wars, most notably the Indian Mutiny, British administrators sought to close the ritual spaces that had served as sites of negotiation since the earliest days of the British Empire.[205] These processes of cultural appropriation had difficulty isolating local political traditions because they were not the static and ancient customs they were imagined to be. Local politics were elusive, slippery, and always in the making. British officials often misunderstood them – or delegitimised them by adapting them to the purposes of British rule, making local elites little more than tax collectors and labour recruiters. Local hereditary elites used similar tactics, of incorporating imperial culture or constructing counter-discourses of identity, to challenge these efforts. Over time, for these very reasons, the challenges to the royal tour as a cultural practice were articulated less by hereditary elites, who became dependent on the British Empire as their reason for existence, and more and more by the educated *respectables* who came to dominate local political discourses.

These Western-educated elites, who serve as the leading historical actors of Chapter 4, criticised the excesses of imperial rule and the conceptual instability between the language of British imperialism and the practices of imperial rule. By and large, however, they did not challenge empire as an idea or the importance of the British Empire as their political, cultural, and social universe. They embraced an imperial citizenship, centred on Queen Victoria and their status as British people, to challenge the injustices of British rule as fundamentally un-British. While colonial administrators focused on methods of indirect rule, these historical actors relied on methods of modern politics, namely print culture, to adapt and remake local political cultures. In identifying themselves with the imperial, they came to dominate local political discourses, even if their voices were largely ignored by the British. As colonial subjects looked forward to an inclusive, liberal empire, colonial administrators were mired in their own fantasies of traditional cultures.

Notes

1 Lord Lytton to Queen Victoria, 4 May 1876, *The Letters of Queen Victoria*, ed. G. E. Buckle, Second Series, *1862–85* (London, 1926–28), vol. 2, 460–8.

2 David Cannadine, *Ornamentalism: How the British Saw Their Empire* (London, 2001).

3 The use of the term 'technology' in this context reflects an understanding of colonial rule inspired by scholars such as Nicholas Dirks, Bernard Cohn, Michel Foucault and others – namely, that empire was sustained by a diverse constellation of methods from machine-guns and naval power to ritual, propaganda, and surveillance. The royal tours, while they appealed to ritual practices and ideas about political legitimacy that were not new, emerged during a particular moment during the nineteenth century (as I describe here) and were made possible by technological innovations.

4 See James Belich, 'Empire and Its Myth', in *Amongst Friends: Australian and New Zealand Voices from America*, ed. Patty O'Brien and Bruce Vaughan (Dunedin, 2005), 149; James Belich, *Making Peoples: A History of New Zealanders* (Honolulu, 1996), 230.

5 This naturalisation of imperial rule was then reflected back on to history of the empire, as represented in the *Cambridge History of the British Empire* (1929–61). The volume on 'British India', for instance, started in 1498 with Vasco da Gama!

6 Historical anthropologists such as Bernard Cohn and Nicholas Dirks have focused on the intimate relationship between knowledge and power in the colonial encounter, arguing that the accumulation of British knowledge about local peoples was appropriated, bastardised, and employed for the purposes of colonial rule. Bernard Cohn, 'Representing Authority in Victorian India', in *The Invention of Tradition*, ed. Eric Hobsbawm and Terence Ranger (Cambridge, 1983), 165–210; Bernard Cohn, *Colonialism and Its Forms of Knowledge* (Princeton, 1996); Nicholas Dirks, *Castes of Mind: Colonialism and the Making of Modern India* (Princeton, 2001). See also Colin Newbury, *Patrons, Clients, and Empire: Chieftaincy and Over-rule in Asia, Africa, and the Pacific* (Oxford, 2003); Terence Ranger, 'The Invention of Tradition in Colonial Africa', in *The Invention of Tradition*, ed. Eric Hobsbawm and Terence Ranger (Cambridge, 1983), 211–62.

7 John Richards, *The Mughal Empire* (Cambridge, 1996), 100–1.

8 Major John Cowell to Albert, 16 August 1860, RA VIC ADD/20/69.

9 Inga Clendinnen, *Dancing with Strangers: Europeans and Australians at First Contact* (Cambridge, 2005).

10 Thomas Metcalf, *Imperial Connections: India in the Indian Ocean Arena, 1860–1920* (Berkeley, 2008).

11 Andrew Apter, *The Pan-African Nation: Oil and the Spectacle of Culture in Nigeria* (Chicago, 2005); George Ferguson Bowen, *Thirty Years of Colonial Government: A Selection from the Despatches and Letters*, vol. 1, ed. Stanley Lane-Poole (New York, 1889), 364.

12 Eric Hobsbawm, 'Introduction: Inventing Traditions', in *The Invention of Tradition*, ed. Eric Hobsbawm and Terence Ranger (Cambridge, 1983), 1–14; Terence Ranger, 'The Invention of Tradition Revisited: The Case of Africa', in *Legitimacy and the State in Twentieth-Century Africa: Essays in Honour of A.H.M. Kirk-Greene*, ed. Terence Ranger and Olufemi Vaughan (London, 1993), 62–111. For a useful, but brief, overview of imperial rituals and the durbar, see Barbara N. Ramusack, *The New Cambridge History of India*, vol. 3.6, *The Indian Princes and Their States* (Cambridge, 2004), 90–2. According to Ramusack, Lord Amherst (1823–28) was the first governor to tour India, but Lord Canning (1856–62) was the first to visit the Indian princes 'systematically' in the aftermath of the 1857 war.

13 Cannadine, *Ornamentalism*, 4.

14 Joseph Schumpeter, *Imperialism and Social Classes* (New York, repr. 1955). Schumpeter's sociological assessment of empire challenged the conceptualisations of his contemporaries, John Hobson and V. I. Lenin. Schumpeter argued that imperialism was not a function of industrial or financial capitalism, but an atavism of a previous age.

15 This does not mean to suggest that a powerful tradition of chiefship did not continue to profoundly influence local and national politics after 1901, particularly in the countryside and on African reserves. The argument here is one about British and imperial politics, the African voices of which became overwhelmingly urban and Western-educated. See Paul Landau, *Popular Politics in the History of South Africa, 1400–1948* (Cambridge, 2010).

16 Elizabeth Eldredge, *Power in Colonial Africa: Conflict and Discourse in Lesotho, 1870–1960* (Madison, WI, 2007), 28–32.

17 Thomas Arbousset, *Missionary Excursion into the Blue Mountains, Being an Account of King Moshoeshoe's Expedition from Thaba-Bosiu to the Sources of the Malibamatso River in the Year 1840*, ed. and trans. David Ambrose and Albert Brutsch (Morija, 1991), 107.

18 Scott Rosenberg, 'Promises of Moshoeshoe: Culture, Nationalism, and Identity in Lesotho, 1902–1966' (PhD dissertation, Indiana University, 1998); Scott Rosenberg, 'Monuments, Holidays, and Remembering Moshoeshoe: The Emergence of National Identity in Lesotho, 1902–1966' *Africa Today* 46, no. 1 (Winter 1999): 49–72.

19 Eldredge, *Power in Colonial Africa*, 28.

20 Elizabeth Eldredge, *A South African Kingdom: The Pursuit of Security in Nineteenth-Century Lesotho* (Cambridge, 2002), 48–9.

21 Eldredge, *South African Kingdom*, 50.
22 Laura Benton, 'The Geography of Quasi-Sovereignty: Westlake, Maine, and the Legal Politics of Colonial Enclaves', *International Law and Justice Working Papers* 5 (2006), 46.
23 Eldredge, *South African Kingdom*, 51.
24 Leonard Thompson, *Survival in Two Worlds: Moshoeshoe of Lesotho, 1786–1870* (Oxford, 1975), 175; See also Peters Sanders' conceptually similar work on Moshoeshoe, published the same year, *Moshoeshoe, Chief of the Sotho* (Portsmouth, NH, 1975).
25 Thompson, *Survival in Two Worlds*, 169.
26 Thompson, *Survival in Two Worlds*, 268.
27 Saul Solomon, *The Progress of His Royal Highness Prince Alfred Ernest Albert through the Cape Colony, British Kaffraria, the Orange Free State, and Port Natal in the Year 1860* (Cape Town, 1861), 75.
28 Solomon, *The Progress of His Royal Highness*, 76; *Natal Mercury*, 11 October 1860.
29 Solomon, *The Progress of His Royal Highness*, 76.
30 Solomon, *The Progress of His Royal Highness*, 76.
31 *Cape Argus*, quoted in Solomon, *The Progress of His Royal Highness*, 77.
32 *Natal Mercury*, 11 October 1860.
33 Solomon, *The Progress of His Royal Highness*, 77.
34 Solomon, *The Progress of His Royal Highness*, 77.
35 Solomon, *The Progress of His Royal Highness*, 77.
36 Solomon, *The Progress of His Royal Highness*, 78.
37 *Cape Argus*, quoted in Solomon, *The Progress of His Royal Highness*, 78; quoted almost verbatim in *Natal Mercury*, 11 October 1860.
38 *Natal Mercury*, 10 October 1860. Some of this performance was conducted by Moshoeshoe's son, Isekelo. The settler newspapers, such as the *Mercury*, described these performances as spontaneous expressions of loyalty rather than choreographed imperial rituals. The *Mercury* also reported natives singing, 'Our chief has come whom we longed for' (presumably about Alfred).
39 From the first encounters, Europeans understood gift exchanges to be a requirement of local ritual cultures. The culture of gift giving was adopted as a standard ritual practice of imperial rule across the empire from the its earliest days and might be better understood as a co-invention, made in the colonial encounter, rather than a British invention or a local 'imposition'.
40 *King William's Town Gazette*, 4 September 1860.
41 Solomon, *The Progress of His Royal Highness*, 79.
42 John Cowell to Albert, 19 August 1860, RA VIC ADD/20/69.
43 Thomas Spear, 'Neo-Traditionalism and the Limits of Invention in British Colonial Africa', *Journal of African History* 44 (2003), 9.
44 *Natal Mercury*, 10 October 1860.
45 Solomon, *The Progress of His Royal Highness*, 80.
46 *Natal Witness*, 12 October 1860.
47 Paul Landau, 'Introduction: An Amazing Distance: Pictures and People in Africa', in *Images and Empires: Visuality in Colonial and Postcolonial Africa*, ed. Paul Landau and Deborah Kaspin (Berkeley, 2002), 1–40.
48 Moshoeshoe to Alfred, 18 August 1860, *Basutoland Records*, ed. G. M. Theal (Cape Town, 1883), 568.
49 John Cowell to Albert, 19 August 1860, RA. It is unclear if Moshoeshoe was pandering to his audience by celebrating past British justice or if the period of British annexation now appeared to be, relatively speaking, a more promising arrangement.
50 Major John Cowell to Albert, 14 August 1860, RA VIC ADD/20/69.
51 Moshoeshoe's skilful foreign policy with Europeans is clearly illustrated in his meeting with President Boshof of the Orange Free State and Governor George Grey of the Cape Colony in 1855. There is a clear narrative disjuncture between Moshoeshoe's challenges to the political legitimacy of European complaints against him and the self-legitimising evolution of European policy toward war against him. See André du

Toit and Hermann Giliomee, *Afrikaner Political Thought: Analysis and Documents*, vol. 1, *1780–1850* (Berkeley, 1983), 188–94.

52 Eldredge, *South African Kingdom*, 82.

53 Sandra Burman, *Chiefdom Politics and Alien Law: Basutoland under Cape Rule, 1871–1884* (New York, 1981).

54 Benton, 'The Geography of Quasi-Sovereignty', 47–8.

55 Jeff Guy '"A Paralysis of Perspective": Image and Text in the Creation of an African Chief', *South African Historical Journal* 47 (2002), 54.

56 John Robinson, the first Prime Minister of Natal (1893–97), called a 'henchman of Mr. Shepstone'. John Robinson, *A Life Time in South Africa: Being Recollections of the First Premier of Natal* (London, 1900), 108. The index of his book refers to Ngoza as 'Zulu attendant on Mr. Shepstone'.

57 Guy, '"A Paralysis"', 54.

58 John W. Colenso, *Ten Weeks in Natal: A Journal of a First Tour of Visitation among the Colonists and the Zulu Kafirs of Natal* (London, 1855), 45–46.

59 Solomon, *The Progress of His Royal Highness*, 97; *The Visit of His Royal Highness Prince Alfred to the Colony of Natal* (London, 1861), 19.

60 *Visit of His Royal Highness*, 18.

61 *Visit of His Royal Highness*, 97–8. This passage is reproduced in Guy, '"A Paralysis"', 56.

62 *Visit of His Royal Highness*, 97–8.

63 *Natal Mercury*, n.d.

64 *Natal Mercury*, n.d.

65 John Lambert, 'Chiefship in Early Colonial Natal, 1843–1879', *Journal of African Studies* 21, no. 2 (June 1995): 269–85.

66 Thomas McClendon, 'Interpretation and Interpolation: Shepstone as Native Interpreter', in *Intermediaries, Interpreters, and Clerks: African Employees in the Making of Colonial Africa*, ed. Benjamin N. Lawrance, Emily Lynn Osborn, and Richard L. Roberts (Madison, WI, 2006), 77–93; Jeff Guy, *The View across the River: Harriette Colenso and the Zulu Struggle against Imperialism* (Charlottesville, 2002); Jeff Guy, *Theophilus Shepstone and the Forging of Natal: African Autonomy and Settler Colonialism in the Making of Traditional Authority* (Scottsville, 2013); Thomas McClendon, *White Chief, Black Lords: Shepstone and the Colonial State in Natal, South Africa, 1845–1878* (Rochester, 2010). Notably, the Victorian novelist Rider Haggard's work, informed by his time working as a colonial administrator under Shepstone, powerfully mythologised Shepstone as the 'great white chief'.

67 McClendon, *White Chief, Black Lords*, 79–80.

68 Guy, '"A Paralysis"', 37.

69 Guy, '"A Paralysis"', 35. See also Norman Etherington, 'The "Shepstone System" in the Colony of Natal and beyond the Borders', in *Natal and Zululand from Earliest Times to 1910: A New History*, ed. Andrew Duminy and W. R. Guest (Pietermaritzburg, 1989), 170–92; See Mahmood Mamdani, *Citizen and Subject: Contemporary Africa and the Legacy of Late Colonialism* (Princeton, 1996), 62–108.

70 Carolyn Hamilton, *Terrific Majesty: The Powers of Shaka Zulu and the Limits of Historical Invention* (Cambridge, MA: 1998), 72–5.

71 Hamilton, *Terrific Majesty*, 75.

72 McClendon, *White Chief, Black Lords*, 90.

73 McClendon, *White Chief, Black Lords*, 90.

74 By 1869, the colonial government determined policy toward Kingitanga, not the governor, though he presumably had some discretionary powers as the Queen's representative in New Zealand.

75 See Alan Ward, *A Show of Justice: Racial 'Amalgamation' in Nineteenth-Century New Zealand* (Auckland, 1974); James Belich, *The New Zealand Wars and the Victorian Interpretation of Racial Conflict* (Auckland, 1989).

76 Angela Ballara, 'Introduction', in *Te Kingitanga: The People of the Maori King Movement*, ed. Angela Ballara (Auckland, 1996), 1.

77 Two other pan-Maori movements emerged in Taranaki during the 1850s: Kai Knarara, a religious movement, and the 'anti-land selling' movement. See Belich, *Making Peoples*, 232.
78 Jenifer Curnow, 'A Brief History of Maori-Language Newspapers', in *Rere atu, taku manu! Discovering History, Language, and Politics in the Maori-Language Newspapers*, ed. Jenifer Curnow, Ngapare Hopa, and Jane McRae (Auckland, 2002), 21–2, 26–8. George Grey, the Governor of New Zealand, was so concerned at *Te Hokioi o Niu Tireni e Rere atu na* that he organised an alternative Maori-language newspaper called *Te Pihoihoi Mokemoke I runga I te Tuanui*.
79 See Paul Clark, *'Hauhau': The Pai Marire Search for Maori Identity* (Auckland, 1975); Bronwyn Elsmore, *Mana from Heaven: A Century of Maori Prophets in New Zealand* (Tauranga, 1989).
80 Vincent O'Malley, *Beyond the Imperial Frontier: The Contest for Colonial New Zealand* (Wellington, 2014), 125, 127.
81 While Kingitanga aspired to be pan-Maori, many Maori communities withheld support. For instance, the neighbouring Te Arawa abstained from the movement and later supported the Crown as loyalist, or *kupapa*, Maori.
82 Ballara, 'Introduction', 11.
83 Belich, *Making Peoples*, 235–6.
84 Belich, *Making Peoples*, 231. Grey even alleged that the Maori were working in concert with French missionaries. For a forensic analysis of Grey's case for war, see Vincent O'Malley, 'Choosing Peace or War: The 1863 Invasion of Waikato', *New Zealand Journal of History* 47, no. 1 (2013): 39–58.
85 Evelyn Stokes, 'Te Waharoa, Wiremu Tamihana Tarapipipi', in *Dictionary of New Zealand Biography* (Wellington, 1990–2000).
86 Waitangi Tribunal, *Te Rohe Potae War and Paupatu*, by Vincent O'Malley. Wai 898, #A22 (unpublished, 2010), 750–7.
87 Bowen to Colonial Office, 2 May 1869, NA CO 209/211/158–62.
88 Bowen to Colonial Office, 2 May 1869, NA.
89 Bowen to Colonial Office, 2 May 1869, NA.
90 Bowen to Colonial Office, 2 May 1869, NA.
91 Bowen to Colonial Office, 2 May 1869, NA.
92 Bowen to Colonial Office, 2 May 1869, NA.
93 *Daily Southern Cross*, 5 July 1869, quoting *Wanganui Times*, 24 June 1869; *Daily Southern Cross*, 10 May 1869. See also Judith Binney, *Redemption Songs: A Life of Te Kooti Arikirangi Te Turuki* (Honolulu, 1997).
94 Bowen to Colonial Office, 3 June 1869, NA CO 209/211/334–400.
95 Bowen to Colonial Office, 3 June 1869, NA.
96 Bowen to Colonial Office, 30 March, 1869, NA CO 209/210/565–8.
97 Bowen to Colonial Office, 2 May 1869, NA CO 209/211/172–8.
98 Kaitangata was a Maori man who was sought after by a woman in the sky named Whaitiri (Thunder) because she mistakenly thought he was a cannibal. For an early anthropological account of Kaitangata, see J. F. H. Wohlers, 'The Mythology and Traditions of the Maori in New Zealand', *Transactions and Proceedings of the Royal Society of New Zealand* 7 (1874), 15. Bowen reported to the Colonial Office that Alfred had been given 'the Kai-tangata' (literally 'Man-eater')'.
99 Bowen to Colonial Office, 2 May 1869, NA.
100 Bowen to Colonial Office, 2 May 1869, NA.
101 Bowen to Colonial Office, 2 May 1869, NA.
102 Steven Oliver, 'Tamihana Te Rauparaha', *Dictionary of New Zealand Biography*.
103 Oliver, 'Tamihana Te Rauparaha'.
104 Oliver, 'Tamihana Te Rauparaha'.
105 Oliver, 'Tamihana Te Rauparaha'.
106 Bowen to Colonial Office, 2 May 1869, NA.
107 Bowen to Colonial Office, 3 June 1869, NA CO 209/211/334–400.
108 Bowen to Colonial Office, 3 June 1869, NA.
109 Bowen to Colonial Office, 3 June 1869, NA.

110 *West Coast Times*, 11 June 1869.
111 *Taranaki Herald*, 10 September 1870.
112 Bowen to Colonial Office, 3 June 1869, NA.
113 Bowen to Colonial Office, 3 June 1869, NA.
114 Bowen to Colonial Office, 3 June 1869, NA.
115 *Taranaki Herald*, 5 June 1869; *Daily Southern Cross*, 4 June 1869.
116 *Taranaki Herald*, 9 June 1869
117 Northbrook to Queen Victoria, 14 June 1875, Prince of Wales in India, 1875–76, vol. 1, 1875, RA VIC/MAIN/Z/468/23; Knollys to Ponsonby, 14 November 1875, Prince of Wales in India, 1875–76, vol. 1, 1875, VIC/MAIN/Z/468/102.
118 William Howard Russell, *The Prince of Wales' Tour: A Diary in India* (London, 1878), 148. The British considered the Gaekwad of Baroda to be among the most important Indian princes, a twenty-one-gun prince in ceremonial terms. According to legend, General Archibald Wavell, the last Indian Viceroy before Lord Mountbatten, used the mnemonic 'Hot Kippers Make Good Breakfast' (Hyderabad, Kashmir, Mysore, Gwalior, Baroda) to help him remember the twenty-one-gun princes.
119 J. Drew Gay, *The Prince of Wales in India; or, from Pall Mall to Punjaub* (New York, 1877), 85. Gay was the special correspondent for the *Daily Telegraph* during the tour.
120 Gay, *The Prince of Wales in India*, 82–98.
121 Wodehouse to Salisbury, n.d., Prince of Wales in India, 1875–76, vol. 1, 1875, RA VIC/MAIN/Z 468/110.
122 Northbrook to Queen Victoria, no. 39, 14 November 1875, BL MSS Eur C144/8; Wodehouse to Salisbury, n.d., Prince of Wales in India, 1875–76, vol. 1, 1875, RA VIC/MAIN/Z 468/110; Northbrook to Wodehouse, enclosure, 3 August 1875, Wodehouse Papers, BL MSS Eur D726/7.
123 Philip Wodehouse to Northbrook, 22 October 1875, BL MSS Eur C 144/17.
124 Philip Wodehouse to Northbrook, 22 October 1875, BL.
125 Northbrook to Queen Victoria, no. 39, 14 November 1875, BL MSS Eur C144/8; Wodehouse to Salisbury, n.d., Prince of Wales in India, 1875–76, vol. 1, 1875, RA VIC/MAIN/Z 468 CFP.
126 Gay, *The Prince of Wales in India*, 41.
127 General Samuel James Browne, Memorandum to Accompany the Draft Program of the Tour of HRH the Prince of Wales to India, Enclosure C, Proposed Program on the Occasion of the Visit of HRH the Prince of Wales to Ajmere, BL MSS Eur F486/3.
128 Alfred to Queen Victoria, 9 January 1870, RA VIC/ADD/A/20/1304.
129 Prince of Wales to Queen Victoria, 14 November 1875, Prince of Wales in India, 1875–76, vol. 1, 1875, RA VIC/MAIN/Z 468 CFP/98.
130 One of the best examples is such encounters, between Jung Bahadur Rana and Prince Alfred in 1870, is richly documented in *The Prince of Edinburgh in the Oudh and Nepal Forests: A Letter from India* (Private Circulation, 1870).
131 This incident appears in the Victorian and more traditional twentieth-century imperial historiography, but is not covered by the more recent historiography of empire. In the nineteenth century, it became a milestone event in an intellectual discourse on British paramountcy and 'feudal' Indian states. Mihir Kumar Ray, *Princely States and the Paramount Power, 1858–1876: A Study on the Nature of Political Relationship between the British Government and the Indian State* (Delhi, 1981); William Lee-Warner, *The Native States of India* (Delhi, 1893); C. L. Tupper, *Indian Political Practice: A Collection of Decisions of the Government of India in Political Cases*, 4 vols (Delhi, 1895); Edward C. Moulton, *Lord Northbrook's Indian Administration, 1872–1876* (New York, 1968); I. F. S. Copland, 'The Baroda Crisis of 1873–77: A Study in Government Rivalry', *Modern Asian Studies* 2, no. 2 (1968): 97–123.
132 Benton, 'The Geography of Quasi-Sovereignty'. See also Lauren Benton, *A Search for Sovereignty: Law and Geography in European Empires, 1400–1900* (New York, 2009).
133 See Benton, 'The Geography of Quasi-Sovereignty', 7–8, 34.

134 C. L. Tupper, *Our Indian Protectorate: An Introduction to the Study of Relations between the British Government and its Indian Feudatories* (London, 1893), 143. Cited in Benton, 'The Geography of Quasi-Sovereignty', 15. The British were not completely delusional to think that they were emulating the practices of Mughal rule. Local princes, who functioned as the imperial governors of Mughal rule, were subject to removal and annexation by the imperial core. Under Akbar and Jahangir, a sophisticated playbook of rule – from royal rituals to surveillance – was developed, foreshadowing in some ways the developments of British rule. Richards, *The Mughal Empire.*

135 *The Collected Papers of John Westlake on Public International Law*, ed. L. Oppenheim (Cambridge, 1914), 220. Quoted in Benton, 'The Geography of Quasi-Sovereignty', 7.

136 Benton, 'The Geography of Quasi-Sovereignty', 9.

137 The state's ruling dynasty dated to the eighteenth century, and it had come under British protection in 1802. During the Mutiny of 1857, Gaekwad Khande Rao remained loyal to the British. In 1870, Khade Rao died, leaving his younger brother Malhár Rao, released from prison by the British, to serve in place of the unborn heir.

138 Under the Mughals, a diwan was a chief revenue officer. Later, the term was used to describe a chief minister (sometimes compared by Western scholars to a prime minister in a parliamentary system) or even the prince himself.

139 Moulton, *Lord Northbrook's Indian Administration*, 131–2.

140 'Crisis in Baroda', BL MSS Eur D870.

141 Moulton, *Lord Northbrook's Indian Administration*, 133.

142 Quoted in Moulton, *Lord Northbrook's Indian Administration*, 134.

143 Copland's well-known 1968 article on the 'Baroda crisis' framed the dispute as one between two British governments, largely ignoring the gaekwad as an independent historical actor. Copland, 'The Baroda Crisis of 1873–77'.

144 Moulton, *Lord Northbrook's Indian Administration*, 137.

145 Dadabhai Naoroji, *Poverty and Un-British Rule in India* (London, 1901).

146 Moulton, *Lord Northbrook's Indian Administration*, 139.

147 Moulton, *Lord Northbrook's Indian Administration*, 141.

148 As Laura Benton amusingly notes, 'Reading [Phayre's] correspondence, one begins to suspect that there were others besides the Baroda ruler who took pleasure in imagining him dead.' Benton, 'The Geography of Quasi-Sovereignty', 25.

149 Moulton, *Lord Northbrook's Indian Administration*, 147.

150 Pelly was shocked by the resentment directed toward him and the sympathy for the gaekwad. He asked Northbrook, 'What in your opinion is the real feeling of the people in the Gaekwad's dominions on the whole affair? Is the sympathy of which I read in the newspapers real or bought? And if real, from what does it arise? ... From an English view of the case it seems to be that the course the Government of India has taken has been calm and just, and that the sympathy expressed for a man who, in addition to more than the ordinary vices of an Asiatic ruler, and besides having oppressed his people, has brought himself, to say the least of it, under the strong suspicion of a cowardly act of trying to poison the British Resident, is either disloyalty to the British Government ... or arises from some idiosyncrasy of the Native mind beyond my comprehension.' Pelly to Northbrook, 27 March 1875, BL MSS Eur C 144/17.

151 Moulton, *Lord Northbrook's Indian Administration*, 149.

152 Benton, 'The Geography of Quasi-Sovereignty', 23.

153 BL MSS Eur F/12/88/4. Cited in Benton, 'The Geography of Quasi-Sovereignty', 33.

154 'Arrest of the Gaekwar of Baroda', *Bombay Gazette*, BL MSS Eur D870.

155 The Prince of Wales wrote to his mother, 'Natives of all classes in this country will, I am sure, be more attached to us and to our rule, if they are treated with kindness and with firmness at the same time, but not with brutality and contempt.' Prince of Wales to Queen Victoria, 14 June 1875, Prince of Wales in India, 1875–76, vol. 1, 1875, RA VIC/MAIN/Z/468/23.

156 Some of the independent newspapers, most notably the *Moorshedanad Patriká* (Brahmapur, Orissa), defended the Indian administration's even-handed reform in Baroda. *Moorshedanad Patriká*, 18 December 1874, in *Indian Newspaper Reports, c. 1868–1942, from the British Library, London* (Marlborough, 2005–), no. 1, 1.
157 *Rájshahye Samáchár*, 6 August 1875, *Indian Newspaper Reports*, no. 34 of 1875, 1.
158 *Rájshahye Samáchár*, 31 August 1875, *Indian Newspaper Reports*, no. 34 of 1875, 2.
159 *Saptahik Samachar*, 9 January 1875, *Indian Newspaper Reports*, no. 3 of 1875, 4.
160 Pelly to Northbrook, 20 February 1875, BL MSS Eur C 144/17.
161 Meade to Northbrook, 23 November 1875, BL MSS Eur C 144/17.
162 Extract from a Confidential Report from Sir H. Daly to Northbrook, no. 29, Prince of Wales in India, 1875–76, vol. 1, 1875, RA VIC/MAIN/Z 468/29.
163 *Rájshahye Samáchár*, 6 August 1875, *Indian Newspaper Reports*, no. 33 of 1875, 7–8.
164 Moulton, *Lord Northbrook's Indian Administration*, 125. Northbrook apparently expressed a long-standing distrust of Muslim rulers.
165 Harriet Ronken Lynton and Mohini Rajan, *The Days of the Beloved* (Los Angeles, 1974), 28–33.
166 Northbrook to Wodehouse, 9 October 1875, Wodehouse Papers, BL MSS Eur D726/7.
167 Northbrook to Queen Victoria, 13 September 1875, no. 36, BL MSS Eur C144/8.
168 *Sulabh Samáchár*, 30 November 1875, *Indian Newspaper Reports*, no. 52 of 1875, 2.
169 Captain John Clerk to Northbrook, 10 September 1875, BL MSS Eur C 144/17. He omitted this suggestion from his final draft to the British Resident, fearing that he would make the sick boy travel even farther.
170 *Sulabh Samáchár*, 30 November 1875, *Indian Newspaper Reports*, no. 52 of 1875, 2. See also Russell, *The Prince of Wales' Tour*, 76.
171 *Native Opinion*, 28 November 1875, 2.
172 Captain John Clerk to Northbrook, 10 September 1875, BL MSS Eur C 144/17.
173 Captain John Clerk to Northbrook, 10 September 1875, BL.
174 Lord Napier to Northbrook, 18 August 1875, BL MSS Eur C 144/17.
175 Captain John Clerk to Northbrook, 10 September 1875, BL.
176 *Native Opinion*, 31 October 1875, 1.
177 Ponsonby to Queen Victoria, 3 January 1876, Prince of Wales in India, 1875–76, vol. 2, 1876, RA VIC/MAIN/Z 469 CFP/4. British authorities feared that he would file a grievance against the British government upon returning to Britain.
178 *Bhárat Sangskárak*, 3 December 1875, *Indian Newspaper Reports*, no. 51 of 1875, 1.
179 Knollys to Ponsonby, 14 November 1875, Prince of Wales in India, 1875–76, vol. 1, 1875, RA VIC/MAIN/Z/468/102.
180 Ponsonby to Queen Victoria, 3 January 1876, Prince of Wales in India, 1875–76, vol. 2, 1876, RA VIC/MAIN/Z 469 CFP/4; Salar Jung to Saunders, 15 December 1875, BL MSS Eur E 190 1/32/4.
181 Joseph Watson, *The Queen's Wish: How It Was Fulfilled by the Imperial Tour of T.R.H. the Duke and Duchess of Cornwall* (London, 1902), 227–9.
182 Watson, *The Queen's Wish*, 232.
183 *The Colonist*, 20 March 1901.
184 Watson, *The Queen's Wish*, 240.
185 Watson, *The Queen's Wish*, 254–5.
186 Watson, *The Queen's Wish*, 254–5.
187 *Poverty Bay Herald*, 14 May 1901.
188 *Poverty Bay Herald*, 25 June 1901. The sentiment that Maori artefacts were more easily located at the British Museum than in New Zealand reflects a nascent national consciousness, whereby New Zealand was more than an overseas extension of Great Britain. Curiously, the *Herald* compared New Zealand's plight to that of Greece!
189 Donald Mackenzie Wallace, *The Web of Empire: A Diary of the Imperial Tour of Their Royal Highnesses the Duke and Duchess of Cornwall and York in 1901* (London, 1902), 232.
190 *Bay of Plenty Times*, 29 May 1901.

191 *Hawera & Normanby Star*, 24 April 1901; *Wanganui Herald*, 18 May 1901.
192 *West Coast Times*, 29 May 1901.
193 Arthur Bigge to Governor Walter Hely-Hutchinson, 23 August 1901, NA CO 48/553/881; Watson, *The Queen's Wish*, 328.
194 Neil Parsons, *King Khama, Emperor Joe, and the Great White Queen: Victorian Britain through African Eyes* (Chicago, 1998).
195 Richard Clay, 'Review of Anthony Sillery, *Founding a Protectorate: History of Bechuanaland, 1885–1895*', *Bulletin of the School of Oriental and African Studies* 29 (1966), 664. Basutoland, a British protectorate from 1868 and a Crown colony ruled by a British governor from 1884, had been forced to cede its arable land west of the Caledon River to the Boers, reducing the size of Moshoeshoe's original kingdom by half. Bechuanaland south of the Molopo River came under British protection in 1885 and was governed by the High Commissioner of South Africa from 1891.
196 Watson, *The Queen's Wish*, 329–30.
197 Watson, *The Queen's Wish*, 329.
198 Watson, *The Queen's Wish*, 350. While Dinuzulu, the last king, had returned to Zululand in 1898 from banishment at St Helena, he was not presented to the duke.
199 Watson, *The Queen's Wish*, 322.
200 See Jeff Guy, *The Destruction of the Zulu Kingdom: The Civil War in Zululand, 1879–1884* (New York, 1979), 61–78.
201 Watson, *The Queen's Wish*, 322.
202 Watson, *The Queen's Wish*, 324.
203 Again, it is important to note that chiefship remained a vibrant and important political tradition at the local level.
204 Jeff Guy, *The Maphumulo Uprising: War, Law and Ritual in the Zulu Rebellion* (Scottsville, 2005); Hamilton, *Terrific Majesty*.
205 See, for instance, the performance of the drunken Zulu king Solomon ka Dinuzulu at an imperial ritual in 1930. Shula Marks, 'The Drunken King and the Nature of the State', in *The Ambiguities of Dependence: Class, Nationalism and the State in Twentieth-Century Natal* (Baltimore, 1986), 14–42.

CHAPTER THREE

Building new Jerusalems: global Britishness and settler cultures in South Africa and New Zealand

Prince Alfred performed the crowning achievement of his visit to South Africa in 1860 when he tipped a truck of stone into Table Bay, ceremonially beginning the construction of a great modernisation project, the Cape Town breakwater. Around the same time, his older brother the Prince of Wales was inaugurating the Victoria Bridge over the St. Lawrence River in Canada. For British subjects at home and in the empire, both projects represented the progress and development of an expanding British world. Cape Town newspaper writers and colonial officials celebrated this day as one of the most important in all the history of South Africa. It was a historic day, they would suggest, a day when the Cape Colony began to transform from a backwater of the British Empire to an important depot of commerce and trade.[1]

Despite these celebrations, the settler societies of British South Africa were deeply divided over the project, between colonial politicians and merchants in the Western Cape, who would most benefit from the improvement project, and the settlers of the Eastern Cape, who were painfully far away from the harbour at Cape Town. In the midst of a royal visit, the settler newspapers of the Eastern Cape protested the injustice of being bullied into funding a harbour for Cape Town that would not benefit them from the general revenue of the colony. Part of the reason Governor George Grey sought to bring Alfred to South Africa, in a royal tour modelled on his brother's planned visit to Canada, was to force the legislature's hand on the issue of the breakwater.[2] This struggle revived the spectre of Cape separatism and reflects the importance of Britishness and imperial citizenship in the language of politics and protest.[3]

During Alfred's visit to Canterbury, New Zealand, in 1869, local newspapers constructed a mythology of the settlement that centred on its faithful reproduction of British society. Edward Gibbon Wakefield's

Canterbury association imagined the settlement, founded in 1850 as an Anglican colony, as a faithful if idealised reproduction of British society, where everyone knew their place in society. According to the provincial superintendent William Rolleston, 'nowhere' in his mother's empire would Alfred find British institutions 'more firmly implanted' than in Canterbury.[4] Without even a foundation stone for the prince to lay, the provincial capital Christchurch could not compete with the splendour and wealth of Australian cities, yet its settlement 'resemble[d] England more than any other portion of the colony'.[5] In other words, they claimed that the duke would feel most at home and most welcome in Canterbury as the most authentic 'little Britain' in the empire.

Despite the rhetorical appeals to inclusion and democracy by colonial elites in New Zealand and elsewhere in the empire during royal visits, Alfred's visit to the province of Canterbury shared another characteristic of metropolitan society – it was a 'class act'. As elsewhere, events were planned by provincial elites, who limited and controlled attendance by charging an entrance fee and discouraging contact between the prince and lower class publics. The Canterbury Popular Entertainment and Amusements Committee established the entrance fee to the public festival at sixpence, and proposals to invite local Maori or to distribute free tickets to the poor were soundly defeated.[6] These measures did not prevent a massive crowd pressing at the entrances to be let in, nearly causing 'a disturbance'.[7] A local settler, writing under the populist pseudonym 'Vox Populi' ('voice of the people'), complained that seats in the gallery of the Provincial Council, *'public property'*, were being sold for 'half-a-guinea each'.[8] Elites' ability to control the symbolic space of the royal visit was openly and loudly contested by another British political tradition: radical and public protest.

In the empire, the narrative of the royal tour was taken up and remade by the colonial press and by social elites as a means of developing local mythologies of order and belonging.[9] They, and the colonial subjects who challenged and contested their elite-constructed mythologies, interpreted the royal tour through a lens of Britishness and imperial citizenship, through which they demanded British liberty as their endowed rights as citizen-subjects. In this context, what it meant to be a Natalian Briton or a Auckland Briton, or to be a New Zealander or a British South African, was shaped and informed by class cooperation and conflict, social status and identity, ethnic and cultural heritage, local politics, and cultural and economic contact with a larger world.

As John Darwin has argued, empires have been 'the default mode of political organisation throughout most of history'.[10] Historians of the nineteenth century often fetishise the nation-state as an inevitable endpoint, but this was not how those who lived in the nineteenth-century British Empire imagined their places in the world. In the context of the royal tour, this chapter advocates for the dynamism of Britishness and imperial citizenship among the settler populations of South Africa and New Zealand. It proposes that settler communities across the southern British world – or, specifically, the colonial press and the social elites of those communities – imagined unique mythologies of belonging that connected the social, political, and cultural worlds of the local with a much larger imperial one. For the settlers of the British world, the imperial connection – and the regional and class lenses through which it was interpreted – dominated notions of belonging. Settlers of virtually all classes, regions, and ethnic heritages took pride in the British traditions of political progress and liberty and co-ownership in a global empire to claim the rights and responsibilities of a British-imperial citizenship. It was from the political, cultural, and intellectual milieu of an imperial culture that the sinews of colonial nationalism began to emerge by the turn of the twentieth century.

While the royal tours garnered little attention in Britain, they became defining moments in local mythologies of imperial community in the empire.[11] Alfred, who visited the Cape twice during the 1860s, became memorialised as South Africa's prince, a tradition that appealed to both local and imperial narratives of belonging. To this day, long after South Africa declared itself a republic, the waterfront in Cape Town is named for Prince Alfred and his mother. For many years, a portrait of the sailor prince hung in the Alfred Room of the South African Library and Museum that he inaugurated during his 1860 visit.[12] In the Western Cape, a Dutch farmer named Johannes Cornelis Goosen christened the town he founded Prince Alfred's Hamlet. These examples reflect the ways that royal visitors were appropriated into local mythologies of imperial identity and citizenship.

The royal tours also demonstrate that imperial and national identities were mutually dependent rather than exclusive. The nationalist histories of the settlement colonies tend to frame the national stories of New Zealand or Australia or South Africa as one of inevitable independence and nationhood, colonial children grown into able-minded adults capable of self-rule. There is also a tendency to craft unique mythologies that separate child from mother: a social democracy of New Zealand or republicanism and white rule in South Africa. The role of Britishness and empire in these national stories, long underplayed, has recently been revisited by scholars of the British diaspora. Britishness and the 'imperial connection' were profoundly important to many nineteenth-century colonial subjects, including those who were not ethnically British or who had touched the soil of the British Isles. This chapter, then, proposes to understand how a diverse array of colonial subjects of European descent understood their sense of political, cultural, and social belonging in local and imperial contexts on the occasion of royal tours.

The history of the British diaspora and the mythology of Britishness has only recently been seriously considered by scholars. While the *Cambridge History of the British Empire*, a magnum opus of a traditional approach to empire, dedicated entire volumes to the colonies of settlement, the emergence of new schools of imperial history in the aftermath of the First World War – post-colonial theory, Marxist-inspired social history, and the New Imperial History – did not consider the white dominions as worthy sites of analysis in their own right. Historians of empire, however, have recently turned their attention to the British colonies of settlement, in a project aimed at reassessing the role of Britishness and imperial identities in the political, cultural, and social worlds of colonial settlers.[13] For these scholars, the colonial societies of the 'British world' were neither mere extensions of metropolitan society nor foreordained nation-states but transnational cultural spaces that were informed both by local circumstances and contingencies and by a political, cultural, social, and historical relationship with Britain and the British diaspora. In this context, British national identity must not be understood as a set of ideas and beliefs packed in a suitcase and carried to 'Greater Britain' but a competing collection of identities made in and of the imperial experience.[14] Britishness was a 'composite, rather than exclusive, form of identity', which was appropriated and adapted, made and remade by British and non-British colonial subjects around the world.[15]

In more traditional historical narratives, historians located proto-nationalist and nationalist narratives and mythologies in nineteenth-century settler societies, where Australians, New Zealanders, and South Africans awoke from the slumber of empire to become aware of their uniqueness as citizens of nation-states.[16] However, as recent scholarship has demonstrated, imperial identities and notions of citizenship remained for some time ascendant, even among many 'other' settlers (e.g. Dutch-speaking Boers or South Asian immigrants); the Scots, Welsh, and Irish of the 'Celtic fringe' who had historically complex relationships with an English 'core' at home; and non-white *respectables* who appealed to their rights as loyal subjects and imperial citizens. At the same time, within colonial states and the larger diasporic community, competing communities of empire, in Dunedin and Otago, Cape Town and Natal, articulated unique discourses of Britishness and citizenship that claimed more perfect understandings of Britishness and challenged other cores and even the mother country as 'better Britains'.[17] It is historically important, in this context, to consider and compare the cultural spaces between the values and beliefs of urban settlers in government cities such as Cape Town and Wellington and the miners of Otago or the frontier ranchers of the Eastern Cape.

For settlers, the royal tours and the associated mythology of Queen Victoria inspired a notion of imperial citizenship that demanded both local autonomy (responsible government) and expanded connections to a broader empire, especially the markets and financial resources of the metropole. Settler political discourses, as we shall see, both complained of the metropolitan government's reluctant imperialist drive and challenged imperial meddling in local affairs (sometimes within the same breath). Despite disagreements with the 'home' government, and often because of them, unique visions of Britishness and imperial citizenship thrived in the political and cultural discourses of the late nineteenth-century British world. The ascendance of imperial identities was nurtured by a sense of ethnic and historical heritage and, in particular, by the development of a transnational imperial monarchy as a symbol of that heritage.

Over time, the languages of nationalism and whiteness came to culturally overwhelm discourses of imperial citizenship, even if they were deeply imbricated in its language and history. Imperial identities were undermined by the conceptual dissonance between local manifestations of Britishness and the action (or inaction) of the metropolitan government. Settler discourses also took on a more overtly racial tone, with discourses of whiteness coming to more effectively counteract local and ethnic differences at the expense of non-white 'others' and, to a lesser degree, the imperial connection. In the emerging post-colonial world, local attachment to Britain and the empire evolved, or dissipated, in dramatically different but often comparable ways across the British world.

Yet, as the examination of the royal tours over time will demonstrate, imperial identities remained vitally important to local politics and mythologies during the second half of the nineteenth century. With the decline of provincialism and localism, the competition and rivalries which bolstered imperial identities over national ones were slowly undone by technological change and political contingencies. While these changes reflect the slow evolution of colonial identities toward the languages of nationalism, settler responses to the royal tours demonstrate the cultural vitality of imperial citizenship as a discourse and the historical problem of a post-imperial world as a foregone conclusion in the nineteenth-century colonies of settlement.

Colonial print cultures

The British diaspora brought not only British people to sites of settlement around the world but also British institutions, ideas, and things – the common law, football or rugby, and the English language.[18] The printed word served as the means by which the British reified knowledge of local customs and peoples, made colonies of laws and legislation, and imagined new narratives of community. Colonial settlers brought with them distinctly British notions of civil society, of which the newspaper was a core institution. In print, settler editors and writers espoused narratives of belonging and identity, that is, imagined communities. These communities were rarely singular in nature (e.g. national or proto-national) but multiple and overlapping. One could be Natalian, South African, and a citizen-subject of the British Empire without internal conflict.

Print culture spread almost as rapidly as people into sites of settlement. The emergence of a local newspaper was considered evidence that the community was of cultural or political significance, on the map, as it were. So important was the press to the New Zealand Company that the *New Zealand Gazette* was published in London in 1839 before its printing press was transported to Wellington, where it was 'set up on a beach', and the first edition published New Zealand in 1840.[19] The *Nelson Examiner* was published two months after settlement, the *Otago News* nine months after arrival, and the *Lyttelton Times* (Canterbury) 'immediately after the landing'.[20] As the collections of the British Library and the National Library of New Zealand demonstrate, nineteenth-century New Zealand had a remarkably rich print culture, particularly for a colony that had been founded to all intents and purposes less than thirty years before the first royal visit.[21]

Southern Africa had a longer and equally rich history of print culture. In Cape Town, the government published the *Cape Town Gazette and African Advertiser* in English and Dutch starting in 1800, five years after the British had claimed the Cape. The first privately published newspapers in Cape Town were the *South African Commercial Advertiser* (1824–69) and *South African Chronicle* (1824–26), followed by the *Cape Argus* (1857–present) and the *Cape Times* (1876–present), among others. Print culture spread to the British 'cores' outside of Cape Town with the movement of people: the *Graham's Town Journal* (1831–present), the *Natal Mercury* (1852–present), and the *King William's Town Gazette* (1856–75). From the earliest days of British settlement, newspapers were an important part of settler communities and how settlers imagined themselves.

Of course, there are limits and problems in using colonial newspapers to understand settler cultures. Newspapers often served as mouthpieces for social elites whose interests may or may not have represented the larger community. Moreover, their audience tended to be town-dwelling and educated.[22] As Alan Lester argues, colonial newspapers served 'the free, the propertied, and the "respectable"'.[23] Even if British settler populations of the late nineteenth century were surprisingly literate, and the influence of a single newspaper copy might have been multiplied an unknown number of times through word of mouth, life in a nineteenth-century British colony was not always conducive to daily newspaper reading. Distances were great, and many settlers did work that severely limited their leisure time, regardless of literacy. And even when settlers did read, it is extremely difficult to gauge how they interpreted and responded to what they read.

Despite these limits, it is clear that newspapers were important sites of political and cultural discourse in colonial civil societies. Relative freedom of the press allowed for fierce debates about local and imperial politics. The *Cape Argus* declared, in 1856, that it 'emanated from no party, will connect itself with no section of the community, and its first great care will be to secure free expression for the opinions of all, with a view to reconcile rather than stir up party differences'.[24] On the whole, British settler communities considered criticising the local or imperial government, particularly on grounds of British traditions and history, to be patriotic. Questioning the bonds of empire or the Queen was considered out of bounds by most, a discursive boundary motivated by genuine devotion, fear of being labelled disloyal, or some combination of both. More importantly in the context of this study, local mythologies of belonging were made and disseminated through the medium of print. They were the means of establishing a local story of what it meant to be British, a Capetonian, a New Zealander, a loyal citizen-subject of the Queen, or any other number of identities.

By decentring the empire and understanding British identity from the perspective of settler communities, we can better understand Britishness and imperial citizenship as a transnational political and cultural discourse. British national identity must be similarly understood, as forged in and of the imperial experience. This observation importantly reflects on the ways in which, as Sir John Seeley contended during the late nineteenth century, British history has been a story of expansion and of the dissemination of British ideas, institutions, and people across a global 'Greater Britain'.[25] In the second half of the nineteenth century, Britishness became a transnational identity that became as important to the neo-Britons of the empire as it was to the old Britons at home, if not more so. It came to transcend other identities in a way that it never had before and never would again.

Britishness and citizenship

Local mythologies of Britishness and imperial identity developed in colonial cores throughout the empire. Even if people talked about South Africa, Australia, or New Zealand, there was little obvious at the time about these geographical entities' futures as unified states. The federation of Australia took over twenty years to negotiate. As late as 1901 the *Otago Witness* predicted that the Duke of York's visit would 'quicken the growing desire' of New Zealanders to join the Australian Commonwealth.[26] Several movements to federate South Africa into a single British-controlled polity were stillborn; only British victory in the South African War (1899–1902) gave way to the Union of South Africa (1910).[27]

On the other hand, these cores frequently pulled away from one another and sometimes from the metropole, often appealing to a more genuine Britishness against a perceived injustice or incredulity. During the middle decades of the nineteenth century, politicians in Graham's Town, Uitenhage, and Port Elizabeth sought to form a new British colony in the Eastern Cape, separate from the government at Cape Town.[28] English-speaking frontier ranchers in South Africa perhaps had more in common with their *trekboer* neighbours than with the merchants and officials of the capital, just as the miners of the New Zealand boomtown of Dunedin looked toward Auckland or Wellington on the North Island with suspicion and even scorn. Even colonial officials recognised the differences in local cultures. During the 1901 tour, the Earl of Ranfurly, Governor of New Zealand (1897–1904), complained to Joseph Chamberlain that 'the old provincial centres are unfortunately extremely jealous, the one of the other'.[29] From these competing cores came emerging colonial cultures and visions of British-imperial citizenship.

While the development of whiteness as the dominant social and political discourse of the British world lies somewhat outside of the limits of this study, understanding the ways in which race and 'otherness' informed definitions of Britishness and citizenship during the royal tours helps us understand the fluidity and heterogeneity of imperial culture. Over time, whiteness became increasingly central to definitions of citizenship in the settler communities, transcending ethnic and local rivalries at the expense of non-white peoples.[30] In the context of the royal tours, this transformation manifested itself in the incorporation of Maori or African places and people into a mythology of white settlement – what Vivian Bickford-Smith has called 'local colour'.[31] While Britishness and imperial citizenship remained politically and culturally robust by the royal tour of 1901, for instance, they were waning not waxing, demonstrating the long-term effects of responsible government, the decline of provincialism and localism, the emergence of national networks of transportation and communication, and the development of national political cultures. By the end of the nineteenth century, however, these processes were just getting underway.

As British colonies of settlement, South Africa and New Zealand offer fertile conceptual terrain for comparison. Yet, in many ways, they were vastly different places. The Cape of Good Hope had been settled by the Dutch East India Company (VOC) in 1652, only to be taken over by the British at the turn of the nineteenth century as a consequence of the French Wars. European settlement of New Zealand was of much more recent vintage, with systematic colonisation as a territorial extension of New South Wales beginning only in 1840 by the British New Zealand Company. British emigration to New Zealand was comparatively robust, and settlers of British origin were the largest European ethnic group by far. In southern Africa, the British encountered a large population of European settlers whose kin had arrived from the Netherlands, France, or Germany generations earlier, and immigration schemes aimed at peopling Africa with British people, as we shall see, never effectively took root. The Cape Colony was positioned on one of history's greatest maritime trade routes, while New Zealand sat almost literally at the edge of the earth. If New Zealanders imagine their society to be progressive, peaceful, and democratic, South Africa is best known for racial unrest and apartheid. While the British South African colonies and New Zealand were both granted what amounted to home rule during the second half of the nineteenth century, New Zealanders overwhelmingly embraced the 'imperial connection' into the twentieth century. The relationship between metropole and colony in the South African context was far more complicated, and hostile. The differences appear stark.

At the same time, these two colonies of settlement share much in common. Both South Africa and New Zealand experienced mineral revolutions during the nineteenth century, whose rushes lured new immigrants and resulted in makeshift boomtowns that became important urban centres. In 1861, a Tasmanian miner named Gabriel Read discovered gold in Otago, starting a rush that temporarily swelled Dunedin into New Zealand's largest city.[32] In southern Africa, the discovery of diamonds (1867) and gold (1884) unleashed social and economic revolution that would for ever transform a backwater of the British Empire into a global depot of wealth and make Johannesburg, in the Boer republic of Transvaal, a metropolis. Gold-rush New Zealand attracted thousands of settlers and sojourners from the Pacific Rim, including a considerable population of Chinese immigrants. In South Africa, settler mining magnates acquired cheap, 'unskilled' labourers through agreements with local chiefs, native labour bureaus, as well as the importation of South Asian 'coolies'.

In southern Africa, local peoples experienced dispossession and destruction on a vast scale. Since the arrival of the Dutch in 1652, the Khoisan-speaking people of the Western and Northern Cape suffered under the biological, military, and cultural plague of European contact, particularly as the balances of power began to weigh heavily on the side of Europeans. A 1713 smallpox epidemic completed the processes by which these people had largely been destroyed by disease, were incorporated in the European labour pool, or fled beyond the Dutch pale. Over the course of the eighteenth and nineteenth centuries, Xhosa, Tswana, Sotho, and Zulu peoples confronted expanding European settlement, resulting in religious conversion, warfare, trade, epidemics, dispossession and resettlement, and physical and political control. For the Xhosa, in particular, who engaged in a century of land wars with white settlers, the consequences were horrific. The British never recognised these original South Africans as a people, as they had with the Maori in the double-dealing Treaty of Waitangi, so the diverse political traditions of the subcontinent never established a single, symbolic treaty with the British Empire. The double language of the British in their relations with local people – simultaneously claiming liberal rule and respect for local politics while dispossessing local peoples through military and legal force – nevertheless bore a remarkable resemblance to what happened in New Zealand.

In measure of Britishness, too, the two might be more comparable than first examinations suggest. While New Zealand's reputation as the 'Britain of the South' creates little question of its heritage, the presence of a large Dutch-speaking settler population and a comparatively small number of British settlers has resulted in less historical attention to the Britishness of South Africa.[33] Even Charles Dilke and J. R. Seeley, two of the nineteenth century's greatest imperial theorists, 'were sceptical of South Africa's potential as a British colony of settlement'.[34] Yet New Zealand's population was not homogeneous. It had growing communities of German and Chinese settlers, for instance. Moreover, by 1901, Scottish and Irish settlers accounted for about half of the immigrant population born in the British Isles. South Africa had important enclaves of British settlement in Cape Town, Natal, and the Eastern Cape. The British government made several attempts to supplement these numbers, most notably settling 4,000 British immigrants in 1820, and even had a plan to transport British convicts to the Cape in 1850.[35]

Despite extensive marketing, which often described distant Britains as lands of milk and honey, the creole British settlers of the colonies of settlement could never overcome the stigma that they were provincial cousins of the 'real' Britishers at 'home'. They could never become 'English English', to use Benedict Anderson's turn of phrase, and only in rare cases served the empire outside of their provinces in Natal or Otago or in colonial capitals at Cape Town or Wellington.[36] In Britain, humanitarians fiercely criticised their abuse of local peoples as radical politicians condemned the costs of colonial defence and frontier wars instigated by land-hungry settlers. In the eyes of many at home, creoles were second-rate Britishers, provincial carbon copies of the original. The British historian and imperial thinker J. A. Froude, for instance, described the Liberal Cape politician John X. Merriman as one of those 'Cape politicians [who] strut about with their constitution as a schoolboy newly promoted to a tail coat'.[37] While some scholars have stressed the romanticisation of colonial Britishness – as perfected in the open spaces and less depressing environments of the southern hemisphere – the sense that creole Britons were inauthentic informed the metropolitan attitudes and policies about the colonies of settlement.

Thus, fighting for the empire during the South African War or the Great War or expressing loyalty to Queen and country in rhetoric and action could heighten the already natural tendency to imagine and construct über-British societies on the edges of the world. Settlers competed with the motherland and other cores to make 'better Britains' and to be more perfect Britishers – whether by building a prosperous commercial entrepôt at the Cape of Good Hope or by imagining a more democratic – even classless – society in New Zealand. These distant Britains also possessed their own imperialist drives, looking to possess and dispossess in a manner that was often, to colonial officials, distasteful at best, crisis-inducing at worst. The failure of Britishness and imperial citizenship as a binding and long-term identity in the colonies of settlement has its origins in this cultural, social, and geographic chasm between Britain and neo-Britains overseas.

The royal tours presented unique moments for settlers to express identification with both a British world and with locality or province. In 1860, Prince Alfred was baptised 'our' South African prince by the colonial press, symbolising a nascent imperial-national identity. An Australian colonist wrote a 'seditious proposal published and suppressed on the eve of the Prince's [1868] visit', advocating a federation of the Australian colonies under the kingship of Alfred.[38] The *South African Commercial Advertiser* similarly advocated 'each of the royal children [be] made viceroys of the important colonies, such as India, Australia, Canada, and the Cape'.[39]

While colonial administrators at home and abroad imagined the royal visits as a form of imperial propaganda, local social elites in the empire used the visits as an opportunity to promote class cohesion, to protect and enhance their own status, and to develop local mythologies of identity as tools of social control. As Saul Dubow has noted in the case of the Cape Colony, there was no conservative gentry – outside of colonial officials – in the colonies of settlement to 'pour scorn on the jumped-up middle classes'.[40] While most immigrants to New Zealand had social roots in the rural working classes of Britain, the colony's emigration schemes attracted a surprising number of university-educated doctors, lawyers, and clergy.[41]

This altered social order meant that colonial elites, the 'town fathers' of Cape Town or Auckland, embraced a belief in Whiggish constitutionalism and improvement that was not unlike the beliefs articulated by the ruling classes at home, and they were more likely to be involved in commercial enterprises that depended on the development of colonial infrastructure and imperial networks of trade. Local organising committees were dominated by town fathers, who used the royal visits to their own ends. The colonial press, typically owned or influenced by local elites, used the royal tours to project a façade of social cohesion and harmony. In 1860, for instance, the *Graham's Town Journal* celebrated that 'high and low, rich and poor have combined in showing honour to the son of our Queen, and in doing justice to that spirit of genuine attachment to the Crown which is the boast of British subjects all the world over'.[42] Loyalty to the Great Queen and her empire was not only used by colonial administrators to nurture an imperial culture but also by local social elites to justify and promote class cohesion and social order.

While local elites gave particular meanings to the royal tours through the settler press, for many settlers, imperial rituals offered an opportunity to let loose, 'to dance until midnight and drink till morning'.[43] The 'Hermit of Adderley-Street' reported, during Alfred's 1860 tour of South Africa, that he had not thought of sleeping for three nights.[44] In New Zealand, the *Timaru Herald* reported that 'business of all kinds being suspended, and the citizens joining with the country residence ... seem to have had but one thought, that of giving pleasure and doing honour to the Royal visitor'.[45] This is not to say that colonial subjects did not express their loyalty or identify with a British colonial empire but that they did so in a way that was informed by personal beliefs and experience, social class and profession, and locality. Local people vehemently protested when their employers refused to close their stores and workshops to celebrate the royal visitor or when events were closed to the general public or charged admission. Through this participation and activism, settlers challenged elite control of civic culture and demanded the rights and responsibilities of British citizenship. At the same time, the celebration was also an opportunity to drink and party in the streets, to contest social mores and hierarchy, and to have fun.

For their part, colonial administrators, social elites, and the press incorporated local peoples into the ritual practices of the royal tour and the mythology of settlement as 'local colour'. While the literature on the national myths of New Zealand and, in particular, South Africa, has focused on the emergence of whiteness as the dominant cultural discourse of the nineteenth- and early twentieth-century colonial world, the symbolism of non-white subjects, from the imagery of a Maori canoe to the 'war dances' of Zulu or Sotho peoples, was vital to the construction of local, imperial, and ultimately national origins stories. The royal tours created an opportunity to highlight the loyalty and submission of former enemies.[46] They were used to nurture an ideology and mythology of empire that suppressed a history of violence, projected the illusion of consent, and legitimise the idea of white rule over 'native peoples'.[47]

Although tour planners developed and perfected the rituals of the royal tour over time, public celebrations in the British colonies, whether the visit of a governor or prince, the Queen's birthday, royal jubilees, or Bonfire Night, shared a set of ritual practices that culturally distinguished empire feast days, as it were, from every other day. There were illuminations, addresses, bonfires, fireworks, balls, parades, triumphal arches, military drills, and native performances. Emblazoned across the pages of local newspapers were phrases such as 'Prince Alfred's Edition' and 'God Save the Queen!' Addresses to and from visiting dignitaries were frequently lampooned for their triteness and repetitiveness. Local settler performances sought both to reproduce British practices – proving that they were just as good as or better than metropolitan Britons – and to appeal to local origin stories, of the settlement of 1820 in the Eastern Cape or the making of a more democratic 'Britain of the South' in New Zealand. They also reflected rivalries within colonies – the geographical, cultural, and political space between urban Cape Town and the rural Eastern Cape, for instance – and between colonies – illustrated by the image of New Zealand as a younger, but better, version of Australia. While the ritual practices were shared across the space of empire, settler responses to the royal tour reflect the complexities of imperial culture and the ways in which the imperial and the local informed settler mythologies and worldviews.

The narratives of the royal visit were contested and remade across the social, political, and cultural terrains of New Zealand and British South Africa. Across the chasm of class and status, settlers may have expressed loyalty to the Queen, but opposition to the powers that be in the Cape or Wellington. Or they may have used the opportunity of the royal tour to dance, and celebrate, and drink. The point is not to unravel and expose every possible remaking of Britishness and citizenship in the context of the royal tour, but to show how fluid and malleable these discourses were across the imperial networks of the British world. What this chapter aims to prove is that colonial subjects read their attachment to Britain and the empire through multivalent geographical, social, and political lenses in a way that has been underappreciated by the extant literature on the colonies of settlement.

South Africa (1860)

Historians had long understood the story of settlers in South Africa during the long nineteenth century as an enduring struggle between the British and descendants of Dutch settlers whose families became 'Afrikaners'. The narrative of this mythology, itself the backbone of the South African national story, begins with the Great Trek of Boer settlers out of the British pale during the 1830s and into the interior of southern Africa and concludes with two Anglo-Boer Wars (1880–81, 1899–1902) and the emergence of a white-dominated Union of South Africa. Recent historiography, however, has destabilised, if not toppled, these assumptions by reassessing the role of Africans in 'white' conflict (e.g. the South African War) and the complex, and conflicting, political and cultural discourses of settler societies that defy the notion of shared interests among colonial settlers or between settlers and the metropolitan government.[48]

In the context of this study, the languages of Britishness and imperial citizenship were made and remade by the diverse settler populations of southern Africa to imagine their communities (local and imperial), to claim British rights and responsibilities, and to protest against unfairness and injustice. As the examination of the breakwater controversy and other settler petitions for imperial justice demonstrate, settler discourses on colonial politics were informed by unique visions of what it meant to be a citizen-subject of a larger British world. Political and cultural battles were often fought in the rhetoric of Britishness and imperial loyalism, even by many non-British people. During royal tours, settler communities appealed to their intense loyalism and adherence to British traditions and principles, as 'better Britons'. They used the forum of the royal tour to protest or advocate causes and to imagine what it meant to be a 'Natalian Briton' or 'British Kaffrarian', rather than simply to be South African.

Cape Town

Cape Town has long held a unique status in the history of southern Africa and in the popular memory of modern Capetonians as a progressive and cosmopolitan urban space, where an ethnically diverse population socially and culturally intermingled, before the Afrikaner-inspired politics of whiteness and apartheid forcibly displaced this tradition.[49] Capetonians and historians have contrasted the so-called Cape liberal tradition with the racially driven political and social exclusion of the Boer republics and even the Eastern Cape, understanding the Western Cape as a forward-looking, enlightened place in the dark seas of South African history. As Vivian Bickford Smith and other scholars of South Africa have been apt to note, however, this brand of exceptionalism is not backed by the historical evidence.

In the context of imperial politics, Cape Town was an imperial core in southern Africa to both the subaltern classes of the city and to many peoples of the Eastern Cape, the Boer republics, and beyond.[50] As the home of the British government in the Cape Colony, it represented to many settlers the politics of an irresolute Colonial Office that was often influenced by humanitarian activists and reluctant to support costly expansionist efforts. It was also the home of a small but influential cadre of progressive politicians, 'friends of the native', and was the South African source of the limited non-racial franchise and legislation regarding the control and treatment of labourers. On the other hand, Government House at Cape Town also served as the residence for colonial governors such as Benjamin D'Urban, Harry Smith, and George Grey, who were responsible for some of the most egregious acts of warfare and dispossession in the history of the British Empire. Cape Town was ruled by an elite that was propertied, white, and English-speaking, who sought to control and define discourses on citizenship and status.

For Capetonians and other British subjects in southern Africa, Cape Town came to symbolise many different things, both the enlightenment of colonial rule and its worst excesses. By the last decades of the century, they had come to advocate, in the face of rapid economic and social change, segregationist policies in the guise of urban progress. The ruling classes of Cape Town tended to represent their town as an emblem of civilisation in southern Africa and a hub for all communication and commerce on the subcontinent. One leading Cape 'liberal' was Saul Solomon, who published the *Cape Argus*. His narrative of the royal visit, *The Progress of His Royal Highness Prince Alfred Ernest Albert through the Cape Colony, British Kaffraria, the Orange Free State, and Port Natal, in the Year 1860*, framed the tour's importance in the material and political progress of southern Africa since the advent of British rule. Solomon, along with other politicians and newspaper editors in Cape Town, tended to represent British South Africa as an organic whole, with Cape Town as its heart. They spoke in the language of respectability and progress:

> Before [the British, the Cape] was a military settlement: a port of call.... Since then it has advanced at a rate as rapid as was consistent with the due consolidation of each advancing improvement effected. From the original Colony no fewer than four extensive offshoots – British Kaffraria, Natal, the Orange Free State, and the Transvaal Republic – have sprung into vigorous and lusty life.... Regularly-constituted courts of law and trial by jury on the English model soon succeeded. The curse of slavery was removed.... And in the fulness [*sic*] of time came the boon of the Free Constitution granted by Her Majesty nine years ago, under which the Cape possesses now the amplest privileges of constitutional self-government. And among the fruits of this new and liberal system the Colonists have been emboldened to venture upon undertakings for advancing the material prosperity of the county.... The first of these was the railway from Cape Town to Wellington, now approaching completion; while the most recent of them, the Breakwater, with the other great harbour improvements in Table Bay, has given occasion to the gratifying visit.[51]

The breakwater, in this context, represented a key historical moment in the progress of not just the Cape but all of South Africa.

The Scotsman John Fairbairn, editor and sole proprietor (by 1860) of the Cape's first independent newspaper, the *South African Commercial Advertiser*, was a prominent member of the Cape elite, espousing a worldview centred on free trade, self-help, and a notion of Britishness that embraced respectability.[52] He had helped establish a free press at the Cape, after a long struggle with Governor Charles Somerset, in 1828.[53] Fairbairn supported the campaign of Dr John Philip, who would later be his father-in-law, for 'Hottentot emancipation' and criticised 'British settler and government expansionism on the colony's eastern frontier' in the *Commercial Advertiser*, inspiring the ire of white settlers on the frontier and in Cape Town.[54] The conservative *Zuid-Afrikaan*, in Cape Town, and the *Graham's Town Journal* were founded, in part, in response to Fairbairn's politics and power. In the language of Britishness, he opposed a metropolitan scheme to import convicts to the Cape in 1849 and advocated an elected assembly.[55] In age Fairbairn grew conservative and became 'more and more pessimistic about the efficacy of the British mission' or the ability of the British government to control land-hungry British settlers.[56]

Prince Alfred's visit in 1860 came near the end of Fairbairn's life, by which time he had come to question British progress in southern Africa. He would die in 1864. The coverage of the tour in the *Commercial Advertiser* hardly reflected this intellectual evolution in its focus on British civilisation at the Cape but did demonstrate Fairbairn's reconciliation with Dutch-speaking Afrikaners. More important, perhaps, was the fact that the *Commercial Advertiser* sought to transcend, or overlook, regional identities and to celebrate the organic unity of British South Africa. It was Cape Town, its institutions and symbols of progress, its editors argued, that stood at the political, cultural, and economic centre of the subcontinent. In this context, the political discourses surrounding the visit – in particular, by naming the new breakwater after Alfred – transformed the controversy over the improvement from one about sectionalism and class into an issue of loyalty and disloyalty. This elite-constructed Capetonian imperialism, which borrowed from the languages of Britishness and imperial citizenship, was appropriated and turned on its head by frontier settlers, Cape Town labourers, and people of colour, as we shall see.

Cape Town was celebrated as a superbly British community, from its works of progress to its loyal citizenry. The *Commercial Advertiser* wanted Capetonians to remind Alfred of 'the good stuff which makes Englishmen the most loyal as well as the most earnest of their kind' to such a degree that he would forget that he had ever left Britain![57] It was duly noted that, as Alfred commenced the construction of a breakwater at Table Bay and other works of progress in the colony, his older brother was ceremonially opening the Victoria Bridge in Canada.[58] This moment demonstrated the spread of British civilisation and progress across a vast global space, from the British Isles across the world and from Cape Town across southern Africa. In appealing to Britishness, the social elites of Cape Town imagined a community that reinforced and justified their own place in Cape society and that of Cape Town in South Africa and the British Empire.

According to the *Advertiser*, the royal tour also transcended the everyday boundaries of class and ethnicity. In this context, the propertied of Cape Town, through the newspaper, used the visit to reinforce their social control of society with the language of loyalty. While some scholars have argued that the politics of whiteness came to transcend the divisions of language, ethnicity, and class, the cultural discourses of the 1860 tour were, arguably, more inclusive, even if non-whites had a markedly subordinate status in the imagined community of loyalism. The *Commercial Advertiser* urged: 'Let no foolish nationalities stand in the way of a general rejoicing. No one need be ashamed to own himself a subject of the British crown, and one good subject is as good as another, whatever may be his origin, creed, or calling'.[59] The address to Alfred from the representatives of the Municipality of Cape Town similarly framed progress in the Cape in terms of a loyalism that transcended ethnicity.[60]

It was also important for the propertied in the Cape that their importance to the empire be recognised. In particular, they hoped that the son would return to his mother, the Great Queen, with reports of the Cape's progress and wealth.[61] According to the *Advertiser*, Britons at home were all but completely ignorant of South Africa, imagining that 'lion hunts are as common just outside of Cape Town as fox-hunting is in Leicestershire; that naked Kaffirs and Hottentots eat raw meat in our streets; and that the environs of our city are not very unlike the Desert of Zahara'.[62] The trip would make '19,999,990 of 20,000,000' British people more knowledgeable about South Africa.[63] The editors argued that the Cape had been long neglected, a black sheep in an imperial system that favoured 'purer' British colonies such as Australia and New Zealand.[64] It was because of the Cape's diverse population and lack of British institutions that the metropole had disregarded her, but it was now time for the colony to be recognised as a thoroughly British place, home of progress and trade and of efforts to colonise the region with British people.[65] Capetonians then, they argued, must put forward an 'honest and hearty welcome' 'as evidence of our love and loyalty as the most magnificent preparations of wealthier lands'.[66] In competition with other colonies, the Cape needed to prove itself to be a little, and better, Britain to the mother country.

Graham's Town

In Graham's Town (Grahamstown today), the settler press used the opportunity of the royal tour to celebrate British civilisation in the Eastern Cape and to lambast the political dominance of Cape Town over the rest of southern Africa. The editors also used the opportunity of the royal tour to describe the competition between colonial towns to demonstrate their loyalty, that Graham's Town and King William's Town would 'do their upmost to exceed each other in fervent expressions of enthusiasm, by producing everything which is in their power to exalt themselves above the Table Mountain merchants and farmers of the West'.[67] Despite any grievances between east and west, they could agree on the majesty of the British monarchy and their loyalty to Queen Victoria. The Cape frontier most significantly represented the vanquishing of uncivilised savages and the spread of British civilisation and progress, of industrious farmers and merchants building neo-Britains in the rugged frontier of southern Africa. The debates over the breakwater, specifically, and the perceived imbalance of political power between the west and east, offered a radically different interpretation from that of the press of the Western Cape.

Founded as a military outpost on the Xhosa frontier in 1812, Graham's Town was situated northeast of Port Elizabeth in the Eastern Cape, some 900 kilometres from Cape Town. As part of a government settlement scheme, funded by a £50,000 grant from parliament, 4,000 British (mostly Scottish) settlers arrived in Albany to farm the land with free labour and consolidate the frontier in 1820.[68] Many of these 1820 settlers, as they were called, abandoned farming and moved into towns, including Graham's Town. The mythology of 1820, which was celebrated with its own ritual ceremonies, and life in a frontier town far away from the colonial capital at Cape Town nurtured unique local narratives of belonging.[69] According to Saul Solomon, Graham's Town 'pride[d] itself, and not quite unreasonably, [as] the most thoroughly English town in Southern Africa'.[70] Yet, as Clifton Crais has argued, settlers who came to build 'England in the miniature', complete with a 'manor house on the hill', required 'growing markets, plentiful land, docile labourers and a cooperative colonial state'.[71] These needs created a matrix of interconnected social, cultural, and political conflicts – between white masters and servants, institutionalised in the immigration scheme itself, between European settlers and local peoples, and with Cape Town and the imperial government.

In the pages of the *Graham's Town Journal* (later, simply *The Journal*), political and cultural discourses appropriated the languages of Britishness and imperial citizenship, particularly through the mythology of 1820, to justify a particular political and social order in the Eastern Cape, which transcended ethnicity and class, legitimised and empowered social elites, and justified the subjugation of local peoples. The *Journal*, founded in 1831, was edited by an 1820 settler named Robert Godlonton. A former London printer, Godlonton defended the Eastern settlers against liberal-humanitarian claims that they were acting in a very un-British way in their relations with the Xhosa and petitioned for greater imperial security and control against local peoples.[72] Godlonton's paper possessed a near-monopoly in Albany, and its distribution reached as far as Britain and North America.[73] Godlonton's politics and mythology of Britishness were deeply entrenched in the 'collective biography of the settlement', particularly conflict with local peoples.[74] His paper was founded in opposition to the 'liberal' papers in Cape Town and with the distinct interests of the Eastern Cape in mind.[75] While alternative political and cultural narratives existed, Godlonton's mythology, as expressed in the *Graham's Town Journal*, was the most widely disseminated and read.

In the pages of the *Journal*, the symbolic meaning of the visit was glossed from the memories and legacy of the 1820 settlers. The *Journal* argued that this frontier ethos ought to be reflected in welcoming Alfred. While the settlers at Cape Town could afford a much more elaborate display of loyalty, the paper argued, Graham's Town could 'gratify the Prince to a much greater extent' with a greeting befitting the colonial frontier: a welcome ceremony featuring between 800 and 1,000 'rough and ready' commandants, police, and the Cape Corps – accompanied by local 'Fingoes and Kaffirs' performing in 'war' dances.[76] At the Healdtown Institution, Alfred paid special attention (according to the *Journal*) to paintings of

> the landing and the ... encampment of the first party of British Settlers. This event took place rather more than 40 years ago. At that time there was no fixed property of any value in Port Elizabeth or Graham's Town; there was no trade carried on with the mother country; no wool sent home in exchange for British manufactures; the land was peopled by barbarians, who revelled in heathenish customs and rights.... But England sent forth from her shores the pioneers of civilisation ... as he visits town after town, and native locations under the care of Christian ministers, [he] will see how well England has done her duty – how well British ideas and habits are spreading amongst the population, and how deeply rooted is the love of loyalty in the hearts of those who were sent by their government forty years ago to establish a new colony.[77]

Absent from this mythology was the Western Cape or a larger South Africa. It was framed by the relationship between the hearty, rugged settlers of Albany and the spread of British civilisation. To the Graham's Town settlers, Prince Alfred's most celebrated act, the inauguration of the Table Bay breakwater, was the end result of a contentious dispute over the fairness of the Eastern Cape helping fund an improvement project for Cape Town. In the end, they felt bullied by the Western Cape-dominated government, Cape merchants, and Sir George Grey. According to the *Journal*, Capetonians at a public meeting about the plan in July 'would have us believe that *Capetown* is the whole colony'.[78] According to Godlonton, Graham's Town would have 'no interest in, and will receive no benefit from, the proposed harbour works', yet principled Eastern opposition to the plan was portrayed by the Cape press as 'factious' and disloyal.[79] The farmers of Albany who used Algoa Bay in Port Elizabeth, a mere 100 kilometres from Graham's Town, saw the need for the construction of a breakwater *there* as much if not more than at Cape Town. Moreover, the far more useful bill to construct a railway between Graham's Town and Port Elizabeth had already been 'thrown overboard', as an expendable 'Eastern measure'.[80]

Opposition to the breakwater was framed in the language of British constitutional traditions. In the pages of the *Journal*, the settler community appealed to British ideas about fair play and the importance of representative government. The Eastern Cape legislators were not completely opposed to the project, they indicated, but wanted it to be reasonable and well planned (not 'unlimited' in its use of the colony's general revenue).[81] Moreover, the *Journal* appealed, responsible government and a legislature for the Cape Colony were without meaning to the Eastern Cape if their opposition was futile and their long and expensive travels to Cape Town a 'farce'.[82] As British subjects, they perceived a right to protest and to have a legitimate voice, rather than it being silenced by the commercial and government elites of Cape Town.

During the royal tour, the *Journal* also revived the idea of Eastern Cape separatism – that is, the Eastern Cape as an independent Crown Colony, liberated from the corruption of the Western Cape – as a possibility. Albany had been home, in the 1820s, of 'radicals' who sought larger land grants, greater control of labour, public offices, and official patronage, 'to replicate the privileges and patronage of English rural society' in conflict with the policies of the British governor, Charles Somerset.[83] The politics of separatism, while admittedly unorganised and often fleeting, were not the monopoly of Dutch-speaking *trekboers* nor had their embers been doused by the 1860s, as Le Cordeur suggested. Even if pursued as an option, however, separatism, the *Journal* claimed, would most certainly be sabotaged by Western Cape legislators, 'so long as it is advantageous to the Cape people to remain as a united colony – so long as money can be borrowed upon the credit for improvement of the *West*'.[84] Careful in his use of language, Godlonton never explicitly advocated separation, but only hinted at it. He did foresee neighbouring British Kaffraria's possible future as a semi-independent colony, rather the personal fiefdom of the Cape governor, as prosperous and successful.[85] In expressing loyalty to the Queen and articulating a unique vision of imperial citizenship, the settlers of Graham's Town found Prince Alfred's breakwater to be a very unfair and therefore un-British project.

The dominant narrative of the traditional historiography, of Britons and Boers, whites and blacks, conceals a more complex and fluid collection of identities. Within communities, social strife was reflected in rhetorical struggles over the definitions of loyalty, Britishness, and imperial citizenship. Moreover, the settlers of the Eastern Cape, Kaffraria, and Natal had much in common with the *trekboers* who had fled British control of the Cape. They often imagined their communities as profoundly connected in the British Empire, yet often firmly disconnected from and hostile to Cape Town. As the discussion of the South African War and the royal tour of 1901 will demonstrate, these discourses moved slowly away from identification with the empire and toward a greater recognition of a white settler identity – even if these processes remained decidedly incomplete by the turn of the century.

New Zealand (1869–71)

In 1869, Prince Alfred, by then Duke of Edinburgh, visited New Zealand in the midst of a brutal war of colonial conquest between local settlers and the Maori. He was originally scheduled to visit the colony during his 1868 tour of Australasia, but this itinerary was cut short by an Irish Fenian assassin's bullet. (In response, New Zealanders expressed an outpouring of sympathy for the Queen and her son and asked that the duke return when he had recovered.) When he did return to the islands in 1869, the North Island was threatened by the attacks of a guerrilla fighter and religious leader named Te Kooti (see Chapter 2), who had led a daring escape from his imprisonment on the Chatham Islands. This 'little war' was as much a civil war as a colonial conflict; pro-British 'Queenite' Maori fought on the colonial side of the conflict, and Te Kooti was ultimately given refuge by the Maori king.[86] This context of warfare and violence informed the meaning of Alfred's visit, which became a forum for criticisms of the imperial government. Te Kooti's campaign against the colony also destabilised the illusion of Maori consent that the visit was designed to nurture, heightening the obsessive pursuit of the Maori leader on the part of the government.

The war affected not only the mood of the visit but also the itinerary. The New Zealand press complained that the Duke of Edinburgh's delayed visit had been drawn back, 'so shortened that the chief towns only of the provinces will be honoured with a visit'.[87] This limited engagement denied people in the countryside or in smaller cities the opportunity to express their loyalty without travelling long distances to witness the visit. The *Otago Daily Times* also expressed concern over the very timing of the royal tour:

> It is much to be regretted that the visit of His Royal Highness to New Zealand should have occurred at so inopportune a time. Not only does he find the colony harassed by the difficulties of a savage war, but he comes among a people so much occupied with the disasters that have befallen them that public rejoicings become a mockery. With the recollection of so many massacres still before us, it is not in human nature that we

> should give way to joyous demonstrations in the spirit of a Roman populace at the approach of Carnival. Every member of our community is in mourning.... If his tour through the Islands should afford slight material for another descriptive volume in the shape of triumphal arches and public banquets, [Alfred] will not fail to remember the circumstances in which the colony is placed.[88]

Thus, the New Zealand settler press used the visit to express their discontent with the imperial government and to make demands as British citizens. The *Wellington Independent* claimed that, despite their unwavering loyalty to the Queen, 'the people of New Zealand have very great reason to resent ... the Imperial Government'.[89] The *Otago Times* similarly complained that the relationship between New Zealand and the mother country was strained over the 'refusal' of support from the imperial government and that this separation would inform the festivities.[90] Some editors went as far as to suggest that the duke had been coached by his imperial advisers to avoid explicit references to New Zealand's suffering.

Like the responses to the royal tour in southern Africa, this contestation across social, political, and geographic divisions was framed in the language of Britishness and imperial citizenship. The newspaper editors appealed to British citizenship in their case against the colonial metropole, celebrating their loyalty to the monarchy and to the empire while noting their disaffection, caused by imperial bungling and hesitance in the struggle against the Maori. After a long dispute with the colonists, the imperial government had withdrawn all imperial troops from the islands, with the exception of one contingent, in 1865–66.[91] Many members of the settler community, as the newspapers argued, were disappointed with the metropolitan government's decision to financially and militarily abandon the colony in the midst of a 'rebellion'. Imperial policy not only failed to 'protect the lives of British subjects from cannibals' but 'seriously compromise[ed] the credit of the mother country'.[92] The settler press imagined a friendly relationship with the Maori that had been sabotaged by imperial 'mismanagement' and the 'impolitic actions of Imperial officers stationed in the colony', sparking a powder keg of unending wars.[93] The visit was defined as a new beginning, when New Zealand was finally remembered by the mother country. Learning of New Zealand's 'sacrifices and hardships', Alfred would return to his mother with their pleas for imperial justice.[94]

The settler press also used the opportunity of the royal tour to exalt egalitarianism and a notable lack of social strife as a unique 'national characteristic' of New Zealand Britons.[95] Building a new Britain in a more temperate land ('The English climate kills excessive cheerfulness'), New Zealanders were more free-spirited and playful.[96] This notion of New Zealand as a particularly democratic and equal society remains central to the mythology of the post-imperial nation. In the 1860s, however, the emergence of this national narrative was framed within British traditions and imperial culture, particularly the idea of a 'better Britain'. New Zealand's leader writers emphasised that, despite the extreme distance between their colony and the motherland, 'sterling, true-hearted and loyal Englishmen are to be found in this distant dependency of the British Empire'.[97] New Zealand was an egalitarian 'far off Britain of the south'.[98]

New Zealanders, they claimed, lacked the puritanical sternness and intolerance of Britain and America, balancing 'the equality of social conditions that prevails in the United States' with 'the English ideas and prejudices we have brought with us from the old country'.[99] The *Lyttelton Times* gloated that even the working classes 'lived in plenty' and could afford an occasional luxury, representing an equality of opportunity that did not exist 'home' in Britain or in the United States.[100] The *Wellington Times* proposed the best welcome for the prince would involve settlers of all classes and standings, from 'our leading merchants and traders' down to 'our mechanics and labourers'.[101] In Christchurch, local men paraded with trade or fraternal organisations: the fire brigade ('Ready, always ready!'), the Ancient Order of Foresters, butchers ('The Roast Beef of Old England'), engineers and iron workers, the Independent Order of Oddfellows of the Manchester Union, 'Lancashire and Cheshire men', and a group of Maori, a dose of 'local colour', dressed in blue coats and scarlet sashes and carrying the British flag.[102] While the notion of a democratic planning process and popular participation in events is not completely unfounded, it glossed over the political and social fault lines revealed by the occasion of the royal visit.[103]

Local critics of these processes challenged the royal tour as an elitist production constructed by the colonial government and social elites to exclude the working public. Settler publics in New Zealand's major towns protested at Alfred's limited and controlled interactions with the people of New Zealand; attempts by local elites to charge entrance fees to see the prince or to limit entry to 'respectable' colonists; and the use of public buildings and spaces for private events. New Zealand's poverty in relation to the Australian colonies was also a constant point of contestation. The fact that New Zealanders could not and should not pay for a grand welcome in the style of the Australian visit and in the face of communal and individual poverty was repeated again and again in editorials and letters.[104] As in South Africa and elsewhere in the empire, the propaganda of the royal tour and the mythology of New Zealand as a democratic Britain of the South, disseminated by social elites and the colonial press, were frequently contested, in counter-discourses that appealed to imperial citizenship and British liberty.

While the sense of cultural and political difference across geographic spaces was less pronounced in New Zealand than in South Africa, provincialism played an important role in how colonial subjects interpreted the royal tour. In the days before 'Vogelism', the public works schemes of Colonial Treasurer Julius Vogel during the 1870s that developed networks of infrastructure and communication that connected the provinces together, the settlements of New Zealand were separated by geography and the divergence of local interests.[105] An extension of Vogelism was the abolishment in 1876 of the New Zealand's 'quasi-federal system', which had nurtured sectional conflict between the Provincial Councils and the General Assembly and led to occasional campaigns for separatism.[106]

There were, undoubtedly, tensions and feelings of resentment between different regions and towns, not to mention conflict among people and groups of different social or political standings *within* these communities: between the more developed South Island and the more recently settled North Island; between town and frontier; and between centres of political and cultural importance, such as Auckland or Wellington, and provincial settlements. Henry Armstrong, a member of the Southland Provincial Council, complained that proper emigration could never be promoted until the Maori were neutralised and 'provincial jealousies and selfishness die out, and our provincial politicians work together for the common good of the whole colony'.[107] These conceptions of cultural and political difference across the geographical spaces of New Zealand profoundly informed notions of empire, Britishness, and citizenship on the occasion of the royal tour.

Auckland

In the North Island, Auckland had served as the capital of the colony from 1841 until 1865. Auckland was made the booms of the 1860s, promoted by immigrant schemes, the presence of imperial troops during the Waikato War, and the Thames gold rush in 1868.[108] It was a planned settlement and administrative hub that served as a launching point for both the wars of the 1850s and 60s and the expansion of settlement into the hinterland. It was a port town dominated by a mercantile elite who sought to project an image of the settlement as a commercial and progressive place of economic growth and civic improvement. In 1869, this mythology was immediately threatened, as local social elites understood the situation, by Te Kooti's raids on North Island settlements and the neglect of the imperial government.

Auckland had recently lost its status as the colonial capital to Wellington – the decision to move made by a commission appointed by the governor, Sir George Grey. The mood was further darkened by conflict with the Maori and a commonly articulated belief that the imperial government was not sufficiently providing for the colonists' defence. Thus, the editors made significant efforts to contrast Auckland with the new capital at Wellington while using the opportunity of the royal tour to criticise a neglectful imperial government. The *Daily Southern Cross* compared the excess and waste of Wellington's royal welcome to Auckland's more sombre and efficient plans to welcome Alfred.[109] While New Zealanders were loyal to their Queen and their homeland, given the circumstances, they were in no mood to expend precious funds on triumphal arches and welcome dinners. Other writers lampooned the local celebration of Aucklanders as the most loyal citizen-subjects of Queen Victoria in all the empire, positing that Aucklanders were 'as loyal as the average subjects of the empire, and neither less nor more'.[110] This was not merely a jesting comment about the most common trope of the royal tour, that 'we' are the Queen's most loyal subjects; it also reflected a tinge of anger in the coverage of the visit, directed at an imperial government that was neglecting to fulfil its obligations to its colonial children.

The welcome for Alfred was bungled when the prince's ship *Galatea* arrived days ahead of schedule with little notice. Local organising committees were shocked by this development and scrambled to complete the construction of stages and triumphal arches as far as possible in a very short period. Workers were 'engaged from midnight', preparing the decorations so that they would be ready in time.[111] The *Daily Southern Cross* lamented that 'his Royal Highness may be deprived of some of the special treats he had in store for him if he had waited another day'[112] This frustration reflects the careful choreography of the visits, the performances of which were carefully planned by colonial officials and town elders in advance, and the lack of coordination and communication between imperial, colonial, and local officials. The example of Auckland in 1869 offers no historical drama but does show how relatively mundane controversies and problems – debates about loyalty and addresses or the early arrival of a visiting dignitary – became important topics of discussion in civic culture, reflecting on the exaggerated significance attached to the visits at the local level.

Wellington

Located on the southern end of the North Island, Wellington was founded as the first organised settlement in New Zealand, in 1840, with the settlement of several hundred settlers at the mouth of the Hutt River called Britannia. When this was flooded and destroyed the New Zealand Company moved the settlement to Lambton Harbour, the site of modern Wellington. It rapidly became a trade centre that survived through trade with the Maori and benefited from local production of wool. It became the colonial capital in 1865, moved to reflect the developments of new settlements and the discovery of gold on the South Island. By 1867, it had a population of only 7,460 residents. Wellington was a fledging urban centre that was only starting to benefit from the attraction of capital and business brought on by its establishment as the capital. The mythology of Wellington came to focus on its role as the 'Empire City', as the first British settlement in New Zealand and the capital of a British Empire in the Pacific.[113]

In 1869, the settler press contrasted the people of the Empire City with their brethren in Australia, the older and more celebrated colony of the region. Waiting for Alfred to arrive, the *Wellington Independent*, for instance, compared the character of youthful New Zealand with that of its older cousin Australia, arguing that New Zealand's continued provincialism was inhibiting progress.[114] The Australian colony of Victoria, they noted, possessed networks of railroads and communications that New Zealand lacked in the days before Vogelism. This infrastructure integrated the provinces and connected them to other major population centres on the continent, creating an environment that promoted 'nation over province'. Moreover, Victoria had a 'real capital' – 'Marvelous Melbourne' – where 'the bulk of wealth and business is centred'.[115] New Zealand, on the other hand, was 'made up of a number of distinct provinces, each with its capital town on the seaboard'.[116] The *Independent* imagined New Zealand to be a collection of outward-looking cores rather than a united whole (and they were quite right).

In this emerging mythology, Wellington would become New Zealand's Melbourne, a political and economic centre, which would lead the colony into a future of prosperity and progress. At the same time, because of the motherland's neglect, New Zealand was not developed enough to compete with Australia. In this context, Wellington, as the capital, could not compete with Australia or even 'give His Royal Highness such a welcome as would do justice to the whole of the colony'.[117] Thus the *Independent* asserted that the people of Wellington should forsake the 'scores of triumphal arches', which the prince had seen in every other colony, to offer more austere but authentic expressions of loyalty to Queen and Empire.[118] The royal tour was framed by local elites as an opportunity for Wellington to live up to local values and its unique destiny as the (British) Empire City of New Zealand.

The visit did elicit a language of contestation, but it was one articulated by the 'haves' rather than the 'have-nots' of Wellington's social order. The Wellington papers complained that Governor George Bowen was conspiring to 'not allow the Duke to mix with the general public more than can be possibly helped', denying the duke opportunities to inspire loyalty among his mother's subjects and the general public the opportunity to express their loyalty.[119] The requests of loyal friendly societies to meet with the duke, for instance, were answered at the last possible moment, giving little opportunity for members to organise and assemble in time.[120] Upon witnessing crowds gathered the meet the prince, Bowen failed to stop the carriages so that Alfred might spend a few moments interacting with his mother's subjects.[121] In the language of social control, the editors of the *Evening Standard* asserted: 'where Kings, Queens, and Princes are concerned, these people are easily pleased, and it is therefore a greater pity to lose any opportunity of pleasing the people during a visit like the present'.[122] As far as they were concerned, the governor had missed crucial opportunities not only for binding New Zealand closer to Britain but also, and perhaps more importantly, for securing the obedience of the lower classes. In Wellington, Alfred's visit served local ends, to contribute to the mythology of the Empire City and its people as well as an imagined method of social control.

South Africa and New Zealand (1901)

The South African War was a transitional moment in the history of the British Empire. The imperial war effort represented both the strengths of the British Empire, when young men from across the empire came to serve Queen and Empire, and its darkest moment, the near-defeat of the greatest empire the world had ever known by some 'farmers', the use of brutal tactics and concentration camps under Kitchener, and the emergence of discontent in the colonies of settlement over the lack of imperial gratitude for their contributions and sacrifices.

In a way, the stories of South Africa and New Zealand after this moment, during the first half of the twentieth century, could hardly be more different. The settlement of the South African War and the Union of South Africa in 1910 reconciled the white populations of the subcontinent, setting in motion the decline and end of British influence in southern Africa: the Maritz (Boer) Rebellion in 1914 and controversy over South Africa's participation in the British war effort during both World Wars; the Statute of Westminster in 1934; and the declaration of a republic in 1961. The national story of New Zealand, on the other hand, remained intertwined with a British one even after the establishment of dominion status in 1907. It was forged in the blood of ANZAC troops during the First World War, it is often claimed, and only quietly drifted away from British influence though remaining proud of its British roots.

Although the British colonies in New Zealand and southern Africa developed into modern nation-states over the second half of the nineteenth century and the first decades of the twentieth century in profoundly different ways, the language of Britishness and ideas about British traditions of liberty and citizenship continued to inform political and cultural discourses of New Zealand and among English-speaking South Africans into the twentieth century. This may not be a surprising claim in the context of New Zealand, but it is an undervalued truth about the history of South Africa.[123] The story of the Duke and Duchess of Cornwall and York's world tour of 1901 reflects both the changes and continuities in imperial culture, of colonies that had largely overcome their sectional divisions evident in the 1860s and had developed more self-confident and independent national identities. At the same time, while non-imperial identities were clearly on the move, Britishness and imperial citizenship continued to shape how people in the empire imagined themselves and their communities.

In the aftermath of Queen Victoria's death in January 1901, the idea of her as an imperial mother, uniting the global offspring of Great Britain, became particularly meaningful to the cosmology of imperial citizenship. New Zealand celebrated its unique place in this history as the first colony founded during the reign of Queen Victoria.[124] This mythology was localised further when combined with the notion that New Zealand was a particularly egalitarian and democratic society. Appealing to a concept that might be termed imperial democracy, the *Lyttelton Times* proposed that the British monarch was, in fact, the elected 'President of the Commonwealth', chosen 'as though we had a quinquennial election'.[125] The *Evening Post* (Wellington) explained that the coexistence of monarchy and democracy, nation and empire was no paradox:

> The youthful colonial democracy, untrammeled as it is by the long-drawn traditions of the past, is suddenly brought to a vivid realisation of the historical associations which centre round a throne, and because that throne is now the symbol of ordered liberty, no less than national unity, it feels stirring within it the inherited sentiment of loyalty which for the Briton suggests no servility, and leads to no loss of self-respect.[126]

In celebration of the Great Queen's reign, the duke laid the foundation stones for statues of the late Queen, paid for by local subscriptions, in an act that was repeated across the empire.[127]

Public discourse in New Zealand also focused on competition with newly federated Australia and New Zealand's place in the Australasian British Empire. On the eve of the royal visit, the *Otago Witness* argued that the royal tour could 'hardly fail to quicken the growing desire to join the Commonwealth'.[128] Despite this expressed desire to join the Australian Commonwealth, there was constant discussion, as there had been during the earlier tours, of how New Zealand could compete with their richer and older Australian cousins. There was wide consensus in the settler press, however, that New Zealand could not compete with the spectacle of the Australian visit, nor could the provincial cities of the islands do more than repeat the performances of Auckland; yet Dunedin or Canterbury, local papers argued, were more genuine in their loyalty and patriotism than Marvelous Melbourne or even Auckland.[129] In this context, the *Otago Daily Times* of Dunedin opposed the government's plan to put on a military show to compete with, even 'go one better' than, New Zealand's 'more powerful neighbours', New South Wales and Victoria.[130] These sentiments reflect a complexity about New Zealand's emerging national identity, which became decreasingly provincial in character but reflected multiple allegiances: with a colony-nation of New Zealand, with an Australasian British world, and with Home and the British Empire.

In this context, the complicated politics of the South African War figured importantly during the New Zealand royal tour, particularly the importance of New Zealand's service to the imperial war cause. Ten contingents and some 6,500 New Zealanders soldiers journeyed to South Africa to serve the war effort, paid for by settler donations.[131] Contrasted to the cultural discomfort of metropolitan Britons with standing armies, colonial cultures were comparatively militarised spaces, a characteristic than was amplified by conflict in South Africa. Military parades and inspections dominated the itinerary, with New Zealand volunteers travelling hundreds of kilometres to attend these functions. The most anticipated moment came when the Duke of Cornwall and York pinned medals for valour and service on New Zealand's imperial troops, which one paper suggested would prevent the volunteers from ever removing their uniforms again.

In pro-war discourses, protest against the war was dismissed, loyalty and service to the empire against Afrikaner despotism celebrated.[132] Moreover, most of the papers affirmed the imperial solidarity that the war had stirred, symbolised in the 'blood, mingling in a common stream on the South African field, of Imperial soldier and imperial trooper'.[133] 'When the Mother Country is in danger or difficulty we send our young men to fight for her, or it may be to die for her if the sacrifice is required.'[134] New Zealand could be counted on to give a hand when the mother country and the empire were threatened.

At the same time, some elements of the settler press condemned the neglect of the imperial soldier, the young New Zealander fighting for the empire in southern Africa, while the papers were filled with accounts of the royal visit. There were, of course, the medals awarded by the Duke of Cornwall, but the tour planners had apparently forgotten about the war effort abroad. The editors of the *Lyttelton Times* complained that imperial and colonial officials were neglecting their boys in South Africa.[135] Parents awaited news of the fate of their sons.[136] Lord Kitchener's plea for supplies 'is utterly ignored, and the men are left to get through a particularly severe winter with none of the assistance that was considered so necessary twelve months ago'.[137] This was a failure of both the government and the public, the *Times* argued, and did not reflect opposition to the war but a general apathy.[138] While veterans and empire were celebrated, it was claimed, those who were suffering and dying on the frontlines of an imperial war were forgotten.

Moreover, the colonial press frequently complained about how New Zealand's volunteer brigades, many of whom had seen war service and who were important players in the performance of the royal tour, were treated poorly and unfairly by the tour planners. The volunteers who attended the festivities in Wellington, for instance, complained that their sleeping quarters were a 'veritable mudhole' and their meals were 'underdone and scanty'.[139] For the troop review at Christchurch, volunteers had to take nine days' leave from their jobs, travel in open trucks in blistering heat to the city, and sleep in uncomfortable and inadequate living conditions.[140] This concern over the treatment of the volunteers reflected the specific grievance about the relationship between a colony-nation and its motherland.

More than on previous tours, the Maori represented 'local colour' during the visit and were firmly appropriated by the emerging national mythology of New Zealand. The age of Maori wars behind them, tour planners incorporated, and the colonial press celebrated, Maori people and customs a part of the story of New Zealand. As Chapter 2 demonstrated, the appropriation of local peoples into imperial culture sought simultaneously to prove the benefits of British civilisation on vanquished peoples and to contrast the heights of British progress (the future) with quaint but no longer dangerous cultures of superstition and barbarism (the past). Moreover, their presence propagated an illusion of consent and what James Belich calls the 'myth of empire', that white settlement and conquest was New Zealand's destiny.[141]

There were also more subtle expressions of this mythology: welcome signs welcoming the prince in both English and Maori; 'Haeremai', or 'Welcome', painted on the Harbour Board Arch; Maori children singing 'God Save the King'.[142]

This narrative sounds remarkably similar to that of southern Africa, but this discourse was different. It reflected a settler mythology of racial harmony and even cooperation, symbolised in the Treaty of Waitangi. The *Otago Daily Times* described 'Natives, the descendants of a race that proved the worthy foemen in bygone days' who 'mingled freely with pioneer colonists and their native-born children'.[143] Symbolically, expressions of loyalty to the British monarchy, in addresses or performance, proved most important in this mythology – as if the Maori were admitting their errors and willingly giving in to the greater and better power. The *Otago Daily Times* even suggested that 'there are no more loyal Britishers in all the Empire' than the Maori.[144] Despite their convergences, the histories of 'white–native' relations in New Zealand and South Africa had much in common – warfare, dispossession, tribalisation, alcoholism, and poverty – and ended up variations of conquest, segregation, and control.

The settler press also argued that imperial loyalism and national pride transcended the social and political chasms of local politics. In the presence of royalty, 'even an anarchist might permit himself to cheer'.[145] In Otago, the *Otago Daily Times* celebrated the crowds who assembled as representing a cross-section of colonial society: 'the miner and the farmer had thrown down their implements, the teacher closed his school and the business man his store … from remote corners of Otago' to pay their respects.[146] In a related vein, Premier John Seddon planned the erection of special stands for elderly pensioners, 'the men who have made the colony with their toil', and reflected on the specialness of New Zealand within the empire: while other colonies were busy preparing arches and designing pageantry, New Zealanders were caring for their founding settlers in old age.[147] While the *Otago Witness* complained that such representations of New Zealand as a 'working man's paradise' duped new workers into settling in New Zealand, only to find the same conditions they would find anywhere else in the empire, they also articulated a vision for what the royal tour ought to represent to the democratic social order of New Zealand:

> Here is a splendid opportunity for drawing a contrast between New Zealand and all the other colonies of the Empire. They spent their ingenuity upon arches and designs of various kinds. We can show a spectacle that will be as pathetic, as significant of the progress we have been making.… There are our pensioners, the men who have made the colony with their toil, and now we provide for their old age.[148]

The myth of democracy and social harmony was contested and challenged across New Zealand, but the idea became central to the apparatus of an emerging nationalism, which focused on these unique attributes of New Zealand's national character. These traits simultaneously served to underline New Zealand's peculiarity as an egalitarian society and to trace the colony-nation's roots in the British diaspora.

The limits of this social harmony, even in the elite settler press, demonstrate the instabilities of the constructed narrative. Two authors ('Tea and Sugar' and 'A Member of the MUIOOF') complained that the Employers' Association of Canterbury had decided to open their shops on the Saturday of the royal visit, denying members of the 'various friendly societies of this city' and others the chance to participate in the festivities.[149] In Wellington, the *New Zealand Free Lance* criticised the 'bungling' and elitism demonstrated by the local planning committees in their welcome to the duke and duchess. The process, dominated by local elites, was characterised by a series of 'squabbles, bickerings, and cross-purposes', what the *New Zealand Free Lance* called 'too many cooks spoiling the broth'.[150] The local committee had committed more money to the festivities than they had in their coffers and proceeded with a 'dictatorial spirit' that was unworthy of a democratic community.[151] The *New Zealand Free Lance* argued that putting up arches was contrary to the egalitarian spirit of New Zealand and that citizens should be encouraged, instead, to decorate their homes and businesses to their own liking.[152] And the editors were enraged when they learned of plans to rope off the streets and erect barricades, which they argued might be a necessary practice in Russia or Germany but not among 'free and loyal' 'Anglo-Saxon peoples'.[153]

The narrative of democracy and egalitarianism both produced and challenged the mythology of New Zealand as a nation. *The Observer* of Auckland challenged the boundaries of acceptable discourse when it encouraged the citizen-subjects of the city to demonstrate restraint and self-respect, representing not only a fierce criticism of excessive celebration of the visit but also an emerging understanding of what it meant to be a New Zealander:

> 'Please don't!' Imagine a horde of Dervishes wildly dancing round you, eager to shake a hand that has only just recovered from the previous town's manipulatory efforts; imagine the frightful fawning and sickening sycophancy a democratic community has subjected this lady and gentleman to, who have done nothing to merit the horror of it all. And Auckland is prepared to do the thing on the same servile scale as the ridiculous multitude of the Commonwealth. It is good to be loyal ... but is it worth while destroying in Royal eyes the qualities that have individualised us?[154]

The editors continued:

> In this matter the reputation of the Auckland people is at stake.... To those favoured individuals who are permitted to wear the bell-topper of distinction or the frockcoat of fealty, we humbly ask that they desist from kissing the royal hand, even if the Royal hand is in so helpless a state as to be of no assistance as a defence. New Zealand is an example to all the world (in its own imagination) of progress.... The Duke's name is not Baal, and he doesn't want to be worshipped.... [I]n coming to New Zealand's fortunately first and fairest city, the recollection we would like him to carry away is that Auckland's citizens had not established a reputation made in a day for fawning, sycophancy, or ill-manners.[155]

This commentary reflects the complex and conflicted nature of national identity in New Zealand. Many themes were the same in 1901 as they were in 1869: the role of social class in discourses and counter-discourses of belonging, a mythology of democracy and egalitarianism, and the legacy of the British diaspora in the traditions and mythologies of the colony-nation. There were also differences.

The end of the land wars and the spread of the European population had neutralised a large proportion of the Maori population, who became more than 'local colour'. They emerged as principal actors in a story of New Zealand, from which the brutal and violent past was largely excised. In the context of declining provincialism and the development of infrastructure and technologies that resulted in a better-connected New Zealand, there also emerged a more independent and self-confident national identity and politics that was based in both the uniqueness of New Zealand and its relationship with a British homeland.[156] While New Zealand and South Africa had much in common, a significant divergence can be detected during the era of the South African War, of a New Zealand that would retain a certain political, economic, and cultural closeness with the motherland and a South Africa that began to more aggressively push away.[157] At the same time, while New Zealand grew increasingly reliant on British trade and capital, the goldfields and diamond mines of southern Africa were thoroughly saturated in British capital. Moreover, the traditions and mythologies of Britishness and empire continued to inform political and cultural discourses for both British settlers and 'colonial others' in both places well into the twentieth century.

The South African leg of the world tour was nearly cancelled because of an epidemic of bubonic plague in Cape Town.[158] In response, the editors of the *Graham's Town Journal* asserted that 'Capetown is not the Colony, and that a railway trip throughout the other ports and the chief inland towns would give their Royal Highnesses a better idea of the country, and bring them in touch with most of the loyal population'.[159] This public relations nightmare, as the Colonial Office understood the situation, led to a hurried exchange of letters between London and the Cape. The visit was important as pro-empire propaganda in the midst of the South African War.[160] Upon hearing of the possibility that HMS *Ophir*, with royal passengers on board, would coal at Simonstown and depart without a visit, W. F. Hely-Hutchinson, the governor at the Cape, encouraged the Colonial Secretary Joseph Chamberlain of the great political importance of the visit, that the '[Afrikaner] Bond' was quite *fearful* 'that the visit may weaken their position'.[161] The British High Commissioner Alfred Milner also apparently worried that 'the disloyal section of the people would make great capital out of its abandonment'.[162] Thus, after expert opinion asserted that the health of the royal visitors would not be at risk, the duke and duchess travelled across South Africa, from Natal to Pietermaritzburg and on to Cape Town in the middle of a colonial war.

In the history of colonial South Africa, the South African War represents the end of an era of Anglo-Boer hostility and aggression, and the emergence of a white unity and dominance that these antagonisms had staved off. It also marked the symbolic end of the 'imperial factor' in South African history, the beginnings of a united and independent nation-state that came to be dominated by Afrikaans-speaking settlers and would not take its cues from London. On the other hand, British political and cultural traditions profoundly informed the body politic of post-Union South Africa. The example of Jan Christian Smuts, the grand old man of early twentieth-century South African politics and two-time prime minister (1919–24, 1939–48), is instructive in this regard. While he was an Afrikaner who had fought on the Boer side during the South African War, he ended up leading the suppression of the Maritz Rebellion during the Great War and serving as a British field marshal during the Second World War. In Parliament Square, he is immortalised in bronze as an imperial hero and Commonwealth statesman. For the English-speaking populations of South Africa, particularly those who lived in the cultural bastions of Britishness, in Cape Town, Natal, and the Eastern Cape, and those ethnic and racial 'others' with whom the language of British liberty and citizenship resonated, Britishness and imperial citizenship remained vibrant political and cultural discourses. Thus, the way that 'British' settlers imagined the 1901 royal tour reflected the decline of regional identities and the continued relevance of Britishness and the 'imperial factor'.

The war and the recent death of Queen Victoria amplified the use of her mythology as a symbol of British liberty and progress, as the patriot Queen. In this mythology, she represented all that was good about the British cause in the war and the continued relevance of Britain and the empire to South Africa. The tour was a sombre affair, with its principal actors and their colonial observers to mourn the Queen and the war dead. Tour organisers instructed men and women to wear dark or black clothing and discouraged shouting and cheering. Yet Victoria also represented the triumph of British rule in southern Africa in this discourse, the 'freedom and progress' brought on by her rule.[163] Her subjects, 'the only Queen most of them had ever known', universally respected and loved her regardless of race or ethnicity.[164] The *Natal Mercury* claimed that she had 'discerned true Colonial and Imperial policy long before many of her most eminent statesmen' and that her rule had convinced republicans across Britain and the empire to renounce their beliefs and embrace constitutional monarchy.[165] This was a rosy picture that glossed over a history of violence, warfare, and dispossession, but it projected a powerful myth about what it meant to be a British citizen-subject in southern Africa.

In a related vein, the inauguration of the federal parliament of Australia represented a future possibility for South Africa in these discourses of imperial identity, with the colony rising from the ashes of war to achieve status as the third 'great federation' of the British Empire.[166] The progress of the Australian visit was carefully reported by the English-speaking press of South Africa and came to represent what the country might become, a federation that 'will only be too readily granted to South Africa when the bitterness of war has passed, and Boer and Briton agree to pursue the ideal that has made the great Commonwealth in the South viz., "one people, one destiny"'.[167] However, the editors of the *Cape Argus* argued that it 'rests with the Boers and Afrikanders to decide when the era of self-government will be inaugurated'.[168] The *Natal Mercury* prophesied the possible benefits of the royal tour, that it would cause the Boers to 'better understand what British rule is, and what advantages it offers to all who are willing to accept it'.[169] While there was considerable foresight in this vision, of a rapprochement between the British colonies and the Boer republics, it was wrong in predicting which side would come to dominate a federated South African state. The leader writers of the British South African press did not have the benefit of retrospect, of knowing that the country would become an Afrikaner-dominated state, so there is little fairness in dismissing their compelling appeals to Queen and Empire as inconsequential.

In fact, the English-language press portrayed the rebellious Dutch-speaking population as a defeated people. The *Natal Mercury* asserted that the Afrikaner cause was effectively crushed during the First Anglo-Boer War: 'As they failed, the future South Africa will be an all-British South Africa.'[170] The *Cape Argus* argued that the Boers had failed to effectively climb the civilisational ladder and now the British subject-citizens of South Africa had passed them to possess a political and cultural monopoly on progress and civilisation:

> When the Cape Colony passed into the Empire it was peopled by settlers a century behind the times. They had left Europe and its civilisation in the 17th century and ever since then they had lived outside and beyond the reach of current progress.... All labour ... was performed by the aborigines.... There was little or no education.... Their isolation at the Cape ... made their ignorance hereditary.... Such were the subjects Great Britain acquired in the beginning of the last century. They were the antithesis of Englishmen in habits both of life and of thought.[171]

One popularly conceived way of countering the influence of the Afrikaners in the post-war state was to promote British immigration, but multiple immigration schemes, the editors of the *Graham's Town Journal* contested, had been sabotaged and cancelled by successive colonial governments, which feared angering the Boers.[172] After the war, this had been Alfred Milner's project in the Transvaal. Post-war South Africa was foreseen to be a very British place.

The colonial press of South Africa also highlighted the importance of empire and imperial citizenship to a post-war South African political and social order. To them, the war effort and the royal tour exemplified the 'solidarity of the empire' and the 'liberties of the people'.[173] With the outpouring of loyalty to the duke and duchess by the people of the South African colonies, the editors of the *Natal Mercury* suggested that:

> [T]he idea that the Colonies were like fruit growing on the parent stem, readying to drop whenever ripe, was dispelled, and the simile of a great oak throwing out its mighty branches never to fall or rot away while the roots of the parent tree held the ground, was found to be more appropriate.[174]

Rather than drifting away from empire, these English-speaking leader writers argued that an emerging national identity was 'perfectly compatible with attachment to the broader ideal of empire'.[175] The *Cape Argus* even appealed to the democracy and equality of New Zealand society as proof, arguing that New Zealand was more of a republic under Queen Victoria than the Boer republics were in their hostility to empire.[176] Here, New Zealand became a model of what South Africa ought to become!

The British colonial press also constructed a mythology of the war that emphasised an imperial identity over or in concert with a national one. The *Natal Mercury* celebrated the imperial war effort in celebratory language:

> No call to arms was needed, no request of help had to be made. At the first note of danger, Britain's sturdy sons in the 'seven seas' shouldered their rifles, read and willing to do or die for Queen and Empire. Form north to south, from east and west they flocked around the grand old flag, and gave the world the most convincing spectacle it had ever seen of the firm foundation of the British Empire, and of the whole-souled devotion of the Colonies to the Crown.... Colonial and Home-born have fought and died side by side for the common cause of Empire, and their blood has consecrated the great ideal of Imperial unity.[177]

In this context, the duke's tribute to those who had suffered and died in the siege of Ladysmith, where he could not visit for security reasons, contributed to a mythology of imperial identity forged in the war effort.[178] Alongside the World Wars, the South African War was a formative moment in the making of imperial and national identities in the colonies of settlement, processes that were more pronounced in the warzone, where the languages of Britishness and imperial citizenship justified the war and served as a vision for the future.

While it is completely reasonable for scholars to underscore the development of a national identity in the South African War and its aftermath, this narrative suppresses a counter-narrative that was not unfounded in its prophecies. It may have been wishful thinking on the part of the British settler community to assume that a minority of the English-speaking population would dominate the majority Afrikaner population in a federated state, yet the risks of imperial withdrawal and Afrikaner domination were well understood:

> South Africa is necessary to the preservation of the Empire.... England can never again think to shirk the responsibility of the defence of this country; nor can she afford to permit legislation or administration here that is not heartily Imperialist.... The situation is not like that in, say New Zealand, where the loyalty of the whole population is undoubted, and where the stability of the Empire does not hang upon the retention of that very valuable dependency. Here, however, it is a very dangerous fooling to lose Imperial control over local government, and to place power in the hands of a faction who do not disguise their intention for using it against the Empire.[179]

This understanding of South Africa's future and the importance of Britishness was darker and more cynical than those discourses that focused on the almost natural progress of British liberty in South Africa, but it reflected the same fundamental principle: that the imperial connection was crucial to the South African body politic and could be abandoned neither by English-speaking South Africans nor the imperial government. This understanding was reflected later in pleas to the imperial government and the monarchy to refuse approval of the Union of South Africa in 1910.

While the royal tour was celebrated for bringing together the late Queen's subjects, their loyalty, ethnic, racial, and geographical divisions profoundly informed perceptions of the visit. The *Natal Mercury* worried that the government-appointed planning commission suffered from a bad case of 'officialdom' and neglected the needs and wants of the public.[180] There were other protests – over where duke and duchess would visit and how long they would spend in each locale; over the appropriateness of a royal visit during a war; and over the suspension of the constitution and the institution of martial law. In Graham's Town on the Eastern Cape, the *Journal* worried about the prospect of a royal tour in the middle of a bloody conflict, that time and resources were being unnecessarily used and that celebration was inappropriate in these sombre times.[181] They argued that the communities of South Africa 'have been depleted of their best men, are impoverished through the war and many of them are still under Martial law'.[182] They argued that while Cape Town had profited richly from the war, even that city could not offer a proper welcome to royal visitors.[183] South Africa was a 'sad sister in the great colonial family' and not prepared for guests.[184]

Moreover, the spectre of Cape separatism and Eastern Cape provincialism survived the progress of the war, even if it posed little threat to the political order of a British-dominated South Africa. On the Eastern Cape, the *Graham's Town Journal* invested its politics in the language of British loyalism, particularly against the imperial and settler interests in Cape Town that failed to push forward completely against 'the chronic and bitter conspiracy of Africanderism'.[185] They condemned the editors of the *Cape Argus*, who, they argued, observed their suffering with a spirit of apathy and condescension:

> Nothing is more charming than the calm, untroubled attitude of the *Cape Argus* in regard to the present war. It shows no sign of weariness or discouragement, and indeed expresses decided satisfaction at the slowly sure, and surely slow progress of the campaign.... The *Argus* man's calm is unruffled, and he is sure that the highest military authorities also, do not care a tinker's anathema what the opinion of the plundered and imperiled population ... may be.... [Imperial military planners have] forced [themselves] generally upon the loyal inhabitants of the Midland and Northern districts of this Colony.... Capetown ... cares remarkably little about the sufferings of the rest of the Colony.[186]

As in an earlier age, the editors of the *Journal* remained hostile to the Western Cape, now seen as a hotbed of disloyalty and irresolution in a time of war.[187] They condemned 'a Bond ministry of weaklings and traitors', 'the disastrous session of Parliament last year, which very greatly encouraged disloyalty and rebellion', a lack of 'foresight and resolution ... [in] calling out the available force and volunteers of the Colony, and planting them on the south bank of the Orange', and the 'failure to prevent the seditious from holding meetings and publishing falsehoods'.[188]

In particular, these editors challenged the extension of martial law to all of South Africa while the 'focus of treason', the Cape Town settler press, was left to 'belch forth its lies and sedition'.[189] The suspension of the constitution and the proposed imposition of martial law was condemned by many politicians and journalists as contrary to a British tradition of liberty. In response, the editors of the *Graham's Town Journal* argued that the current system was 'dangerous and unworkable' and that most of the population was neither 'so loyal or so politically intelligent' as to be trusted with the privilege of responsible government.[190] These echoes of Cape separatism were not anti-imperialist but were, in fact, couched in a language of Britishness and loyalism. These protests had much in common with the language of contestation used by their enemies, the Boers, of the imperialism and meddling of the imperial government and Cape Town.

Despite the *Graham's Town Journal*'s pronounced hostility toward Cape Town and its inhabitants, British South Africa had largely overcome the dominance of provincial identities to establish a more national British identity, developed through the emergence of responsible government and the development of railways and telegraph wires and forged in war. The Treaty of Vereeniging (1902) and the Union of South Africa (1910) created the political and cultural conditions for a reconciliation between the hostile colonial populations of southern Africa. Of course, the reconstruction scheme of Sir Alfred Milner and his Kindergarten after the war sought to 'Anglicise' South Africa through British immigration, education, and modernisation, but he failed to overcome Boer political and cultural dominance.[191] While these developments also cultivated the end of the so-called imperial connection and an emerging national identity, the end of empire and British influence in South Africa was not a foregone conclusion. British traditions and mythologies of belonging, that 'forgotten nationalism', continued to shape South African political culture, and an attachment to empire remained a cultural force well into the twentieth century. Moreover, as the next chapter demonstrates, these discourses were not limited to settlers of English or British ancestry but to diverse populations who cast their lot with the British monarchy and the British Empire.

Conclusion

Over time, the provincialism and localism of these British cores, in Otago and Natal, the Eastern Cape and Wellington, were transcended by new political orders, responsible government, and new networks of communication and transportation, all of which encouraged the development of national mythologies of belonging over local and imperial ones. Despite these changes, which posed significant challenges to the 'imperial factor' in colonial societies, Britishness and imperial citizenship continued to inform the political and cultural lives of twentieth-century South Africans and New Zealanders. While the two colony-nations diverged in obvious and well-known ways, they also continued to share the political and cultural traditions of Britishness and an imperial culture.

While New Zealand is a more obvious example of this phenomenon than the far more complicated case of South Africa, Vivian Bickford-Smith has rightly characterised Britishness as South Africa's 'forgotten nationalism'.[192] British flags, for instance, were flown at city halls in Natal and the Eastern Cape until the 1990s![193] Even if British-imperial identities might have been more diffuse in southern Africa, the modern national identities of both South Africa and New Zealand emerged out of the political and cultural milieu of British imperial culture. In the long term, the former came to dominate the latter, but this was – as this chapter suggests – a process rather than a foregone conclusion.

While these trends might be examined usefully in another – or perhaps larger – context, the multivalent ways in which colonial subjects responded to and made sense of the royal tours offer particularly fertile terrain for assessing loyalism, Britishness, and citizenship in the settler empire. Even as colonial officials and local elites in sought to use royal visits to promote colonial loyalty to Queen and Empire and social solidarity, the various counter-discourses that were produced by colonial subjects – of provincialism, class conflict, and disagreements between metropole and colony – clearly exhibit the geographical, political, and social fault lines that characterised nineteenth-century settler societies. While more firmly local and national identities displaced imperial ones over time, as a result of responsible government, the decline of provincialism, and technological change, these new identities were not constructed on the ashes of a British-imperial culture but on the social, political, and cultural foundation that colonial subjects had built during the nineteenth century.

Notes

1 While southern Africa stood at the verge of the mineral revolutions that would transform its political economy forever, the Cape experienced its own economic boom, the result of surging wool production and (as James Belich points out) importation. James Belich, *Replenishing the Earth: The Settler Revolution and the Rise of the Anglo-World, 1783–1939* (Oxford, 2009), 374–7.

2 Nigel Worden, E. Van Heyningen, and Vivian Bickford-Smith, *Cape Town: The Making of a City* (Cape Town, 1998), 166; Saul Solomon, *The Progress of His Royal Highness Prince Alfred Ernest Albert through the Cape Colony, British Kaffraria, the Orange Free State, and Port Natal, in the Year 1860* (Cape Town, 1861), xi.

3 On Cape separatism, see Basil A. Le Cordeur, *The Politics of Eastern Cape Separatism, 1820–1854* (Cape Town, 1981).

4 *Star*, 14 April 1869.

5 *Lyttelton Times*, 22 April 1869.

6 *Star*, 17 April 1869.

7 *Star*, 23 April 1869.

8 *Star*, 21 April 1869.

9 See Benedict Anderson, *Imagined Communities: Reflections on the Origin and Spread of Nationalism* (New York, 1983); Alan Lester, *Imperial Networks: Creating Identities in Nineteenth-Century South Africa and Britain* (New York, 2001); Jane McRae, '"Ki nga pito e wha o te ao nei" (To the four corners of this world): Maori Publishing and Writing for Nineteenth-Century Maori-Language Newspapers', in *Agent of Change: Print Culture Studies after Elizabeth L. Eisenstein*, ed. Sabrina Alcorn Baron, Eric N. Lindquist, and Eleanor F. Shevlin (Amherst, 2007), 287–300.

10 John Darwin, *After Tamerlane: The Rise and Fall of Global Empires 1400–2000* (London, 2008), 23.

11 David Cannadine, *Ornamentalism: How the British Saw Their Empire* (London, 2001), 105.

12 Solomon, *The Progress of His Royal Highness*, 126–36; also see Saul Dubow, *A Commonwealth of Knowledge: Science, Sensibility, and White South Africa, 1820–2000* (Oxford, 2006), 68–70.

13 Carl Bridge and Kent Fedorowich, eds, *The British World: Diaspora, Culture, and Identity* (London, 2003); Phillip Buckner and R. Douglas Francis, eds, *Rediscovering the British World* (Calgary, 2005).

14 Krishan Kumar, *The Making of English National Identity* (New York, 2003); Robert J. C. Young, *The Idea of English Ethnicity* (New York, 2008).

15 Saul Dubow, 'How British Was the British World? The Case of South Africa', *JICH* 37, no. 1 (2009), 7.

16 Richard Jebb, *Studies in Colonial Nationalism* (London, 1905); Doug Cole, 'The Problem of "Nationalism" and "Imperialism" in British Settlement Colonies', *Journal of British Studies* 10 (1971): 160–82.

17 John Darwin, *The Empire Project: The Rise and Fall of the British World-System, 1830–1970* (Cambridge, 2009), esp. 11–12, 177–87; Belich, *Replenishing the Earth*, esp. 466–73.

18 Niall Ferguson, *Empire: The Rise and Demise of the British World Order and the Lessons for World Power* (New York, 2003).

19 J. Reginald Tye, 'New Zealand', in *Periodicals of Queen Victoria's Empire: An Exploration*, ed. J. Don Vann and Rosemary T. VanArsdel (Toronto, 1996), 208.

20 Tye, 'New Zealand', 208.

21 Many of the National Library of New Zealand's newspapers have been digitised as part of the *Papers Past* project: http://paperspast.natlib.govt.nz. See also David Hastings, *Extra! Extra! How the People Made the News* (Auckland, 2013).

22 Tye, 'New Zealand', 209.

23 Alan Lester, 'British Settler Discourses and the Circuits of Empire', *History Workshop Journal* 54 (2002), 30.

24 *Paging through History: 150 Years with the 'Cape Argus'* (Cape Town, 2007), 7.
25 J. R. Seeley, *The Expansion of England: Two Courses of Lectures* (Boston, 1883). Also see Kumar, *The Making of English National Identity*; Young, *The Idea of English Ethnicity*, 1.
26 *Otago Witness*, 20 March 1901.
27 Governor George Grey had advocated South African federation during the early 1860s, and the Colonial Secretary Lord Carnarvon made efforts to federate the South African colonies on a Canadian model during the 1870s. Christopher Saunders and Ian R. Smith, 'Southern Africa, 1795–1910', in *OHBE*, vol. 3, *The Nineteenth Century* (Oxford, 1999), 606.
28 See Le Cordeur, *The Politics of Eastern Cape Separatism*.
29 Ranfurly to Chamberlain, 4 July 1901, NA CO 209/262/435–40.
30 See, for instance, Damon Slesa, *Racial Crossings: Race, Intermarriage and the Victorian British Empire* (Oxford, 2011).
31 Vivian Bickford-Smith, 'Providing Local Colour? "Cape Coloureds" and Cape Town's Identity from the Late Nineteenth Century to the Near Present', American Historical Association, 8 January 2010.
32 Philippa Mein Smith, *A Concise History of New Zealand* (Cambridge, 2005), 78–82.
33 John Lambert, '"An Unknown People": Reconstructing British South African Identity', *JICH* 37, no. 4 (December 2009): 599–617; Andrew Thompson, 'The Language of Loyalism in Southern Africa, c. 1870–1939', *English Historical Review* 118, no 477 (2003): 617–50; Dubow, 'How British Was the British World?'; John Lambert, 'The Last Outpost: Natalians, South Africa, and the British Empire', in *Settlers and Expatriates: Britons over the Seas*, OHBE Companion Series, ed. Robert Bickers (Oxford, 2010), 150–77. For analysis of Britishness in post-apartheid South Africa, see Daniel Conway and Pauline Leonard, *Migration, Space and Transnational Identities: The British in South Africa* (London, 2014).
34 Dubow, 'How British Was the British World?', 4.
35 Worden *et al.*, *Cape Town*, 176.
36 Anderson, *Imagined Communities*, 92–3. Jan Smuts is perhaps the best-known example of colonials transcending the political and cultural space of the periphery.
37 W. H. Dunn, *James Anthony Froude; A Biography*, vol. 2, *1857–1894* (Oxford, 1963); cited in Dubow, 'How British Was the British World?', 6, 9.
38 A Colonist, *A Proposal for the Confederation of the Australian Colonies, with Prince Alfred, Duke of Edinburgh, as King of Australia* (Sydney, 1867).
39 *South Africa Commercial Advertiser*, 1 August 1860.
40 Dubow, 'How British Was the British World?', 6.
41 Raewyn Dalziel, 'Southern Islands: New Zealand and Polynesia', in *OHBE*, vol. 3, *The Nineteenth Century*, 582.
42 *Graham's Town Journal*, 15 August 1860.
43 *South African Commercial Advertiser*, 4 August 1860.
44 *South African Commercial Advertiser*, 28 July 1860
45 *Timaru Herald*, 28 April 1869.
46 *Evening Post*, 17 April 1869. These understandings of the royal tour did not go unchallenged. For instance, the *Evening Post* of Wellington satirised the celebration of 'loyal Maori', who they claimed had been bribed with promises of alcohol and food.
47 A similar argument is made in the context of American history in Philip Deloria, *Playing Indian* (New Haven, 1999).
48 Christopher Saunders, 'African Attitudes to Britain and the Empire before and after the South African War', in *The South African War Reappraised*, ed. Donal Lowry (New York, 2000), 140–9; Elizabeth Elbourne, 'Indigenous Peoples and Imperial Networks in the Early Nineteenth Century: The Politics of Knowledge', in *Rediscovering the British World*, ed. Phillip Buckner and R. Douglas Francis (Calgary, 2005), 59–86.
49 For a discussion of this tradition, see Vivian Bickford-Smith, *Ethnic Pride and Racial Prejudice in Victorian Cape Town* (Cambridge, 1995), 1–2. For an example,

see George Frederickson, *White Supremacy: A Comparative Study in American and South African History* (Oxford, 1981), 262–82.

50 The *South African Commercial Advertiser* condescendingly noted that the 'great unwashed of our town will live for some months to come, if on nothing else, at least on the gorgeous memories of that blessed period [the royal tour], which for them has secured so many cheap out door exhibitions', 1 August 1860.

51 Solomon, *Progress of His Royal Highness*, viii–ix; Asa Briggs, *The Age of Improvement, 1783–1867*, 2nd edn (New York, 1999).

52 Worden *et al.*, *Cape Town*, 132.

53 Saul Dubow argues that this achievement, along with the work of missionary John Phillip to improve the conditions and treatment of Khoisan people, the anti-slavery movement, and agitation for representative government, are the founding myths of Cape liberalism. Dubow, *A Commonwealth of Knowledge*, 27.

54 Stanley Trapido, 'John Fairbairn (1794–1864)', *Oxford DNB*.

55 Trapido, 'John Fairbairn'.

56 Trapido, 'John Fairbairn'.

57 *South African Commercial Advertiser*, 25 July 1860.

58 Solomon, *Progress of His Royal Highness*, 113.

59 *South African Commercial Advertiser*, 25 July 1860.

60 *South African Commercial Advertiser*, 25 July 1860.

61 *South African Commercial Advertiser*, 8 August 1860.

62 *South African Commercial Advertiser*, 28 July 1860.

63 *South African Commercial Advertiser*, 8 September 1860.

64 *South African Commercial Advertiser*, 28 July 1860.

65 *South African Commercial Advertiser*, 28 July 1860.

66 *South African Commercial Advertiser*, 28 July 1860.

67 *South African Commercial Advertiser*, 1 August 1860.

68 Francis Fleming, *Kaffraria, and Its Inhabitants* (London, 1853), 16.

69 Frank Riet, *The Settler Celebrations of 1870: Compiled from Contemporary Accounts* (Grahamstown, 1970).

70 Solomon, *Progress of His Royal Highness*, 37.

71 Clifton Crais, *White Supremacy and Black Resistance in Pre-Industrial South Africa: The Making of the Colonial Order in the Eastern Cape, 1770–1865* (Cambridge, 1992), 88.

72 Lester, *Imperial Networks*, 61–2.

73 Lester, *Imperial Networks*, 61–2.

74 Lester, *Imperial Networks*, 48.

75 Le Cordeur, *The Politics of Eastern Cape Separatism*, 63–8.

76 *Graham's Town Journal*, 17 July 1860.

77 *Graham's Town Journal*, 15 August 1860.

78 *Graham's Town Journal*, 10 July 1860.

79 *Graham's Town Journal*, 10 July 1860.

80 *Graham's Town Journal*, 31 July 1860.

81 *Graham's Town Journal*, 21 July 1860.

82 *Graham's Town Journal*, 24 July 1860, 31 July 1860.

83 Timothy Keegan, *Colonial South Africa and the Origins of the Racial Order* (Charlottesville, 1996), 61–74. Le Cordeur, *The Politics of Eastern Cape Separatism*, 1–36; Alan Lester, 'Reformulating Identities: British Settlers in Early Nineteenth-Century South Africa', *Transactions of the Institute of British Geographers* 23, no 4 (2004), 518. Lester notes that many of these notables were 'betrayed' by their white servants, who often abandoned their indentures and dared to venture out on their own.

84 *Graham's Town Journal*, 10 July 1860.

85 *Graham's Town Journal*, 24 July 1860.

86 Dalziel, 'Southern Islands', 587.

87 *Timaru Herald*, 10 April 1869.

88 *Otago Daily Times*, 19 April 1869.

89 *Wellington Independent*, 13 April 1869.
90 *Otago Daily Times*, quoted in the *Evening Post*, 30 April 1869.
91 Dalziel, 'Southern Islands', 585–6.
92 *Otago Daily Times*, 19 April 1869.
93 *Otago Daily Times*, 19 April 1869.
94 *Wellington Independent*, 13 April 1869.
95 *Lyttelton Times*, 24 April 1869.
96 *Lyttelton Times*, 24 April 1869.
97 *Timaru Herald*, 28 April 1869.
98 *Bruce Herald*, 12 May 1869.
99 *Lyttelton Times*, 24 April 1869.
100 *Lyttelton Times*, 24 April 1869.
101 *Wellington Independent*, 13 April 1869.
102 *Timaru Herald*, 28 April 1869.
103 At a March meeting organised to discuss the royal welcome, no fewer than 700 people attended. *Star*, 10 March 1869.
104 *Daily Southern Cross*, 22 April 1869.
105 See Raewyn Dalziel, *Julius Vogel, Business Politician* (Auckland, 1986).
106 R. C. J. Stone, *From Tamaki-Makau-Rau to Auckland* (Auckland, 2001); Dalziel, 'Southern Islands', 584.
107 *Evening Post*, 5 May 1869.
108 Belich, *Making Peoples*, 368.
109 *Daily Southern Cross*, 15 April 1869.
110 *Daily Southern Cross*, 7 May 1869.
111 *Daily Southern Cross*, 10 May 1869.
112 *Daily Southern Cross*, 10 May 1869.
113 Ironically, Wellington had been settled in defiance of the British government, and its settlers resisted the rule of Auckland-based governors for a time after 1840.
114 *Wellington Independent*, 13 April 1869.
115 *Wellington Independent*, 13 April 1869.
116 *Wellington Independent*, 13 April 1869.
117 *Wellington Independent*, 13 April 1869.
118 *Wellington Independent*, 13 April 1869.
119 *Evening Standard*, 14 April 1869.
120 *Evening Standard*, 17 April 1869.
121 *Evening Standard*, 17 April 1869.
122 *Evening Standard*, 17 April 1869.
123 Vivian Bickford-Smith, 'Writing about Englishness: South Africa's Forgotten Nationalism', in *Empire and After: Englishness in Postcolonial Perspective*, ed. Graham MacPhee and Prem Poddar (Oxford, 2007), 57–72. For a more traditional approach, see John Bond, *They Were South Africans* (Oxford, 1956).
124 *Otago Daily Times*, 12 June 1901.
125 *Lyttelton Times*, 11 June 1901; *Otago Witness*, 12 June 1901.
126 *Evening Post*, 8 June 1901.
127 *Otago Witness*, 3 July 1901.
128 *Otago Witness*, 20 March 1901.
129 *Otago Witness*, 19 June 1901.
130 *Otago Daily Times*, 31 May 1901.
131 A. J. Harrop, 'New Zealand and the Empire, 1852–1951', in *The Cambridge History of the British Empire*, vol. 7, *New Zealand* (Cambridge, 1936), 219.
132 *Otago Daily Times*, 14 June 1901.
133 *Otago Daily Times*, 31 May 1901, 14 June 1901.
134 *Otago Witness*, 12 June 1901.
135 *Lyttelton Times*, 11 June 1901.
136 *Lyttelton Times*, 11 June 1901.
137 *Lyttelton Times*, 11 June 1901.
138 *Lyttelton Times*, 11 June 1901.

139 *Bruce Herald*, 25 June 1901.
140 *Otago Witness*, 29 May 1901.
141 James Belich, 'Empire and Its Myth', in *Amongst Friends. Australian and New Zealand Voices from America*, ed. Patty O'Brien and Bruce Vaughn (Dunedin, 2005), 146–61.
142 *Otago Witness*, 12 June 1901.
143 *Otago Witness*, 12 June 1901.
144 *Otago Daily Times*, 15 June 1901.
145 *Lyttelton Times*, 11 June 1901.
146 *Otago Daily Times*, 26 June 1901.
147 *Otago Witness*, 12 June 1901.
148 *Otago Witness*, 12 June 1901.
149 *Lyttelton Times*, 17 June 1901.
150 *New Zealand Free Lance*, 8 June 1901.
151 *New Zealand Free Lance*, 15 June 1901.
152 *New Zealand Free Lance*, 8 June 1901.
153 *New Zealand Free Lance*, 15 June 1901.
154 *Observer*, 15 June 1901.
155 *Observer*, 15 June 1901.
156 The emergence of national political parties is perhaps the best indicator of this change. The Liberal Party as a national party was able to transcend and dominate New Zealand politics in a way that provincial parties or stitched-together regional and national alliances never could.
157 Dalziel, 'Southern Islands', 592.
158 William Beinart and Lotte Hughes, 'Plague and Urban Environments', in *Environment and Empire* (Oxford, 2007), 167–83.
159 *Graham's Town Journal*, 13 June 1901.
160 Joseph Watson, *The Queen's Wish: How It Was Fulfilled by the Imperial Tour of T.R.H. the Duke and Duchess of Cornwall and York* (London, 1902), 306–37.
161 Governor W. F. Hely-Hutchinson to Joseph Chamberlain, 25 April 1901, JC 11/12/69.
162 Joseph Chamberlain to Edward VII, n.d., JC 11/12/04.
163 *Cape Argus*, 24 May 1901.
164 *Natal Mercury*, 19 July 1901.
165 *Natal Mercury*, 15 August 1901.
166 *Natal Mercury*, 13 August 1901.
167 *Natal Mercury*, 13 August 1901.
168 *Cape Argus*, 29 June 1901.
169 *Natal Mercury*, 13 August 1901.
170 *Natal Mercury*, 3 August 1901.
171 *Cape Argus*, 16 April 1901.
172 *Graham's Town Journal*, 28 July 1901.
173 *Natal Mercury*, 15 August 1901.
174 *Natal Mercury*, 15 August 1901.
175 *Cape Argus*, 10 May 1901.
176 *Cape Argus*, 10 May 1901.
177 *Natal Mercury*, 15 August 1901.
178 *Natal Mercury*, 16 August 1901
179 *Graham's Town Journal*, 27 August 1901.
180 *Natal Mercury*, 12 June 1901.
181 *Graham's Town Journal*, 3 August 1901.
182 *Graham's Town Journal*, 16 May 1901.
183 *Graham's Town Journal*, 18 May 1901.
184 *Graham's Town Journal*, 18 May 1901.
185 *Graham's Town Journal*, 7 March 1901.
186 *Graham's Town Journal*, 28 May 1901.
187 *Graham's Town Journal*, 7 March 1901.
188 *Graham's Town Journal*, 7 March 1901.

189 *Graham's Town Journal*, 7 March 1901. In particular, they were angered at the lack of outrage on the part of the Cape Town papers when the northern towns of Colesburg and Aliwal were invaded.
190 *Graham's Town Journal*, 9 March 1901.
191 Saunders and Smith, 'Southern Africa', 619–20.
192 Bickford-Smith, 'Writing about Englishness'.
193 Lambert, '"An Unknown People"', 604.

CHAPTER FOUR

'Positively cosmopolitan': Britishness, respectability, and imperial citizenship

In 1901, Francis Z. S. Peregrino, an African man representing the native peoples of South Africa, addressed the future King George V and Queen Mary, during their globe-trotting tour of the British Empire. Moved by the presence of the future King during the royal visit, Peregrino noted that the Duke of York 'dwelt not on any distinctions of race and colour' and was 'deeply touched by the display of loyalty' from his father's subjects of colour.[1] In the person of the duke and in the memory of the duke's grandmother the Great Queen, Peregrino invested in the promise of an inclusive, non-racial imperial citizenship, the rights and responsibilities of which would be shared by all of Britain's colonial subjects regardless of colour or creed.

Born in Accra in Gold Coast, Peregrino moved to the United States around 1890, editing and publishing 'coloured' newspapers in Buffalo and Pittsburgh before emigrating to the Cape Colony in 1900. He came to the Cape in the midst of the South African War, he said, to 'devote his pen and brain to the service of the native people'.[2] As editor of the Cape Town-based *South African Spectator*, Peregrino articulated a belief in British constitutionalism and loyalty to the British Empire. As a cosmopolitan writer, activist, and intellectual, Peregrino understood himself as being simultaneously 'native' and British and consequently made sense of his political and cultural universe in an idiom of Britishness and imperial citizenship.

This chapter focuses on the intermediaries of empire, on Western-educated *respectables*, who made and were made by the contact zone of empire.[3] They developed deep-seated political and cultural connections with empire and often came to see themselves as part of an imperial culture. Many of them recognised certain benefits of British rule, and a few even imagined themselves to be British people. At the same time, they were intensely aware of the dominance, dispossession, and exclusion of colonial rule, where the promises of the

British constitution and imperial citizenship uncomfortably coexisted with an empire of violence, dispossession, and disenfranchisement.

During the second half of the nineteenth century, and well into the twentieth century, these *respectables* often imagined and even agitated for a future in the empire, rather than outside it. Nationalist organisations such as the Indian National Congress and the South African Native National Congress clung to the language of imperial citizenship into the early decades of the twentieth century.[4] It may be easy, in retrospect, to condemn these historical actors as out of touch with the zeitgeist of history, but they did not have the luxury of knowing what was to come. This chapter examines the reception of nineteenth-century royal tours to the Cape Colony and the British Raj by 'respectable' people of colour, reflecting the ways that ideologies and mythologies of imperial culture were refashioned by *respectables* of colour through a lens of shared imperial citizenship, an alternative vision of imperial culture whereby all 'civilised' and loyal (male) subjects shared the rights and responsibilities of the British constitutional tradition.[5] While formal citizenship in a legal sense did not exist in Britain or the Empire until 1948, *respectables* professed a membership in the political and cultural community of empire, embodied in the rights and responsibilities of the British constitution, reinforced by the rhetoric of the liberal empire, and displayed through loyalty to the monarchy.[6]

British missionaries, administrators, and intellectuals broadly recognised a transnational class of 'educated natives' who were nurtured and educated in Western culture through missionary efforts and 'Anglicisation' movements. During the nineteenth century, colonial schools such as Elphinstone College in Bombay (f. 1824), the Lovedale Missionary Institution (f. 1840), and Zonnebloem College (f. 1858) in South Africa were founded with distinct if related intentions – namely to 'civilise' an intermediary class of indigenous people who could multiply efforts to evangelise the masses, translate cultures and languages for religious and administrative purposes, and mediate colonial governance. Most famously, in the case of India, Thomas Babington Macaulay's Minute on Indian Education (1835) advocated the formation of 'a class who may be interpreters between us and the millions whom we govern; a class of persons, Indian in blood and colour, but English in taste, in opinions, in morals, and in intellect'.

Historian have ably described the transformation of nineteenth-century imperial culture, from a liberal-humanitarian discourse of Anglicisation during the early part of the century to one that that privileged 'traditional' indigenous elites over Western-educated *respectables*, a rejection of liberal-humanitarianism in the aftermath of the abolition of slavery, the Indian Mutiny, and the Morant Bay 'Rebellion'.[7] The educated native came to represent, among other caricatures, 'the Dangerous Native', 'a misadjusted, urbanised, male agitator, his lips dripping with wild and imperfectly understood rhetoric about rights' or the 'money-grubbing', acquisitive, and effeminate *babu*.[8] This literature, while quite compelling, does not properly account for the ongoing contributions of colonial *respectables* to imperial politics and culture. The shifting attitudes of many colonial officials, politicians, and intellectuals of European descent toward a more racialised and 'traditional' imperial culture represent only one part of the story. As evidenced by the deeply personal connections to the British Crown and their reactions to the royal tours, *respectables* envisioned a community of empire based on loyalty, civilisation, and respectability rather than one based on race or ethnicity. Moreover, while the historical actors of this chapter imagined a political and cultural community that was uniquely imperial and framed their rights in the language of British traditions, they also participated in a broader struggle for human rights against the rising tide of racism and the 'global colour bar'.[9]

Scholars, however, have rarely presented these Western-educated people of colour in such light. Post-colonial and other area studies scholars have treated the historical actors presented here in skilful and sophisticated ways but struggle perhaps too diligently to excise them from the spectre of collaboration, to really see them as sly subverters of the colonial order or to understand 'mimicry' as a form of anti-colonial resistance.[10] On the other hand, scholars of British history and British imperial history fail to see them as relevant to their political discourses.[11] With these historical traditions in mind, Saul Dubow has proposed a more inclusive understanding of Britishness, as a global cultural space open to borrowing, appropriation, and redefinition, arguing for the usefulness of:

> a concept of Britishness that dispenses, as far as is possible, with connotations of racial or ethnic ancestry and which decouples the idea of Britishness from a British state or the 'ethnological unity' of Greater Britain hankered after by J. R. Seeley. It does so by challenging the unstated assumption that the British Empire refers to territories and peoples which were somehow *owned* or collectively possessed by the United Kingdom and proposes instead a more capacious category capable of including elective, hyphenated forms of belonging.... Britishness, in this sense, is better seen as a field of cultural, political, and symbolic attachments which includes the rights, claims, and aspirations of subject-citizens as well as citizen-subjects – 'non-Britons' as well as neo-Britons' in today's parlance.[12]

This chapter aims to explore the responses of pro-empire, 'respectable' people of colour in the British Cape Colony and the British Raj – specifically, a comparatively small group of cosmopolitan newspaper writers who claimed British rights and imperial citizenship derived from their loyalty to the empire and the monarchy. The newspaper editors of this analysis were advocates of a non-racial respectable status and identity, who saw themselves as the (more) authentic heirs of British constitutionalism.

The royal tours offer a fascinating lens through which to write a global history of loyalism and Britishness in the British Empire. Respectable people of colour in South Africa and India shared a basic worldview with a global class of respectable subjects across the British Empire, all of whom commented on and responded to the royal tours in comparable languages of loyalty. This global history of Britishness and imperial citizenship serves to provincialise the British Isles in rather profound ways, to demonstrate that many people of colour could and did embrace an imperial identity despite the racial determinism, violence, and dispossession that came to dominate the colonial experience during the nineteenth century. During the royal tours, they appealed to the liberal-humanitarian rhetoric of empire, which cloaked the more brutal reality that often lay beneath the surface, to demand their rights as imperial citizens and loyal subjects of the Queen.

While the failure of Britain to fulfil the promises of imperial citizenship or the rising socio-cultural dominance of imperial 'whiteness' (see Chapters 3 and 5) may have pushed these communities away from an imperial identity, this failure could not have been foreseen by the historical actors at the time. Destabilised and delegitimised by events such as the Union of South Africa (1910) or the Amritsar Massacre (1919), these counter-discourses of identity and belonging survived well into the twentieth century, used by African and Indian nationalists to appeal for imperial justice, by colonial soldiers to challenge the military colour bar during the World Wars, and by the *Windrush* generation to contest racial discrimination at 'Home'.[13]

Respectability in world history

The rise of the bourgeoisie was long an accepted framework for nineteenth-century European history. It was central to the Marxist conception of history that a commercial and professional capitalist middle class displaced the feudal aristocracy as the ruling elite of society. Over the last several decades, historians have skilfully deconstructed this paradigm, displacing it with a new orthodoxy that reflects both social continuity and change.[14] While the rise of the middle class thesis in Europe has been challenged and largely displaced (or revised), the ethos of respectability associated with bourgeois attitudes and values remains relevant, particularly in the context of empire.

There were many ways for one to visualise, articulate, and represent respectability, through social networks, gender roles, dress, manners, consumption, and language. Vivian Bickford-Smith defines respectability, 'that ubiquitous Victorian value', as 'the acceptance of the values of the English elite: thrift, the sanctity of property, deference to superiors, belief in the moralising efficacy of hard work and cleanliness'.[15] The notion of respectability in Britain as a malleable and empowering cultural form can and should be extended to the study of the British Empire, where both settlers of European descent and people of colour often imagined themselves to be respectable people. In particular, the historical actors of this chapter embraced 'civilised' behaviour and dress, the value of the English language, cleanliness, education, the ballot box, and social conservatism, best illustrated by paternalism toward their social inferiors (and in the case of South Africa, derision toward 'traditional' chiefly elites).

While definitions of citizenship in the late nineteenth- and early twentieth-century British world were increasingly defined along ethnic and racial lines, there also persisted more open-ended and universalist discourses of imperial citizenship. They centred, in particular, on a mythologised image of Victoria the Good, the maternal, justice-giving Queen. Colonial societies were inundated with this mythology, which was a fundamental 'component of the ideological apparatus of the imperialist state'.[16] While the African and Asian intelligentsias of this chapter were fundamentally social conservatives, interested in protecting and enhancing their own power and status, they also demanded a radical transformation of imperial culture by demanding the inherent rights and responsibilities of loyal subjects and imperial citizens.

In expressing the social position of such *respectables*, Max Weber's distinction between class and status proves to be most helpful. To Weber, status (*ständische Lage*) meant:

> an effective claim to social esteem in terms of positive or negative privileges; it is typically founded on: 1. style of life, hence 2. formal education, which may be (a) empirical training or (b) rational instruction.... Status *may* rest on class position of a distinct or ambiguous kind. However, it is not solely determined by it.... A '*status group*' means a plurality of persons who, within a larger group, successfully claim: 1. a special social esteem, and possibly also 2. status monopolies.[17]

The claims of the colonised to respectable status might be considered an aspiration-to-class, to a non-racial, universal middle class, but not class in itself. Moreover, they did not aspire to be white or to be *ethnically* British. They did not, as Leo Switzer argues, 'participat[e] in choral and reading groups, debating societies, sewing and singing groups, and in ... tennis, croquet, and cricket ... rugby, and even horse racing' because they aspired to British 'middle-class culture'.[18] They saw themselves to be modern and cosmopolitan, observers and readers of a larger world. They could understand themselves as both 'natives' and 'British' without contradiction. Moreover, as respectable, civilised British subjects, they simultaneously claimed to be advocates for indigenous peoples and often peered down at those whom they considered socially and culturally beneath them, regardless of race. These public men inherited, in a very real sense, the tangled and complicated legacy of British liberalism. They believed, as Uday Singh Mehta has argued in the context of British liberals, in both individual freedoms and political representation as well as a 'cosmopolitanism of reason' that failed to successfully confront difference in the absence of comparable rationality and respectability.[19] They argued for what Theodore Koditschek defines as a Macaulian constitutionalism, 'representative government, individual rights, the right to bear arms, "no taxation without representation," [and] institutional checks and balances'.[20] As a related set of global political discourses, Victorian liberalism broadly embraced a universalism that sought to impose its own limited conception of civilisation on others. For British liberals, this meant that empire was not a paradox, but a natural and logical extension of their worldview. The South Asian and African intelligentsia of this chapter imagined their own citizenship and respectability, related to other social and cultural groups, with a similar brand of cosmopolitanism, that is, with their own imperial eyes. As C. A. Bayly argues about Indian intellectuals, 'they cannibalised, reconstructed and re-authored those ideas, often using them in an intellectual assault on the policies, moral character, and culture of their rulers.... [They] believed that they could rewrite liberal discourse so as to strip it of its coercive colonial features and re-empower it as an indigenous ideological, but one still pointing toward universal progress.'[21]

There is an obvious danger in interpreting the development of Asian and African intelligentsias as a function of modernising 'Angloglobalisation', as an imposition of the British civilising mission rather than as the result of a complex and multi-faceted set of encounters across the world.[22] Niall Ferguson, perhaps the most brash proponent of such an outlook, argues for the modernising legacy of the British Empire against those who identify instead the 'racism, racial discrimination, xenophobia, and related intolerance', all of which, he argues, 'existed long before colonialism'.[23] British governance,

Ferguson believes, brought great benefits, including 'the English language', 'representative assemblies', 'the triumph of capitalism', and 'the Anglicisation of North America and Australasia'.[24] From the opposite side of the political and intellectual spectrum, post-colonial scholars, most notably Frantz Fanon, have described the processes by which the colonised internalise their inferiority by trying to be white (e.g. wearing a white mask), by dressing, talking, and acting 'white'.[25] In a related if less polemical vein, the cultural anthropologists Jean and John Comaroff described the 'colonisation of the mind' of African peoples by evangelical missionaries, inoculating potential converts with the 'quotidian' practices of a middle-class, industrialising British society.[26]

Rather than understanding the practices and behaviours of respectability as a British imposition, it makes more sense to understand them as part of a more complex field of cultural encounters. The cosmopolitan newspaper writers of this chapter were avid readers of the political and cultural currents of a larger world and saw themselves to be modern people. Victorian-era imperialism and globalisation created innumerable sets of cultural connections and borrowings whereby local actors could participate in multiple political, cultural, and social universes without paradox. They could also borrow, embrace, and appropriate cultures, politics, and social norms from multiple sources without abandoning their own histories and experiences.

Men of the (British) world

The cosmopolitan publishers of independent African and South Asian newspapers were bi- or multi-lingual men, who were well-versed in the political discourses of the larger British world, and beyond.[27] The *South African Spectator* boasted on its masthead that it was 'positively cosmopolitan. We know a man and not colour: principles, and not creed.'[28] John Tengo Jabavu, for instance, was a founder of Imbumba Yama Nyama (South African Aborigines' Association) and was in contact with the Aborigines' Protection Society in Britain, which included Charles Dilke and Thomas Fowell Buxton among its members, and frequently wrote letters to their newspaper the *Aborigines' Friend*.[29] He was a leader of a 'Native Combination' in 1885 that agreed, unsuccessfully, to form a branch of the Empire League and considered himself a proud 'Gladstonian Liberal'.[30] He petitioned and corresponded with government officials in Britain, mailing copies of *Imvo Zabantsundu* to British MPs.[31] Yet, as Peregrino's life story demonstrates, South African culture was not only shaped by Britain and the British Empire but by the United States, pan-Africanism, and other transnational currents. The South Asian writers were perhaps more deeply enmeshed in an Anglo-Indian culture, but they demonstrated an avid interest in the history and politics of Britain and the British Empire.[32] Viswanath Narayan Mandalik translated Elphinstone's *History of India* into Marathi and Gujerathi, translated works of Hindu law into English, gave several papers at the Royal Asiatic Society, and edited the transactions of the Literary Society of Bombay.[33] Similarly, Kristo Das Pal was an important member of the British Indian Association and often allied himself with local British merchants and settlers.

These South Asian and African intellectuals were creating and participating in an imperial political culture that was often communicated in both the vernacular (Xhosa and Marathi, for instance) and the lingua franca of empire (English). Their message was accessible to the imperial stakeholders, to colonial administrators and sympathetic parties in Britain and the empire, and to the local, to literate and non-literate people in their local communities. During the royal tours, they negotiated, contested, and remade the national, or transnational, 'imagined community' of empire in print.

Colonial officials were deeply concerned by the politicisation of Africans and South Asians in the empire. The writers of the independent South African and Indian newspapers were socially conservative in the sense that they sought to protect and enhance their own social power and status. While their politics were often radical, particularly in challenging the dominant racial discourses of imperial culture, they always framed their notions of citizenship in loyalty to the monarchy and the British Empire. Importantly, both the Indian National Congress (f. 1885) and the South African Native National Congress (f. 1912), seen as the foremost anti-colonial and nationalist political organisations of the twentieth century, swore allegiance to the British monarch. Colonial officials, however, conflated politicisation with disloyalty.

The British government carefully watched the independent press, with local agents charged with reporting Indian opinion.[34] During the 1875 royal tour, the Viceroy of India, Lord Northbrook, wrote to Philip Wodehouse, the Governor of Bombay, asking him to make a secret inquiry about intentions of the 'Native newspapers in Bombay', whom he later accused of spreading false rumours and of 'exceeding what is consistent with the conduct of loyal subjects'.[35] As we shall see, *Imvo Zabantsundu* was shut down as a traitorous organ of enemy propaganda by the military government of the Cape.

Officials also worried that the dissemination of news and information from the newspapers, through the gossip of the local bazaar or 'the Native school master who read it to them', would inevitably lead to the politicisation of non-literate people of colour.[36] In 1878, the colonial government of India sought to crack down on 'seditious writings' of the native newspapers that constantly complained of the 'injustice and tyranny' of the British government in India.[37] The Viceroy's Council under Lord Lytton passed Act IV of 1878, through which newspapers were subject to seizure if found to 'contain any words, signs, or visible representations likely to excite disaffection to the Government established by law in British India, or antipathy between any persons of different races, castes, religions, or sects in British India'.[38] While this rather extreme measure was repealed in 1881 by Lord Ripon's government, the concern reveals the cultural potency that the native press really had. At the same time, the fact that such virulent political discourses, ones that often criticised colonial or imperial rule, could survive in an empire where, for instance, mutinous sepoys were attached to cannons and blown to bits, says something rather curious about the Janus-faced nature of British rule.

The independent press: India

Independent Indian newspapers began to proliferate in British South Asia during the second half of the nineteenth century. While these newspapers had a circulation of only about 100,000 readers in 1873, the highest single circulation totalling 3,000, they articulated and disseminated a powerful political message that, despite fervent loyalty to the Crown and the British Empire, frightened many colonial officials.[39] Independent vernacular or native newspapers, as they have been called, were typically owned by British-educated, town-dwelling, English-speaking Indians.[40] The newspaper writers of *Native Opinion* and the *Hindoo Patriot* combined political activism against local and imperial injustice and corruption with celebration of India's place in the British Empire. Although the social origins of Viswanath Narayan Mandalik, the founder of *Native Opinion*, differ from those of Harish Chandra Mukherjee and Kristo Das Pal, the successful editors of the *Hindoo Patriot*, all three men combined service and loyalty to the empire, local political interests, journalism, and literary endeavours.[41] All three were part of elite political cultures in large urban centres, where the British offered a degree of self-governance, and thus part of a sub-imperial culture that sought to improve its own status and power through its connections to Britain and by controlling local wealth and politics. They generally looked down on those socially and culturally beneath them but celebrated the princely elites of South Asia as heroes and leaders. While several other publications will be incorporated into the analysis of the independent South Asian press, these organs of 'native opinion' are featured mostly prominently.

Native Opinion was a weekly published in both English and Marathi between 1867 and 1889, founded and edited by Viswanath Narayan Mandalik; a man named Narayan Mahadeo Paramanand took over editorial duties soon after the paper's founding, though Mandalik continued to contribute many or most of the articles.[42] Mandalik was a *chitpávan* Brahmin born in Murud on the Konkan Coast, south of Bombay, in 1833.[43] He took a law degree at the Elphinstone Institution, the predecessor to Elphinstone College, before beginning a career in the colonial service, working in the Sindh for the (in)famous and widely travelled colonial official Bartle Frere, who subscribed to *Native Opinion*, in addition to working as an educational inspector, as a sub-judge at Bassein, as director of the government book depot in Bombay, and as the assistant to the Income Tax Commissioner.[44] He was also a political activist and politician in municipal and imperial politics, becoming mayor of Bombay and serving as a member of the city's exclusive legislative council.[45]

The newspapers in the Bombay Presidency, home of *Native Opinion* and one of the most populated urban spaces on the subcontinent, acted as organs for local educated natives, who were generally excluded by the high property and wealth requirements of municipal citizenship.[46] By 1885, there were already forty-three Indian newspapers in Bombay, and the municipality was characterised by a vibrant but socially exclusive local political culture.[47] The extension of commercial and property rights to local elites under the East India Company and development of limited self-governance by means of a series of Municipal Acts (1865, 1872, 1888) under the Raj were designed to produce a local class of intermediaries and to reduce the financial burden of the imperial government.[48] Local politics and the Bombay Municipal Corporation were dominated by Anglo-Indian settlers and by an elite cadre of Indian traders, industrialists, and landlords.[49] On the whole, Bombay's Indian newspapers 'campaigned for an extension of the municipal franchise as well as for greater and more direct Indian representation on both provincial and imperial legislative councils; they also focused on exposing corruption among the dominant *shetia* (i.e. magnate) class, while keeping up attacks on the colonial state on a range of civil rights' issues'.[50] Mandalik's politics transcended this social bifurcation of Bombay political discourse, between property-owning 'colonial-indigenous' elites and an activist intelligentsia, reflecting a radicalism on his part that is not suitably reflected in the historical literature.[51]

The *Bengal Recorder* (f. 1849) of Calcutta was renamed the *Hindoo Patriot* in 1853 and purchased by Harish Chandra Mukherjee in

1855.[52] Mukherjee was born in 1824 to a 'high-caste Brahmin' family of 'poor circumstances' in Bhowanipore.[53] While the editorship of the paper was in the hands of Kristo Das Pal by the time of the royal tour in 1875, Mukherjee's political activism as editor established the *Patriot* as an important voice in local and imperial politics, most notably for supporting the indigo *ryots* (peasants or farmers) against landowning planters during the 1859 Indigo Revolt, after which he spent the rest of his life (d. 1861) fighting the planters' libel suits against him.[54]

Kristo Das Pal was born in 1839 in Calcutta to a family of the Teli professional caste, and like Mukherjee was celebrated in the Indian literature of his time as a self-made man.[55] He studied at the Oriental Seminary, a non-denominational English-language school for Hindu boys, and at Presidency College, Calcutta, the oldest college in India and an important cultural centre for early nineteenth-century Anglicisation.[56] As a member of the British Indian Association, a loyalist political organisation dominated by Bengali zamindars, he drafted the congratulatory letter to the British government in India following the suppression of the 1857 revolt and later became the organisation's secretary.[57] Much like Viswanath Narayan Mandalik, he came to serve imperial and municipal governments, as a municipal commissioner and on the legislative council of Bengal.[58] As a follower of Mukherjee, he combined fierce criticism of local and imperial corruption and injustice with empire loyalism and respectability.

The capital of the Raj, Calcutta had a configuration of 'colonial-indigenous' *respectables* and municipal governance similar to Bombay. Calcutta, like Bombay, was spatially organised into a central White Town and a peripheral Black Town.[59] P. J. Marshall has argued that 'the whites of Calcutta lavished money and effort on creating for themselves the amenities of what they regarded as civilised British urban life on a scale that left abundant pickings for Indians who were minded to take advantage of their prodigality'.[60] As the cosmopolitan, urban writers of the *Hindoo Patriot* (and *Native Opinion* in Bombay, for that matter) demonstrate, 'an Indian intelligentsia ... responded in a most creative way to aspects of European culture that became available to them in the city'.[61] That is not to say that they mimicked or sought to emulate European settlers, but that they embraced certain aspects of European social and cultural life, building styles, voluntary associations, music, and dress, for instance, as acts of self-fashioning or self-ascription. For the Indian elites of the city, and for those who sought political and social inclusion in municipal politics, their notions of respectability formed the very core of how they imagined themselves as people.

South Asian scholars and Indian nationalists have long identified the municipal politics of Bombay and Calcutta as the hotbeds of proto-nationalism, where future nationalists learned and practised politics. Hugh Tinker argued in his *Foundations of Local Self-Government*:

> When the Indian National Congress was formed, almost all its front rank leadership was recruited from the municipal corporations of the Presidency capitals, to the exclusion of the rest of India. These men alone had acquired experience of public debate, they had formed some kind of philosophy of political action, and through encounters with senior British officials, they had learned something of the art of dealing with the bureaucracy.[62]

During the 1870s and 80s, the 'colonial-indigenous' oligarchy represented by the generation of Mandalik and Pal was being challenged and transcended in both cities by a new generation of more radical young politicians. In Calcutta, the future nationalist Sisir Kumar Ghose, editor of the *Amrita Bazar Patrika*, referred to the entrenched interests that dominated the Calcutta Municipal Corporation, Hindu zamindars, the intelligentsia of the British Indian Association, and local Anglo-Indian traders and settlers, a 'self-seeking plutocracy'.[63] After Bombay was granted a partly elective municipal corporation in 1872, Ghose and his newly founded Indian League began a campaign in 1875, months before the Prince of Wales' visit, for municipal reform; they framed their campaign in populist language but ended up demanding 'equitable and well devised representation'.[64] Ghose's perceived radicalism alienated him from most of his supporters in the Indian League, many of whom came to support the British Indian Association's opposition to the government's proposed reform on the grounds that it restricted the rights of ratepayers by giving the imperial government increased rights of intervention.[65] The ruling BIA compromised with the young men of the Indian League by proposing a reduced property franchise for voters while maintaining the price tag on respectability.[66]

Post-colonial and nationalist historiographies frame the 1870s and 1880s as a period of transition when political figures such as Mandalik and Pal, who represented an old guard of loyalism and elitism, were being transcended by a new vanguard of proto-nationalists. This belief in intellectual change or political awakening is not wrong but belongs to an older historiographical tradition that largely ignores the ambiguous cultural space between collaboration and resistance. On one hand, the old guard's politics, during the royal tour, for instance, were far more radical than the nationalist historiography admits; for alleged mouthpieces of entrenched colonial-indigenous elites, they certainly offered scurrilous criticisms of corrupt and unjust British rule in India.

On the other, the so-called radical proto-nationalist intelligentsia of Calcutta and Bombay continued to couch their politics in the language of loyalism and respectability through the World Wars.

India (1875–76)

Colonial officials imagined, or invented, Queen Victoria to be a true heir to the Mughal emperors. The ritual and spectacle of the Prince of Wales' visit of 1875 was designed to recreate a feudal Mughal past, to visualise a cosmic connection between past and present that would legitimise and justify British rule in India.[67] For the *respectables* who wrote for *Native Opinion*, the *Hindoo Patriot*, and other independent newspapers, however, the royal tour was not about Mughal-style spectacle, but about modern, imperial politics. During the royal tour, the writers of the South Asian native press imagined themselves to be imperial citizens who possessed British rights and responsibilities, a counter-discourse through which they defined their politics against the very *un*-British rule of the Raj.

The independent press participated in a vibrant imperial political culture, openly contesting the unjust policies and practices of British rule. While editorial biases may have differed – based on place, status, patronage, and political outlook – the discourses of imperial citizenship were widely embraced across Indian print culture. They challenged the mercantilist suppression of Indian industry; the 'despotism' of British magistrates and the police; the inaction of the British government to widespread famine; and the heavy burden of taxation.[68] During the tour, they challenged the costs and purposes of the events and defended the Indian princely elite, whom they saw as victimised by the visit. Despite this contestation, they generally expressed a loyalty to the empire and a hope that the Queen's son would convey India's plight to his great mother and to the British people.

For British settlers and administrators, politicisation of this kind was a symptom of ingratitude and disloyalty. During the tour, the editors of the native press were derided for their alleged disloyalty to the Queen by the settler press, who were encouraged by Raj officials to correct their 'mistruths'.[69] The Anglo-Indian *Bombay Gazette* identified the native press, singling out the editors of *Native Opinion*, as 'the chief mischief makers in India ... who, while professing loyalty to the British Government, lose no opportunity of trying to excite ... the bitterest antipathy to British rule and British civilisation'.[70] The editors of *Native Opinion* understood politics as vital to loyalism and citizenship and thus celebrated the attacks by the Anglo-Indian press as 'a very high compliment'.[71] *Rajshahye Samáchár* defended Indian loyalty against such criticism:

> We do not understand how loyalty can be impeached ... or how the omission of a particular act can be construed as disrespect to the British Crown; or how it can be thought that the Prince of Wales is not honoured if some particular part of the town be not illuminated on a particular day; or how natives can be supposed wanting in proofs of good-will to the British Government, because they do not expend a certain sum of money for the purpose.... We do not understand why, thus hankering after a feigned loyalty, Government betrays the levity of its heart; except it be for the object of making a parade before others of its popularity with the natives.[72]

In general, the authors of the independent Indian press argued that the British rule in India was carried out under a veil of secrecy and that the anti-native rhetoric of the Anglo-Indian newspapers, often as the mouthpieces of Raj officials, was a source of Indian hostility to the British government rather than the political agitation of Indian newspapers.[73] This heated debate with the settler press reflects the activism and contestation of the independent Indian press, to which Act IV was a response. They defended themselves as the British government's 'most valuable friends' in India and challenged the ineptitude and mean-spiritedness of the colonial officials who chose to ignore their advice.[74] While professing their loyalty to the Queen and the British Empire, they criticised the tour – the costs, the corruption, and the heavy-handedness – and demanded investments and reforms that would benefit the citizen-subjects of British India.

The South Asian intelligentsia who wrote for *Native Opinion*, the *Hindoo Patriot*, and other newspapers professed their pride in India and its prominent place in the British Empire and understood the empire as their political and cultural universe. *Native Opinion* celebrated India as 'the brightest jewel in the Empire's Crown' without which Britain 'would sink to the level of a second rate power in Europe and [lose] all her Asiatic influence'.[75] They identified the conceptual space between the British political tradition, as 'the mother of law and the nursery of freedom', and British rule in practice, which denied 'citizens of a free empire' the rights and privileges of Britishness.[76] These men did not criticise the Raj because they were disloyal or because they opposed the idea of empire. To the contrary, they challenged the practices and policies of the British government in India because they imagined themselves to be loyal and respectable subjects of the Queen.

In this context, South Asian journalists identified the royal visit as an opportunity for the Indian government to enact fundamental reforms toward a more just rule. Mandalik's *Native Opinion* saw the royal tour as a fitting occasion for the British to extend 'constitutional rights and privileges' to their Indian subjects.[77] While they identified the importance of graciously welcoming their Queen's son, the editors challenged the royal tour – the spectacle of illuminations, fireworks, and dinners – as empty and expensive ritual practices without constructive results, including guaranteed rights for the Queen's Indian subjects.[78] They complained that the government of India acted in a principally un-British way, by making laws 'in defiance of all public opinion and in the aggressiveness observable in every department of the administration', in the style of an 'enlightened despotism'.[79]

These *respectables* were deeply invested in the Prince of Wales as a transformational figure. They generally recognised that the British monarchy had 'no power whatever and can therefore not reduce any kind of taxes, nor remove any kind of grievance' but believed, in the cultural tradition of the patriot Queen, that Victoria the imperial matriarch could exert influence on the government to change their ways.[80] The *Amrita Bazar Patrika* proposed the formation of associations in every district 'to represent the wants and grievances of the people as the wealthy and well-to-do inhabitants of Calcutta will only take care to make everything appear in brilliant colours'.[81] To them, the prince's interest in India was genuine and well intentioned, but the realities of poverty and misrule would be veiled by the ritual stagecraft of the visit:

> But the way in which His Royal Highness has resolved to travel in India is not likely to make him acquainted with the country and its people. For under the present arrangement he will only be able to come in contact with the leading men, who will doubtless seek to appear before the Prince in gay and glittering apparel suited to their rank.... Thus it will be impossible for [the prince] to know whether natives have any grievance at all. He will see through official eyes, and will be made to think after the officials.... The Prince will return and tell his mother that there is no nation so happy as the people of India, and the English papers will proudly proclaim that under the British rule India is flowing with wealth and corn.[82]

They and their countrymen needed to challenge colonial control of the visit and articulate their grievances to the prince. Only then could their imperial citizenship be redeemed, in the benevolence and love of the justice-giving Great Queen.

While educated elites wanted the royal tour to be an opportunity for the British to extend rights and privileges, to see an improved standard of living for loyal subjects of the Queen, they instead witnessed the corruption and meanness of the Raj. The collection of subscriptions on the part of local organising associations to fund tributes to the prince was carried out through 'extortion and oppression' and demands for 'minimum donations'.[83] According to several testimonies, voluntary subscriptions were cajoled out of everyone from the princes to the poorest Indians by bullying and force: 'scores of poor clerks, who could ill afford it, had to come down handsomely or incur the displeasure of their chiefs'.[84] The *Grámbártá Prakáshiká* (West Bengal) argued that the local zamindars would recoup their tour expenses by 'squeezing out ... the hard-earned income of a poverty-stricken tenantry who have barely recovered from the ravages of the recent famine'.[85] The criticism of these practices was directed at the princes, landowners, and organising committees that collected money, but the more fundamental critique pointed toward the financial demands of the Indian government.

While the British government subsidised the tour, paying for the costs of the voyage and the gifts, local communities funded the lion's share of the visit. The South Asian intellectuals of the independent press questioned the costs of the tour on 'this poor country', as the taxed riches of India flowed to British officers and civil servants or back to Britain, and the livelihoods of local weavers were 'sacrifice[d] for the benefit of the Manchester merchants'.[86] The native press criticised exorbitant spending by the government and the princes if not directed toward 'some permanent institution' as a monument to the visit.[87] They argued that fixing roads and bridges, draining dirty, bacteria-infested water, and executing other improvements, even if only within the prince's eyesight, would be far more useful than fireworks. These demands were not symptoms of nationalism or even resistance to empire as an idea. These men were demanding, as loyal subjects, building projects and education, a government responsive to the needs and opinions of its subjects, and the right to critique and challenge the government – that is, a brand of citizenship made in and of the empire.

The *respectables'* conceptualisation of citizenship sought to transcend the differences between Briton and Indian but did not propose democratic or social equality among South Asians. To the contrary, it was deeply informed by notions of respectability and status. The *respectables* wrote in populist rhetoric but often peered condescendingly downward at the unrespectable masses. Mandalik's paper, for instance, was disappointed by the lack of Oriental spectacle in Bombay during the tour. Before the tour began, *Native Opinion* had proposed that the Prince of Wales appear in the kind of 'grandeur and ceremony' that would impress 'the oriental mind', that is, riding an elephant in the manner of 'the Grand Mogul', 'throwing gold and silver pieces to the poor'.[88] They lamented after the procession that their suggestions were ignored. For the masses, it seems, they advocated not for rights and citizenship but for spectacle that would inspire loyalty and 'Asiatic reverence' for the heir to the throne (a somewhat confusing contradiction).[89]

As the 'most valuable friends' of the British, they understood themselves to represent the Indian people.[90] As a social and cultural conduit between the rulers and the ruled, these men imagined that they had a special and important place in Anglo-Indian society as South Asian *respectables*. Their claims to populism were not completely unfounded, however. They lamented the profound poverty of India and the plights of the *ryots* and the weavers. They challenged the structures of rule, the police and the courts system, that affected the lives of all Indians within the reach of imperial rule. However, women, who were the subject of intense debate by British officials, humanitarians, and activists, were wholly absent from their discussions.

As the stories of the Gaekwad of Baroda and the Nizam of Hyderabad demonstrate (Chapter 2), this South Asian press intelligentsia looked to the princes and chiefs as the natural leaders of Indian society and scorned their treatment by Raj officials. The royal tours, many of them argued, were 'only intended to create an impression of power of the British, and to wound the feelings of Native Princes'.[91] The British government and the Anglo-Indian press, they contested, failed to honour the hereditary elites of the Raj and instead questioned their motives and loyalty. With the recent past in mind, both *Native Opinion* and the *Hindoo Patriot* appealed to the faithful devotion of the Indian princes as expressed to the Prince of Wales, which was

> not show loyalty, for it they had chosen they could have backed the revolted soldiery in '57 and turned their own arms against the British government.... It is extremely doubtful that the English could have successfully resisted the sweeping tide of opposition from the natural leaders of the people.[92]

Despite having been 'wronged, robbed, and degraded', the South Asian princes remained loyal to the British Crown.[93] In exchange for their loyalty, the rajahs and nawabs were treated with contempt and abuse. They were pushed and prodded by colonial officials during the royal tour, much to the chagrin of the independent press. To the South Asian *respectables*, the problem with British rule was not disloyalty on the part of South Asian people, but the ineptitude and abuse of the Raj.

The papers argued that relationship between India's 'natural leaders' and the British government had devolved since 1857, from one of relative equality to one between masters and servants. Before the rebellion, the hereditary elite could 'dream that they were the allies and equals of the British government'.[94] By 1875, Britain's South Asian rulers had been 'curtailed', 'reduced to mere shadows'.[95] Their power had been appropriated – and misused – by the British. One of the most important rituals of the tour, the distribution of the Star of India, was seen as a fundamentally empty gesture. Beyond the 'profuse distribution of empty titles', the authors of *Native Opinion* wondered, 'has the prince to do nothing in return for the millions that will be spent in his honour, except the giving of a few paltry presents?'[96] Unlike the South African writers, who saw in princes and chiefs an atavism of a savage past, the editors of the independent Indian press celebrated and honoured hereditary political elites as natural leaders, whose legitimacy had been undermined and reduced by British rule.

The Prince of Wales left the subcontinent in 1876, the same year Queen Victoria became the Empress of India. In many ways, the analysis of the Great Queen's new title by the independent South Asian press mirrored their coverage of the royal tour. To the editors, elevating Queen Victoria to the role of empress was 'calculated to produce in our minds a feeling of pride and grandeur and renown of the Empire'.[97] While arguing that 'the progress of the country in civilisation and modern appliances during the last twenty years has been immense', the writers of *Native Opinion* suggested that a new title meant little 'without any rights or privileges being granted or promised to the people of India'.[98] These are obviously not the sentiments of opposition to British rule in itself, but the protests of loyal subjects and imperial citizens.

The Indian National Congress (INC) was founded a decade later in 1885, not as an agent of nationalism or anti-colonialism but as a loyalist organisation. Dadabhai Naoroji, the second president of the INC, declared in his 1886 inauguration speech:

> It is our good fortune that we are under a rule which makes it possible for us to meet in this manner *(Cheers.)* It is under the civilizing rule of the Queen and people of England that we meet here together, hindered by none, and are freely allowed to speak our minds without the least fear and without the least hesitation. Such a thing is possible only under British rule, and British rule only. *(Loud cheers.)* Then I put the question plainly: Is this Congress a nursery for sedition and rebellion against the British Government? *(Cries of 'No, no'.)* Or is it another stone in the foundation of the stability of that Government?[99]

Later INC 'Radicals' belittled pro-British 'Moderates', or 'Loyalists', as collaborators disconnected from the true feelings of the Indian people.[100] The notion of imperial citizenship, of South Asians who identified with and embraced the British Empire, does not fit comfortably in the nationalist narrative. Empire loyalism on part of Indian *respectables* such as Viswanath Narayan Mandalik, Kristo Pal, and other educated elites had radical implications for their politics. They were, in a very real sense, the intellectual predecessors of the nationalist politicians of the twentieth century. Yet their intellectual contributions to both imperial (and British) political culture and Indian nationalism illustrate the cultural and political vitality of empire loyalism and imperial citizenship.

These Indian discourses of imperial identity and citizenship failed to resonate with the British, even as imperial activists at home were imagining a global community of imperial federation. Despite the rejection, many South Asians held tightly to the historical relationship between Britain and India and the cultural remnants of imperial citizenship. Their approach became delegitimised more and more by the excesses of British rule, such as the Amritsar Massacre and the failure of the British government to enact substantial political reforms. Still, these discourses survived. Mohandas Gandhi's career as a human rights activist began with a Victorian lawyer in Natal, not the dhoti-wearing 'traditionalist' of the 1930s and 40s. Bill Nasson points to the Indian Royal Air Force pilot of the Second World War who named his Hurricane fighter *Amritsar*, a reflection of imperial rule's complex legacy.[101] South Asian immigrants who arrived in post-war Britain experienced conflicted and dualistic notions of belonging, their loyalty to Britain still challenged. These encounters demonstrate the strange and convoluted legacy of British imperialism that can be defined neither by the language of collaboration or resistance nor by identity politics of modern nationalism.

The independent press: South Africa

In South Africa, independent African newspapers were the products and by-products of evangelical missionary schools. In fact, the editors of *Imvo Zabantsundu*, the *South African Spectator*, and *Izwi Labantu* were all Christian mission students, and two were the sons of prominent African clergymen. Unlike the South Asian editors, they were excluded from service in colonial or local governments, yet all three actively participated in the local and imperial politics of South Africa.[102] As missionary students, their brand of social and cultural imperialism centred on a civilising mission to those socially beneath them. Through education, they argued, all people of colour might achieve civilisation and citizenship. And, unlike their South Asian counterparts, they looked toward hereditary and colonial-appointed chiefs with scorn, as atavisms in a modern age. During the royal tour, they appealed to *British* constitutionalism and justice, investing their status as African *respectables* in promoting the vote, education, and loyalty to the British monarchy and the empire.

This brand of respectable politics became acutely pronounced, and challenged, during the South African War (1899–1902), an imperial war fought between the British Empire, including thousands of African and Coloured subjects, and the Afrikaner republics. Colonial administrators, politicians, and intellectuals cast the war as an ideological struggle between British liberty and Afrikaner tyranny (and republicanism). The Prime Minister, Lord Salisbury, appealed to the mythology of the Great Queen when he told the House of Lords in October 1899 that:

> [T]he moment has arrived for deciding whether the future of South Africa is to be a growing and increasing Dutch supremacy or a safe, perfectly established supremacy of the English Queen.... With regard to the future there must be no doubt that the Sovereign of England is paramount; there must be no doubt that the white races will be put upon an equality, and that due precaution will be taken for the philanthropic and kindly and improving treatment of those countless indigenous races of whose destiny, I fear, we have been too forgetful.[103]

People of colour overwhelmingly recognised this difference and served the imperial war effort in great numbers, through 'irregular armed service, scouting, spying and intelligence, supplying crop, livestock, and other goods, and in providing remount, transport riding, and other labour for logistical services'.[104] While local *respectables* challenged the practices of British rule, they broadly attested to the centrality of the British constitution and their great patron the Great Queen as bulwarks against colonial and Afrikaner abuse: 'for them, Britain and its Empire stood for justice, fairness and equality before the law, which meant above all non-racialism in the sense of "equal rights for all civilised men"'.[105] Through the royal tour of 1901, British colonial administrators sought to reinforce this propaganda and to thank colonial subjects across the world for their service to the empire.

The year 1901 also marked the first negotiations aimed at ending the war. When the Boer general Louis Botha tried to negotiate the non-racial franchise out of the war settlement, he posed a threat not only to the franchise, but to respectable status itself, serving to crystallise the difference between British liberty and Afrikaner tyranny. The Cape's non-racial franchise was one of the most prized possessions of African *respectables*. It was remarkably democratic for the nineteenth century: the 1853 constitution required property worth £25 or a salary of £50 in order to vote.[106] The non-racial franchise slowly eroded through a series of registration and voting acts (1887, 1892, 1894), which purged many African and Coloured voters from the voting rolls.[107] Yet, even after 1892, nearly half the voters in the colony were people of colour.[108] John Tengo Jabavu, editor of *Imvo Zabantsundu*, Francis Z. S. Peregrino, of the *South African Spectator*, and Alan Kirkland Soga, editor of *Izwi Labantu*, differed in their political allegiances and in their opinions on the war, but all celebrated and promoted the importance of formal politics within the bounds of the British constitution.

Imvo Zabantsundu (*Native* or *Black Opinion*) of King William's Town was the first newspaper published independently by a person of colour in South Africa. It was a weekly newspaper published in English and Xhosa by a twenty-five-year old Methodist lay preacher named John Tengo Jabavu, starting in 1884, with around 10,000 readers in the Cape, Natal, Basutoland, and the Afrikaner republics.[109] Jabavu's family identified themselves as Mfengu ('Fingo') people, but he was educated at the Methodist mission station at Healdtown and took up a teaching post at Somerset East. He was an avid student and teacher of languages, including English, Latin, and Greek, and wrote for the liberal settler newspaper *Cape Argus* under a *nom de plume*.[110]

Between 1881 and 1884, he had edited *Isigidimi Sama Xosa* (*Xhosa Messenger*) for the Scottish missionaries at Lovedale but was ousted for openly criticising the Cape government one too many times.[111] Jabavu became an important and active figure in Cape politics, campaigning for white politicians and advocating a brand of non-racial, respectable liberal politics. He was allied with a group of progressive Cape politicians, which included John X. Merriman, James-Rose Innes, Saul Solomon, and J. W. Sauer, and was a sought-after electioneer in districts where African votes affected election outcomes. His political allies also provided the funding for the newspaper, which was printed on the presses of the *Cape Mercury*.[112]

Framing South African politics as a struggle between British liberty and Afrikaner tyranny and republicanism, he was, until 1898, a staunch and vocal opponent of the Afrikaner Bond, the Cape political party that represented Boer interests, and worked tirelessly to organise an English-speaking progressive coalition in order to defeat it.[113] In 1897, his dream of a broad-church British party emerged in the form of the Progressive Party, led by Cecil Rhodes, with whom he briefly allied. Political disagreements with the Progressives and the alliance of his friends John X. Merriman and J. W. Sauer with the Bond, however, pushed him toward a shift of allegiance.[114]

In March 1898, Jan Hofmeyr, the Bond leader, proclaimed that he was not and never had been hostile to African political rights, beginning his campaign to vie for African voters.[115] Jabavu declared Hofmeyr the new standard-bearer for 'true British principle' in South African politics, in opposition to Cecil Rhodes' 'equal rights for white men only'.[116] His allegiance to the Bond, combined with his pacifism during the South African War, would make him a lightning rod of political controversy, to the point that his voice, *Imvo Zabantsundu*, was silenced in August 1901 by the military government of the Cape.

Francis Z. S. Peregrino, editor of the Cape Town English-language newspaper the *South African Spectator*, came to South Africa only in 1900 because, he said, 'at the outbreak of war ... [he] turned his thoughts to South Africa and anticipating that when peace had been proclaimed and the whole country is under the British flag, progress and prosperity are bound to follow, [and] he made up his mind to come here to devote his pen and brain to the service of the native people'.[117] He had been born in Accra in Gold Coast to a family involved with local Wesleyan missionaries: his uncle was one of the first Wesleyan missionaries of African descent.[118] He was educated in England and lived there until around 1890, when he moved to the United States.[119] He demonstrated particular interest in the African Methodist Episcopal (AME) Church, an evangelical missionary organisation founded by African Americans in Philadelphia, and pan-Africanist ideology. He often deferred to his colleagues at *Izwi* on local matters he considered controversial, such as the suppression of *Imvo*, but always stressed the need for cooperation among people of colour. Despite only coming to South Africa a year before the royal tour, he was chosen by a committee of other respectable men of colour to present the 'native address' to the Duke and Duchess of Cornwall. Having widely travelled in the British world, Peregrino articulated his belief in British citizenship through education, the ballot box, and empire loyalism.

Within fifteen months of the paper's founding in 1897, Alan Kirkland Soga became editor of *Izwi Labantu* (*Voice of the People*), founded by Walter Benson Rubusana and published in Xhosa and English from East London. Soga's mother was Scottish, and he was educated in Scotland.[120] His father Tiyo Soga, an important adviser to the Xhosa chief Sandile during the royal tour of 1860, was trained at the University of Glasgow and became the first African Presbyterian minister.[121] Alan Soga was a clerk in Tembuland as late as 1897 when he resigned, according to the *Cape Argus*, because he could not

> consistently with the position he occupied in the service, render the Natives the assistance which is desirable in the present crisis.... He charges that his action, which has been taken on his own initiative, will act as an incentive to Native and Coloured friends to vote solidly for the British party and the maintenance of that supremacy which is necessary for their welfare in the future.[122]

Izwi Labantu was founded, in a very real sense, to counter the dominance of Jabavu and his paper, which was by then seen by many of his opponents as an organ of the Afrikaner Bond.[123] Soga apparently had a distaste for Jabavu, as a Mfengu, but this ethnic rivalry was a minor sub-plot to a far more vibrant political one. While subsidised by the arch-imperialist Cecil Rhodes and his Progressive Party, Soga's paper maintained a stridently independent editorial perspective.[124] He loudly supported the British cause in the war against his nemesis Jabavu, who also claimed to be pro-British, and could hardly contain his satisfaction when *Imvo Zabantsundu* was banned.

South Africa (1901)

Constructions of race and difference profoundly informed the making of modern South Africa. Scholars have long sought the origins of the twentieth-century racial order in the nineteenth-century British Empire in southern Africa. They have searched the cosmopolitan world of Cape Town, the frontier farms and mission stations of the Eastern Cape, and the goldfields of the Rand, producing a thoughtful and useful historical literature that has reshaped the contours of South African historical studies.[125] Urban segregation, spatial controls and native reserves, pass cards, and political disenfranchisement all emerged, not in the 1948 victory of the National Party or even in the 1910 Union of South Africa, but in the British colonial state of the nineteenth century.

The non-racial politics of the South African newspapermen – John Tengo Jabavu (*Imvo Zabantsundu*), Alan Soga (*Izwi Labantu*), and Francis Z. S. Peregrino (*South African Spectator*) – demonstrate that this modern racial order was not a foregone conclusion. While they and their progressive settler allies were characterised by what might be described as imperialist tendencies, to transform others in their own image, the notions of citizenship they articulated cannot be conflated with the more racialist and exclusionary politics of imperial culture. They invested their notion of imperial citizenship in the politics of respectability and in the medium of an independent print culture. They imagined a future in the empire, where all respectable citizen-subjects of the Queen shared the same rights and privileges.

The most prized possession of their respectability – the 'liberal' Cape franchise – came under attack during the late nineteenth century. In this context, these *respectables* understood the South African War to be a defining moment in the future social and political order of southern Africa. They feared, rightly so, that the post-war settlement would solidify white dominance, a union of British and Boer, over the non-white populations of southern Africa. And the Cape franchise was one of the earliest and most controversial impasses during the negotiations to end the war. Jabavu foresaw, appealing to the language of the *Aborigine's Friend*, that *white* settlers would 'come together ... over the body of "the nigger"', to subjugate all people of colour.[126] Jabavu, Soga, and Peregrino sought to avert this fate and to make a new future for South Africa by claiming their rights as British subjects. Alan Soga fiercely disagreed with John Tengo Jabavu's pacifism, and their fierce political rivalry only developed further over the course of the war. While they disagreed with each other over the politics of the war, they all interpreted its meaning through the lens of an imperial citizenship.

The Duke and Duchess of Cornwall – the future King George V and Queen Mary – visited South Africa less than a year after the death of George's grandmother, Victoria. The tour itself was a by-product of the South African War, designed by Joseph Chamberlain, the Colonial Secretary, to convey thanks for imperial service in the war and to bolster loyalty during troubled times for the empire. The future King's visit to war-torn South Africa was nearly cancelled, because of an outbreak of bubonic plague.[127] The death of the Great Queen and the ongoing conflict profoundly informed the responses by people of colour to the royal tour. They had firmly stood by the empire in a time of war and appealed, as loyal subjects of the Great Queen and their new King, and future subjects of the Duke of Cornwall, for a post-war South Africa where all people shared the rights and responsibilities of imperial citizens.

'The vaunted teleology of the Queen's rule' – the promise of 'the mother's compassion and justice' – was a product of colonial propaganda that was appropriated by local *respectables*.[128] In her death, they sought to redeem this promise by promoting a social order that did not deny any of her loyal subjects their rights. *Imvo Zabantsundu* expressed grief over the loss of this Queen 'so precious to all of her subjects because of her transcendent virtues, and *not less* to her Native subjects in South Africa'.[129] Jabavu celebrated the Victorian era as an age of improvement, of 'increasing comfort and well-being for the masses', liberty 'advancing in all directions', new and improved technology, the advance of education and Christianity, and less crime.[130] Of course, the *Pax Britannica* was also an era of violence, dispossession, and even disenfranchisement for people of colour in South Africa and the empire. But, Victoria the 'Mother, wife, and Queen' as a symbol represented progress toward justice and equality for *all* of her subjects, an unfulfilled promise.[131] The *South African Spectator* predicted, as a consequence of her death, 'the dawn of a new era, one of understanding and perfect concord between the races'.[132]

In the face of intense criticism, most notably from Soga, the 'pro-Boer' Jabavu sought to prove his loyalty to the empire through expressions of grief. In a letter to *Imvo Zabantsundu*, 'N.S.B.' complimented Jabavu's impeccable loyalism and his deep, heartfelt articulation of grief (the author also noted that the paper's black border of mourning was much more pronounced than that of other King William's Town journals).[133] 'Whatever may be said of the loyalty of the newspapers and their Editors', N.S.B. wrote, John Tengo Jabavu was 'not surpassed by any'.[134] The South African War was a rather dark period in Jabavu's political career, and his need to express loyalty was particularly acute. The political discourses over his loyalty in the days following Queen Victoria's death, particularly his very public disagreements with Soga, reflect on the complexities of 'native politics'.

Jabavu's 'support' for the Afrikaner Bond was framed without a discourse of British politics. While Soga identified him as a traitor, the real danger Jabavu represented to the wartime British government of the Cape was in demanding the rights of citizenship and in rejecting the jingoism of the war, arguing that, from the perspective of the colonised, there was *very* little difference between British and Boer settlers. Despite the intense criticism, *Imvo* claimed to be the most authentic voice of *British* political culture in South Africa and participated in a larger imperial political discourse about loyalty, jingoism, and the war.

Both Soga and Peregrino strongly supported the British war effort. The pacifism and pro-Boerism of *Imvo* was unacceptable to Soga, who belittled Jabavu's politics as treason in a time of war. He condemned those who, like Jabavu, dared to conflate Briton with Boer. Both of the pro-war papers (*Izwi Labantu* and the *South African Spectator*) advertised Boer atrocities and promoted African service to the empire. In this context, Peregrino confidently asserted that

> the loyalty of the coloured people during these troublons [*sic*] times has been spontaneous and unquestionable. From all parts of the Colony they appeal to be allowed to bear their share in the responsibilities, and to participate in the sacrifices necessary to the firm, and permanent establishment of His Majesty's beneficent rule under which the coloured people, are afforded full protection.[135]

As an advocate of the war, Soga was also a militant supporter of men such as Cecil Rhodes and Alfred Milner, the brand of arch-imperialist who represent the empire's most xenophobic and expansionist tendencies. Few histories of the British Empire account for such complexities – of pro-empire, pro-Boer, even pro-imperialist people of colour. These *respectables* did not support British rule as the better of two evils, but as an investment in a just and more equitable future that lived up to the promises of Britishness.

An analysis of the debates and issues, always legitimised and justified within a frame of loyalism, of these months between Victoria's death and the arrival of the Duke of York is telling. The pages of the newspapers, for instance, debated the value of literary education for 'Natives', which proved to be vitally important to the status-based vision of such *respectables*. Letters articulating the dangers of 'Native education' were fiercely refuted. The editors even advocated that the 'Native memorial' to the late Queen Victoria ought to be a scholarship for worthy African students, in order to celebrate the 'progress of education and religion during Queen Victoria's reign'.[136] That said, their point was not that all Africans deserved a 'literary education', but that no subject of the King should be denied one on the basis of his or her race. At the same time, these discourses reflected a belief in the 'civilising mission', a desire to raise up their savage brethren to the heights of civilisation and to transform South Africans in their own image.

Cape politics figured most importantly in the pages of the papers. The editors of the independent South African press were by and large not democrats; they generally believed that only *men* of a certain education and status ought to possess the vote. In the months before the royal visit, the planned resignation of Richard Solomon, the (white) representative in the Cape Parliament for Tembuland, infuriated Jabavu.[137] Jabavu has been criticised by nationalist historians for accepting, even advocating, white representation for African constituencies, as might be evidenced in the discussion over Solomon's seat. Jabavu's vision for the South African future, and that of the 'better class' of Africans, was distinctly centred on non-racial status, and his politics reflected both this bias and his sense of political pragmatism. As African liberals, they emphasised the need to work within the political and legal bounds of the constitution. Solomon was chastised by *Imvo Zabantsundu* for resigning mid-term and for making the announcement in advance, which would engender 'excitement' and would give time for the electorate to be 'vigorously canvassed'.[138]

These concerns demonstrate the complex political discourses of educated elites in South Africa. On one hand, the concern over 'excitement' was presumably classist, distaste for the possibility of popular reaction and disorder in the towns and countryside of Tembuland, even though the franchise itself was rather limited. On the other, it reflects the concern that 'sojourners in the territories [settlers, missionaries, business interests?] will claim to be heard before the *permanent* residents'.[139] Jabavu advocated that the voters of Tembuland should be allowed 'the freest possible scope in selecting a representative', without outside interference and manipulation, and that they should 'insist on their undoubted rights, and put forward their own candidate'.[140] In this context, the issue was not *specifically* African rights, but that of just and fair elections in which 'irrespective of race' all of 'His Majesty's [qualified] subjects' could vote.[141] Racial politics would serve only to 'retard the true progress of the country'.[142]

These men also promoted respectability by emphasising the virtues of cleanliness and sobriety. The *Spectator* published an editorial on that most ubiquitous Victorian value, cleanliness, titled, 'Let Us Be Clean': a tirade against 'the picturesque filth which is permitted to strut about the streets to the delight of the enemies of the race, and the advocates for the inferior treatment of the race but to the disgust of the *decent and respectable citizen*'.[143] Elsewhere Peregrino worried that 'the rising generation [which was being allowed] to sink to the level of the Hooligan' and the 'contagion' of lawlessness.[144] 'Cleanliness, honestly, industry, and self-respect', he argued, 'are habits which sit as well on [whites] as on [people of colour].'[145] Self-fashioning themselves as respectable and modern, these men of the (British) world advocated rights for all loyal and respectable subject-citizens, regardless of race or ethnicity.

On the eve of the royal visit, Jabavu's *Imvo Zabantsundu* was suppressed by the military government of the Cape. Colonial officials kept a careful eye on independent African newspapers, and Jabavu's pacifism and 'pro-Boer' politics were deemed too dangerous for the royal visit and the war effort. Soga was elated by the silencing of Jabavu. *Izwi* celebrated its rival's demise with the headline, 'IMVO R.I.P.':

> NEMESIS – which publishes arrogant and tyrannical abuse of prosperity, has found out our native contemporary at last.... Frankly, we have consistently opposed the pro-Boer policy of 'Imvo', and its unfriendly attitude towards those friends of progress and good Government, who made it possible for that paper to establish itself.... We feel deeply the humiliation cast upon the native press, just entering on the threshold of life.... What an opportunity for our enemies to seize upon!... The magnanimity of the British race is wonderful. Perhaps the moral lessons to be gained by this serious blow, will not be altogether lost, but will work out for the good to the future of the native press that has to be.[146]

Soga, in haste to judge an old rival, unfairly concluded that Jabavu was disloyal, the same error that was often made by settlers and colonial officials about the African press as a whole. They confused independent political opinions with disloyalty.

In the context of this political crisis, the royal tour represented an important opportunity for the South African intelligentsia to mourn the loss of the Great Queen, to celebrate their new King, and to demonstrate loyalty to *their* empire. Peregrino looked forward to the 'spontaneous outbursts of loyalty' that would remind the King's subjects why they were fighting and inform the rebels as to the futility of their exercise.[147] These men were particularly heartened by the inclusion of notable *respectables* such as Peregrino in the tour. *Imvo Zabantsundu* celebrated that loyal Africans would be recognised as important members of the imperial community.[148] Despite this inclusion, the independent press came to question imperial dedication to the King's loyal subjects of colour, in part because they were marginalised in royal ceremonies in favour of hereditary elites.

Peregrino, who had arrived in South Africa only a year earlier from the United States, was chosen by the community to deliver a 'native address' to the Duke and Duchess of Cornwall. He denied rumours that the Colonial Office had screened his address or that a 'white man' had presented it to the duke.[149] The address was overwhelmingly directed not at the duke's father, Edward VII, but to the memory of his grandmother, Victoria the Good, under whom 'the shackles of slavery were struck off our feet'.[150]

While encouraged by this encounter, all three men were concerned that the stagecraft of colonial officials would suppress demonstrations of spontaneous loyalty by common people and misrepresent the character of South Africa's native population.[151] Specifically, they were concerned that the people of South Africa would be represented by 'chiefs and headmen', rather than 'the most enlightened of our people'.[152] To Soga, this exclusion would deny the duke and duchess a 'fair opportunity of gauging the true state of civilisation and improvement arrived at by the natives'.[153] Much of their scorn was directed at the ornamental rituals described in Chapter 2, the durbar-like rituals and war dances, and the hereditary elites who performed in them.

They argued that these rituals misrepresented the progress of South Africa during the reign of Queen Victoria and focused the duke's attention on a corrupt and dependent aristocracy. The *Spectator*, for instance, mocked plans for the performance of a Zulu war dance as 'buffoonery', a cultural relic of an uncivilised past'.[154] *Izwi Labantu* shared the 'amazement and feelings of disgust at the perpetuation of customs that are condemned by all civilised natives' and suggested that natives ought to sing the national anthem instead.[155] They argued that the genuine loyalty of both the lower classes and of the enlightened, respectable classes was being suppressed by the colonial officials.[156] It was, they suggested, the African intelligentsia, who 'fully realise[d] the trend of British policy, and the advantage that loyalty offers'.[157]

In the aftermath of the tour, Soga and Peregrino pressed for a war settlement that considered the service and loyalty of South Africa's non-white population. In this, the intelligentsia of the independent South African press were articulating a brand of imperial citizenship and identity, even so far as to advocate imperial federation! Loyalty to the monarchy was framed in a vision of British rights and respectable status. The editors of these papers were not only claiming Britishness but also arguing that their understanding of it was more authentic, closer to its *true* ideals, as clearly articulated in their debates over the terms of peace. In April 1901, the *Spectator* had argued that the settlement must be ended on 'amicable' terms, but that

> it would be contrary to all precedent and altogether at variance *with British traditions* to surrender the rights and endanger the safety of the loyal native and coloured citizen even to that end. We believe that in view of all the circumstances precedent to the assumption of hostilities, an unconditional surrender would have been in order, but failing that, we believe that the conclusion of peace on any basis other than that of equal rights to all His Majesty's *civilised subjects*, would be a retrogression.[158]

When the *Imvo Zabantsundu* returned to the presses in October 1902, over a year after being proscribed, Jabavu began not with a defence of his politics but with an ode to Queen Victoria and the profound progress accomplished during her reign.[159] He went on to imagine a post-war South African politics where 'Dutch, British, and Natives have a right to be' and all 'should be accorded the common rights of *citizenship*', of shared 'prosperity' and 'responsibility'.[160] This imperial political culture survived its betrayal during the South African War intact. Yet its message continued, with few exceptions, to fall on deaf ears, both in Cape Town and London.

The alternative print culture of South Africa expanded rapidly in the decade following the war. No fewer than nine new African, Coloured, and Indian newspapers began publication between 1901 and 1910.[161] Jabavu and Soga remained fierce political rivals. When Soga helped found the Native Press Organisation (NPA), Jabavu refused to participate.[162] They participated in separate political organisations and organised separate protests.[163] In April 1901, *Izwi Labantu* closed.[164] *Imvo Zabantsundu* survived, with the editorship passing to Jabavu's son Alexander in 1921, but Jabavu's consistently erratic politics (which was nothing new) and the emergence of a new generation of political leaders limited his influence. F. Z. S. Peregrino continued to publish the *South African Spectator* until 1908, but he has left little in terms of a historical record.[165]

The end of the South African War brought about a transformation of South African politics that would effectively shut out non-whites and inspire a nationalist politics. The Treaty of Vereeniging (1902) brought the whole of South Africa effectively under British rule, with promises of local rule under the British Crown for the former Boer republics. The issue of African voting rights was temporarily avoided, and the pre-war franchises remained largely intact. The Union of South Africa (1910) created a federal state that abandoned the enfranchisement of non-whites in the name of '[white] unity and reconciliation'.[166] Jabavu, who would travel with an African and Coloured delegation to petition the imperial government in 1909 (see Chapter 5), wrote, 'That cow of Great Britain has now gone dry.'[167]

Conclusion

Bill Nasson has demonstrated in his excellent studies of African service to the empire during the South African War and the First World War that a 'vigorous, Western-educated minority' 'retain[ed] their optimistic faith in the British imperial project, despite its palpably wounding betrayal of their tenuous rights and interests', until the end of empire and beyond.[168] These people were neither, as older generations of historical literature have presented them, colonial collaborators nor proto-nationalists, but pro-empire African and Asian liberals whose identities often centred on loyalism and respectability. Loyalism was not so simply a means to an end. Patriotism and service to the empire, specifically, was a 'chance to acquire ... a just and recognised status as loyal subjects of the Crown'.[169] Demonstrations of loyalty and patriotism were not inauthentic – a 'subversive' ploy – nor were they articulated without knowledge of the obvious inequality and abuses of colonial rule.

These *respectables* claimed British political traditions and claimed Britishness in an effort to transform the very *un*-British practices of colonial rule. As Leon de Kock argues, they demonstrated 'evidence of *desired identification* with the colonizing culture as an *act of* affirmation, a kind of publicly declared "struggle" that does not oppose the terms of a colonial culture but insists on a *more pure* version of its originating legitimation'.[170] They imagined their political, cultural, and social universe as an imperial and transnational one. Educated in missionary and other British schools, these elites were nurtured by the British to be the intermediaries of empire. In embracing an imperial culture, however, the 'native' intelligentsia of India and South Africa, and other locales across the British Empire, articulated a vision of imperial citizenship that challenged the conceptual space between the theory and reality of British rule.

This emergence of this imperial political culture paralleled the development of the ritualistic practices described in Chapter 2. As British rule sought to appropriate one form of politics, which they imagined to be traditional and hierarchical, local *respectables* were forging a new one, which they imagined to be modern and cosmopolitan. While the colonial experiences of India and South Africa were unquestionably different, the development of comparable political practices and traditions and the emergence of a transnational class of Western-educated elites suggest the shared experiences of colonial rule across the global spaces of the British Empire. The historical actors of this chapter also demonstrate the limits of collaboration and resistance as ways of describing the colonial past.

Imperial citizenship represents a vibrant cultural and political tradition of the nineteenth- and early twentieth-century British world. Its failure as a discourse was as much about British inaction to live up to the promises of the liberal empire as violent and illiberal action. As a transitional period, the late nineteenth-century empire was a dynamic and interconnected political space where a modern, global politics of respectability and imperial citizenship was made. In this context, the nationalist political movements of the twentieth century have their origins in local political traditions as well as the intellectual milieu of imperial politics. The cosmopolitan and modern authors, intellectuals, and activists of this chapter are relevant and important to the history of Britain and Britishness, even if their claims to Britishness and citizenship fell on deaf ears. In the imperial networks of empire, their message was short-circuited, even if it importantly paralleled the efforts to foster a white imperial citizenship in Britain and the settler empire.

Notes

1 *South African Spectator*, 24 August 1901.

2 *South African Spectator*, 7 September 1901.

3 There is a rich and important historiography emerging on this topic. In particular, see Benjamin N. Lawrance, Emily Lynn Osborn, and Richard L. Roberts, eds, *Intermediaries, Interpreters, and Clerks: African Employees in the Making of Colonial Africa* (Madison, WI, 2006).

4 This is not to say that Indian nationalism was a creation of British imperial culture in the sense suggested by an older generation of historians such as David Washbrook or Anil Seal. While Seal has been framed, perhaps with some justification, as an imperial apologist, this study argues that imperial culture was ripped from its conceptual foundations and reappropriated by local peoples; the emergence of Indian nationalism out of imperial culture, then, was not an accidental consequence of British importation of ideas about nationhood or modernity. Moreover, its focus on 'elites', rather than the 'subaltern masses', is a reflection of their intimate relationship with

British rule, not a conceptual elitism. For more on this older historiography, see Anil Seal, *The Emergence of Indian Nationalism: Competition and Collaboration in the Later Nineteenth Century* (Cambridge, 1968); David Washbrook, *The Emergence of Provincial Politics: The Madras Presidency 1870–1920* (Cambridge, 1976).

5 The role of Britishness in South African has been the subject of many recent studies. See Vivian Bickford-Smith, 'Writing about Englishness: South Africa's Forgotten Nationalism', in *Empire and After: Englishness in Postcolonial Perspective*, ed. Graham MacPhee and Prem Poddar (Oxford, 2007), 57–72; Vivian Bickford-Smith, 'Revisiting Anglicisation in the Nineteenth Century Cape Colony', in *The British World: Diaspora, Culture and Identity*, ed. Carl Bridge and Kent Fedorowich (Portland, OR, 2003), 82–95; Vivian Bickford-Smith, *Ethnic Pride and Racial Prejudice in Victorian Cape Town* (Cambridge, 1995); John Lambert, 'Britishness, South Africanness and the First World War', in *Rediscovering the British World*, ed. Phillip Buckner and R. Douglas Francis (Calgary, 2005), 285–304; Bill Nasson, *Abraham Esau's War: A Black South African War in the Cape, 1899–1902* (Cambridge, 1991); Bill Nasson, 'Why They Fought: Black Cape Colonists and Imperial Wars, 1899–1918', *International Journal of African Historical Studies* 37, no. 1 (2004): 55–70; Andrew Thompson, 'The Languages of Loyalism in Southern Africa, c. 1870–1939', *English Historical Review* 118, no. 477: 617–50; Elizabeth Van Heyningen and Pat Merrett, '"The Healing Touch": The Guild of Loyal Women of South Africa 1900–1912', *South African Historical Journal* 47 (November 2003): 24–50.

6 While legal citizenship did not exist until 1948, colonial subjects could (in theory) freely move within the British Empire and to and from the British Isles, suggesting that the empire was understood by British politicians and administrators as a single political community.

7 See, for instance, Catherine Hall, *Civilising Subjects: Metropole and Colony in the English Imagination, 1830–1867* (Chicago, 2002); Mrinalini Sinha, *Colonial Masculinity: The 'Manly Englishman' and the 'Effeminate Bengali' in the Late Nineteenth Century* (Manchester, 1995).

8 Michael Oliver West, *The Rise of an African Middle Class* (Bloomington, IN, 2002), 14; Sinha, *Colonial Masculinity*, 15–6.

9 Marilyn Lake and Henry Reynolds, *Drawing the Global Colour Line: White Men's Countries and the International Challenge of Racial Equality* (Cambridge, 2008).

10 Leon de Kock, *Civilising Barbarians: Missionary Narrative and African Textual Response in Nineteenth-Century South Africa* (Johannesburg, 1996); Homi Bhabha, *The Location of Culture* (New York, 1995). On the problem of authenticity, see Carol A. Breckenridge and Peter van der Veer, 'Orientalism and Postcolonial Predicament', in *Orientalism and the Postcolonial Predicament*, ed. Carol A. Breckenridge and Peter van der Veer (Philadelphia, 1993), 14–16.

11 For Ronald Robinson and Jack Gallagher, local 'collaborators' functioned as agents of imperial rule in exchange for a specific set of social and economic benefits. The most developed statement of this approach is Ronald Robinson, 'Non-European Foundations of European Imperialism: Sketch for a Theory of Collaboration', in *Studies of the Theory of Imperialism*, ed. Roger Owen and Robert B. Sutcliffe (New York, 1972), 117–42.

12 Saul Dubow, 'How British Was the British World? The Case of South Africa', *JICH* 37, no. 1 (2009), 2–3.

13 This profound, if often conflicted identification with Britain and Britishness on the part of colonial and Commonwealth immigrants has been prominently featured in literature and film. See Zadie Smith, *White Teeth* (New York, 2001); Andrea Levy, *Small Island* (New York, 2005).

14 P. J. Cain and A. G. Hopkins, 'Gentlemanly Capitalism and British Overseas Expansion II: New Imperialism, 1850–1945', *Economic History Review* 40, no. 1 (1987), 1; David Cannadine, *The Decline and Fall of the British Aristocracy* (New York, 1999); Richard Price, *British Society, 1680–1880: Dynamism, Containment and Change* (Cambridge, 1999).

15 Bickford-Smith, *Ethnic Pride*, 39.

16 Hugh Cunningham, 'The Languages of Patriotism, 1750–1914', *History Workshop Journal* 12 (Autumn 1981), 22.
17 Max Weber, 'Status Groups and Classes', in *The Essential Weber*, ed. Sam Whimster (New York, 2004), 177–8.
18 Les Switzer, 'The Beginnings of African Protest Journalism', in *South Africa's Alternative Press: Voices of Protest and Resistance, 1880–1960*, ed. Les Switzer (Cambridge, 1997), 61.
19 Uday Singh Mehta, *Liberalism and Empire: A Study in Nineteenth-Century British Liberal Thought* (Chicago, 1999), 20.
20 Theodore Koditschek, *Liberalism, Imperialism, and the Historical Imagination: Nineteenth-Century Visions of a Greater Britain* (Cambridge, 2011), 287.
21 C. A. Bayly, *Recovering Liberties: Indian Thought in the Age of Liberalism and Empire* (Cambridge, 2012), 3–4.
22 Niall Ferguson, *Empire: The Rise and Demise of the British World Order and the Lessons for World Power* (New York, 2003).
23 Ferguson, *Empire*, xxv.
24 Ferguson, *Empire*, xxiii–xxv.
25 Frantz Fanon, *Black Skin, White Masks*, trans. Charles Lam Markmann (New York, 1967).
26 Jean and John Comaroff, *Of Revelation and Revolution: Christianity, Colonialism, and Consciousness in South Africa*, vol. 1 (Chicago, 1991).
27 Elizabeth Elbourne has written rather skilfully on the development of a broader 'Aborigine' consciousness across the 'imperial networks' of the British world. See Elizabeth Elbourne, 'Indigenous Peoples and Imperial Networks in the Early Nineteenth Century: The Politics of Knowledge', in *Rediscovering the British World*, ed. Phillip Buckner and R. Douglas Francis (Calgary, 2005), 59–86.
28 *South African Spectator*, 23 August 1902.
29 Catherine Higgs, *The Ghost of Equality: The Public Lives of D.D.T. Jabavu of South Africa, 1885–1959* (Cape Town, 1997), 12; *Imvo Zabantsundu*, 30 April 1901, 3; Stanley Trapido, 'White Conflict and Non-White Participation in the Politics of the Cape of Good Hope' (PhD dissertation, University of London, 1970), 290–7.
30 Trapido, 'White Conflict and Non-White Participation', 291–2.
31 Trapido, 'White Conflict and Non-White Participation', 290, 297.
32 I use the term Anglo-Indian to mean a hybrid British-Asian culture, not its more traditional definition of British culture in India.
33 *Eminent Indians on Indian Politics*, ed. Chunilal Lalubhai Parekh (Bombay, 1892), 173.
34 See *Indian Newspaper Reports, c. 1868–1942, from the British Library, London* (Marlborough, 2005–). These reports from the India Office collection at the British Library reproduce many newspapers that have been otherwise lost for ever.
35 Northbrook to Wodehouse, 3 June 1875, 8 January 1876, 4 December 1876, BL MSS Eur D726/7.
36 H. S. Caldecott to Gordon Sprigg, 11 February 1896, Rhodes Papers, Bodleian Library, Oxford, vol. 6.2, no. 96. Cited in Stanley Trapido, 'White Conflict and Non-White Participation', 321.
37 Uma Das Gupta, 'The Indian Press 1870–1880: A Small World of Journalism', *Modern Asian Studies* 11 (Spring 1977), 213.
38 Act for the Better Control of Publications in Oriental Languages, Act IX of 1878.
39 Gupta, 'The Indian Press', 229.
40 Gupta, 'The Indian Press', 216.
41 *Native Opinion* and the *Hindoo Patriot* have been identified for the purposes of this study because they were available and their origins can be traced. Many of the independent newspapers no longer exist outside of British intelligence on them.
42 Gupta, 'The Indian Press', 217.
43 *Eminent Indians on Indian Politics*, 171.
44 *Eminent Indians on Indian Politics*, 171–2.
45 Gupta, 'The Indian Press', 228.

46 *Eminent Indians on Indian Politics*, 801.
47 Sandip Hazareesing, 'The Quest for Urban Citizenship: Civic Rights, Public Opinion, and Colonial Resistance in Early Twentieth-Century Bombay', *Modern Asian Studies* 34 (October 2000), 801.
48 Hazareesing, 'The Quest for Urban Citizenship', 798–801.
49 Hazareesing, 'The Quest for Urban Citizenship', 800–2. For the thirty-five years between 1888 and 1923, the municipal franchise remained virtually unchanged, with 1 per cent of the population (11,500 municipal residents) enfranchised in 1914. According to Hazareesing, of seventy-two members of the Bombay Municipal Corporation, there were seventeen landlords, fifteen mill owners, seven merchants, and twelve European businessmen in 1914. Also see A. D. Gordon, *Businessmen and Politics: Rising Nationalism and a Modernising Economy in Bombay 1918–1933* (Delhi, 1978).
50 Hazareesing, 'The Quest for Urban Citizenship', 801.
51 Hazareesing, 'The Quest for Urban Citizenship', 801.
52 Charles Edward Buckland, 'Harish Chandra Mukerji' and 'Grish Chandra Grose' in *Dictionary of Indian Biography* (London, 1906), 162, 304.
53 Srikanta Roy, *Bengal Celebrities* (Calcutta, 1906), 75; Buckland, 'Harish Chandra Mukerji', 304–5.
54 Buckland, 'Harish Chandra Mukerji', 305.
55 Charles Edward Buckland, 'Kristo Das Pal', in *Dictionary of Indian Biography*, 326–7.
56 Buckland, 'Kristo Das Pal'.
57 Nagendra Nath Ghosh, *Kristo Das Pal: A Study* (Calcutta, 1887), 9, 14.
58 Ghosh, *Kristo Das Pal*, 15.
59 See Swati Chattopadhyay, 'Blurring Boundaries: The Limits of "White Town" in Colonial Calcutta', *Journal of the Society of Architectural Historians* 59 (June 2000): 154–79; P. J. Marshall, 'The White Town of Calcutta under the Rule of the East India Company', *Modern Asian Studies* 34 (May 2000): 307–31.
60 Marshall, 'The White Town of Calcutta', 307. In this vein, see Dane Kennedy, *The Magic Mountains: Hill Stations of the British Raj* (Berkeley, 1996).
61 Marshall, 'The White Town of Calcutta', 307.
62 Hugh Tinker, *Foundations of Local Self-Government in India, Pakistan and Burma* (London, 1954). Cited in Chris Furedy, 'The Bhadralok and Municipal Reform in Calcutta, 1875–1900', Working Paper of the Institute of Asian and Slavonic Research, University of British Columbia (August 1972), 2.
63 Furedy, 'The Bhadralok and Municipal Reform', 6–9.
64 Furedy, 'The Bhadralok and Municipal Reform', 10.
65 Furedy, 'The Bhadralok and Municipal Reform', 12.
66 Furedy, 'The Bhadralok and Municipal Reform', 12.
67 David Cannadine, *Ornamentalism: How the British Saw Their Empire* (London, 2001); Bernard Cohn, 'Cloth, Clothes, and Colonialism', in *Colonialism and Its Forms of Knowledge: The British in India* (Princeton, 1996), 106–62.
68 These sentiments were most clearly articulated by the Calcutta-based *Amrita Bazar Patrika* on the eve of the royal visit. *Amrita Bazar Patrika*, 5 August 1875, *Indian Newspaper Reports*, no. 33 of 1875, 4.
69 Northbrook to Wodehouse, 4 December 1875, 18 January 1876, BL MSS Eur D726/7.
70 *Bombay Gazette*, quoted in *Native Opinion*, 28 November 1875.
71 *Native Opinion*, 28 November 1875.
72 *Rajshahye Samáchár*, 6 August 1875, *Indian Newspaper Reports*, no. 34 of 1875, 1.
73 *Native Opinion*, 28 November 1875.
74 *Sádhárani* (Chinsurah), 7 August 1875, *Indian Newspaper Reports*, no. 37 of 1875, 1.
75 *Native Opinion*, 5 September 1875.
76 *Hindoo Patriot*, 4 October 1875.
77 *Native Opinion*, 13 February 1876.
78 *Native Opinion*, 17 October 1875; *Hindoo Patriot*, 16 August 1875.
79 *Native Opinion*, 31 October 1875.

80 *Native Opinion*, 29 August 1875; *Hindoo Patriot*, 8 November 1875.
81 *Amrita Bazar Patrika*, 5 August 1875, *Indian Newspaper Reports*, no. 33 of 1875, 4.
82 *Amrita Bazar Patrika*, 27 November 1875, *Indian Newspaper Reports*, no. 48 of 1875, 3. The *Hindoo Patriot* hoped that, if the Prince of Wales were able to see 'the real truth about [Indians'] conditions', 'the million which will be expended in his honour will not have been expended in vain', *Hindoo Patriot*, 4 October 1875. Similarly, the *Dacca Prakásh* argued that Indians should 'lay before His Royal Highness all their wants and grievances, the poverty of India, the disgrace and humiliating position of the Native Princes, the ruin of the arts, manufactures, and the natural industries of the country, through the selfishness of foreign merchants, and the misery of the upper classes', *Dacca Prakásh*, 8 August 1875, *Indian Newspaper Reports*, no. 33 of 1875, 5.
83 *Native Opinion*, 29 August 1875.
84 *Native Opinion*, 12 December 1875.
85 *Grámbártá Prakáshiká*, 20 November 1875, *Indian Newspaper Reports*, no. 48 of 1875, 4.
86 *Hindu Hitoishiní* (Decca), 7 August 1875, *Indian Newspaper Reports*, no. 33 of 1875, 5; *Som Prákash* (Changripottah), 9 August 1875, no. 33 of 1875, 6; *Sáptahik Samáchár* (Ranaghat), *Indian Newspaper Reports*, no. 33 of 1875, 7.
87 *Native Opinion*, 17 October 1875; *Hindu Ranjiká*, 18 August 1875, *Indian Newspaper Reports*, no. 35 of 1875, 1.
88 *Native Opinion*, 14 November 1875.
89 *Native Opinion*, 17 October 1875.
90 *Sádháraní* (Chinsurah), 7 August 1875, *Indian Newspaper Reports*, no. 37 of 1875, 1.
91 *Rajshahye Samáchár*, 6 August 1875, *Indian Newspaper Reports*, no. 34 of 1875, 1.
92 *Hindoo Patriot*, 4 October 1875 and *Native Opinion*, 17 October 1875. The language of the two passages is virtually identical.
93 *Native Opinion*, 17 October 1875.
94 *Native Opinion*, 17 October 1875.
95 *Native Opinion*, 31 October 1875; *Bishwa Dút*, 23 December 1875, *Reports on Native Papers*, no. 1 of 1875, 2.
96 *Native Opinion*, 17 October 1875.
97 *Native Opinion*, 19 March 1876.
98 *Native Opinion*, 19 September 1876.
99 Dadabhai Naoroji, 'The Inaugural Address of the Second Indian National Congress', in *Inaugural Addresses by Presidents of the Indian National Congress*, ed. Dinker Vishnu Gokhale (Bombay, 1895), 7.
100 See Robert N. Minor, 'Sri Aurobindo's Dismissal of Gandhi and His Nonviolence', in *Indian Critiques of Gandhi*, ed. Harold Coward (Albany, 2003), 89–90.
101 Bill Nasson, *Britannia's Empire: Making a British World* (Stroud, 2004), 169.
102 Robert Ross, *Status and Respectability in the Cape Colony, 1750–1870: A Tragedy of Manners* (Cambridge, 1999), 174.
103 HL Deb. 17 October 1899 vol. 77 cc21–2.
104 Bill Nasson, *The South African War, 1899–1902* (Oxford, 1999).
105 Christopher Saunders, 'African Attitudes to Britain and the Empire before and after the South African War', in *The South African War Reappraised*, ed. Donal Lowry (New York, 2000), 141–3. South African nationalists remained dedicated to this principle into the 1930s. See also Charles V. Reed, 'Imperial Citizenship and the Origins of South African Nationalism, 1902–1923', in *Crossing Boundaries: Ethnicity, Race, and National Belonging in a Transnational World*, ed. Brian Behnken and Simon Wendt (Lanham, MD, 2013), 103–22.
106 Ross, *Status and Respectability*, 174; Stanley Trapido, 'The Origins of the Cape Franchise Qualifications of 1853', *Journal of African History* 5 (Winter 1964), 37
107 Ross, *Status and Respectability*, 174.
108 Ross, *Status and Respectability*, 174.

109 Switzer, 'The Beginnings of African Protest Journalism', 60. Jabavu apparently focused on the English-language columns while his subeditors generally wrote the Xhosa-language pieces.
110 D. D. T. Jabavu, *The Life of John Tengo Jabavu, Editor of 'Imvo Zabantsundu', 1884–1921* (Lovedale, 1922), 11–12.
111 Les and Donna Switzer. *The Black Press in South Africa and Lesotho: A Descriptive Bibliographic Guide to African, Coloured, and Indian Newspapers, Newsletters, and Magazines 1836–1976* (Boston, 1979), 4. Higgs, *The Ghost of Equality*, 11.
112 Switzer, 'The Beginnings of African Protest Journalism', 60–1.
113 Trapido, 'White Conflict and Non-White Participation', 290, 304. It should be noted that the Bond itself expressed loyalty to Queen Victoria. But the rhetoric of Cape politics often conflated the political party and Cape Afrikaners with the Afrikaner republics. See Mordechai Tamarkin, *Cecil Rhodes and the Cape Afrikaners: The Imperial Colossus and the Colonial Parish Pump* (New York, 1996), 61; Hermann Giliomee, *The Afrikaners: Biography of a People* (Charlottesville, 2003).
114 Trapido, 'White Conflict and Non-White Participation', 309; de Kock, *Civilising Barbarians*, 336–77.
115 Trapido, 'White Conflict and Non-White Participation', 331.
116 De Kock, *Civilising Barbarians*, 336–77, citing *Imvo Zabantsundu*, 31 March, 1898; Jeff Pieres, 'John Tengo Jabavu', *Oxford DNB*, online edn, May 2006. www.oxforddnb.com/view/article/53763, accessed 31 July 2015; Trapido, 'White Conflict and Non-White Participation', 331.
117 *South African Spectator*, 7 September 1901.
118 *South African Spectator*, 7 September 1901.
119 *South African Spectator*, 7 September 1901.
120 George M. Fredrickson, *Black Liberation: A Comparative History of Black Ideologies in the United States and South Africa* (Oxford, 1995), 41; Trapido, 'White Conflict and Non-White Participation', 333.
121 Trapido, 'White Conflict and Non-White Participation', 333. On Tiyo Soga, see Mcebisi Ndletyana, ed., *African Intellectuals in 19th and Early 20th Century South Africa* (Cape Town, 2008).
122 *Cape Argus*, 23 July 1898, cited in Trapido, 'White Conflict and Non-White Participation', 333.
123 Switzer, 'The Beginnings of African Protest Journalism', 65.
124 Switzer, 'The Beginnings of African Protest Journalism', 65.
125 Timothy Keegan, *Colonial South Africa and the Origins of the Racial Order* (Charlottesville, 1996); Nigel Penn, *The Forgotten Frontier: Colonist and Khoisan on the Cape's Northern Frontier in the Eighteenth Century* (Athens, OH, 2006).
126 *Imvo Zabantsundu*, 30 April 1901, 3. Quotation from the *Aborigines' Friend*. By 1908, Soga conceded the same point, condemning 'white civilisation' for 'its history ... laid in a trail of blood and savagery'. *Izwi*, 24 October 1908, cited in Saunders, 'African Attitudes to Britain and the Empire', 143.
127 For more on the outbreak of plague, see Myron J. Echenberg, *Plague Ports: The Global Urban Impact of Bubonic Plague, 1894–1901* (New York, 2007), 299.
128 De Kock, *Civilising Barbarians*, 139.
129 *Imvo Zabantsundu*, 28 January 1901.
130 *Imvo Zabantsundu*, 28 January 1901, 18 March 1901. On 18 February 1901, *Imvo Zabantsundu* humorously noted that 'the Queen was the salt of the British constitution': 'The laws may be good, but like food required salt.'
131 *Imvo Zabantsundu*, 28 January 1901, 3.
132 *South African Spectator*, 23 February 1901.
133 *Imvo Zabantsundu*, 11 February 1901, 3.
134 *Imvo Zabantsundu*, 11 February 1901, 3.
135 *South African Spectator*, 4 February 1901.

136 *Imvo Zabantsundu*, 18 March 1901, 3; 1 April 1901, 9 April 1901.
137 Solomon was the son of a missionary, educated at the South African College and Cambridge, served as Attorney-General of the Cape (1898–1900), and was knighted by the Queen. Walter H. Wills, *The Anglo-African Who's Who and Biographical Sketchbook, 1907* (Johannesburg, repr. 2006), 342. He was apparently leaving his post to join the government of Transvaal.
138 *Imvo Zabantsundu*, 18 February 1901.
139 *Imvo Zabantsundu*, 18 February 1901.
140 *Imvo Zabantsundu*, 18 February 1901.
141 *Imvo Zabantsundu*, 18 February 1901.
142 *Imvo Zabantsundu*, 18 February 1901.
143 *South African Spectator*, 9 February 1901. Emphasis added.
144 *South African Spectator*, 23 February 1901, 23 November 1901.
145 *South African Spectator*, 8 February 1902.
146 *Izwi Labantu*, 27 August 1901. The *Spectator* deferred to *Izwi*, citing Soga as a 'greater authority' on the issue of *Imvo* but criticised 'the ingratitude and abuse' shown toward 'a friend'. *South African Spectator*, 7 September 1901.
147 *South African Spectator*, 24 August 1901.
148 *Imvo Zabantsundu*, 21 June 1901, 3.
149 *South African Spectator*, 24 August 1901. It would be highly unusual for such an address *not* to be screened by the colonial government before the event. Colonial officials strictly disallowed political commentary (as they saw it) by any person put before a royal visitor.
150 *South African Spectator*, 24 August 1901
151 *Imvo Zabantsundu*, 21 June 1901.
152 *Imvo Zabantsundu*, 21 June 1901.
153 *Izwi Labantu*, 27 August 1901.
154 *South African Spectator*, 13 July 1901.
155 *Izwi Labantu*, 2 July 1901.
156 *Imvo Zabantsundu*, 21 June 1901.
157 *Izwi Labantu*, 20 August 1901.
158 *South African Spectator*, 20 April 1901.
159 *Imvo Zabantsundu*, 8 October 1902.
160 *Imvo Zabantsundu*, 8 October 1902.
161 Les Switzer, 'Introduction', in *South Africa's Alternative Press: Voices of Protest and Resistance, 1880–1960*, ed. Les Switzer (Cambridge, 1997), 4–5.
162 Switzer, 'The Beginnings of African Protest Journalism', 67.
163 Switzer, 'The Beginnings of African Protest Journalism', 68–9.
164 Switzer, 'The Beginnings of African Protest Journalism', 68–9.
165 Manu Herbstein, 'F.Z.S. Peregrino and *The Fortnightly Spectator*: Query', 27 May 1998, H-Albion. http://h-net.msu.edu/cgi-bin/logbrowse.pl?trx=vx&list=h-africa&month=9805&week=d&msg=j0jnngZeA9jKnvRNLFS5qg&user=&pw=, accessed 8 May 2009.
166 M. Wilson and L. M. Thompson, eds, *The Oxford History of South Africa*, vol. 2, *South Africa, 1870–1966* (Oxford, 1971), 358. Quoted in Ronald Hyam and Peter Henshaw, *The Lion and the Springbok: Britain and South Africa since the Boer War* (Cambridge, 2003), 77. Hyam and Henshaw argue that 'African interests ... were [not] sacrificed [by the British] at the altar of Anglo-Afrikaner reconciliation' and that the British did not consider African interests in their policy toward South Africa, but that the British government possessed a limited realm of action if they wished to maintain southern Africa as part of the British Empire. Also see Nasson, *The South African War*, 232–3.
167 *Imvo Zabantsundu*, 31 August 1901. Quoted in Hyam and Henshaw, *The Lion and the Springbok*, 77.
168 Nasson, 'Why They Fought', 55. On African participation in the Anglo-Zulu War and the 1906 Zulu rebellion, see P. S. Thompson, *Black Soldiers of the Queen: The Natal Contingent in the Anglo-Zulu War* (Tuscaloosa, 2006) and P. S. Thompson,

'"Loyalty's Fair Reward": The Natal Native Horse in the Zulu Rebellion of 1906', *South African Historical Journal* 66, no. 4 (2014): 656–76.

169 Nasson, 'Why They Fought', 60.

170 Leon de Kock, 'Sitting for the Civilisation Test: The Making(s) of a Civil Imaginary in Colonial South Africa', *Poetics Today* 22 (Summer 2001), 392.

CHAPTER FIVE

The empire comes home: colonial subjects and the appeal for imperial justice

During the second half of the nineteenth century, imperial activists and intellectuals in Britain struggled to redefine the ideological apparatus of British imperialism, to push back against the shifting winds of colonial politics and the widespread failures of imperial governance: rebellions in Canada (1837–38), India (1857–58), and Jamaica (1865); growing agitation for increased local governance in the colonies of settlement and India; and the declining value of an 'empire of free trade' in a world where Britain's unilateral dominance was threatened by the growing political, economic, and military potency of the United States and Germany. In response, imperial stakeholders sought to cement the importance of the empire to British subjects at home and abroad. The development of responsible government in the colonies of settlement, the imperial federation movement, empire exhibitions, Empire Day, the education system, and the royal tours were part of this apparatus.[1]

Prince Albert's efforts in 1860 to promote imperial unity and to make an imperial culture through the invention of the royal tour reflect an early attempt to cement the fragile pieces of empire, which became largely defunct in the monarchy as an institution with the death of Albert in 1861. Benjamin Disraeli's often-quoted Crystal Palace speech (1872) conceptually linked modern Toryism and the fate of Britain to empire in a way that suggested a new importance of empire in British political culture.[2] Sir John Seeley's *The Expansion of England* (1883) proposed, in support of greater imperial political and cultural unity, an understanding of British history that emphasised the expansion of England, first in the British Isles then overseas to the neo-Britains of America, Africa, and the Pacific, as the defining attribute of Britain's past, present, and future.[3] Advocates of imperial federation at the turn of the century, most notably the former Birmingham radical Joseph Chamberlain, agitated for a global political union of British states in order to maintain Britain's relevance in a changing world and to preserve the political, cultural, and economic unity of the 'British world'. Others, such as Charles Dilke and even Cecil Rhodes, imagined a 'Greater Britain' of English-speaking peoples including the United States, a 'utopian dream' of Anglo-Saxon global hegemony and peace.[4] All of these intellectual movements reflected a profound uncertainty about the future of Britain and its empire as well as a desire to education the public at home and abroad about the importance of imperial relationship.

During the same period, colonial subjects of colour sought inclusion in the political, legal, and cultural community of empire. Through what Alan Lester and Elizabeth Elbourne term 'imperial networks', circuits of culture, ideas, trade, and politics both between metropole and colony and across the British world, these activists, intellectuals, and politicians sought to engage with and appeal to the British people, the government, and the monarchy.[5] As they discovered, however, these cultural and political networks were not open, democratic, or evenly distributed. These 'webs of trade, knowledge, migration, military power, and political intervention', as Tony Ballantyne and Antoinette Burton argue, 'allowed certain communities to assert their influence and sovereignty over other groups'.[6] In the British Empire, information itself, neither free nor evenly distributed, was regulated and controlled by the growing cultural resonance of racialised settler discourses, recently empowered both by the delegitimisation of the humanitarian mission and by the advent of responsible government in the colonies of settlement. In other words, these networks were 'governed' by modalities of power.

This chapter explores the visits of two delegations to Britain, the first a group led in 1884 by the Kingitanga leader Tawhiao to petition Queen Victoria and the imperial government for intervention against the New Zealand government's violations of the Waitangi treaty, the second a 1909 delegation of white, African, and Coloured activists who sought parliamentary amendments to the proposed Union of South Africa Act that would protect British subjects of colour in the Cape Colony and beyond. While these episodes may seem far removed from one another, they both represent moments when colonial subjects touched by the royal tours brought their claims to the imperial metropole.

None of the historical actors mentioned in this chapter explicitly articulated any connection between the royal tour and their journeys to the heart of empire, but they were clearly inspired by the notion of the Queen (in Tawhiao's case) and Britain as sources of justice in the face of settler aggression. They, too, represent different archetypes of colonial subjects, a chief in the case of Tawhiao (though his entourage was more diverse) and *respectables* of colour (with the exception of

William Schreiner) in the case of the South African delegation. Both, however, were subject to the evolution, or devolution, of an imperial culture that increasingly privileged the concerns of colonial settlers over those of other subjects. By 1909, of course, white solidarity had crystallised, and British concerns over the drift of the white colonies of settlement away from the metropolitan sphere of influence had only heightened. In both cases, the networks of empire were short-circuited when colonial subjects of empire brought their concerns home.

How empire informed the political, cultural, and social lives of Britons was a contentious debate for contemporary observers of British society – and has continued to be for modern historians. The social history of British imperialism produced a rich historical conversation that explored the intersection between class, imperial consciousness, and popular politics.[7] More recent historians of British imperialism, among them New Imperial historians, have searched British domestic culture to find consciousness or sub-consciousness of empire and the construction of racial and gender difference throughout British society over time.[8] Against this literature, the historian Bernard Porter has challenged its historical foundations in a more empirical way, searching carefully through the dusty archives, through school lesson books, the popular press, memoirs, and other sources to find what he sees as limited evidence of empire outside of governing elites.

These competing visions of Britain's imperial past speak conceptually and theoretically 'over and under' one another rather than seriously engaging with one another. Duncan Bell has very ably critiqued this 'either/or' approach to understanding the role of empire in British society:

> Arguments about the lack of an imperial national identity set the bar very high, demanding that in order to classify an identity as imperial there has to exist pervasive and explicit (hence empirically demonstrable) support for the empire. Arguments about the imperialism of British culture tend to be based on far less stringent criteria, and thus on a different account of identity construction. Here a collective identity is regarded as imperial if the material and discursive contexts in which people are embedded are permeated with imperial themes and imagery. In such a society, individuals cannot easily escape being imperial – they are inflected, inscribed, interpellated, constituted, by the imperial encounter.... The former eschews the role of the empire in shaping non-measurable, sometimes subconscious, perceptions and understandings of the self and world. The latter is based on a set of generalisations that are often unwarranted, and, as Porter highlights, often mines a shallow evidentiary seam.[9]

Following Bell's line of thought, this chapter tries to understand British culture as an imperial culture through a more nuanced lens by tracing the projection and reception of visits by colonial delegations to the metropole. The chapter concludes that the visits, and empire itself, were both celebrated and ignored, contested and domesticated in a way that does not conceptually square with the conceptual polarities of either historiographical camp. The tours often piqued the interest of the British press and public and garnered support in certain political circles. At the same time, they were largely ignored or dismissed by the metropolitan stakeholders who were, in other moments, most likely to leap to the defence of the empire project.

While the events described herein were 'small events' in the context of domestic British history, given attention in Britain for only fleeting moments, their narratives were disseminated to the British public in different forms and elicited specific responses and reactions from the press, MPs in the Houses of Parliament, and fascinated crowds on the streets. These visits did not create the same outpouring of responses as did imperial crises such as the sieges of Khartoum (1884–85) or Mafeking (1901), or the carefully crafted celebrations of Queen Victoria's Golden (1887) and Diamond (1896) Jubilees, which were arguably imperial in the ways that they were received. These visits reflect how the British public responded to the more subtle waves of imperial culture. Like the royals of the book's first chapters, the British people domesticated empire, a usually unsaid and often unnoticed part of metropolitan British culture. As Bill Schwarz argues (describing Stanley Baldwin's imperial consciousness), '[The empire] was simply there, like God or Shakespeare, testament to civilisation of the English, a matter not of passion but of faith.'[10]

Petitioning the monarchy for justice and bringing claims of injustice to the metropole were an important tradition of the nineteenth- and twentieth-century empire. The records of the Colonial Office and Royal Archives are filled will numerous petitions from colonised subjects, for instance. As Duncan Bell's work demonstrates, Queen Victoria – 'or at least an idealised representation of her – acted as the linchpin for a sense of global national identity'.[11] The construction of the royal tours centred on projecting the idea of an 'imperial matriarch, presiding with maternal devotion over the greater British family spread around the globe'.[12] The tours were, of course, a component of a broader, if often piecemeal and unsustained, cultural and ideological project that was designed to inspire obedience and loyalty among colonial subjects through the imagery of the Great (White) Queen – a brand of imperial propaganda. This conception of the Queen (and King) as a fount of justice was also a logical consequence of Anglicisation and the promises of the liberal empire. As Macaulay put it, 'having becoming instructed in European knowledge, [our subjects] may, in some future age demand European institutions,... Whenever it comes, it will be the proudest day in English history.'[13] As the previous chapters demonstrate, however, colonial subjects demanded 'European institutions' within the empire rather than independent from it. Moreover, while Douglas Lortimer and others have suggested that such visits must be read as performances meant to appeal to Britishers' preconceptions of colonial people of colour, I argue below and elsewhere in the book that these historical actors were not simply playacting their Britishness.[14]

Queen Victoria received countless petitions and delegations over her reign. The Maori King movement was, for instance, consciously modelled after Queen Victoria, the story goes, inspired by the 1852 encounter of Tamihana Te Rauparaha, the son of chief Te Rauparaha, with Queen Victoria during a visit to Britain.[15] The visit of Tawhiao was inspired by that of the Zulu chief Cetshwayo in 1882, which resulted in similarly limited gains for the petitioner. Neil Parsons argues for the significance of King Khama's later (1895) tour of the imperial metropole, against claims that the Jameson Raid and its consequences preserved what remained of the Tswana kingdoms; for Parsons this 'half a loaf' was secured by the visit.[16] Of course, delegations and petitions rarely achieve even half a loaf. In most cases, Queen Victoria willingly acted as little more than a mouthpiece for the Colonial Office and the government. Petitions that she received were forwarded on to the Colonial Office, and her meetings with colonial subjects relayed the government's decisions. While colonial subjects might have imagined the Great (White) Queen as a mediator between themselves and the imperial government, a notion that itself was reinforced by the mythology and propaganda of British imperialism, the monarchy functioned by and large as an extension of the government's will.

As the sight of colonial subjects became more common in Britain, they became increasing domesticated by British society. As royal visitors often viewed the presence of empire as a banality – it simply *was* – so colonial visitors in Britain became less exotic and newsworthy over time. As the London *Morning Advertiser* explained – with some exaggeration – in 1884:

> Black kings and princes are no longer the *rarae aves* [rare birds] that they were when his swarthy Majesty King Cetewayo first dawned upon an astounded London drawing room. Now an African of noble birth is to be met with at most fashionable receptions during the season, and black bishops talk theology with British deans at garden parties.[17]

Of course – as the crowds who gathered around Tawhiao in the streets in 1884 demonstrate, colonial 'others' remained a curiosity, albeit one that was to be expected in the metropole of the British Empire. This sense of banality was, in a sense, an important ideological component of British-imperial culture.

Curiously (or not), the imperial stakeholders who were most likely to pound the drums for empire at home, a discourse represented by the imperial federation movement and later the Round Table and imperial preference movements, were the least likely to come to the defence of non-white colonial subjects. Politically, this makes sense of course, but it also demonstrates a dissonance in British-imperial culture. Those most likely to defend British subjects of colour represented the liberal-humanitarian discourse of the Aborigines' Protection Society (which had a hand in both visits described in this chapter), missionaries, the humanitarian lobby, and the so-called pro-Boers. But, as this work and others demonstrate, the ideology of the liberal empire – propagated by a complex constellation of political, intellectual, and cultural movements during the nineteenth century – was on the wane. Stakeholders of empire, and therefore British policy, demonstrated a preference for the white empire.[18] This empire was drifting away from the metropole's orbit, with colonial subjects of colour persuasively but unsuccessfully arguing for renewed bonds of empire. Their voices, while sympathetically received in Britain, were drowned out by proponents of the white empire and ignored by a British society with an unsustained and sometimes fleeting interest in empire.

The Maori King in London

In 1883, the Kingitanga leader Tawhiao abandoned his policy of isolation and ventured out of King country in an effort to reinvigorate the Maori cause. In 1881, Tawhiao and his people 'symbolically laid down their weapons before the Resident Magistrate (RM) at Alexandra (Pirongia) and returned to the Waikato', with the king allegedly declaring, 'this is the end of warfare in this land'.[19] Inspired by the 1882 visit of the Zulu king Cetshwayo to London – which resulted in a limited restoration of his authority in South Africa – Tawhiao decided to take his case to his treaty partner, Queen Victoria. The chief Tawhanga had visited London in the same year as the Zulu king as well but was rebuffed by Lord Kimberley, the Colonial Secretary. By demonstrating his loyalty to the Queen and explaining the injustices that his people had experienced under the government of New Zealand, he hoped that she would intervene to restore the agreements of the Treaty of Waitangi.

In July 1883, the Maori MPs Wi Te Wheoro, Hone Mohi Tawhai, Henare Tomoana, and H. R. Tairoa informed F. W. Chesson of the Aborigines' Protection Society (APS) in London that 'it is the intention of Tawhiao whom we recognise as the head of our race, to visit your world shortly for the purpose of petitioning Her Majesty on these things'.[20] The APS served as Tawhiao's point of contact with the British government for the duration of his travels. Tawhiao's party included Major Wiremu Te Wheoro, a Maori MP and loyalist major during the Waikato wars; Patara Te Tuhi, the king's second cousin and secretary as well as former editor of the King newspaper *Te Hokioi e Rere Atu Na*; the wealthy Whanganui chief Topia Turoa; Hori Ropihana; and an interpreter, 'a half-caste named George Skidmore'.[21] Before departing for Britain, he travelled around the North Island, mustering support and fundraising. The party also met with Sir George Grey, who told them that 'if their object was to see famous places, and persons they would be kindly entertained by the English people' but 'if they were going to urge any political object, in all probability the Imperial Government would decline to interfere'.[22]

At the departure ceremony in April 1884, Tawhiao wore an 'extraordinary head-dress, in the shape of an imperial Crown ... constructed of wire, covered with brilliantly coloured flax to imitate gold and gems'.[23] The group travelled from Auckland to Sydney and on to Melbourne, arriving at Plymouth on 31 May 1884 aboard the Orient steamer *Sorata*. They intended to stay two months, but – waiting hopefully for an audience with Queen Victoria – they stayed eighty-one days (Te Wheoro and Skidmore stayed on longer). They took up residence with a Mrs Saintsbury at Demeter House, near Russell Square. It was there that Tawhiao and his entourage held court every day, where it was understood by the press, politicians, and other people of interest that the King would be 'on view' and available for introductions and business.[24]

Tawhiao was greeted with fascination by the British press, and he was frequently hounded by crowds seeking to catch a glimpse of the Maori King. As a kind of living exhibition, the Maori delegation was portrayed as strange and exotic – there was much obsessing over Tawhiao's facial tattoos – but also domesticated, because the Maori had been both 'tamed' by British civilisation and broken by British conquest. There also existed some sense that it was somewhat normal, in the imperial metropole, to witness on occasion the presence of a colonial subject. While the press and politicians expressed some sympathy with Tawhiao's complaints *in principle*, few suggested any sort of imperial intervention. Interest in Tawhiao's cause, too, dissipated in all but humanitarian circles and the minds of a few close allies as soon as he departed for New Zealand. While Tawhiao came to London with a political purpose in mind, metropolitan Britons treated his visit largely as a colonial spectacle, reflecting a limited interest in the politics and policies of Britain's empire.

The press lavished much attention on Tawhiao's behaviour and appearance, focusing on the perceived shabbiness of his dress, bringing to mind Homi Bhabha's failed mimicry of 'almost the same, but not quite'.[25] He could style himself in European ways and reject alcohol, but his tattoos and manners revealed him as the unredeemed savage that he was. The *Illustrated London News* described him as:

> Dresse[d] plainly in the European fashion, and his shark's tooth suspended by a black ribbon from his right ear, and a bunch of fish-bones hanging from his buttonhole, are his only distinguishing ornaments. He is a man of middle height, fairly robust, and with a face deeply scarred with tattoo marks in a minute scroll-pattern, which covers the entire forehead and features except just below the eyes.[26]

The *Colonies and India* focused more on his physical features; he was 'a man of middle height, fairly robust, and with a face deeply scarred with tattoo-marks in a minute scroll-pattern. He has a large, intelligent head, and a mild aspect, and has been described as the most uncommunicative of men.'[27] Perhaps channelling settler efforts to discredit his legitimacy, the *Pall Mall Gazette* described his dress as decidedly unkingly: 'Old frieze coat reaching down to his ankles, and comforter round his neck, a very bad hat, an old pair of shoes, and yellow stockings. A dirty handkerchief was stuffed into the bosom of his shirt. The clothes did not make the King – that was evident.'[28]

In the manner of amateur anthropologists, the London press sought to make sense of the Maori King by observing his dress and manner, demonstrating the supremacy of British civilisation and culture in New Zealand. Despite the decidedly modern nature and method of Tawhiao's claims, he could only be understood as an exotic exhibition or relic of the past rather than a vehicle of modern politics.

The Maori delegation engaged with London and Londoners in ways that did not neatly align with the 'othering' propagated by the British press. They attended the theatre a number of times and were invited onstage at the Victoria to 'cheering, clapping, yelling, hooting, stamping, and catcalling'.[29] Tawhiao shopped for shawls, for his wives, and the press found much humour in Tawhiao's frequent visits to the shop of a tailor named Young on Oxford Street.[30] On one occasion, Tawhiao fled an ensuing mob and protested on a couch in the tailor's shop, the crowd's 'noses against the windowpanes'.[31] The delegation took in the sights: the British Museum (according to press accounts, Tawhiao fled in fear of the Egyptian mummies after fifteen minutes), St Paul's, the Strangers' Gallery of the Commons (the press reported that one member of the delegation nodded off), the Tower of London, the Royal Colonial Institute at South Kensington Museum, Windsor Castle, and

Westminster Abbey (where they apparently experienced some trouble gaining entrance). At one point, the Maori participated in a cleansing ritual in the Thames. By one account, Tawhiao was visited by a sculptor but could not sit long enough. He accepted gifts of bon-bons and prayer books and apparently demonstrated his 'regard for full-bodied charms' on more than one occasion.[32] While the New Zealand papers, which were far more likely to publish embarrassing or bizarre episodes, found comedic value in the Maori visit, the imperial capital would be an intimidating and foreign encounter for the overwhelming majority of colonial subjects.

The delegation also made the political rounds, seeking political support for the Maori cause in the Houses of Parliament.[33] They politicked and socialised with the social and political elites of London. In his speeches, Tawhiao emphasised loyalty to and the supremacy of the Queen. He visited the National Temperance League at Crystal Palace, had lunch with the Lord Mayor, and attended soirées planned to celebrate his visit and provide him with access to important people. On 4 July, the Liberal MP Theodore Fry organised a reception for the delegation at his residence, and on 8 July Tawhiao met with dignitaries in a conference at the Salisbury Hotel. He met with press and other guests during his daily sessions at the Russell Square house of Mrs Saintsbury. According to the Auckland *Star*, Tawhiao would send his translator away when he was done with any given interview.[34] During these times, the delegation would have some cigars and play cribbage.[35] Despite the party's dedication to temperance (George Grey had warned them about the perils of 'the drink' before their departure), the *Star* reported that the group (except Te Wheoro) took to drinking champagne and claret cup.[36]

The delegation briefed the Colonial Secretary, Lord Derby, on their intentions through a memorial submitted on their behalf by the APS:

> We, the Maori Chiefs of New Zealand, have come to this distant land into your presence, on account of the great disaster which has overtaken your Maori race, which is beloved by the Queen and the people of England. Accordingly we have now swum the ocean of Kiwa which lies between us, and have reached England in safety, the source and fountain of authority, to the place where the Queen lives, that she may redress the ills of the Maori race inflicted on them by the Government of New Zealand.[37]

In their memorial, they asked that the imperial government arrange 'that they may have power to make laws regarding their own lands and race'; the 'appointment of a Maori Commissioner, appointed by the Queen'; that 'the greater portion of the taxes levied on your Maori subjects to be returned to them'; 'that the European Judges in the Native Land Court be superseded, and that your Maori race be then permitted to direct their own affairs in that court'; and that 'the lands wrongly obtained by the Government be returned to us'.[38] Appealing to the 'tender regard displayed by the Queen to Her Maori race, as show in the treaty of Waitangi', they laid out a detailed list of grievances that they asserted were committed against them by the government of New Zealand against the Treaty of Waitangi.[39] They focused on land and, in particular, the injustices of the Native Land Courts, and their requests sought to alleviate the worst excesses of colonisation, not to roll back European settlement. But before their steamer arrived at Portsmouth, the deck had already been stacked against Tawhiao's mission by the New Zealand settler lobby.

The New Zealand press presented Tawhiao as an imposter, and worse. In March, the *Wairarapa Daily Times* on the North Island condemned Tawhiao's mission, his character, and those who sympathised with him in Britain:

> [Tawhiao] is a fair spoken, well meaning man, but a sot and a libertine. His determination to proceed to England has naturally caused some consternation among Maori sympathisers. What would the Exeter Hall party, which believes in the noble Maori, and almost canonised a year or two ago one of our worst native specimens, do if Tawhiao cuts capers in London after the style which has been recorded at each point of his late pilgrimage through the North Island.[40]

More damning, however, was the political work done by William Jervois, Governor of New Zealand, and Dillon Bell, an old ally of George Grey and former Minister of Native Affairs. In April 1884, the Under-Secretary of State for the Colonies, John Bramston, wrote to Bell inquiring about the 'specific objects of Tawhiao's visit' and the views of the New Zealand government.[41] Bell responded, in one of his more diplomatic letters of the visit, advising Bramston that:

> I entertain no doubt that Tawhiao intends to approach Her Majesty's Government with representations upon political questions, which he will claim to make on behalf of all Her Majesty's Native subjects in New Zealand. The position of the Maori King among the tribes is, I need hardly say, very different from the one held by the so-called chiefs who came to England in 1882; and Lord Derby may perhaps consider how far it would be expedient to recognise him as being entitled to speak for the tribes.[42]

He also expressed his 'confidence that the Imperial Government would not desire to embarrass your Government ... referring all political questions for settlement in New Zealand'.[43] Elsewhere, he dismissed their claims as 'sheer nonsense'.[44] Jervois similarly emphasised that Tawhiao hardly represented the Maori and that his following had 'dwindled down to about two thousand including women and children'.[45] He complained that the Minister of Native Affairs had offered him lands, a seat in the legislature, a pension among other benefits, without success, and that European advisers and stories of Cetshwayo's visit were giving the Maori King false hope.

Despite the outward face of the government, William Gladstone's Colonial Secretary Lord Derby did consider – it seems – Tawhiao's appeal for imperial intervention. In this context, he sought Jervois' opinion on the powers granted to Queen Victoria by Section 71 of the New Zealand Constitution Act to 'provide by Letters Patent that the laws enacted by the Legislature of the Colony should not extend to the Native Territory, and that the native laws, customs, and usages, modified as might be thought desirable, should prevail therein to the exclusion of all other law'.[46] Jervois contended that Section 71 was not intended to be permanent stipulation hanging over the head of New Zealand. Moreover, the government indicated that the land courts were necessary and that protections were provided to avoid injustice, providing policy and legal documents that served to sanction the legal processes of dispossession.[47] Jervois argued that, with Maori scattered across the islands, there existed no practical way to grant them self-governance and that there was 'no ground for the statement that the Maoris are oppressed'.[48] Responding to the governor's request for information, the John Bryce, Minister of Native Affairs, complained of the 'inconvenience in being required to make an official memorandum … for it appears to be an admission, that a defence on the part of the New Zealand Government is necessary in response to an attack made from an irresponsible quarter in London, prompted, there is little doubt, by some tenth-rate politician in New Zealand'.[49] Blaming Europeans in Britain and New Zealand was a common theme of the campaign against Tawhiao. The Minister of Native Affairs, John Ballance, condemned those in Britain who sought to take issue with the treatment of indigenous peoples: 'There is a demand in England for Native grievances.'[50]

With the government of New Zealand and the New Zealand press doing everything in their power to undermine Tawhiao's goals and legitimacy, the Colonial Office lost interest in Tawhiao's mission by the middle of summer. By July, the *Star* reported that 'the Colonial Office has put an effectual extinguisher on the social prestige of our native visitors by sending round to the newspapers, and other interested parties, a private memo, stating that neither in New Zealand, nor anywhere else, is Tawhiao recognised as "King" of the Maoris'.[51]

As a result, the goal of a grand reception planned at Mrs Saintsbury's house was stifled by the government's efforts to delegitimise the Maori King's mission. Invited MPs and 'literary "swells"' who had accepted later reported than they could no longer attend because of 'business engagements or ill-health'.[52]

Ultimately, the delegation was informed that the Queen was sick and could not meet with them, but they did secure a meeting with Lord Derby. According to *The Times*, Derby informed them that, 'New Zealand is very far off.... It is for us, as I am sure the members of this deputation are fully aware, a very difficult and complicated matter to interfere in questions which we have practically, whether legally or not, handed over for many years past to be dealt with by local authority.'[53] At their departure, they received from the Colonial Office a framed portrait of the Queen.[54] Tawhiao and the other Maori took away from this meeting an understanding of certain promises from Lord Derby, though it is unclear from the record what if anything Lord Derby promised them. Te Whero would later complain, for instance, that 'the word that the Government of New Zealand said to Lord Derby, that they would allow more native members in the Parliament of New Zealand, they have not carried out'.[55] While Lord Derby did in fact urge the government of New Zealand to 'not fail to protect and to promote the welfare of the Native by just administration and the law and by a generous consideration of all their reasonable representations', little came of this encouragement.[56] For Bell, the lesson of Tawhiao's visit was clear:

> The whole thing from first to last has been a sham. Everybody knew perfectly well that the control of Native Affairs had long ago passed away from the Imperial Government, and nobody imagined that Lord Derby had the least intention of interfering now. The preposterous notion of creating a Maori District under section 71 of the Constitution Act, was only part of the make-believe that has been going on.... [The chiefs] will go back to their homes having learnt the lesson that for any purpose of Imperial interference in the politics of New Zealand, their visit to this country has been a waste of time.[57]

On the other hand, Tawhiao returned to New Zealand expecting some form of imperial intervention. John Gorst wrote to Derby in May 1885, complaining that the Maori, while 'waiting anxiously [for] the reply to the appeal which has been made to the British Government', had been victimised by the 'continued mistaken action of the New Zealand Government'.[58] Robert G. W. Herbert of the Colonial Office wrote back to Gorst, indicating that his letter and the Maori signatures that he enclosed would be added to 'the papers about to be presented to Parliament in connexion with that memorial'.[59] Finally, in 1885, Derby told Jervois to inform Tawhiao of the government's decision, one that had been established, seemingly, before the delegation ever met with the Colonial Secretary:

> The questions to which the Memorial relates have also been discussed in the House of Commons with many expressions of sympathy for the Maori race, and of the belief that their interests and their customs would be guarded and respected by the Government of New Zealand. The feeling at the same appeared to be general that while the Government of the Queen in this country has no longer its former power and responsibility in regard to the internal affairs of New Zealand, it should use its good offices with the Colonial Government with the view of obtaining for the Natives all of the consideration which can be given to them.[60]

For Tawhiao, the promise of imperial justice – of the Great White Queen – went unredeemed. According to the *Otago Daily Times*, 'the chiefs composed and sang a song, expressing their regret at only having seen the "shadow of the Queen"'.[61] It would seem the Tawhiao never gave up on his hope that one day that justice would come to his people, and to the British:

> God has been gracious to me wherever I have been, in turning the hearts of the English people toward me. I have met with nothing but kindness and consideration, and not a single bad word has been said to me.... Be strong, be strong.... When the obstacles are removed we shall be one again, and peace and justice and righteousness shall flow like a river through the island from end to end, and also extend to Australia and England.[62]

Despite his seeming lack of disillusionment, Tawhiao faced a Britain that valued him as an exhibition of exoticness, or savagery – of the local flavour expected of the imperial metropole – not for the political message of loyalism and injustice that he brought. Those imperial networks were uneven and unfair, they favoured the flow of information from settlers, even as those societies drifted away from imperial influence. Imperial whiteness trumped loyalty to Queen and Empire. In Tawhiao's case, the empire was out of sight and out of mind, and most of the coverage reflects a general lack of seriousness about his claims.

South Africans against Union

Sol Plaatje described the Act of Union in 1910 in terms of loss:

> With the formation of the Union, the Imperial Government, for reasons which have never been satisfactorily explained, unreservedly handed over the Natives to the colonists, and these colonists, as a rule, are dominated

> by the Dutch Republican spirit. Thus the suzerainty of Great Britain, which under the reign of Her late Majesty Victoria, of blessed memory, was the Natives' only bulwark, has now apparently been withdrawn or relaxed, and the Republicans like a lot of bloodhounds long held in the leash, use the free hand given by the Imperial Government not only to guard against a possible supersession of Cape ideas of toleration, but to effectively extend through the Union the drastic native policy pursued by the Province which is misnamed 'Free' State, and enforce it with the utmost rigour.[63]

The Union of South Africa (1910) created a unitary state (unlike Australia and Canada) that abandoned the enfranchisement of non-whites in the name of white unity and reconciliation. It failed to extend the non-racial franchise of the Cape Colony and limited membership in the Union Parliament to people 'of European descent'. The Union itself represented a long-term effort by colonial administrators and politicians to unify the Cape, Natal, the Orange Free State, and the Transvaal under British rule and represented a logical consequence of British strategic goals during the South African War. The South Africa Act that went before and was passed by the British parliament in 1909 was a direct result of a 1908–09 National Convention. The principal concern for the African and Coloured populations of South Africa was that the Cape's non-racial franchise was not protected or extended and that the connection between British subjects of colour and the mother country would be broken, effectively abandoning them to deal with the white settlers of South Africa on their own.[64] As Sol Plaatje complained, the majority of South Africans, most of whom wished to retain British sovereignty over local affairs, would be left without the vote.[65]

In 1908, Cape Prime Minister John X. Merriman suggested in a letter to General Jan Smuts of the Transvaal a high educational requirement to prevent non-white voters from outnumbering white ones.[66] Merriman and Smuts agreed before the convention that the individual states would retain their franchises but that the European population would determine representation.[67] The Governor of the Transvaal, Lord Selbourne, proposed a 'civilisation qualification' whereby a non-European man who committed to monogamy, spoke a European language, met property or income requirements, 'habitually' wore clothing, and lived in a house would secure a ninth of a vote (his children an eighth, etc.).[68] At the convention, Colonel Sanford, former chief magistrate in Transkei, advocated that Africans should be allowed to prove themselves as 'good and worthy citizens and able to bear their full share of the burden of citizenship'.[69] Afrikaner Cape liberal J. W. Sauer echoed Sanford's comments although he qualified the Cape delegation's advocacy for political equality, indicating that they were not advocating for social equality, which could not be legislated.[70] Like Sanford, he argued that, whatever 'civilisation test' was chosen, it should be applied consistently across the Union. Moreover, the Cape's non-white voters, he contended, were the 'most contented group in the British Empire'.[71] With a bit of political manoeuvring by Merriman, by appointing Sauer to the relevant sub-committee, the Cape's franchise was protected but not extended, and the convention delegates agreed that only a two-thirds majority in the Union parliament could tamper with it. Non-whites were barred from sitting in parliament without contest. Clause 26 of the Act (Qualifications of Senators) required any senator elected to the Union Parliament to 'be a British subject of European descent'.[72]

The Act thus established a colour bar for election to the new Union parliament and the possibility that what remained of the non-racial franchise could be 'taken away' by a two-thirds vote in the same legislative body.[73] In the Cape parliament, the former Prime Minister of the Cape, W. P. Schreiner (who made sixty-four speeches), and others introduced amendments to the Cape's bill on the draft constitution (as a 'recommendation for the Convention to consider') that condemned potential disenfranchisement of non-white voters and the colour bar, but all were voted down.[74] As John Tengo Jabavu assessed in a letter to Theo Schreiner (brother of W. P.), 'there seems no help for it but to appeal to the British Government and the House of Commons and the British public'.[75]

From early on, black liberals and 'friends of the native' appealed to – or threatened to appeal to – the imperial government. During the debates in the Cape legislature, when 'one member [Cartwright] stated that a gentleman of high position [presumably Schreiner] was ready to proceed to England to advocate for the cause of the natives', David Graaff 'denounced such a course as handicapping the efforts of the best friends of the natives [in South Africa]'.[76] Abdullah Abdurahman's African Political Organisation promised on 16 April: 'in the event of no redress being obtained from the National Convention, a delegation will be sent to England to interview the Imperial Government'.[77] A committee appointed by the Transkeian Territories General Council, which included 'representatives of nearly all the Native Tribes resident in the Native Territories of His Majesty's Colony of the Cape of Good Hope', petitioned the British government to consider the 'effects on the political status of His Majesty's subjects of African descent ... 1. By the deletion from Clause (d) Section 25 of the words "of European descent". 2. By the deletion from Clause 1, Section 33, of the word "European". 3. By the deletion from Clause (c), Section 44, of the words "of European descent".'[78]

The Transkei natives continued, appealing to their loyalism to the Crown and to empire and their rights as British subjects:

> [T]o express to Your Excellency the devotion and loyalty of themselves and the people whom they represent … [who] under the benign and fostering rule of the British government [have] acquired rights and privileges of subjects of the British Crown which to them are of inestimable value and that foremost among these are that equality … conferred upon all British subjects, and the possession of the franchise.[79]

Funded by African subscriptions and at a political dead end in South Africa, a group that included Schreiner, the Cape Coloured politician and doctor Abdullah Abdurahman, and the African newspaper editors, activists, and intellectuals John Tengo Jabavu and Walter Rubusana took their concerns to London in order to submit their protest at the South Africa Act to the imperial government in person. Pressured by the government of Natal to avoid political entanglements, John Dube travelled to London under the guise of a fundraising trip for his school, Ohlange, and left after Schreiner's delegation had already departed.[80] He attended events and provided support without offering the appearance of active campaigning.[81] They were also joined by Pixely kaIsaka Seme, who was at Oxford, and Alfred Mangena, a South African lawyer working in London.[82] Their strategy sought to appeal to an imperial constitution from which the South African draft constitution diverged, taking advantage of the legal ambiguities that existed in a South Africa still within the orbit of British influence. Before leaving, Abdurahman collected resolutions passed by local branches of the African Political Organisation, participating in a long tradition of petitioning the British government.[83] In advance of their arrival, Schreiner received letters of support from Ramsay MacDonald, Charles Dilke, and W. T. Stead, among others.[84]

The delegation met with the Colonial Secretary, the Earl of Crewe, on 22 July, who expressed sympathy but made no promises and brought the South Africa Act to the floor of the House that afternoon.[85] Travers Buxton of the Aborigines' Protection Society, through Dilke, arranged for Schreiner to meet with members of the APS during a breakfast at the Westminster Palace Hotel on 27 July.[86] Dilke, as well as the official members of the delegation (i.e. not Dube), spoke. Despite the sympathy of certain political circles, their arguments were not seriously considered by the Asquith government.

The metropolitan response to the delegation focused almost entirely on Schreiner, despite the fact that Abdurahman, Jabavu, Rubusana, and Dube were important political figures in their own right. While the press paid some attention to their plight, but also emphasised the importance of the Union to peace and stability in South Africa, it was a different kind of attention than that given to Tawhiao. As *respectables*, the African members of the delegation lacked the exoticism and cultural difference imposed on Tawhiao (some of which was exaggerated and unfair). In the mirror of empire, they were 'almost but not quite', yet 'almost' enough and a common enough sight in the imperial metropole by the twentieth century not to elicit attention. In fact, beyond the rhetoric of a few Liberal, Radical, and Labour MPs, they were virtually invisible to the political establishment and the press.

British policy toward the white colonies of settlement had also crystallised over the past three decades. While Tawhiao had come decades after the advent of responsible government in New Zealand (1852), there was some reason for Tawhiao, the APS, and other 'friends of the native', to hope for imperial intervention against the perceived violations of the Treaty of Waitangi. Although Lord Derby had publicly toed the line, he had asked for the consideration of the government of New Zealand and even inquired about the relevance of Section 71 of the New Zealand constitution. By 1909, British policy had hardened across the empire and particularly in South Africa, where British geostrategic goals and a desire to placate the previously rebellious Afrikaners outweighed the political and constitutional objections expressed by Schreiner's delegation. Arthur Balfour, former Conservative Prime Minister and Leader of the Opposition, demonstrating a consensus across party lines, argued that the Union fulfilled the 'dream of successive statesmen belonging to all parties, and belonging to the different white races in South Africa, a dream which has been indulged for more than a generation, and which now, I hope, is going to receive its final consummation'.[87] While the rhetoric of liberal empire, its heyday having passed, remained compelling to British subjects in the empire, it was stillborn at home.

The South African delegation smartly framed the issue of 'native rights' as not a uniquely South African problem but an empire problem. For Jabavu, the South Africa Act would undermine the bonds of unity between Britain and its subjects of colour across the empire. As he argued, metropolitan intervention in the South African case was the only way for Britain to 'retain the confidence of its coloured subjects of the King across the Empire'.[88] In a letter to *The Times*, Abdurahman appealed directly to the people of Great Britain in the name of 'the millions of loyal British subjects whom we have been delegated to represent' to challenge the act's clauses barring non-whites from election to the Union parliament on grounds that:

(a) They are illiberal, unjust, and unreasonably offensive to the King's subjects.
(b) They deprive the coloured people and the natives of the Cape Colony of existing rights granted them in 1852 and embodied in the Cape Constitution ... rights of every duly qualified civilised British subject in a self-governing colony.
(c) They originate for South Africa a disqualification based upon colour which has never yet been embodied in any Imperial Act of Parliament, and they reverse the principle of equal rights for all qualified civilised men ... affirmed by the late Hon. Cecil Rhodes.[89]

A few weeks later, Jabavu wrote to *The Times* arguing that 'the native races abroad, though far away from England, are attached to British rule by strong cords of loyalty; and delight and pride themselves on having a great King who rules in equity from this the centre of the Empire'.[90]

Contextualising the motions approved by Abdurahman's African Political Organisation, Walter Hely-Hutchinson, the Governor at the Cape, explained to the Colonial Office that, while he 'wished ... that the provisions of the draft Constitution, as regards the Native Franchise, had been somewhat different from what they are', efforts to impose better terms on the convention would have 'wreck[ed]' the Union.[91] This became a common thread in his letters to the home government. The arguments against the draft constitution, 'the only possible compromise', were 'overstated and exaggerated'.[92] Moreover, he argued that, by requiring a two-thirds majority of both houses to dismantle the non-racial franchise, the new constitution provided greater protections to the King's subjects of colour and that no person of colour had ever been elected to the Cape parliament anyway. He also condemned Schreiner, arguing that he had opposed in the past John Merriman's work, 'for more than a generation, defend[ing] the reasonable rights of the Natives in the Cape Parliament'.[93] *The Times* echoed this sentiment, arguing that:

> A large section of the coloured people definitely repudiate [Schreiner]. If the state of the natives is one of alarm – of which there is no evidence whatever – this is largely due to the alarmist statements made by Mr. Schreiner himself. His denial that there is danger to the Union in his proposals must proceed either from blindness or from wilful misrepresentation.... [Imperial intervention] would itself be the greatest blow ever struck at the Empire.[94]

In a series of letters to *The Times*, Schreiner defended his mission, arguing that the requested changes would not impose the 'Cape system' on Transvaal and the Orange Free State but would simply protect the rights of British subjects in the Cape Colony.[95] He contested that, 'it is frankly inconceivable that either those colonies or Natal would refuse to enter the Union because of the contingency that a man not of European descent might at some time be elected for the Province of the Cape of Good Hope as a member of the Senate or the House of Assembly'.[96] During the parliamentary debates, Asquith's Under-Secretary of State for the Colonies, Colonel John Seeley, referencing Schreiner's letter, argued that such an intervention would be 'entirely unprecedented and so obviously unreasonable.... What he wants to ensure is that the Government of this country shall have a say in the matter under all circumstances.'[97]

During the debate, some MPs expressed sympathy with the delegation's plight. In order to avoid stamping a 'seal of racial inferiority upon the masses of the people of South Africa' and committing Britain 'to a new principle in local government and human rights', Ellis Griffith, a Liberal MP and future Under-Secretary for the Colonies under Asquith, contended that 'we are not asking for what we think the coloured and native men are entitled to; we are only asking for them to retain that which they are entitled to now'.[98] He contended that any amendment to protect the native franchise did not represent 'a new departure in British statesmanship' (as some MPs had characterised such an intervention) but merely protected the status quo. Scottish MP George N. Barnes mocked the practicality of barring non-Europeans from the rolls:

> Is the man in South Africa who aspires to a position in an assembly of this character to be armed with a certificate with a sort of genealogical tree in his pocket? If so, how far is he to go back?... I believe there are one or two who are Members of it now, who are quite good enough for the Mother of Parliaments, but who, forsooth, would not be sufficiently high in the scale of the human family, and not sufficiently good for the people out in South Africa.[99]

The African and Coloured delegates received mention during the parliamentary debates. The MP Charles Dilke argued that:

> Mr. Rhodes's civilised coloured man should be let in.... We were told that one of the main objects of the war, and one of the dominating factors in any peace that could be made, would be the assertion of the Cape principle as against the Boer principle. In the two Colonies we gave up the Cape principle for the Boer principle. I will mention the case of Dr. Abdurahman, who was a supporter of the war, and who was one of those who supported vehemently Mr. Rhodes's view, and who, like many others who are doubtful about this ineligibility, supports the Cape ideal, although he does not want to go into Parliament himself, and never did.

> In the Transvaal they have been, I know, rather easygoing in this matter, but by this Bill you are taking a man like Dr. Abdurahman, who was three times elected chairman of the most important municipal committee of Cape Town, and saying to him, 'You shall never be a member of Parliament'. Are you going to pass an Act of Parliament containing these ill-chosen words under which you do not know whether you are going to exclude such men as Dr. Abdurahman?[100]

The former pro-Boer and Liberal MP William Byles appealed to the example of John Tengo Jabavu:

> The natives of South Africa have put together their money in order to send over this delegation, and one of them, Mr. J. Tengo Jabavu, the editor of a newspaper at the Cape, is as cultivated a man and as capable a citizen as any white man there is, but his skin is as black as a hat, and that is the only thing against him. He has written an article which I regard as of some importance, as bringing before the country rather emphatically the views of the natives themselves – the opinions they hold with regard to the proposals under our consideration. He says the proposals have occasioned deep and widespread alarm and anxiety among the natives from one end of South Africa to the other. He continues: – Civilised and uncivilised, black and coloured (half-castes); partisans of opposing parties in politics; men women and children – in a word, elements that have never worked together – have been united in a manner they have never been before by a common grievance; the attack on their colour, qua colour. Mr. Tengo Jabavu leaves that point, and goes on to another, in which he argues that to take away the native franchise and to deprive the Cape native of it would be a flagrant breach of faith. He adds: – Many of those represented by the native delegation came voluntarily under British rule, and not by conquest. They were assured by governors, governors' agents, officials, and missionaries of the absolute justice, freedom, and liberty, without discrimination of colour, they would enjoy under the British Government. Treaties exist which promised them just and even-handed treatment if they did not rebel. These engagements have been observed by them in letter and spirit.... A breach of faith is a very serious matter to charge against the British Parliament.[101]

As the work of the last decade has demonstrated, the liberal-humanitarian discourse of Dilke and Byles – an extension of nineteenth-century abolitionism and missionary work, Macaulayism and Anglicisation efforts, and even the anti-war sentiment of 'pro-Boerism' – had been long on the wane by 1909, transcended by the rise of the settler lobby, imperial preference for the white empire, and racialist discourse. Schreiner, Jabavu, Rubusana, Dilke, and Byles were all appealing to idioms of the liberal empire that were past their sell-by date in the mainstream of imperial culture. In this, the government's geopolitical agenda and concerns about losing the white empire neatly coincided with the larger currents of imperial thought.

For Herbert Asquith, the act represented a practical compromise that resolved the tensions between the British colonies and the former Boer republics over African voting rights. The government was advised by the governor at the Cape, Walter Hely-Hutchinson, that while he wished that 'provisions, as regards the Native Franchise, had been somewhat different and that the words "European descent" … had never been introduced', the new constitution provided greater protections to the franchise by requiring a two-thirds vote by the Union parliament to abolish it.[102] During the Commons debates, Asquith warned: '[Y]ou plunge into the crucible for refashioning or possible destruction this carefully contrived and most delicately balanced arrangement, which represents the deliberate opinion of the four separately consulted Legislatures, and in the case of Natal of the electorate themselves.'[103] Both Asquith and the former Colonial Secretary Alfred Lyttelton provided support with a staged conception of civilisation, one that was perhaps had more in common with the abolitionist mind than twentieth-century racial theory. Asquith justified the proposed Union as a solution to 'this problem of how you are to adapt and to evolve free institutions in a community where two different races in totally different stages of civilisation find themselves sitting side by side and intermixed'.[104] According to Lyttelton, 'neither the prudence nor the elementary common-sense of the Empire can possibly admit the claim that blacks, very likely hundreds and thousands of years behind the whites in civilisation, are to be admitted to the same suffrage with them'.[105] As Marilyn Lake and Henry Reynolds argue, the South African War had 'cause[d] English officials to "come out" as "white men"'.[106]

There was another delegation in London during the summer of 1909. John X. Merriman, Henry de Villiers, Louis Botha, Leander Starr Jameson, Jan Hofmeyr, and Jan Smuts travelled to Britain to lobby the British government and parliament to pass the bill as received. De Villiers argued that he had, as president of the Convention, consulted with the British High Commissioner Lord Selborne 'at every stage' and that the Colonial Office provided input along the way.[107] For the British parliament to refuse it would amount to a rejection of responsible government. Further, he argued that, 'racialism … is fast dying, and the effect of the Union will undoubtedly be to kill it altogether'.[108] This, the claim that the provisions of the Union provided more protection to non-white South Africans than the present arrangements, was a standard line among proponents of the Union.

On both sides of the issue, supporters and opponents of the Union Bill appealed to the needs and health of the greater empire. Lake and

Reynolds argue that proponents of the non-racial franchise faced the opposition of inter-empire and international 'racial solidarity', with settlers across the empire prepared to protest or rebel against imperial intervention.[109] In the Lords, the former colonial official Lord Northcote appealed to the examples of Canada and Australia to assert the principle of 'white rule and white responsibility for the conduct of public affairs' in the empire.[110] Former British Resident and administrator in India John Rees argued that the real 'imperial danger [was of] of self-governing Colonies being coerced by this Parliament into doing that which they do not want to do'.[111]

On the other hand, critics of the bill used, in particular, changes requested by the British government to the Australian Federation Bill, passed in 1900, as a precedent for imperial intervention in the South African case. Similarly, Liberal MP George Cox asserted that he would 'throw back the Union' rather than 'do something which is a violation of the traditions of the British Empire'.[112] Ryland Adkins claimed that there was 'no precedent for the Imperial Parliament consenting to any Act which will take away existing rights and existing securities from fellow subjects of ours over whom this Parliament has responsibility'.[113] Keir Hardie, appealing to Dilke, argued that the consequences of the Act would felt far outside of South Africa:

> An Indian in this country may sit in this House. In South Africa there are Indians of various races and creeds, and a large number of them have been brought there as indentured labourers. Others have gone to Natal as traders. They are already smarting keenly under the treatment which is being meted out to them in some of the Colonies of South Africa. When their compatriots at home learn further that the House of Commons has deliberately set up this colour bar which prevents those men from being returned to the South African Parliament, is that going to increase their sense of loyalty or their faith in the justice of British rule? Therefore the House of Commons in this respect has a direct responsibility, and if acts of this kind lead to a combined native rising in South Africa Imperial troops will be called in, and, in spite of what fell from some hon. Members opposite, the cost will not be wholly borne by South Africa.[114]

The Act overwhelmingly passed the votes that it faced in the Houses of Parliament, and King Edward VII gave the royal assent on 20 September 1909.

Despite this imperial betrayal, the loyalist South African Native National Congress, co-founded by Sol Plaatje, John Dube, and others in 1912 as a response to the political and social order of the Union, continued to agitate the British government – the monarchy, in particular – to redeem the promises of imperial citizenship. The fears of African intellectuals and activists were quickly realised in the Natives

Land Act of 1913, which limited Africans' ability to own land by establishing reserves and prohibited them from buying land outside of these reserves (some 13 per cent of the Union's territory).[115] For Plaatje, this affront denied Africans 'the bare human right to which every man born into the world is entitled, namely the right to occupy and live by tilling the land'.[116] While the Union had denied the most basic right of citizenship, the vote, the newly empowered Union parliament's first significant act of 'native policy' was to institutionalise physical segregation and begin the processes of establishing native reserves.

For those who had fought against the Union (with the exception of Jabavu, who supported it), the Lands Act represented the realisation of their worst nightmares. Plaatje, Dube, and Rubusana led another deputation to London to protest against the Act, having exhausted any means for change within South Africa and wishing to avoid violence in the countryside. Plaatje reported that they encountered sympathy from British politicians, the press, and the public. Asquith's Colonial Secretary, Viscount Harcourt, indicated that his hands were tied but that Louis Botha had assured him that the Act was merely temporary. Plaatje complained, 'The Imperial Government, which went to war against Oom Paul [Krüger] to secure justice for whites, tell us they cannot interfere to secure justice for blacks.'[117] The trip's purpose was suspended with the outbreak of the Great War, after which the delegation determined that their 'duty as British subjects, was to present a united front to the enemies of their King-Emperor'.[118]

Mohandas Gandhi was also in London in 1909. Gandhi argued to Merriman, who was in Britain in support of the Union Act, that Smuts could repeal the Asiatic Act and apply a civilisation test to allow a number of educated Indians into the Transvaal.[119] Gandhi met with the India Secretary, Lord Morley, and the Colonial Secretary, Lord Crewe. Through Crewe, Smuts proposed that six educated Indians could enter Transvaal every year.[120] He would not, however, agree to the principle of equality, giving Gandhi little motivation to offer concessions. For Gandhi, the visit represented a turning point, as he increasingly realised the futility of appealing to the imperial government for justice. On his way back to South Africa aboard the SS *Kildonan Castle*, in 1909, he would write *Hind Swaraj* (*Indian Home Rule*), a rejection of the British liberal empire and European civilisation.[121] In it, he rejects the very core of the kind of respectability and loyalism that in an earlier incarnation he had embraced: 'In effect it means this: that we want English rule without the Englishman. You want the tiger's nature, but not the tiger; that is to say, you would make India English. And when it becomes English, it will be called not Hindustan but Englistan. This is not the Swaraj that I want.'[122]

To sweeten the pill of Union, the Colonial Office proposed that that the Prince of Wales go to South Africa and inaugurate the Union by opening the parliament for the first time, as he had done in Australia in 1910.[123] Edward VII would die in May of 1910, and South Africa was instead visited by Arthur, Duke of Connaught, his wife, and their daughter Princess Patricia in November of the same year. He would perform the ritual tasks expected of every royal tourist since 1860, receiving dignitaries, giving speeches, and inspecting troops. The crowning achievement of his visit was the inauguration of the Union parliament. In Cape Town, the duke shared news of the King's joy that 'the auspicious union of the South African dominions has already made for the social and material progress of his people, and he feels assured that all South Africans will work steadfastly and honourably for the welfare of their great and beautiful country'.[124] As usual, the tour sought to please and appease colonial subjects with the presence of royalty, while ignoring the politics that were afoot in South Asian and African communities. The British Indian Association used the arrival of the duke as an opportunity to 'urge the Union Government to close this painful struggle', following the death of a deported Indian who attempted to return to South Africa in an act of passive resistance, only to die at sea after being refused entrance at several ports.[125] African papers expressed joy about the arrival of the prince but also sought – in the words of *Illanga Lase Natal* – Britain's 'trust'.[126]

While there exist many explanations of the disillusionment of colonial subjects with Britain and the empire – above all that the British establishment increasingly and consistently allied itself with white settler populations in opposition, proving the ideological and cultural work of the nineteenth-century liberal empire a false promise – certainly the loss of the Great Queen, too, had something to do with the decline of these discourses. Nonetheless, the legacy of imperial citizenship survived. In his 1994 autobiography, *Long Walk to Freedom*, Nelson Mandela, one of the world's most famous anti-colonial nationalists, 'confess[es] to being somewhat of an Anglophile'.[127] He continues:

> When I thought of Western democracy and freedom, I thought of the British parliamentary system. In so many ways, the very model of the gentleman for me was an Englishman. Despite Britain being the home of parliamentary democracy, it was that democracy that had helped inflict a pernicious system of inequality on my people. While I abhorred the notion of British imperialism, I never rejected the trappings of British styles and manners.[128]

Mandela recognised, of course, that his case of Anglophilia reflected the complex legacies of imperialism and its 'colonisation of consciousness'.[129] At the same time, Mandela's sentiments are cultural artefacts of imperial citizenship as an idea, of the unredeemed promises of British political traditions in South Africa. The fact that these discourses, or their remnants, have little resonance in the modern world demonstrates one of the fundamental lessons of history: that the past is a strange and incomprehensible place, where we should resist the urge to impose our own values and sensibilities.

While the period between and including the two World Wars was characterised by a growing disillusionment with the promises of British rule, a recognition that the equality of all British subjects would never be realised, colonial subjects continued to take their grievances to Britain and to the monarch. European empires continued to 'come home' as growing and increasingly connected anti-colonial movements fuelled by the failures of the Versailles Conference convened in Brussels, London, and Berlin, among other metropoles, during the 1920s and 30s.[130] Conversely, royal tours continued to be employed well into the post-colonial age, even as policy-makers professed unrealistic expectations of the magic that they could do and failed to understand the complexities of colonial (and post-colonial) politics and identities. This disconnect, between the promises and realities of colonial rule, as well as the disconnect between the fantasies of colonial administrators and the conceptual depth of empire loyalism and imperial politics, had as much to do with the end of empire as violence, warfare, and inequality.

Notes

1 See, for instance, John MacKenzie, *Propaganda and Empire: The Manipulation of British Public Opinion, 1880–1960* (Manchester, 1984).

2 T. E. Kebbel, ed., *Selected Speeches of the Earl of Beaconsfield*, vol. 2 (London, 1882), 529–34. The links between the monarchy and empire in Disraeli's speech were actually quite fragile. It also must be considered to be a response to Charles Dilke's controversial speech on the 'Costs of the Crown' (London, 1871).

3 John Seeley, *The Expansion of England: Two Courses of Lectures* (London, repr. 1931). For the later debate over tariff reform and imperial preference, which itself was an intellectual successor of these nineteenth-century movements, see Frank Trentman, *Free Trade Nation: Consumption, Commerce, and Civil Society in Modern Britain* (Oxford, 2008) and E. H. H. Green, *The Crisis of Conservatism: The Politics, Economics and Ideology of the Conservative Party, 1880–1914* (New York, 1996). Tariff reform as a platform proved to be an absolutely disastrous electoral strategy for the Conservative Party, which lost the 1906 election in a massive landslide.

4 Duncan Bell, *The Idea of Greater Britain: The Empire and the Future of World Order, 1860–1900* (Princeton, 2007); Duncan Bell, 'Dreamworlds of Empire: Race, Utopia, and Anglobal Governance, 1880–1914', presented at Britain and Her World System, 1815–1931: Trade, Migration and Politics, Institut du monde anglophone, Sorbonne nouvelle, Paris, France, 12–13 March 2010.

5 Alan Lester, *Imperial Networks: Creating Identities in Nineteenth-Century South Africa and Britain* (New York, 2001); Elizabeth Elbourne, 'Indigenous People and

Imperial Networks in the Early Nineteenth Century: The Politics of Knowledge', in *Rediscovering the British World*, ed. Phillip Buckner and R. Douglas Francis (Calgary, 2005), 59–86.; Tony Ballantyne and Antoinette Burton, 'Introduction: Bodies, Empires, and World Histories', in *Bodies in Contact: Rethinking Encounters in World History*, ed. Tony Ballantyne and Antoinette Burton (Durham, NC, 2005), 8.

6 Ballantyne and Burton, 'Introduction', 3.

7 J. A. Hobson, *Imperialism: A Study* (New York, 1902); V. I. Lenin, *On Imperialism: The Highest Stage of Capitalism* (1916); Joseph Schumpeter, *Imperialism and Social Classes* (New York, repr. 1951); Richard Price, *An Imperial War and the British Working Class: Working-Class Attitudes and Reactions to the Boer War, 1899–1902* (London, 1972); P. J. Cain and A. G. Hopkins, *British Imperialism, 1688–2000*, 2nd edn (New York, 2001).

8 See Kathleen Wilson, ed. *A New Imperial History: Culture, Identity, and Modernity in Britain and the Empire* (Cambridge, 2004).

9 Duncan Bell, 'Empire and International Relations in Victorian Political Thought', *Historical Journal* 49, no. 1 (2006): 281–98.

10 Bill Schwarz, *The White Man's World* (Oxford, 2011), 107.

11 Duncan Bell, 'The Idea of a Patriot Queen? The Monarchy, the Constitution, and the Iconographic Order of Greater Britain, 1860–1900', *JICH* 34, no. 1 (2006), 3.

12 David Cannadine, *History in Our Time* (New York, 2000), 43.

13 Thomas Macaulay, quoted in Jane Samson, ed. *The British Empire* (Oxford, 2001), 134–5.

14 Douglas Lortimer, *Colour, Class, and the Victorians: English Attitudes to the Negro in the Mid-Nineteenth Century* (Leicester, 1978).

15 Angela Ballara, 'Introduction', in *Te Kingitanga: The People of the Maori King Movement*, ed. Angela Ballara (Auckland, 1996), 1.

16 Neil Parsons, '"No Longer Rare Birds in London": Zulu, Ndebele, Gaza, and Swazi Envoys to England, 1882–1894', in *Black Victorians/Black Victoriana*, ed. Gretchen Holbrook Gerzina (New Brunswick, 2003), 110–44.

17 *Morning Advertiser*, 7 September 1895, quoted in Parsons, '"No Longer Rare Birds"', 110.

18 Daniel Gorman, *Imperial Citizenship: Empire and the Question of Belonging* (Manchester, 2006).

19 Rahui Papa and Paul Meredith, 'Kingitanga – the Maori King Movement – Tawhiao, 1860–1894', in *Te Ara: The Encyclopaedia of New Zealand* (Wellington, 2005–14); 'Tūkāroto Pōtatau Matutaera Tāwhiao', in *Dictionary of New Zealand Biography* (Wellington, 1990–2000).

20 Wi Te Wheoro, Hone Mohi Tawhai, Henare Tomoana, and H. R. Tairoa to F. W. Chesson, Aborigines' Protection Society, 16 July 1883, reprinted in Vincent O'Malley, Bruce Stirling, and Vally Penetito, eds, *The Treaty of Waitangi Companion: Maori and Pakeha from Tasman to Today* (Auckland, 2011), 185–7.

21 Carmen Kirkwood, *Tawhiao, King or Prophet* (Hamilton, 2000), 162. Patara Te Tuhi had travelled to Europe before; he was trained in the use of the printing press in Austria.

22 *Hawke's Bay Herald*, 20 March 1884.

23 Gov. Jervois to Earl of Derby, 28 April 1884, Insert to NA CO 209/243/126–7; *New Zealand Herald and Daily Southern Cross*, 28 April 1884.

24 *Te Aroha News*, 30 August 1884.

25 Homi Bhabha, *The Location of Culture* (New York, 1994), 85–92.

26 *Illustrated London News*, quoted in *Taranaki Herald*, 25 July 1884.

27 *Colonies and India*, quoted in *The Graphic*, 14 June 1884.

28 *Pall Mall Gazette*, quoted in *Nelson Evening Mail*, 11 September 1884.

29 (Auckland) *Star*, 8 September 1884.

30 He apparently visited as many as half a dozen times per day.

31 (Auckland) *Star*, 2 September 1884.

32 *Nelson Evening Mail*, 11 September 1884, quoting *Pall Mall Gazette*.

33 Neil Parsons argues that the visits of African envoys were carefully orchestrated by Colonial Officials to strike awe in the minds of colonial subjects (as was the purpose of the royal tour). This was not the case in either of the visits under examination here. Parsons, '"No Longer Rare Birds in London"', 113.
34 (Auckland) *Star*, 8 September 1884.
35 (Auckland) *Star*, 8 September 1884.
36 (Auckland) *Star*, 8 September 1884.
37 Memorial of the Maori Chiefs, Tawhiao, Wiremu Te Wheoro, Patara Te Tuhi, Topia Turoa, and Hori Ropihana, no. 1, in *Correspondence Respecting a Memorial Brought to this Country by Certain Maori Chiefs in 1884*, Parliamentary Papers (London, 1885).
38 Memorial of the Maori Chiefs.
39 Memorial of the Maori Chiefs.
40 *Wairarapa Daily Times*, 21 March 1884.
41 John Bramston to Gov. F. D. Bell, 8 April 1884, Archives New Zealand (henceforth ANZ), MA 23-4A/NO 84/2310.
42 J. D. Bell to John Bramston, 9 April 1884, ANZ MA 23-4A/NO 84/2310.
43 J. D. Bell to Premier of New Zealand, 27 May 1884, ANZ MA 23-4A/NO 84/2302 No. 269.
44 J. D. Bell to Premier of New Zealand, 28 July 1884, ANZ MA 23-4A/NO 84/3057 No. 352.
45 . Gov. F. D. Jervois to Earl of Derby, 1 April 1884, NA CO 209/243/69–73.
46 Earl of Derby to Gov. F. D. Jervois, no. 3, in *Correspondence Respecting a Memorial Brought to this Country by Certain Maori Chiefs in 1884.*
47 Gov. W. F. D. Jervois to Earl of Derby, Appendix no. 3, in *Correspondence Respecting a Memorial Brought to this Country by Certain Maori Chiefs in 1884.*
48 No. 3, in *Correspondence Respecting a Memorial Brought to this Country by Certain Maori Chiefs in 1884.*
49 John Bryce (Native Minister), Memorandum for His Excellency the Governor, Enclosure 1 in Appendix No. 3, in *Correspondence Respecting a Memorial Brought to this Country by Certain Maori Chiefs in 1884.*
50 John Ballance (Minister of Native Affairs) to Gov. F. D. Jervois, n.d., ANZ MA 23-4A/NO 87/361.
51 (Auckland) *Star*, 1 September 1884.
52 (Auckland) *Star*, 2 September 1884.
53 'The Government and the Maori Chiefs', *The Times*, 23 July 1884.
54 *Otago Daily Times*, 7 October 1884.
55 Te Whero, 6 January 1887, ANZ MA 23-4A.
56 Earl of Derby to Gov. W. F. D. Jervois, in *Further Correspondence Respecting a Memorial Brought to this Country by Certain Maori Chiefs in 1884*, Parliamentary Papers (London, 1885).
57 J. D. Bell to Premier of NZ, 24 July 1884, ANZ MA 23-4A/NO 34 No. 347.
58 J. E. Gorst to the Colonial Office, no. 9, in *Correspondence Respecting a Memorial Brought to this Country by Certain Maori Chiefs in 1884.*
59 Colonial Office to J. E. Gorst, no. 10, in *Correspondence Respecting a Memorial Brought to this Country by Certain Maori Chiefs in 1884.*
60 Earl of Derby to Gov. W. F. D. Jervois, in *Further Correspondence Respecting a Memorial brought to this Country by Certain Maori Chiefs in 1884.*
61 *Otago Daily Times*, 7 October 1884.
62 F. W. Chesson to the Editor, *The Times*, 26 December 1884.
63 Sol Plaatje, *Native Life in South Africa before and since the European War and the Boer Rebellion* (Whitefish, MT, repr. 2004), 12–13.
64 The Colonial Office was actually relieved that the proposal did not restrict the franchise further. Hyam and Henshaw, *The Lion and the Springbok*, 82.
65 Sol Plaatje, 'An Appeal to the British Brotherhoods', *Ilanga Lase Natal*, 28 August 1914. Plaatje mocked the idea that this somehow represented local autonomy. By

his estimates, 1 million South Africans would be eligible to vote; 6 million would be ineligible.

66 Stanley Trapido, 'White Conflict and Non-White Participation in the Politics of the Cape of Good Hope' (PhD dissertation, University of London, 1970), 195. Also see Marilyn Lake and Henry Reynolds, *Drawing the Global Colour Line: White Men's Countries and the International Challenge of Racial Solidarity* (Cambridge, 2008), 223–4.

67 Trapido, 'White Conflict and Non-White Participation', 197.

68 Ramachandra Guha, *India before Gandhi* (London, 2014), 311–12.

69 Quoted in Trapido, 'White Conflict and Non-White Participation', 198.

70 Trapido, 'White Conflict and Non-White Participation', 198.

71 Trapido, 'White Conflict and Non-White Participation', 199.

72 HC Deb. 19 August 1909 vol. 9 c1553.

73 'Native Rights in South Africa', *The Times*, 30 July 1909.

74 W. Hely-Hutchinson to Lord Crewe, 14 April 1909, NA CO 48/601/434–40; *Cape Times*, 17 April 1909; W. Hely-Hutchinson to Lord Crewe, 19 April 1909, NA CO/48/601/495–500.

75 John Tengo Jabavu to Theo Schreiner, 12 June 1909, BC 112/D3.1/file 12 (6.2), Schreiner Papers, University of Cape Town Archives.

76 *Cape Times*, 17 April 1909.

77 Hely-Hutchinson to Crewe, 19 April 1909, NA.

78 Petition from the Transkeian Territories General Council, NA CO 48/602/286–94.

79 Petition from the Transkeian Territories General Council, NA.

80 Heather Hughes, *The First President: A Life of John L. Dube, Founding President of the ANC* (Auckland Park, 2011), 149–51.

81 Hughes, *First President*, 152.

82 Hughes, *First President*, 151.

83 Memo from African Political Organisation General Executive, 11 June 1909, BC 112/D3.1, Schreiner Papers, University of Cape Town Archives.

84 Ramsay MacDonald to W. P. Schreiner, 18 June 1909, BC 112/D3.1/File 12 (10.1), Schreiner Papers, University of Cape Town Archives; Charles Dilke to W. P. Schreiner, 6 July 1909, BC 112/D3.1, Schreiner Papers, University of Cape Town Archives; W. T. Stead to W. P. Schreiner, 10 July 1909, BC 112/D3.1/File 12 (19.1), Schreiner Papers, University of Cape Town Archives.

85 Eric Walker, *W. P. Schreiner: A South African* (Oxford, 1969), 329.

86 Travers Buxton to Charles Dilke, 8 July 1909, BC 112/D.3, Schreiner Papers, University of Cape Town Archives; Hughes, *First President*, 152.

87 HC Deb. 16 August 1909 vol. 9 c1000.

88 John Tengo Jabavu, 'The South Africa Bill', *The Times*, 19 August 1909.

89 Abdullah Abdurahman, 'South African Natives and the Constitution', *The Times*, 28 July 1909.

90 John Tengo Jabavu, 'The South Africa Bill', *The Times*, 19 August 1909.

91 W. Hely-Hutchinson to Lord Crewe, 29 March 1909, NA CO 48/601/323–4.

92 W. Hely-Hutchinson to Lord Crewe, 16 June 1909, NA CO 48/601/218–20.

93 Hely-Hutchinson to Crewe, 16 June 1909, NA.

94 *The Times*, 8 July 1909. Here, *The Times* repeats the claim that, if Schreiner succeeded, he would 'wreck' the Union.

95 W. Schreiner, 'South Africa Bill and the Native Question', *The Times*, 2 August 1909.

96 Schreiner, 'South Africa Bill and the Native Question'.

97 HC Deb. 9 August 1909 vol 9 c1638.

98 HC Deb. 19 August 1909 vol. 9 c1580.

99 HC Deb. 19 August 1909 vol. 9 c1555.

100 HC Deb. 16 August 1909 vol. 9 cc975–81.

101 HC Deb. 16 August 1909 vol. 9 cc1029–30.

102 W. Hely-Hutchinson to Lord Crewe, 29 March 1909, NA CO 48/601/322–4.

103 HC Deb. 19 August 1909 vol. 9 cc1561–4.

104 HC Deb. 16 August 1909 vol. 9 c1009.
105 HC Deb. 19 August 1909 vol. 9 c1584.
106 Lake and Reynolds, *Drawing the Global Colour Line*, 231. See also Schwarz, *White Man's World*, 208–76.
107 *Courier* (Dundee), 5 July 1909.
108 *Courier* (Dundee), 5 July 1909.
109 Lake and Reynolds, *Drawing the Global Colour Line*, 221.
110 HL Deb. 27 July 1909 vol. 2 c770.
111 HC Deb. 19 Aug 1909 vol. 9 1636.
112 HC Deb. 19 August 1909 vol. 9 cc1569–70.
113 HB Deb. 19 August 1909 vol. 9 cc1630–1.
114 HC Deb. 19 August 1909 vol. 9 c1573.
115 Hyam and Henshaw, *The Lion and the Springbok*, 28–9.
116 Plaatje, 'An Appeal to the British Brotherhoods'.
117 Plaatje, 'An Appeal to the British Brotherhoods'.
118 'South African Native National Congress', *Ilanga Lase Natal*, 13 August 1915.
119 Guha, *India before Gandhi*, 335–6.
120 Lake and Reynolds, *Drawing the Global Colour Line*, 228; Guha, *India before Gandhi*, 335–6.
121 Lake and Reynolds, *Drawing the Global Colour Line*, 234–5.
122 Mohandas Gandhi, 'What is Swaraj?' (ch. 3), in *Hind Swaraj, or Indian Home Rule* (Madras, 1921).
123 HC Deb. 16 August 1909 vol. 9 c953.
124 Press Association, printed in *Poverty Bay Herald*, 5 November 1910.
125 *Indian Opinion*, 29 October 1910; Uma Shashikant Mesthrie, 'From Advocacy to Mobilisation: *Indian Opinion*, 1903–1914', in *South Africa's Alternative Press: Voices of Protest and Resistance, 1880–1960*, ed. Les Switzer (Cambridge, 1997), 120.
126 *Ilanga Lase Natal*, 25 November 1910.
127 Nelson Mandela, *Long Walk to Freedom* (New York, 1994), 302.
128 Mandela, *Long Walk to Freedom*, 302. This excerpt has been frequently cited. See, in particular, Tom Lodge, *Mandela: A Critical Life* (New York, 2006), 6; Christopher Saunders, 'Britishness in South Africa', *Humanities Research* 13, no. 1 (2006), 68.
129 See, in particular, Mandela, *Long Walk to Freedom*, 96–7.
130 Tony Ballantyne and Antoinette Burton, 'Empires and the Reach of the Global', in *A World Connecting, 1870–1945*, ed. Emily S. Rosenberg (Cambridge, MA, 2012), 390–1.

Postscript and conclusion

In 1911, King George V was the first and last reigning British monarch to visit Britain's Indian Empire. His coronation durbar in Delhi represented both the political and cultural pinnacle of the ritual apparatus developed during the second half of the nineteenth century, but also the ways in which it was unravelling in the years before the First World War. It also demonstrated how imperial culture was made by complex modes of reception and appropriation, how ideas about empire, citizenship, and identity were forged in encounters and experiences 'on the ground', as it were, and how colonial knowledge was always imperfect and partial.

The Delhi durbar was the greatest act in the performance of imperial culture by British royals. The royal jeweller crafted a lighter model of the imperial crown, costing the Indian treasury £60,000, for the long durbar on a hot Delhi day.[1] Sir Philip Gibbs, the biographer of George V, described the scene at the durbar as 'the most brilliant, the most imposing, the most gorgeous State Ceremony the world has ever known'.[2] The ritual also marked the transfer of the imperial capital from Calcutta to Delhi, a former centre of Mughal power. During one part of the ceremonies, the King and Queen 'sat on the marble balcony ... showing themselves to the [thousands of] people' at Delhi Fort, the palace of the Mughal Emperor Shah Jahan, in a ceremony proposed by the King himself.[3] The 1911 Delhi durbar was one of the grandest ritual performances in the history of the British Empire, a culmination of the royal tours and the British ornamental imagination.

The ritual practices of the royal tour were on full display in Delhi. George V received and gave addresses. The viceroy gave and received visits with the princely elite, and the King granted private audiences to the more important princes. Massive tents were erected to serve as residences for visiting dignitaries. Like his uncle, Prince Alfred, the King went tiger hunting in the Nepal forests.[4] He inspected imperial troops and the living veterans of the Indian Mutiny.[5] Curiously, the great controversy of the durbar involved a familiar character, and his alleged disrespect toward the King-Emperor:

> No incident of the Coronation Durbar at Delhi aroused more interest than did the manner in which the Gaekwad of Baroda played homage. The cinematograph films show that, when coming to perform this, he was swinging a stick in his hand, which to say the least of it, was decidedly unusual, and that, having bowed curtly and retreated a pace or two, he turned his back on the King-Emperor and walked off, instead of leaving the Presence backwards as did others doing homage. Considerable comment having been caused by this, the Viceroy, with his Highness's consent, published a letter in which the Gaekwad assures Lord Hardinge of his loyalty and allegiance to the throne, sets down his failure to observe strict etiquette to nervous confusion in the presence of their Majesties before the great assembly, says that, being second of the Feudatory Princes and failing to see exactly what the Nizam of Hyderabad did, had no chance of observing the others do homage.[6]

The Gaekwad of Baroda was Sayaji Rao III, the young prince whom the Prince of Wales had met in 1875. He had recently converted to a liberal nationalism, making contributions to the Indian National Congress and Dadabhai Naoroji's British parliamentary campaign.[7] As a result, he had been carefully monitored by the British Resident in Baroda. While there is no evidence that the gaekwad purposely snubbed the King, his political sympathies, which transcended the difference between 'traditional' and 'modern' politics, certainly make one wonder. Ritual contestation, after all, had a long tradition in the encounters between British royals and local people.

The coronation durbar represented more than the far reaches of the British ritual imagination. It was a calculated response to the development of a more radical and separatist Indian nationalism during the first decade of the twentieth century. In 1906, the INC split into factions: the *Garam Dal*, the radicals led by Bal Gangadhar Tilak, and *Naram Dal*, the loyalist 'Moderates' under Gopal Krishna Gokhale. On one hand, the 1905 partition of Bengal – a British tactic of divide and conquer – unleashed a firestorm of political contestation from Bengali nationalists. On the other hand, the Indian Councils Act of 1909, the Morley–Minto reforms, instituted political reforms that allowed Indians to be elected to local and provincial councils for the first time, a concession that failed to appease an increasingly mass nationalist movement. In 1911, the visit of George V was used as an opportunity to counter the propaganda of Indian nationalism. The King announced the reunification of Bengal, bonuses for military and civilian servants of the government, and grants for educational advancement.[8]

The durbar invoked the mythology of the patriot king, the Great (White) King who loved and protected his subjects. While the British monarch had long been an object of petitions and demands – to make right the wrongs of other British subjects or governments – this mythology was most carefully and successfully crafted and nurtured during the long reign of Queen Victoria. George V, and the monarchs who followed him, exploited the ritual and ideological apparatus of the nineteenth-century empire to legitimise and justify the monarchy and the empire well into the twentieth century. At the same time, as the coronation durbar demonstrates, these ritual practices, which were limited and unstable from their inception, were increasingly undermined, delegitimised, and challenged by emerging mythologies of belonging and identity politics.

* * *

Royal tourists, colonial subjects and the making of a British world has reflected on a diverse cast of characters, culled from different historical sites and representative of different discourses of British imperial culture: a Great Queen dispossessed of the power to control her own image; royal children bored with the tedium of their royal ambassadorships; African chiefs, Indian princes, and a Maori King who participated in or contested the mythology of the Great Queen; colonial governors who used the visits as opportunities to impress and defeat Britain's enemies; Western-educated *respectables* who used an idiom of British constitutionalism to demand imperial citizenship; colonial settlers who claimed to be 'better Britons'; and loyalist Dutch-speaking South Africans and an Irish assassin who envisioned a future for the Irish in the empire. These examples demonstrate the ways in which imperial culture was made, not at Windsor Castle, or in the halls of the Colonial Office, or in Government House in Calcutta or Cape Town or Auckland, but by human actors in the empire, who made sense of their political, cultural, and social worlds the best they could and with the tools that they had as subjects of a global empire. These encounters demonstrate how imperial culture, fragile and unstable, uncontainable and uncontrollable, was made in the empire.

The First World War has been identified by scholars as a transformative moment in the history of Britain and the British Empire. The war was a breaking point for many 'loyalist' people of colour in Britain's African and Indian empires, who became increasingly disillusioned by the broken promises of imperial service and citizenship during and in the aftermath the war.[9] In India, British soldiers opened fire on civilians protesting against the Rowlatt Act, an extension of the oppressive wartime 'emergency measures', in the Amritsar Massacre (1919), which proved to be a turning point for many Indian nationalists. The white colonies of settlement earned their spurs during the war, as reflected in the Balfour Declaration (1926) and the Statute of Westminster (1931), completing the long evolution from responsible government and home rule to independent Dominion status. In New Zealand and Australia, emerging national mythologies were forged in the blood of ANZAC troops in the trenches of Gallipoli. In the aftermath of the war, however, Britain became more and more dependent on the empire for trade and the maintenance of its global power in a changing world order, symbolised by the Covenant of the League of Nations as well as the financial and political rise of the United States.

The political and cultural wind of change, to borrow Harold Macmillan's 1960 turn of phrase, was already blowing through the empire, however. The changes attributed to the war represented significant continuity with the previous decades rather than a radical break with the past. The development of home rule, designed to avoid another imperial disaster like the American and Canadian revolts, and settler disputes with the imperial government had nurtured these changes for the last half-century. In South Africa, *respectables* of African and Coloured descent were profoundly disillusioned by the failure of the imperial government to intervene against the disenfranchisement of the Union of South Africa (1910) or the dispossession of the Native Lands' Act (1913). In India, the British failed to live up to the promises of the war, encouraging the growth of the mass anti-nationalist movement that had rapidly developed in the decade before the war. The changing politics of Sol Plaatje and Mohandas Gandhi, from imperial citizenship to non-cooperation and contestation, reflect the changing nature of imperial politics for local peoples.

The second half of the nineteenth century was a transitional period in the history of the British Empire, when notions of imperial identity and citizenship came to dominate (however briefly) the cultural and political landscape of imperial culture. This is not to say that local and nationalist identities were not forged, but that they did so in the milieu of imperial politics. By and large, Queen Victoria's English-speaking subjects imagined their political and cultural universes with an inward gaze toward their local communities and an outward gaze toward Britain and the empire. The politics of this era were, overwhelmingly, not separatist or anti-imperial, nationalist in a twentieth-century sense, but embraced Britishness and imperial citizenship, the rights and responsibilities of citizen-subjects of the Queen and the co-ownership of a global empire. While these ideas manifested themselves in diverse and often conflicting ways, they informed the lives of 'overseas Britons', many of whom had no ethnic or racial claim to Britishness, and made an imperial culture that could not be dictated from Britain, from colonial capitals, or by local social elites. During the twentieth century, they would re-emerge in the demands of Second World War veterans, the claims of the *Windrush* generation, and British Muslims in the aftermath of the 7/7 bombings.

In Britain, the revived public consciousness of the empire resulted from the experiences of the war and anxieties about Britain's future as a world power. Between 1903 and the war, for instance, the Tariff Reform League advocated for Imperial Preference, a protectionist zone designed to counter the growing industrial power of the United States and Germany.[10] While the British Empire was at its greatest geographical extent in the aftermath of the war, it was an empire in decline. At the same time, British society was becoming a mass, democratic society – symbolised by the abolition of the House of Lords' legislative veto power (1911), the enfranchisement of women over thirty (1919), and the development of a modern mass media.

As David Cannadine has argued, these transformations made the monarchy a greater novelty, with Buckingham Palace becoming a tourist trap rather than a centre of power, and royal memorabilia, which became popular during the Golden and Diamond Jubilees, transforming a 'sacred' monarchy into a consumer fetish. The development of radio and film made the monarchy more accessible – in some sense making the royal tour obsolete – but during an era when the imperial monarchy and its empire were both on the wane.[11] Today, Elizabeth II may be a symbolic head of state for millions of people across the globe, but she lacks the symbolic influence of the Great Queen.[12] Her people may adore her, but largely because she has no power over them and because they are not her subjects but citizens.

Recent works of the 'imperial turn' represent the imperial experience in a far more sophisticated analytic than their predecessors, often influenced by the important work of area studies scholars in the fields of African, South Asian, and Australasian history (who have as much of a claim on doing a history of empire as British scholars). British imperial history has likewise been influenced and reshaped by scholars of the former colonies of settlement, many of whom have embraced the notion of a British World. The dialectic of collaboration/resistance has been largely rejected and the role of imperial politics more seriously considered. The current work has been profoundly shaped by and (hopefully) contributes significantly to this scholarly milieu by offering a study of the unique encounter and experience offered by the royal tour of empire. It is a book about how the empire was imagined and experienced by different historical actors, representing unique discourses of imperial culture, across the space of the nineteenth-century

British Empire. It importantly recentres the making of imperial culture, locating the empire itself in the centre of these processes, and offers for consideration – standing on the shoulders of several recent scholars – the centrality of Britishness and imperial citizenship to Queen Victoria's colonial subjects.

Notes

1 A. N. Wilson, *After the Victorians: The Decline of Britain in the World* (New York, 2005), 129.
2 Philip Gibbs, *George the Faithful: The Life and Times of King George V* (London, 1936), 212.
3 *Illustrated London News*, 6 January 1912.
4 *The Times*, 21 September 1911.
5 *Illustrated London News*, 6 January 1912.
6 *Illustrated London News*, 6 January 1912.
7 Lawrence James, *Raj: The Making and Unmaking of British India* (New York, 1997), 338.
8 Richard Burn, 'Political Movements, 1909–1917', in *The Cambridge History of the British Empire*, vol. 5, *The Indian Empire, 1858–1918*, ed. H. H. Dowell (Cambridge, 1932), 575–6.
9 Bill Nasson, 'Why They Fought: Black Cape Colonists and the Imperial Wars, 1899–1918', *International Journal of African Historical Studies* 37, no. 1 (2004): 55–70.
10 See Andrew Thompson, *Imperial Britain: The Empire in British Politics, c. 1880–1932* (New York, 2002); David Thackeray, 'The Crisis of the Tariff Reform League and the Division of "Radical Conservatism", c. 1913–1922', *History* 91, no. 301 (2006): 45–61; E. H. H. Green, *The Crisis of Conservatism: The Politics, Economics and Ideology of the Conservative Party, 1880–1914* (New York, 1996). Of course, the years of the tariff reform campaign represented a long time in the wilderness for the Conservatives, making one wonder how much the issue mattered to most voters.
11 The monarchy recovered some of its cultural significance during the Second World War, for instance, but experienced blows to its prestige during the Abdication Crisis (1936) and following the death of Princess Diana (1997). The tabloid press, an invention of the nineteenth century, also contributed to these processes of trivialisation.
12 Philip Murphy persuasively argues that she symbolises and personifies the Commonwealth. *Monarchy and the End of Empire: The House of Windsor, the British Government, and the Postwar Commonwealth* (Oxford, 2013).

BIBLIOGRAPHY

Manuscripts

Archives New Zealand, Wellington

Department of Maori Affairs, Maori political and tribal matters, Tawhiao's Papers

British Library, London

Correspondence of Thomas George Baring, 1st Earl of Northbrook, relating to India
Papers of Sir John Lawrence, 1st Baron Lawrence
Wodehouse Papers
Correspondence and papers relating to administrative arrangements for Prince of Wales's tour, 1875–76; 1877
Maharaja Gaekwad of Baroda Malhar Rao papers

National Archives, Kew

Colonial Office Records

Northwestern University Archives, Evanston, IL

Abdullah Abdurahman Family Papers

Queensland Women's Historical Association, Brisbane

Papers of Sir George Bowen

Royal Archives, Windsor

Victorian Archives
Additional Victorian Archives
Queen Victoria's Journals, Princess Beatrice's copies

Royal Collection, London

Collar of the Order of the Star of India

University of Birmingham

Correspondence, Diaries, and Papers of Joseph Chamberlain

University of Cape Town

Papers of W. P. Schreiner

University of Nottingham

Papers of Henry Pelham-Clinton, Duke of Newcastle

Newspapers and periodicals

Amrita Banar Patrika
Bay of Plenty Times
Bhárat Sangskárak
Birmingham Daily Post
Bishwa Dút
Bruce Herald
Cape Argus
Cape Times
Courier (Dundee)
Daily News (London)
Daily Southern Cross
De Zuid-Afrikaan
Evening Post (Wellington)
Gentleman's Magazine
Graham's Town Journal
Grámbártá Prakáshiká
The Graphic
Hawera & Normanby Star
Hawke's Bay Herald
Hindoo Patriot
Hindu Hitoishiní
Hindu Ranjiká
Illustrated London News
Imvo Zabantsundu
Izwi Labantu
King William's Town Gazette
Lloyd's Weekly Newspaper
Lyttelton Times
Moorshedanad Patriká
Morning Chronicle (London)
Morning Post (London)
Natal Mercury
Native Opinion
Nelson Evening Mail
New Zealand Free Lance
New Zealand Tablet
North Otago Times

Observer (Auckland)
Otago Daily Times
Otago Witness
Poverty Bay Herald
Rájshahye Samáchár
Reynolds's Newspaper
Sádháraní
Saptahik Samachar
Som Prákash
South African Commercial Advertiser
South African Spectator
Star (Auckland)
Star (Wellington)
Sulabh Samáchár
Taranaki Herald
Te Aroha
Timaru Herald
The Times (London)
Treasury of Literature and the Ladies' Treasury
Tuapeka Times
Wairarapa Daily Times
Wanganui Times
Wellington Independent
West Coast Times

Nineteenth-century literature on the tours

Bishop, Walter E. *A Diary of Events kept during the Royal Colonial Tour, 1901*. London, 1901.

A Complete Report of the Attempted Assassination of H.R.H. Prince Alfred. Sydney, 1868.

Dalton, John N. *The Cruise of Her Majesty's Ship 'Bacchante', 1879–1882: Compiled from the Private Journals, Letters, and Note-books of Prince Albert Victor and Prince George of Wales*, 2 vols. London, 1886.

Fayer, J. *Notes on the Visits to India of Their Royal Highnesses the Prince of Wales and Duke of Edinburgh, 1870–1875–76*. London, 1879.

Fenian Revelations: The Confessions of O'Farrell who Attempted to Assassinate the Duke of Edinburgh. London, 1868.

Gay, J. Drew. *The Prince of Wales in India; or, from Pall Mall to Punjaub*. New York, 1877.

Hopkins, John. *The Life of King Edward VII. With a sketch of the career of George, Prince of Wales, and a history of the royal tour of the empire in 1901*. London, 1902.

Horne, Richard. *Galatea Secunda: An odaic cantata, addressed to H.R.H. Prince Alfred, Duke of Edinburgh, on his first arrival in the colony of Victoria*. Melbourne, 1867.

Knight, Edward. *With the Royal Tour a Narrative of the Recent Tour of the Duke and Duchess of Cornwall and York Through Greater Britain, Including His Royal Highness's Speech Delivered at the Guildhall, on December 5, 1901.* Toronto, 1902.

Maxwell, William. *With the Ophir round the empire: an account of the tour of the Prince and Princess of Wales, 1901*. London, 1902.

Milner, John. *The Cruise of H.M.S. Galatea, Captain H.R.R. the Duke of Edinburgh, K.G., in 1867–1868* London, 1869.

Price, Harry. *The Royal Tour of 1901, or, the Cruise of H.M.S. Ophir: being a lower deck Account of their Royal Highnesses, the Duke and Duchess of Cornwall and York's Voyage around the British Empire*. Exeter, 1980.

The Prince of Edinburgh in the Oudh and Nepal Forests: A Letter from India. Private Circulation, 1870.

The Prince in Calcutta; or Memorials of His Royal Highness the Duke of Edinburgh's visit in December, 1869. Calcutta, 1870.

The Prince in India and to India, by an Indian. Calcutta, 1871.

A Proposal for the Confederation of the Australian Colonies, with Prince Alfred, Duke of Edinburgh, as King of Australia. By a Colonist. Melbourne, 1867.

Rees, John David. *HRH the Duke of Clarence and Avondale in Southern India.* London, 1891.

Russell, William Howard. *The Prince of Wales' Tour: A Diary in India.* London, 1878.

Scott, Fabian. *Our Colonies. A Descriptive Fantasia on the Royal Tour.* London, 1901.

Solomon, Saul. *The Progress of His Royal Highness Prince Alfred Ernest Albert through the Cape Colony, British Kaffraria, the Orange Free State, and Port Natal, in the Year 1860*. Cape Town, 1861.

Victoria's Golden Reign: A Record of Sixty Years as a Maid, Mother, and Ruler, by a Lady of the Court. London, 1897.

The Visit of His Royal Highness Prince Alfred to the Colony of Natal. London, 1861.

Wallace, Donald. *The Web of Empire: A Diary of the Imperial Tour of the Duke and Duchess Of Cornwall and York in 1901*. London, 1902.

Watson, Joseph. *The Queen's Wish: How It Was Fulfilled by the Imperial Tour of T.R.H. the Duke and Duchess of Cornwall.* London, 1902.

Reference sources

Dictionary of New Zealand Biography. Wellington, 1990–2000.

Oxford Dictionary of National Biography. Oxford, 2003.

Te Ara, The Encyclopaedia of New Zealand. Wellington, 2005–14.

Published materials

Alexander, Michael and Sushila Anand. *Queen Victoria's Maharajah: Duleep Singh, 1838–93*, 2nd edn. London, 2001.

Anderson, Benedict. *Imagined Communities: Reflections on the Origins and Spread of Nationalism*. New York, 1983.

Apter, Andrew H. *The Pan-African Nation: Oil and the Spectacle of Culture in Nigeria*. Chicago, 2005.

Arbousset, Thomas. *Missionary Excursion into the Blue Mountains, Being an Account of King Moshoeshoe's Expedition from Thaba-Bosiu to the Sources of the Malibamatso River in the Year 1840*, ed. and trans. David Ambrose and Albert Brutsch. Morija, 1991.

Arnstein, Walter L. 'Queen Victoria', *Victorian Studies* 36 (1993): 377–80.

—*Queen Victoria*. New York, 2003.

Aronson, Theo. *Royal Ambassadors: British Royalties in Southern Africa, 1860–1947*. Cape Town, 1975.

Bagehot, Walter. *The English Constitution*. Introduction by Miles Taylor. New York, 2001.

Ballantyne, Tony and Antoinette Burton. 'Empires and the Reach of the Global', in *A World Connecting, 1870–1945*, ed. Emily S. Rosenberg. Cambridge, MA, 2012.

Ballantyne, Tony and Antoinette Burton, eds. *Bodies in Contact: Rethinking Encounters in World History*. Durham, NC, 2005.

Ballara, Angela, ed. *Te Kingitanga: The People of the Maori King Movement*. Auckland, 1996.

Basutoland Records, 3 vols, ed. G. M. Theal. Cape Town, 1883.

Baucom, Ian. *Out of Place: Englishness, Empire, and the Locations of Identity*. Princeton, 1999.

Bayly, C. A. *Birth of the Modern World, 1780–1914: Global Connections and Comparisons*. Oxford, 2004.

—*Empire and Information: Intelligence Gathering and Social Communication in India, 1780–1870*. Cambridge, 1996.

—*Recovering Liberties: Indian Thought in the Age of Liberalism and Empire*. Cambridge, 2012.

—*Rulers, Townsmen, and Bazaars: North Indian Society in the Age of British Expansion, 1770–1870*. Cambridge, 1983.

Beaven, Arthur Henry. *Popular Royalty*. London, 1904.

Beinart, William and Lotte Hughes, *Environment and Empire*. Oxford, 2007.

Belich, James. 'Empire and Its Myth', in *Amongst Friends: Australian and New Zealand Voices from America*, ed. Patty O'Brien and Bruce Vaughan. Dunedin, 2005.

—*Making Peoples: A History of New Zealanders*. Honolulu, 1996.

—*The New Zealand Wars and the Victorian Interpretation of Racial Conflict*. Auckland, 1989.

—*Replenishing the Earth: The Settler Revolution and the Rise of the Anglo-World, 1783–1939*. Oxford, 2009.

Bell, Duncan. 'Empire and International Relations in Victorian Political Thought', *Historical Journal* 49, no. 1 (2006): 281–98.

—'The Idea of a Patriot Queen? The Monarchy, the Constitution, and the Iconographic Order of Greater Britain, 1860–1900', *Journal of Imperial and Commonwealth History* 34, no. 1 (March 2006): 3–21.

—*The Idea of Greater Britain: Empire and the Future of World Order, 1860–1900*. Princeton, 2007.

—*Victorian Visions of Global Order: Empire and International Relations in Nineteenth-Century Political Thought*. Cambridge, 2012.

Benton, Laura. 'The Geography of Quasi-Sovereignty: Westlake, Maine, and the Legal Politics of Colonial Enclaves', *International Law and Justice Working Papers* 5 (2006): 1–51.

—*A Search for Sovereignty: Law and Geography in European Empires, 1400–1900*. Cambridge, 2009.

Bhabha, Homi. *The Location of Culture*. New York, 1994.

Bickford-Smith, Vivian. *Ethnic Pride and Racial Prejudice in Victorian Cape Town*. Cambridge, 1995.

—'Revisiting Anglicisation in the Nineteenth Century Cape Colony', in *The British World: Diaspora, Culture and Identity*, ed. Carl Bridge and Kent Fedorowich. Portland, OR, 2003.

—'Writing about Englishness: South Africa's Forgotten Nationalism', in *Empire and After: Englishness in Postcolonial Perspective*, ed. Graham MacPhee and Prem Poddar. Oxford, 2007.

Binney, Judith. *Redemption Songs: A Life of Te Kooti Arikirangi Te Turuki*. Honolulu, 1997.

Bodelsen, C. A. *Studies in Mid-Victorian Imperialism*. New York, 1968.

Bogdanor, Vernon. *The Monarchy and the Constitution*. New York, 1995.

Bond, John. *They Were South Africans*. Oxford, 1956.

Bowen, George Ferguson. *Thirty Years of Colonial Government: A Selection from the Despatches and Letters*, ed. Stanley Lane-Poole. New York, 1889.

Breckenridge, Carol A. and Peter van der Veer, 'Orientalism and Postcolonial Predicament', in *Orientalism and the Postcolonial Predicament*, ed. Carol A. Breckenridge and Peter van der Veer (Philadelphia, 1993).

Bridge, Carl and Kent Fedorowich, eds. *The British World: Diaspora, Culture, and Identity*. London, 2003.

Briggs, Asa. *The Age of Improvement, 1783–1867*, 2nd edn. New York, 1999.

Bucholz, Robert. *The Augustan Court: Queen Anne and the Decline of Court Culture*. Stanford, 1993.

Buckland, Charles Edward. 'Grish Chandra Grose', in *Dictionary of Indian Biography*. London, 1906.

—'Harish Chandra Mukerji', in *Dictionary of Indian Biography*. London, 1906.

—'Kristo Das Pal', in *Dictionary of Indian Biography*. London, 1906.

Buckner, Phillip. 'Casting Daylight Upon Magic: Deconstructing the Royal Tour of 1901 to Canada', *Journal of Imperial and Commonwealth History* 31 (May 2003): 158–189.

Buckner, Phillip and R. Douglas Francis, eds. *Rediscovering the British World.* Calgary, 2005.

Bunn, David. 'The Sleep of the Brave: Graves as Sites and Sins in the Colonial Eastern Cape', in *Images and Empires: Visuality in Colonial and Postcolonial Africa,* ed. Paul Landau and Deborah Kaspin. Berkeley, 2002.

Burman, Sandra. *Chiefdom Politics and Alien Law: Basutoland under Cape Rule, 1871–1884.* New York, 1981.

—'The Royal Tour of 1901 and the Construction of an Imperial Identity in South Africa', *South African Historical Journal* 41 (1999): 326–48.

Burn, Richard. 'Political Movements, 1909–1917', in *The Cambridge History of the British Empire,* vol. 5, *The Indian Empire, 1858–1918,* ed. H. H. Dowell. Cambridge, 1932.

Butler, Richard W. 'The History and Development of Royal Tourism in Scotland: Balmoral, the Ultimate Holiday Home?', in *Royal Tourism: Excursions around Monarchy,* ed. Philip Long and Nicola J. Palmer. Bristol, 2007.

Cain, P. J. and A. G. Hopkins. *British Imperialism, 1688–2000,* 2nd edn (New York, 2001)

—'Gentlemanly Capitalism and British Overseas Expansion II: New Imperialism, 1850–1945', *Economic History Review* 40, no. 1 (1987): 1–26.

Campbell, Malcolm. 'A "Successful Experiment" No More: The Intensification of Religious Bigotry in Eastern Australia, 1865–1885', *Humanities Research* 12, no. 1 (2005): 67–78.

Cannadine, David. 'The Context, Performance and Meaning of Ritual', in *The Invention of Tradition,* ed. Eric Hobsbawm and Terence Ranger. Cambridge, 1983.

—'From Biography to History: Writing the Modern British Monarchy', *Historical Research* 77 (August 2004): 289–312.

—*The Decline and Fall of the British Aristocracy.* New York, 1999.

—*History in Our Time.* New York, 2000.

—'The Last Hanoverian Sovereign? The Victorian Monarchy in Historical Perspective, 1688–1988', in *The First Modern Society: Essays in English History in Honour of Lawrence Stone,* ed. A. L. Beier, D. Cannadine, and J. M. Rosenheim. Cambridge, 1989.

—*Ornamentalism: How the British Saw Their Empire.* London, 2001.

Cannon, John. *The Modern British Monarchy: A Study in Adaptation.* Reading, 1987.

—'The Survival of the British Monarchy', *Transactions of the Royal Historical Society* 5 (1986): 143–64.

Chattopadhyay, Swati. 'Blurring Boundaries: The Limits of "White Town" in Colonial Calcutta', *Journal of the Society of Architectural Historians* 59 (June 2000): 154–79.

Clark, Paul. *'Hauhau': The Pai Marire Search for Maori Identity.* Auckland, 1975.

Clay, Richard. 'Review of Anthony Sillery, *Founding a Protectorate: History of Bechuanaland, 1885–1895*', *Bulletin of the School of Oriental and African Studies* 29 (1966): 664.

Clendinnen, Inga. *Dancing with Strangers: Europeans and Australians at First Contact*. Cambridge, 2005.

Cohn, Bernard. *Colonialism and Its Forms of Knowledge: The British in India*. Princeton, 1996.

—'Representing Authority in Victorian India', in *The Invention of Tradition*, ed. Eric Hobsbawm and Terence Ranger. Cambridge, 1983.

Cole, Doug. 'The Problem of "Nationalism" and "Imperialism" in British Settlement Colonies', *Journal of British Studies* 10 (1971): 160–82.

Colenso, John W. *Ten Weeks in Natal: A Journal of a First Tour of Visitation among the Colonists and the Zulu Kafirs of Natal*. London, 1855.

Colley, Linda. 'Britishness and Otherness: An Argument', *Journal of British Studies* 31 (1992): 309–29.

—*Britons: Forging a Nation, 1707–1837*. New Haven, 1992.

Colls, Robert and Philip Dodd, eds. *Englishness: Politics and Culture: 1880–1920*. Dover, 1986.

Comaroff, Jean and John Comaroff. *Of Revelation and Revolution: Christianity, Colonialism, and Consciousness in South Africa*, vol. 1. Chicago, 1991.

Conway, Daniel and Pauline Leonard, *Migration, Space and Transnational Identities: The British in South Africa*. London, 2014.

Coombes, Annie E. *Reinventing Africa: Museums, Material Culture, and Popular Imagination in Late Victorian and Edwardian England*. New Haven, 1994.

Cooper, Frederick and Rogers Brubaker. 'Beyond Identity', *Theory and Society* 29 (2000): 1–47.

Copland, I. F. S. 'The Baroda Crisis of 1873–77: A Study in Government Rivalry', *Modern Asian Studies* 2, no. 2 (1968): 97–123.

Correspondence Respecting a Memorial Brought to this Country by Certain Maori Chiefs in 1884, Parliamentary Papers. London, 1885.

Craig, David M. 'The Crowned Republic? Monarchy and Anti-Monarchy in Britain, 1760–1901', *Historical Journal* 46 (March 2003): 167–85.

Crais, Clifton. *White Supremacy and Black Resistance in Pre-Industrial South Africa: The Making of the Colonial Order in the Eastern Cape, 1770–1865*. Cambridge, 1992.

Curnow, Jenifer, Ngapare Hopa, and Jane McRae, eds. *Rere atu, taku manu! Discovering History, Language, and Politics in the Maori-Language Newspapers*. Auckland, 2002.

Curnow, Jenifer and Jane McRae, eds. *He Pitopito Korero no te Perehi Maori: Readings from the Maori Language Press*. Auckland, 2006.

Cunningham, Hugh. 'The Languages of Patriotism, 1750–1914', *History Workshop Journal* 12 (Autumn 1981): 8–83.

Dalrymple, William. *The Last Mughal: The Fall of a Dynasty, Delhi, 1857*. New York, 2006.

Dalziel, Raewyn. *Julius Vogel, Business Politician*. Auckland, 1986.

—'Southern Islands: New Zealand and Polynesia', in *OHBE*, vol. 3, *The Nineteenth Century*. Oxford, 1999.

Darwin, John. *After Tamerlane: The Rise and Fall of Global Empires 1400–2000*. London, 2008.

—*The Empire Project: The Rise and Fall of the British World-System, 1830–1970*. Cambridge, 2009.

Das Gupta, Uma. 'The Indian Press 1870–1880: A Small World of Journalism', *Modern Asian Studies* 11 (Spring 1977): 213–35.

Davis, Mike. *Late Victorian Holocausts: El Niño Famines and the Making of the Third World*. New York, 2002.

De Certeau, Michel. *The Practice of Everyday Life*, trans. Steven Rendall. Los Angeles, 1984.

De Kock, Leon. *Civilising Barbarians: Missionary Narrative and African Textual Response in Nineteenth-Century South Africa*. Johannesburg, 1996.

—'Sitting for the Civilisation Test: The Making(s) of a Civil Imaginary in Colonial South Africa', *Poetics Today* 22 (Summer 2001): 391–412.

Deloria, Philip. *Playing Indian*. New Haven, 1999.

Dening, Greg. *Beach Crossings: Voyaging across Times, Cultures, and Self*. Philadelphia, 2004.

Dilke, Charles. *Greater Britain: A Record of Travel in English-Speaking Countries during 1866 and 1867*. London, 1869.

—*The Problems of Greater Britain*. New York, 1890.

Dirks, Nicholas. *Castes of Mind: Colonialism and the Making of Modern India*. Princeton, 2001.

Drummond, Alison. 'Queen Victoria Had a Maori Godson', *Te Ao Hou: The New World*, no. 24 (October 1958): 60–61

Dubow, Saul. *A Commonwealth of Knowledge: Science, Sensibility, and White South Africa, 1820–2000*. Oxford, 2006.

—'How British Was the British World? The Case of South Africa', *Journal of Imperial and Commonwealth History* 37, no. 1 (2009): 1–27.

Duff, David, ed. *Victoria Travels: Journeys of Queen Victoria between 1830 and 1900, with Extracts from her Journal*. New York, 1971.

du Toit, André and Hermann Giliomee, *Afrikaner Political Thought: Analysis and Documents*, vol. 1, *1780–1850*. Berkeley, 1983.

Echenberg, Myron J. *Plague Ports: The Global Urban Impact of Bubonic Plague,1894–1901*. New York, 2007.

Elbourne, Elizabeth. 'Indigenous People and Imperial Networks in the Early Nineteenth Century: The Politics of Knowledge', in *Rediscovering the British World*, ed. Phillip Buckner and R. Douglas Francis. Calgary, 2005.

—*Power in Colonial Africa: Conflict and Discourse in Lesotho, 1870–1960*. Madison, WI, 2007.

—*A South African Kingdom: The Pursuit of Security in Nineteenth-Century Lesotho*. Cambridge, 2002.

Eley, Geoff. 'Beneath the Skin. Or: How to Forget about Empire without Really Trying', *Journal of Colonialism and Colonial History* 3 (Spring 2002). http://muse.jhu.edu/journals/journal_of_colonialism_and_colonial_history/summary/v003/3.1eley.html, accessed 30 July 2015.

Elsmore, Bronwyn. *Mana from Heaven: A Century of Maori Prophets in New Zealand*. Tauranga, 1989.

English, Jim. 'Empire Day in Britain, 1904–1958', *Historical Journal* 49, no. 1 (March 2006): 247–76.

Etherington, Norman. 'The "Shepstone System" in the Colony of Natal and beyond the Borders', in *Natal and Zululand from Earliest Times to 1910: A New History*, ed. Andrew Duminy and W. R. Guest. Pietermaritzburg, 1989.

Fabb, John. *Royal Tours of the British Empire, 1860–1927*. London, 1989.

Fanon, Frantz. *Black Skin, White Masks*, trans. Charles Lam Markmann. New York, 1967.

Ferguson, Niall. *Empire: The Rise and Demise of the British World Order and the Lessons for World Power*. New York, 2003.

Fleming, Francis. *Kaffraria, and Its Inhabitants*. London, 1853.

Fredrickson, George M. *Black Liberation: A Comparative History of Black Ideologies in the United States and South Africa*. Oxford, 1995.

—*White Supremacy: A Comparative Study in American and South African History*. Oxford, 1981.

Fulford, Roger. *The Prince Consort*. London, 1949.

Furedy, Chris. 'The Bhadralok and Municipal Reform in Calcutta, 1875–1900', Working Paper of the Institute of Asian and Slavonic Research, University of British Columbia (August 1972).

Further Correspondence Respecting a Memorial Brought to this Country by Certain Maori Chiefs in 1884, Parliamentary Papers. London, 1885.

Gandhi, Mohandas. 'What is Swaraj?' (ch. 3), in *Hind Swaraj, or Indian Home Rule*. Madras, 1921.

Geertz, Clifford. *The Interpretation of Cultures: Select Essays*. New York, 1973.

Ghosh, Nagendra Nath. *Kristo Das Pal: A Study*. Calcutta, 1887.

Gibbs, Philip. *George the Faithful: The Life and Times of King George V*. London, 1936.

Giliomee, Hermann. *The Afrikaners: Biography of a People*. Charlottesville, 2003.

Gordon, A. D. *Businessmen and Politics: Rising Nationalism and a Modernising Economy in Bombay 1918–1933*. Delhi, 1978.

Gorman, Daniel. *Imperial Citizenship: Empire and the Question of Belonging* Manchester, 2006.

Green, E. H. H. *The Crisis of Conservatism: The Politics, Economics and Ideology of the Conservative Party, 1880–1914*. New York, 1996.

Grump, James. 'Sir George Grey's Encounter with the Maori and the Xhosa, 1845–1868', *Journal of World History* 9 (March 1998): 89–106.

Guha, Ramachandra. *India before Gandhi*. London, 2014.

Guha, Ranajit. *Dominance without Hegemony: History and Power in Colonial India*. Cambridge, MA, 1998.

—*Elementary Aspects of Peasant Insurgency in Colonial India*. Durham, NC, 1999.

Guy, Jeff. *The Destruction of the Zulu Kingdom: The Civil War in Zululand, 1879–1884*. New York, 1979.

—*The Maphumulo Uprising: War, Law And Ritual in the Zulu Rebellion*. Scottsville, 2005.

—' "A Paralysis of Perspective": Image and Text in the Creation of an African Chief', *South African Historical Journal* 47 (2002): 51–74.

—*Theophilus Shepstone and the Forging of Natal: African Autonomy and Settler Colonialism in the Making of Traditional Authority*. Scottsville, 2013.

—*The View across the River: Harriette Colenso and the Zulu Struggle against Imperialism*. Charlottesville, 2002.

Hall, Catherine. *Civilising Subjects: Metropole and Colony in the English Imagination, 1830–1867*. Chicago, 2002.

Halpern, Rick and Martin J. Dauton, eds. *Empire and the Others: British Encounters with Indigenous Peoples, 1600–1850*. Philadelphia, 1999.

Hamilton, Carolyn. *Terrific Majesty: The Power of Shaka Zulu and the Limits of Historical Invention*. Cambridge, 1998.

Hamilton, Carolyn *et al. Refiguring the Archive*. Norwell, 2002.

Hansard Parliamentary Debates.

Harcourt, Freda. 'Disraeli's Imperialism, 1866–1868: A Question of Timing', *Historical Journal* 23 (1980): 87–109.

—'Gladstone, Monarchism, and the "New" Imperialism, 1868–74', *Journal of Imperial and Commonwealth History* 23 (Winter 1980): 88–109.

—'The Queen, the Sultan, and the Viceroy: A Victorian State Occasion', *London Journal* 5 (Winter 1979): 35–56.

Hardie, Frank. *The Political Influence of the British Monarchy, 1868–1952*. London, 1970.

Harrop, A. J. 'New Zealand and the Empire, 1852–1951', in *The Cambridge History of the British Empire*, vol. 7, *New Zealand*. Cambridge, 1936.

Hastings, David. *Extra! Extra! How the People Made the News*. Auckland, 2013.

Hawkins, Sean and Philip D. Morgan. 'Blacks and the British Empire: An Introduction', in *Black Experience and the Empire*, ed. Philip D. Morgan and Shawn Hawkins. Oxford, 2004.

Hazareesing, Sandip. 'The Quest for Urban Citizenship: Civic Rights, Public Opinion, and Colonial Resistance in Early Twentieth-Century Bombay', *Modern Asian Studies* 34 (October 2000): 797–829.

Herbstein, Manu. 'F.Z.S. Peregrino and *The Fortnightly Spectator*: Query', 27 May 1998, H-Albion. http://h-net.msu.edu/cgi-bin/logbrowse.pl?trx=vx&list=h-africa&month=9805&week=d&msg=j0jnngZeA9jKnvRNLFS5qg&user=&pw=, accessed 8 May 2009.

Hibbert, Christopher, ed. *Queen Victoria in her Letters and Journals*. London, 1984.

Higgs, Catherine. *The Ghost of Equality: The Public Lives of D.D.T. Jabavu of South Africa, 1885–1959*. Cape Town, 1997.

Hobsbawm, Eric and Terence Ranger, eds. *The Invention of Tradition*. Cambridge, 1983.

Hobson, J. A. *Imperialism: A Study*. New York, 1902.

Hodgson, Janet. 'A History of Zonnebloem College, 1858–1870: A Study of Church and Society.' MA thesis. University of Cape Town, 1975.

—'Xhosa Chiefs in Cape Town in the Mid-19th Century', *Studies in the History of Cape Town* 2 (1980): 41–74.

Hofmeyr, Isabel. *Gandhi's Printing Press: Experiments in Slow Reading*. Cambridge, MA, 2013.

—*The Portable Bunyan: A Transnational History of 'The Pilgrim's Progress.'* Princeton, 2004.

Holland, Bernard Henry. *Imperium et Libertas; a Study in History and Politics*. London, 1901.

Homans, Margaret. *Remaking Queen Victoria*. Cambridge, 1997.

Hough, Richard. *Victoria and Albert*. New York, 1996.

Hughes, Heather. *The First President: A Life of John L. Dube, Founding President of the ANC*. Auckland Park, 2011.

Hyam, Ronald and Peter Henshaw, *The Lion and the Springbok: Britain and South Africa since the Boer War*. Cambridge, 2003.

Indian Newspaper Reports, c. 1868–1942, from the British Library, London. Marlborough, 2005–.

Jabavu, D. D. T. *The Life of John Tengo Jabavu, Editor of Imvo Zabantsundu, 1884–1921*. Lovedale, 1922.

Jackson, Ashley. 'Motivation and Mobilization for War: Recruitment for the British Army in the Bechuanaland', *African Affairs* 96, no. 384 (July 1997): 399–417.

James, Lawrence. *Raj: The Making and Unmaking of British India*. New York, 1997.

Jebb, Richard. *Studies in Colonial Nationalism*. London, 1905.

Kantorowicz, Ernst H. *The King's Two Bodies: A Study in Mediaeval Political Theology*. Princeton, repr. 1998.

Kawharu, Ian Hugh, ed. *Waitangi: Maori and Pakeha Perspectives of the Treaty of Waitangi*. Oxford, 1989.

Keay, Anna. *The Magnificent Monarchy: Charles II and the Ceremonies of Power*. New York, 2008.

Kebbel, T. E., ed., *Selected Speeches of the Earl of Beaconsfield*, vol. 2. London, 1882.

Keegan, Timothy. *Colonial South Africa and the Origins of the Racial Order*. Charlottesville, 1996.

—*The Round Table Movement and Imperial Union*. Toronto, 1975.

Kendle, John. *Federal Britain: A History*. New York, 1997.

Kennedy, Dane. 'The Boundaries of Oxford's Empire', *International History Review*, 23, no. 3 (September 2001): 604–22.

—*The Magic Mountains: Hill Stations of the British Raj*. Berkeley, 1996.

Kirkwood, Carmen. *Tawhiao King or Prophet*. Hamilton, 2000.

Koditschek, Theodore. *Liberalism, Imperialism, and the Historical Imagination: Nineteenth-Century Visions of a Greater Britain*. Cambridge, 2011.

Kuhn, William Marshall. 'Ceremony and Politics: The Management of British Royal Ceremonial, 1861–1911'. PhD dissertation, Johns Hopkins University, 1989.

—*Democratic Royalism: The Transformation of the British Monarchy, 1861–1914*. New York, 1996.

—'The Future of the British Monarchy', *Journal of British Studies* 38 (April 1999): 267–72.

Kumar, Krishan. *The Making of English National Identity*. Cambridge, 2003.

Lake, Marilyn and Henry Reynolds. *Drawing the Global Colour Line: White Men's Countries and the International Challenge of Racial Equality*. Cambridge, 2008.

Lambert, John. 'Britishness, South Africanness and the First World War', in *Rediscovering the British World*, ed. Phillip Buckner and R. Douglas Francis. Calgary, 2005.

—'Chiefship in Early Colonial Natal, 1843–1879', *Journal of African Studies* 21, no. 2 (June 1995): 269–85.

—'An Identity Threatened: White English-Speaking South Africans, Britishness, and Dominion South Africanism, 1934–1939', *African Historical Review* 37 (2005): 50–70.

—'The Last Outpost: Natalians, South Africa, and the British Empire', in *Settlers and Expatriates: Britons over the Seas*, OHBE Companion Series, ed. Robert Bickers. Oxford, 2010.

—'"An Unknown People": Reconstructing British South African Identity', *Journal of Imperial and Commonwealth History* 37, no. 4 (December 2009): 599–617.

Landau, Paul. *Popular Politics in the History of South Africa, 1400–1948*. Cambridge, 2010.

—*The Realm of the Word: Language, Gender, and Christianity in a Southern African Kingdom*. Portsmouth, NH, 1995.

Landau, Paul and Deborah Kaspin. eds. *Images and Empires: Visuality in Colonial and Postcolonial Africa*. Berkeley, 2002.

Lawrance, Benjamin N., Emily Lynn Osborn, and Richard L. Roberts, eds. *Intermediaries, Interpreters, and Clerks: African Employees in the Making of Colonial Africa*. Madison, WI, 2006.

Le Cordeur, Basil. *The Politics of Eastern Cape Separatism, 1820–1854*. Oxford, 1981.

Lee, Sidney. *King Edward VII: A Biography*, 2 vols. London, 1925.

Lee-Warner, William. *The Native States of India*. Delhi, 1893.

Lenin, V. I. *On Imperialism: The Highest Stage of Capitalism*. 1916.

Lester, Alan. 'British Settler Discourses and the Circuits of Empire', *History Workshop Journal* 54 (2002): 24–48.

—*Imperial Networks: Creating Identities in Nineteenth-Century South Africa and Britain*. New York, 2001.

—'Reformulating Identities: British Settlers in Early Nineteenth-Century South Africa', *Transactions of the Institute of British Geographers* 23, no 4 (2004): 515–31.

The Letters of Queen Victoria, ed. G. E. Buckle, Second Series, *1862–85*, 3 vols (London, 1926–28).

The Letters of Queen Victoria, ed. G. E. Buckle, Third Series, *1886–1901*, 3 vols (London, 1930–32).

Levy, Andrea. *Small Island*. New York, 2005.

Lodge, Tom. *Mandela: A Critical Life*. New York, 2006.

Lortimer, Douglas. *Colour, Class, and the Victorians: English Attitudes to the Negro in the Mid-Nineteenth Century*. Leicester, 1978.

Louis, William Roger. *The Oxford History of the British Empire*, 5 vols. Oxford, 1999.

Lowry, Donal. 'The Crown, Empire Loyalism and the Assimilation of Non-British White Subjects in the British World: An Argument against "Ethnic Determinism"', *Journal of Imperial and Commonwealth History* 31 (May 2003): 96–120

Lowry, Donal, ed. *The South African War Reappraised*. Manchester, 2000.

Lynton, Harriet Ronken and Mohini Rajan. *The Days of the Beloved*. Los Angeles, 1974.

MacKenzie, John. *The Empire of Nature: Hunting, Conservation and British Imperialism*. Manchester, 1997.

—*Propaganda and Empire: The Manipulation of British Public Opinion, 1880–1960*. Manchester, 1984.

—*The Scots in South Africa: Ethnicity, Identity, Gender and Race 1772–1914* Manchester, 2007.

—*The Victorian Vision: Inventing New Britain*. London, 2001.

MacKenzie, John, ed. *Imperialism and Popular Culture*. Manchester, 1989.

Mamdani, Mahmood. *Citizen and Subject: Contemporary Africa and the Legacy of Late Colonialism*. Princeton, 1996.

Mandela, Nelson. *Long Walk to Freedom*. New York, 1994.

Marks, Shula. *The Ambiguities of Dependence: Class, Nationalism and the State in Twentieth-Century Natal*. Baltimore, 1986.

Marshall, P. J. 'The White Town of Calcutta under the Rule of the East India Company', *Modern Asian Studies* 34 (May 2000): 307–31.

Martin, Theodore. *The Life of His Royal Highness the Prince Consort*, 5 vols. London, 1875–80.

McClendon, Thomas. *White Chief, Black Lords: Shepstone and the Colonial State in Natal, South Africa, 1845–1878*. Rochester, 2010.

McCracken, Donal. *Forgotten Protest: Ireland and the Anglo-Boer War*. Belfast, 2003.

McCreery, Cindy. 'A British Prince and a Transnational Life: Alfred, Duke of Edinburgh's Visit to Australia, 1867–8', in *Transnational Ties: Australian Lives in the World*, ed. Desley Deacon, Penny Russell, and Angela Woollacott. Canberra, 2008.

—'"Long May He Float on the Ocean of Life": The First Royal Visit to Tasmania, 1868', *Tasmanian Historical Studies* no. 12 (2007): 19–42.

—'Telling the Story: HMS *Galatea*'s 1867 Visit to the Cape', *South African Historical Journal* 61 (December 2009), 817–37.

—'The Voyage of the Duke of Edinburgh in HMS Galatea to Australia, 1867–8', in *Exploring the British World: Identity, Cultural Production, Institutions*, ed. Kate Darian-Smith, Patricia Grimshaw, Kiera Lindsey, and Stuart Mcintyre. Melbourne, 2004.

McKinlay, Brian. *The First Royal Tour, 1867–1868*. London, 1971.

McRae, Jane. '"Ki nga pito e wha o te ao nei" (To the four corners of this world): Maori Publishing and Writing for Nineteenth-Century Maori-Language Newspapers', in *Agent of Change: Print Culture Studies after Elizabeth*

L. Eisenstein, ed. Sabrina Alcorn Baron, Eric N. Lindquist, and Eleanor F. Shevlin. Amherst, 2007.
Mears, Natalie. *Queen and Political Discourse in the Elizabethan Realms*. Cambridge, 2005.
Mehta, Uday Singh. *Liberalism and Empire: A Study in Nineteenth-Century British Liberal Thought*. Chicago, 1999.
Mesthrie, Uma Shashikant. 'From Advocacy to Mobilisation: *Indian Opinion*, 1903–1914', in *South Africa's Alternative Press: Voices of Protest and Resistance, 1880–1960*, ed. Leo Switzer. Cambridge, 1997.
Metcalf, Thomas. *Ideologies of the Raj*. Cambridge, 1997.
—*Imperial Connections: India in the Indian Ocean Arena, 1860–1920*. Berkeley, 2008.
Minor, Robert N. 'Sri Aurobindo's Dismissal of Gandhi and His Nonviolence', in *Indian Critiques of Gandhi*, ed. Harold Coward. Albany, 2003.
Mitchell, Timothy. *Colonising Egypt*. Cambridge, 1988.
Morris, Marilyn. *The British Monarchy and the French Revolution*. Princeton, 1998.
Moulton, Edward C. *Lord Northbrook's Indian Administration, 1872–1876*. New York, 1968.
Murphy, James. *Abject Loyalty: Nationalism and the Monarchy in Ireland during the Reign of Queen Victoria*. Washington, DC, 2001.
Murphy, Philip. *Monarchy and the End of Empire: The House of Windsor, the British Government, and the Postwar Commonwealth*. Oxford, 2013.
Naoroji, Dadabhai. 'The Inaugural Address of the Second Indian National Congress', in *Inaugural Addresses by Presidents of the Indian National Congress*, ed. Dinker Vishnu Gokhale. Bombay, 1895.
—*Poverty and Un-British Rule in India*. London, 1901.
Nasson, Bill. *Abraham Esau's War: A Black South African War in the Cape, 1899–1902*. Cambridge, 1991.
—*Britannia's Empire: Making a British World*. Stroud, 2004.
—*The South African War, 1899–1902*. Oxford, 1999.
—*The South African War: The Anglo-Boer War*. Cape Town, 2010.
—'Why They Fought: Black Cape Colonists and Imperial Wars, 1899–1918', *International Journal of African Historical Studies* 37, no. 1 (2004): 55–70.
Ndletyana, Mcebisi, ed. *African Intellectuals in 19th and Early 20th Century South Africa*. Cape Town, 2008.
Newbury, Colin. *Patrons, Clients, and Empire: Chieftaincy and Over-rule in Asia, Africa, and the Pacific*. Oxford, 2003.
Nicolson, Harold. *King George V: His Life and Reign*. New York, 1952.
Olechnowicz, Andrzej. *The Monarchy and the British Nation*. Cambridge, 2007.
O'Malley, Vincent. *Beyond the Imperial Frontier: The Contest for Colonial New Zealand*. Wellington, 2014.
—'Choosing Peace or War: The 1863 Invasion of Waikato', *New Zealand Journal of History* 47, no. 1 (2013): 39–58.
—*Te Rohe Potae War and Paupatu*, Waitangi Tribunal, Wai 898, #A22. Unpublished, 2010.

O'Malley, Vincent, Bruce Stirling, and Vally Penetito, *The Treaty of Waitangi Companion: Maori and Pakeha from Tasman to Today*. Auckland, 2011.

Paging through History: 150 Years with the 'Cape Argus'. Cape Town, 2007.

Parekh, Chunilal Lalubhai, ed. *Eminent Indians on Indian Politics*, ed. Chunilal Lalubhai Parekh. Bombay, 1892.

Parkes, Henry. *Fifty Years in the Making of Australian History*. London, 1892.

Parsons, Neil. *King Khama, Emperor Joe, and the Great White Queen: Victorian Britain through African Eyes*. Chicago, 1998.

—' "No Longer Rare Birds in London": Zulu, Ndebele, Gaza, and Swazi Envoys to England, 1882–1894', in *Black Victorians/Black Victoriana*, ed. Gretchen Holbrook Gerzina. New Brunswick, 2003.

Paxman, Jeremy. *On Royalty: A Very Polite Inquiry into Some Strangely Related Families*. New York, 2007.

Peires, Jeff. *The Dead Will Arise: Nongqawuse and the Great Xhosa Cattle-Killing Movement of 1856–7*. Bloomington, IN, 1989.

—'John Tengo Jabavu', *Oxford Dictionary of National Biography* (Oxford, 2004); online edn, May 2006. www.oxforddnb.com/view/article/53763, accessed 31 July 2015.

Penn, Nigel. *The Forgotten Frontier: Colonist and Khoisan on the Cape's Northern Frontier in the Eighteenth Century*. Athens, OH, 2006.

Pike, Philip W. *The Royal Presence in Australia the Official Royal Tours of Australia, from 1867 to 1986*. Adelaide, 1986.

Plaatje, Solomon. *Native Life in South Africa before and since the European War and the Boer Rebellion*. Whitefish, MT, repr. 2004.

Plunkett, John. *Queen Victoria: First Media Monarch*. Oxford, 2003.

Porter, Bernard. *The Absent-Minded Imperialists: What the British Really Thought About Empire*. Oxford, 2004.

Potter, Simon J. 'Webs, Networks, and Systems: Globalization and Mass Media in the Nineteenth- and Twentieth-Century British Empire', *Journal of British Studies* 46 (July 2007): 621–46.

Price, Richard. *An Imperial War and the British Working Class: Working-Class Attitudes and Reactions to the Boer War, 1899–1902*. London, 1972.

—*Making Empire: Colonial Encounters and the Creation of Imperial Rule in Nineteenth-Century Africa*. Cambridge, 2008.

—'One Big Thing: Britain, Its Empire, and Their Imperial Culture', *Journal of British Studies* 45 (July 2006): 602–27.

'Prince Philip's spear "gaffe"', BBC News: Asia-Pacific. http://news.bbc.co.uk/2/low/asia-pacific/1848813.stm, accessed 30 October 2007.

The Principal Speeches and Addresses of His Royal Highness the Prince Consort. London, 1862.

Prochaska, Frank. *The Republic of Britain: 1760–2000*. New York, 2000.

—*Royal Bounty: The Making of a Welfare Monarchy*. New Haven, 1995.

A Proposal for the Confederation of the Australian Colonies, with Prince Alfred, Duke of Edinburgh, as King of Australia. By a Colonist. Sydney, 1867.

Putnam, Laura. 'To Study the Fragments Whole: Microhistory and the Atlantic World', *Journal of Social History* 39 (Spring 2006): 615–63.

Radforth, Ian. 'Performance, Politics, and Representation: Aboriginal People and the 1860 Royal Tour of Canada', *Canadian Historical Review* 84 (March 2003): 1–32.

—*Royal Spectacle: The 1860 Visit of the Prince of Wales to Canada and the United States*. Toronto, 2004.

Ramusack, Barbara N. *The New Cambridge History of India*, vol. 3.6, *The Indian Princes and Their States*. Cambridge, 2004.

Ranger, Terence. 'The Invention of Tradition in Colonial Africa', in *The Invention of Tradition*, ed. Eric Hobsbawm and Terence Ranger. Cambridge, 1983.

—'The Invention of Tradition Revisited: The Case of Africa', in *Legitimacy and the State in Twentieth Century Africa: Essays in Honour of A.H.M. Kirk-Greene*, ed. Terence Ranger and Olufemi Vaughan. London, 1993.

Ray, Mihir Kumar. *Princely States and the Paramount Power, 1858–1876: A Study on the Nature of Political Relationship between the British Government and the Indian State*. Delhi, 1981.

Reed, Charles V. 'Imperial Citizenship and the Origins of South African Nationalism, 1902–1923', in *Crossing Boundaries: Ethnicity, Race, and National Belonging in a Transnational World*, ed. Brian Behnken and Simon Wendt. Lanham, MD, 2013.

Rees, William Lee. *The Life and Times of Sir George Grey, K.C.B.* Auckland, 1892.

Richards, John. *The Mughal Empire*. Cambridge, 1996.

Ridley, Jane. *The Heir Apparent: A Life of Edward VII, the Playboy Prince*. New York, 2014.

Riet, Frank. *The Settler Celebrations of 1870: Compiled from Contemporary Accounts*. Grahamstown, 1970.

Robinson, John. *A Life Time in South Africa: Being Recollections of the First Premier of Natal*. London, 1900.

Robinson, Ronald. 'Non-European Foundations of European Imperialism: Sketch for a Theory of Collaboration', in *Studies of the Theory of Imperialism*, ed. Roger Owen and Robert B. Sutcliffe. New York, 1972.

Robinson, Ronald and John Gallagher. *Africa and the Victorians: The Climax of Imperialism on the Dark Continent* New York, 1961.

'The role of the Monarchy in the Commonwealth', *The Official Website of the British Monarchy*. www.royal.gov.uk, accessed 12 May 2010.

Rose, Jonathan. *The Intellectual Life of the British Working Classes*. New Haven, 2001.

Rosenberg, Emily, ed. *A World Connecting 1870–1945*. Cambridge, 2012.

Rosenberg, Scott. 'Monuments, Holidays, and Remembering Moshoeshoe: The Emergence of National Identity in Lesotho, 1902–1966', *Africa Today* 46, no. 1 (Winter 1999): 49–72.

—'Promises of Moshoeshoe: Culture, Nationalism, and Identity in Lesotho, 1902–1966'. PhD dissertation, Indiana University, 1998.

Ross, Robert. *The Borders of Race in Colonial South Africa: The Kat River Settlement, 1829–1856*. Cambridge, 2014.

—*Status and Respectability in the Cape Colony, 1750–1870: A Tragedy of Manners*. Cambridge, 1999.

Routh, Jonathan. *The Secret Life of Queen Victoria: Her Majesty's Missing Dairies*. Garden City, NY, 1980.

Roy, Srikanta. *Bengal Celebrities*. Calcutta, 1906.

Rudolph, Susanne Hoeber, Lloyd I. Rudolph, and Mohan Singh Kanota, eds. *Reversing the Gaze: Amar Singh's Diary, a Colonial Subject's Narrative of Imperial India*, 2002.

Rush, Anne. 'The Bonds of Empire: West Indians and Britishness 1900–1970'. PhD dissertation, American University, Washington, DC, 2004.

—*Bonds of Empire: West Indians and Britishness from Victoria to Decolonisation*. Oxford, 2011.

Rutherford, James. *Sir George Grey, K.C.B., 1812–1898: A Study in Colonial Government*. London, 1961.

Said, Edward. *Orientalism*. New York, 1974.

Samson, Jane, ed. *The British Empire*. Oxford, 2001.

Sanders, Peter. *Moshoeshoe, Chief of the Sotho*. Portsmouth, NH, 1975.

Sapire, Hilary. 'African Loyalism and its Discontents: The Royal Tour of South Africa 1947', *Historical Journal* 54, no. 1 (2011): 215–40.

—'Ambiguities of Loyalism: The Prince of Wales in India and Africa 1921 and 1925', *History Workshop Journal* 73 (Spring 2012): 37–65.

Saunders, Christopher. 'African Attitudes to Britain and the Empire before and after the South African War', in *The South African War Reappraised*, ed. Donal Lowry. New York, 2000.

—'Britishness in South Africa', *Humanities Research* 13, no. 1 (2006): 61–9.

Saunders, Christopher and Ian R. Smith. 'Southern Africa, 1795–1910', in *OHBE*, vol. 3, *The Nineteenth Century*. Oxford, 1999.

Schumpeter, Joseph. *Imperialism and Social Classes*. New York, repr. 1951.

Scheider, Miriam. 'Royal Naval Education, Sailor Princes, and the Re-Invention of the Monarchy'. MPhil thesis, University of Cambridge, 2011.

Schwarz, Bill. *The White Man's World*. Oxford, 2011.

Seal, Anil. *The Emergence of Indian Nationalism: Competition and Collaboration in the Later Nineteenth Century*. Cambridge, 1968.

Seeley, John. *The Expansion of England: Two Courses of Lectures*. London, repr. 1931.

Sinha, Mrinalini. *Colonial Masculinity: The 'Manly Englishman' and the 'Effeminate Bengali' in the Late Nineteenth Century*. Manchester, 1995.

—*Specters of Mother India: The Global Restructuring of an Empire*. Durham, NC, 2007.

Slesa, Damon. *Racial Crossings: Race, Intermarriage and the Victorian British Empire*. Oxford, 2011.

Smith, Philippa Mein. *A Concise History of New Zealand*. Cambridge, 2005.

Smith, Zadie. *White Teeth*. New York, 2001.

Spear, Thomas. 'Neo-Traditionalism and the Limits of Invention in British Colonial Africa', *Journal of African History* 44 (2003): 3–27

Starkey, David, ed. *The English Court from the Wars of the Roses to the Civil War*. New York, 1987.

Stone, R. C. J. *From Tamaki-Makau-Rau to Auckland*. Auckland, 2001.

Sunderland, David. *Managing the British Empire: the Crown Agents, 1803–1914*. Rochester, 2004.

Switzer, Les. 'The Beginnings of African Protest Journalism', in *South Africa's Alternative Press: Voices of Protest and Resistance, 1880–1960*, ed. Les Switzer. Cambridge, 1997.

Switzer, Les, ed. *South Africa's Alternative Press: Voices of Protest and Resistance, 1880–1960*. Cambridge, 1997.

Switzer, Les and Donna Switzer. *The Black Press in South Africa and Lesotho: A Descriptive Bibliographic Guide to African, Coloured, and Indian Newspapers, Newsletters and Magazines, 1836–1976*. Boston, 1976.

Tamarkin, Mordechai. *Cecil Rhodes and the Cape Afrikaners: The Imperial Colossus and the Colonial Parish Pump*. New York, 1996.Taylor, Anthony. *'Down with the Crown': British Anti-monarchism and Debates About Royalty Since 1790*. London, 1999.

—'Republicanism Reappraised: Anti-Monarchism and the English Radical Tradition, 1850–1872', in *Rereading the Constitution: New Narratives in the Political History of England's Long Nineteenth Century*, ed. James Vernon. New York: Cambridge University Press, 1996.

Taylor, Miles. *Queen Victoria and India*. New Haven, forthcoming.

—'Queen Victoria and India, 1837–61', *Victorian Studies* 46, no. 2 (Winter 2014), 264–74.

Thackeray, David. 'The Crisis of the Tariff Reform League and the Division of "Radical Conservatism", c. 1913–1922', *History* 91, no. 301 (2006): 45–61.

Thomas, Nicholas. *Colonialism's Culture: Anthropology, Travel and Government*. Princeton, 1994.

Thompson, Andrew. *Imperial Britain: The Empire in British Politics, c. 1880–1932*. New York, 2002.

—'The Languages of Loyalism in Southern Africa, c. 1870–1939', *English Historical Review* 118, no. 477 (2003): 617–50.

Thompson, Dorothy. *Queen Victoria: The Woman, the Monarchy, and the People*. New York, 1990.

Thompson, E. P. *The Making of the English Working Class*. New York, 1996.

Thompson, F. M. L. *The Rise of Respectable Society: A Social History of Victorian Britain, 1830–1900*. Cambridge, MA, 1988.

Thompson, Leonard. *Survival in Two Worlds: Moshoeshoe of Lesotho, 1786–1870*. London, 1975.

Thompson, P. S. '"Loyalty's Fair Reward": The Natal Native Horse in the Zulu Rebellion of 1906', *South African Historical Journal* 66, no. 4 (2014): 656–76.

Thorne, Susan. *Congregationalist Missionaries and the Making of Imperial Culture in Nineteenth-Century England*. Palo Alto, CA, 1999.

Tinker, Hugh. *Foundations of Local Self-Government in India, Pakistan and Burma*. London, 1954.

Trapido, Stanley. 'The Origins of the Cape Franchise Qualifications of 1853', *Journal of African History* 5 (Winter 1964): 37–54.

—'White Conflict and Non-White Participation in the Politics of the Cape of Good Hope'. PhD dissertation, University of London, 1970.

Trentman, Frank. *Free Trade Nation: Consumption, Commerce, and Civil Society in Modern Britain*. Oxford, 2008.

Tye, J. Reginald. 'New Zealand', in *Periodicals of Queen Victoria's Empire: An Exploration*, ed. J. Don Vann and Rosemary T. VanArsdel. Toronto, 1996.

Tyrrell, Alex and Yvonne Ward. '"God Bless Her Little Majesty". The Popularising of Monarchy in the 1840s', *National Identities* 2 (July 2000): 109–25.

Tupper, C. L. *Indian Political Practice: A Collection of Decisions of the Government of India in Political Cases*, 4 vols. Delhi, 1895.

—*Our Indian Protectorate: An Introduction to the Study of Relations between the British Government and its Indian Feudatories*. London, 1893.

Urbach, Karina. 'Prince Albert: The Creative Consort', in *The Man behind the Queen: Male Consorts in History*, ed. Charles Beam and Miles Taylor. London, 2014.

Van Der Kiste, John and Bee Jordaan. *Dearest Affie: Alfred, Duke of Edinburgh, Queen Victoria's Second Son, 1844–1900*. Gloucester, 1984.

Van Heyningen, Elizabeth and Pat Merrett. '"The Healing Touch": The Guild of Loyal Women of South Africa 1900–1912', *South African Historical Journal* 47 (November 2003): 24–50.

Vernon, James. *Politics and the People*. Cambridge, 1993.

Walker, Eric. *W.P. Schreiner: A South Africa*. Oxford, 1969.

Ward, Stuart. 'Transcending the Nation: A Global Imperial History?', in *After the Imperial Turn: Thinking with and through the Nation*, ed. Antoinette Burton. Durham, NC, 2003.

Wade, Henry A. 'Imagining the Great White Mother and the Great King: Aboriginal Tradition and Royal Representation in the "Great Pow-Wow" of 1901', *Journal of the Canadian Historical Association* 11 (2000): 87–108.

Wainwright, Martin. *'The Better Class' of Indians: Social Rank, Imperial Identity, and South Asians in Britain, 1858–1914*. Manchester, 2008.

Walker, Eric. *W. P. Schreiner: A South African*. Oxford, 1969.

Ward, John Manning. *The State and the People: Australian Federation and Nation-Making,1870–1901*, ed. D. M. Schreuder, B. H. Fletcher, and R. Hutchison. Leichhardt, 2001.

Ward, Peter. *A Show of Justice: Racial 'Amalgamation' in Nineteenth-Century New Zealand* Auckland, 1974.

Washbrook, David. *The Emergence of Provincial Politics: The Madras Presidency 1870–1920*. Cambridge, 1976.

Weber, Max. 'Status Groups and Classes', in *The Essential Weber*, ed. Sam Whimster. New York, 2004.

West, Michael Oliver. *The Rise of an African Middle Class*. Bloomington, IN, 2002.

Westlake, John. *The Collected Papers of John Westlake on Public International Law*, ed. L. Oppenheim. Cambridge, 1914.

Weintraub, Stanley. *Uncrowned King: The Life of Prince Albert*. New York, 1997.
Wilentz, Sean, ed. *Rites of Power: Symbolism, Ritual, and Politics since the Middle Ages*. Philadelphia, 1999.
Willan, Brian. *Sol Plaatje: South African Nationalist, 1876–1932*. London, 1984.
Williams, Richard. *The Contentious Crown: Public Discussion of the British Monarchy in the Reign of Queen Victoria*. Brookfield, VT, 1997.
Willis, Justin. 'A Portrait for Mukama: Monarchy and Empire in Colonial Munyoro, Uganda', *Journal of Imperial and Commonwealth History* 34 (March 2006): 105–22.
Wills, Walter H. *The Anglo-African Who's Who and Biographical Sketchbook, 1907*. Johannesburg, repr. 2006.
Wilson, A. N. *After the Victorians: The Decline of Britain in the World*. New York, 2005.
Wilson, Kathleen, ed. *A New Imperial History: Culture, Identity, and Modernity in Britain and the Empire, 1660–1840*. Cambridge, 2004.
Wilson, M. and Leonard Thompson, eds. *The Oxford History of South Africa*, vol. 2, *South Africa, 1870–1966*. Oxford, 1971.
Witz, Leslie. *Apartheid's Festival: Contesting South Africa's National Pasts*. Bloomington, IN, 2003.
Wohlers, J. F. H. 'The Mythology and Traditions of the Maori in New Zealand', *Transactions and Proceedings of the Royal Society of New Zealand* 7 (1874): 3–53.
Worden, Nigel, E. Van Heyningen, and Vivian Bickford-Smith. *Cape Town: The Making of a City*. Cape Town, 1998.
Young, Robert J. C. *The Idea of English Ethnicity*. New York, 2008.

INDEX